Giants in Their Tall Black Hats

John Gibbon. Courtesy of the Wisconsin Veterans Museum

Giants in Their Tall Black Hats

Essays on the Iron Brigade

EDITED BY
ALAN T. NOLAN AND
SHARON EGGLESTON VIPOND

Indiana University Press
BLOOMINGTON AND INDIANAPOLIS

This book is a publication of

Indiana University Press
601 North Morton Street
Bloomington, Indiana 47404-3797 USA

www.indiana.edu/~iupress

Telephone orders 800-842-6796
Fax orders 812-855-7931
Orders by e-mail iuporder@indiana.edu

The paper used in this publication meets the minimum requirements of American National Standard for Information Sciences—Permanence of Paper for Printed Library Materials, ANSI Z39.48-1984.

Manufactured in the United States of America

Library of Congress Cataloging-in-Publication Data

Giants in their tall black hats : essays on the Iron Brigade /
edited by Alan T. Nolan and Sharon Eggleston Vipond.
p. cm.
Includes bibliographical references and index.
ISBN 0-253-33457-8 (alk. paper)
1. United States. Army. Iron Brigade (1861–1865).
2. United States—History—Civil War, 1861–1865—
Regimental histories. I. Nolan, Alan T. II. Vipond,
Sharon Eggleston, date.
E493.5.I7G53 1998
973.7'4—dc21 98-23926

1 2 3 4 5 03 02 01 00 99 98

Contents

Illustrations

Maps

Tables

Acknowledgments

The editors would like to extend their thanks to Lance J. Herdegen for his advice and his encouragement of this project. Thanks also to John Hennessy of the Manassas National Battlefield Park and Don Pfanz of the Fredericksburg and Spotsylvania National Military Park for their guidance and support. Thanks to the Wisconsin Veterans Museum in Madison, the Beloit Historical Society, and the Vernon County Historical Society for permission to use photographs of the Iron Brigade. Special thanks to John Heiser of Gettysburg, Pennsylvania, who designed and produced the maps.

A.T.N.
S.E.V.

Introduction

In early May of 1863, Captain Charles Stevens of Berdan's Sharpshooters stood at a muddy Virginia roadside in a heavy thunderstorm and watched the Army of the Potomac march eastward, in the direction of Fredericksburg:

> Loud cheers were frequently given when some particular regiment or brigade passed by. Especially when . . . the 1st Corps came along with the "full moon" on its banners, and as the great Western or Iron Brigade passed, looking like giants with their tall black hats, they were greeted with hearty cheers. . . . And giants they were, in action. . . . I look back and see that famed body of troops marching up that long muddy hill unmindful of the pouring rain, but full of life and spirit, with steady step, filling the entire roadway, their big black hats and feathers conspicuous. . . .[1]

These "giants," as Stevens called them, were the men of a unique Civil War brigade. Originally called "The Black Hat Brigade" because its soldiers wore the regular army's dress black hats instead of the more typical blue cap, the Iron Brigade was the only all-Western brigade in the Eastern armies of the Union. The brigade was initially made up of the Second, Sixth, and Seventh Wisconsin and Nineteenth Indiana volunteer infantry regiments, and later reinforced by the Twenty-fourth Michigan volunteers. Battery B of the Fourth United States Artillery, composed in large part of infantry detached from these regiments, was closely associated with the Iron Brigade.

Organized on October 1, 1861, the four Wisconsin and Indiana regiments were initially commanded by Brigadier General Rufus King, a West Pointer from New York who, prior to the war, had moved to Wisconsin. Having wintered in camp, the brigade was reassigned from McClellan's Army of the Potomac and missed the Peninsula Campaign of 1862. In May of 1862, while stationed at Fredericksburg, Virginia, the brigade received a second commander in the person of Brigadier General John Gibbon, an artillery regular from West Point who in spite of North Carolina origins had stayed with the old flag. To finish the war as a corps commander after a distinguished career, Gibbon was surely the architect of the brigade. Among other things, he standardized the brigade's uniform, outfitting the Western men in the dress uniform of the regular army, including the tall black felt Hardee hat, trimmed with a plume.

It was at Brawner Farm in Northern Virginia, on August 28, 1862, the eve of Second Bull Run, that the brigade saw its first significant action. In his essay, Alan T. Nolan looks beyond the Iron Brigade's baptism of fire and describes farmer Brawner's effort to gain government compensation for his personal losses during the battle.[2]

Early September of 1862 saw the brigade move north into Maryland under George McClellan and win its famous name. Kent Gramm takes a deeper look at the brigade's flight at Turner's Gap on September 14 and explores the circumstances under which a group of "plain boys from nowhere" underwent the bloody transformation to battle-hardened veterans on the slopes of South Mountain. Gramm details the painful forging of the Iron Brigade which took place over the course of four to five terrible days in September 1862. He then takes us forward, down the road from Turner's Gap, which led the Iron Brigade to the small village of Sharpsburg on the banks of the Potomac and into the battle of Antietam.

Of the tumultuous day at Antietam, Stephen Sears has written: "Of all the days on all the fields where American soldiers have fought, the most terrible by almost any measure was September 17, 1862. The battle waged on that date . . . took a human toll that exceeded that on any other single day in the nation's history."[3] In his essay, Scott Hartwig uses the journals of Rufus Dawes to narrate the Iron Brigade's action during the battle of Antietam and to recount the terrible fight in the "bloody cornfield." He illustrates why the Western men, in the years following the war, would always "dread the thought" of that terrible place.

Alan Gaff and Maureen Gaff trace the bloodstained path traveled by the Iron Brigade from the killing fields of Manassas, Virginia, through Turner's Gap and the cornfield at Sharpsburg, Maryland. These stories demonstrate the "dread reality of war" for the brigade that led all Federal brigades in the percentage of deaths in battle.

On November 5, 1862, Solomon Meredith, another native of North Carolina, originally Colonel of the Nineteenth Indiana Volunteers, was appointed commander of the brigade in place of the promoted John Gibbon. Steven Wright's essay provides new insights about Gibbon, the man who forged the brigade into the remarkable fighting force that it was to become. Drawing upon Gibbon's previously unpublished diaries and letters to his wife, Wright examines the profound transformation in both Gibbon himself and the rough and often undisciplined Western volunteers under his command.

The brigade's next battle was at Fredericksburg in December of 1862. This was followed by Chancellorsville in the spring of 1863. While not caught in the vortex of this event, the men of the brigade made a dangerous crossing of the Rappahannock under fire and would remember the incident as one of the few bright spots in the otherwise dismal campaign that culminated in the army's defeat at Chancellorsville. Marc and Beth Storch recount this great story.

Another of the brigade's great days was the first day of Gettysburg, July 1, 1863. As the First Brigade of the First Division of the First Corps, it defended McPherson's Ridge long enough to assure that the Federals, instead of Lee's outnumbering divisions, would sieze the high ground south of the town. It was from this high ground—Cemetery Hill, Cemetery Ridge, Culp's Hill, and the Round Tops—that the battle was successfully fought on the next two days. Lance Herdegen explains the complex relationship between First Corps Commander John F. Reynolds and the Iron Brigade, a relationship forged in the days before Gettysburg; that battle forever links the memory of Reynolds and his First Corps. The picture of his relationship with the Iron Brigade was substantially altered by that one "shining moment" on the edge of Herbst's woodlot.

Severely reduced by casualties, the Iron Brigade after Gettysburg lost its distinctive all-Western character and its regiments were joined thereafter by regiments from non-Western states. Remnants of the brigade fought on during Ulysses S. Grant's bitter Overland Campaign. Sharon Eggleston Vipond traces the evolution and transformation of the brigade after its devastating losses at Gettysburg and provides an in-depth narrative of the brigade's first fight under Grant, in the Wilderness early in May 1864. As it was for all the men who fought there, the Wilderness remains a confusing and enigmatic battle, an inferno which swallowed up many Iron Brigade veterans and set the stage for the beginning of the end of the Civil War.

On the eve of the Wilderness, pursuant to Grant's reorganization of the army, the First Corps was merged into the Fifth Corps, and the Iron Brigade therefore changed its corps identification to the Fifth Corps. Thereafter, the remnants of its regiments advanced in Grant's Overland Campaign but were from time to time reorganized in the course of that whirlwind. Thus the Nineteenth Indiana was merged with the Twentieth Indiana in October 1863 and was transferred to the Second Corps. The Second Wisconsin of the Iron Brigade was detached at Spotsylvania, and in February 1865, still in the midst of Grant's final campaign, the Twenty-fourth Michigan was withdrawn from the front. There were neverthless veterans of the Iron Brigade and Battery B at Appomattox. Silas Felton examines the supportive and symbiotic relationship between the Iron Brigade and "Bloody B" (as it was affectionately known to the Western men). Felton also profiles James Stewart, the tough Scotsman who helped to build the battery's fighting skills and commanded it with such distinction at Gettysburg and thereafter.

The final essay by Richard Zeitlin shifts the spotlight to the postwar years and the meaning of the flags treasured by Iron Brigade veterans. The old, faded, and torn flags reminded them of the glory they enjoyed as survivors of the legendary Iron Brigade, of the price they had paid for the Union, and of the Wisconsin, Indiana, and Michigan boys they had left buried on fields in Virginia, Maryland, and Pennsylvania.

In collecting these essays, it has been our goal to provide new perspectives on the exploits and nature of the Western men—the individual human beings—who formed this distinctive and distinguished Civil War brigade. Beyond the battle narratives and the analyses of military and political events contained in these essays, we have also sought to focus on *stories*—told in the words of the men who fought and suffered through our nation's greatest trial, *stories* that help us, as modern readers, probe into life in the past and achieve a more authentic connection with those whose actions and motives we seek to understand: the black-hatted "giants" of the Iron Brigade.[4]

Sharon Eggleston Vipond
Woodstock, Georgia

Alan T. Nolan
Indianapolis, Indiana

April, 1997

Giants in Their Tall Black Hats

John Brawner's Damage Claim

ALAN T. NOLAN

The Battle on the Farm

People interested in the Iron Brigade are generally aware of its first full-blown combat on the Brawner Farm on August 28, 1862, the eve of Second Bull Run.[1] It was a stunning engagement in which the brigade and Battery B, surprised and outnumbered, fought to a standstill men of Stonewall Jackson's wing of Lee's army. Jackson's wing had separated from Lee and Longstreet's wing on August 25 at the Rappahannock River. Flanking Major General John Pope's Army of Virginia, Jackson had fallen on Manassas in Pope's rear on August 26. Aware that his wing was vulnerable by itself in northern Virginia, Jackson had moved his 25,000 men to wooded Stony Ridge immediately north of the Brawner Farm. There he waited for Lee and Longstreet to follow him into northern Virginia.

The farm of John C. Brawner, a tenant farmer, was located along the north side of the Warrenton Turnpike between the crossroads villages of Gainesville and Groveton, Virginia. The countryside was rolling with occasional ridges and in 1862 was marked by patches of woods and marginal farms.[2] Brawner's farm was composed of approximately 300 acres. It was owned by the widow Augusta Douglas of Gainesville, and since 1858 had been leased to Brawner. Brawner was sixty-four years old in 1862. Prior to the war, his household included his wife, two sons, and three daughters. In August of 1862, the sons were away in the army. The whereabouts of his wife in 1862 are unknown.[3]

Brawner's farm was not imposing. The farmhouse and barn were located a quarter of a mile north of the Warrenton Turnpike on the crest of a gentle ridge. A farm lane led from the turnpike to the farmhouse. In the yard, extending to the east, was an orchard. Except for the orchard and a small grove of trees at the house and barn, the ground near the buildings was cleared so that the fields in front and behind the buildings were open. Brawner's fields were bordered on the east by a rectangular wood that lay south and east of the farm buildings. The wood was approximately a fifth of a mile long. Its north edge, enclosed by a zigzag rail fence, began seventy-five yards south of the crest of the farm building ridge and extended down to and south of the turnpike. Inside the wood, the ground was rugged and irregular and dipped down to the level of the turnpike at the eastern edge of the wood, where another open field extended to the north from the turnpike.

A Confederate general officer later characterized the Brawner Farm as simply "a farm-house, an orchard, a few stacks of hay, and a rotten 'worm' fence,"[4] but Virginia was a border state and the farm was perilously close to Washington, thirty miles to the east. When the Virginia Convention voted on April 17, 1861, to secede,[5] northern Virginia became a marchland. Confederate troops had advanced toward the Potomac and the Union moved divisions across the river onto Virginia soil.

Brawner's first brush with the war, a near miss for his property, had taken place in July of 1861. The Federals had undertaken their first major offensive in northern Virginia and had been defeated in the First Battle of Bull Run. Sixty thousand soldiers, Northern and Southern, had engaged in a confused and bloody struggle around the Henry House Hill and Bull Run, five miles east of the farm. The Federals had then retreated to the Washington defenses, leaving the Confederates in Brawner's neighborhood until March of 1862. Anticipating another Union advance, the Confederates had then withdrawn southward toward the Rappahannock River and the Federals had moved before marching farther south. For almost four months during the late spring and early summer of 1862, things were quiet around the Brawner Farm.[6] Then in August of 1862, the armies had again marched into northern Virginia and the fighting had moved toward the farm.

Brigadier General Rufus King's Division, including Brigadier General John Gibbon's Brigade of Western men, mustered approximately 10,000 officers and men of all arms[7] and was assigned to Major General Irvin McDowell's Third Corps of Pope's army. On August 28, 1862, the division was marching east on the turnpike en route to Centreville as a part of Pope's inept and ill-informed effort to find Jackson before Lee and Longstreet's wing of the Army of Northern Virginia joined Jackson. The route of march was past the Brawner Farm. Immediately behind Gibbon's Brigade in King's column was the brigade of Brigadier General Abner Doubleday.

From his post on Stony Ridge, Stonewall Jackson saw King's apparently isolated division marching across his front, past the Brawner Farm.[8] It was approximately 5:00 P.M. and the sun was beginning to set. At about the same time, Jackson heard from Lee. Longstreet had reached nearby Thoroughfare Gap, was expected to force it, and was within supporting distance. Jackson

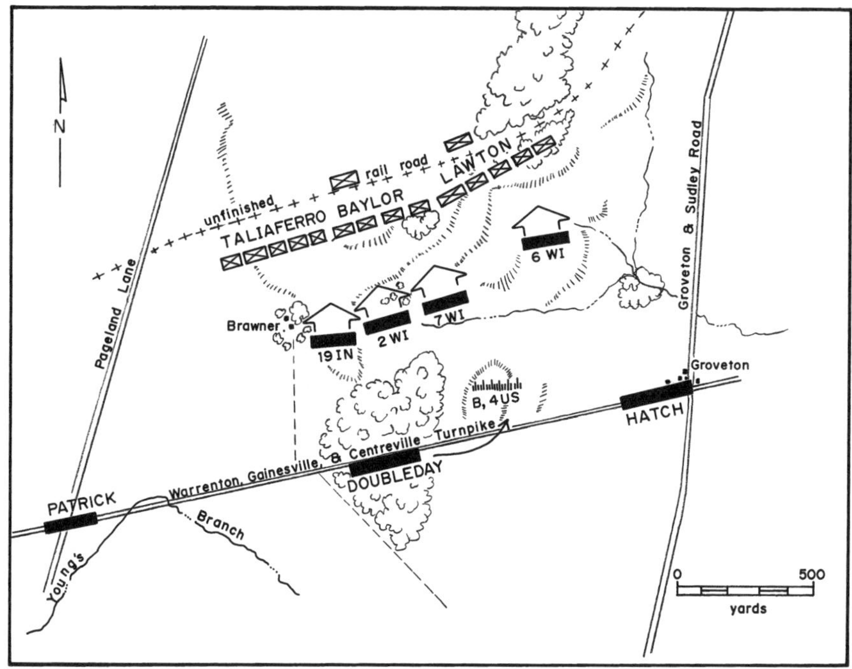

Brawner Farm Battlefield, Manassas, Virginia. Source: Gaff.

immediately disposed his troops to attack. As the head of Gibbon's column emerged from the cover of the wood at the eastern edge of the Brawner property, a Confederate battery fired on it from a position north and east of the farm. Another battery, firing from the north and west of the farm, promptly opened on other brigades of King's Division that were marching to the rear of Gibbon's men. Believing that the enemy guns were unsupported horse artillery, Gibbon ordered Battery B to the head of his column to respond to the battery firing from the east and directed the Second Wisconsin Volunteers, his only combat veterans, to silence the battery firing in his rear.

Battery B drove rapidly up the turnpike, unlimbered, and went into position on a knoll east of the Brawner woods and just north of the turnpike. As the Federal artillery commenced firing, the Second Wisconsin moved through the woods. Having formed line of battle in the open field south of the Brawner farmhouse and barn, it started forward. Approaching the crest of the ridge on which the farm buildings were located, the unsuspecting Federals were suddenly fired on from their right flank by skirmishers from Starke's Brigade of Brigadier General William B. Taliaferro's Stonewall Division. In spite of their surprise, the Wisconsin men did not falter. They wheeled to their right and returned Starke's fire. The flank companies of the Wisconsin regiment were sent forward as skirmishers and Starke's Confederates withdrew over the crest of the ridge followed by the Wisconsin skirmishers. Within a few yards, the Federal skirmishers confronted a larger group of Confederates posted in a small grove of trees. Shots were exchanged as the other Second Wisconsin companies, moving with the skirmish line, reached the crest of the ridge. Looking north from the crest, the Western men at last knew the truth: Long columns of Confederate infantry were filing out of wooded Stony Ridge and advancing on the Brawner property. At once Baylor's Stonewall Brigade, also of Taliaferro's Division, opened fire on the Second Wisconsin. Rejoined by its skirmishers, the embattled Second Wisconsin returned this fire and held its ground.

At last comprehending the force of the Confederate assault, having dispatched calls for help to division commander King and the other brigades of the division, Gibbon sent the Nineteenth Indiana to form on the left of the Second Wisconsin, extending his line toward the Brawner farm buildings. The Seventh Wisconsin went in to the right of the Second. Gibbon committed the Sixth Wisconsin to the right of the Seventh, to a position in the lower ground in the field east of the Brawner woods. Behind the Sixth, the guns of Battery B were at work.

The battle was now joined. Gibbon's line was just south of the crest of the Brawner farmhouse ridge. From left to right it followed the ridge line, passed along the northern edge of the wood and extended into the field east of the wood. There was a large gap in the line between the positions of the Seventh and Sixth Wisconsin. Having driven off the Confederate battery that had begun the affair, Battery B now moved to a new position so that it could fire into this gap. Both of Gibbon's flanks were in the air and were overlapped by the larger Confederate forces, even before Confederate reserves entered the battle.

In addition to Starke's Brigade, the Confederate skirmishers that had surprised the Second Wisconsin, and Baylor's Stonewall Brigade, Jackson now committed the brigade of Colonel A. G. Taliaferro from the same division. He also sent in the brigades of Brigadier Generals Isaac R. Trimble and Alexander R. Lawton from Major General Richard S. Ewell's division, and additional artillery. Although not ordered to do so, Doubleday sent the Seventy-sixth New York and Fifty-sixth Pennsylvania from his brigade into the gap between the Seventh and Sixth Wisconsin. His remaining regiment, the Ninety-fifth New York, moved to the support of Battery B. Battery D of the First Rhode Island Light Artillery of Doubleday's brigade also joined the battle. It appears that Jackson committed between 5,900 and 6,400 infantry. Gibbon was able to field between 2,500 and 2,900 infantry, including the regiments from Doubleday's brigade. The two sides were relatively even in artillery engaged.[9]

Darkness and the tacit consent of the generals terminated the engagement. From the first Confederate artillery fire to the last desultory infantry fire, it lasted for approximately three hours, perhaps two of which were intense. The participants have adequately characterized the nature of the fight. According to Brigadier General Taliaferro, "it was a stand-up combat, dogged and unflinching, in a field almost bare. There were no wounds from spent balls, the confronting lines looked into each other's faces at deadly range, less than a hundred yards apart, and they stood as immovable as the painted heroes in a battle-piece."[10] The Confederates held the farmhouse and the northern edge of the orchard and their line then extended in front of the Brawner wood and into the low ground in the field east of the wood. The Federals clung to the farmyard, the southern edge of the orchard, and the northern face of the wood, extending their line eastward into the same low ground. Gibbon, who was to be in many battles, later said that it was "the most terrific musketry fire I . . . ever listened to."[11] Brigadier General Taliaferro reported it was "one of the most terrific conflicts that can be conceived of." Brigadier General Trimble stated that "I have never known so terrible a fire as raged . . . on both sides." And Doubleday wrote that "there have been few more unequal contests or better contested fields during the war."[12] Perhaps Brigadier General Taliaferro provided the best summary description of the engagement. After the war, and referring to the Federal as well as Confederate participants, he wrote: "out in the sunlight, in the dying daylight, and under the stars, they stood, and although they could not advance, they would not retire. There was some discipline in this, but there was much more of true valor."[13]

And, of course, this kind of fighting exacted a fearful toll. Thirty-seven percent of Gibbon's Western men were casualties, including three of four regimental commanders, the lieutenant colonel of the Seventh Wisconsin, and the majors of three of the four Western regiments. Doubleday's regiments also lost heavily. On the Confederate side, the total losses exceeded those of the Federals, and the Federal rifles accounted for division commanders William B. Taliaferro and Richard S. Ewell. Nine regimental commanders, including three in the Stonewall Brigade, were killed or wounded. Douglas Southall Freeman has written that the battle was one of Jackson's costliest, for the numbers engaged.[14]

Leaving their dead and wounded on the farm, the surviving Federals returned to the turnpike and ultimately made a painful night march to Manassas. Jackson's men returned to Stony Ridge. Confederate physicians tended the Federal wounded as well as their own and Confederate burial parties buried the dead of both sides in shallow graves on Brawner's property. On the next two days, August 29 and 30, Second Bull Run, a major battle and a spectacular Confederate victory, took place just east of the farm. The Confederates remained on the farm and Southern artillery batteries placed there participated in the Confederate victory.

Stonewall Jackson's admiring biographer, the Englishman G. F. R. Henderson, was later to write of Brawner Farm: "The men who faced each other that August evening fought with a gallantry that has seldom been surpassed.

. . . The Federals, surprised and unsupported, bore away the honors. The Western Brigade, commanded by Gen. Gibbon, displayed a coolness and steadfastness worthy of the soldiers of Albuera."[15] Brawner Farm was in fact the prophetic beginning of a storied career for the soldiers from the Old Northwest and for Battery B. Later reinforced by the newly raised Twenty-fourth Michigan Volunteers, the Western brigade went on to earn the sobriquet "Iron Brigade."

The Claim

In 1871, the Forty-first Congress of the United States enacted a war claims statute. The legislation authorized the payment of claims "of those citizens who remained loyal adherents to the cause of the government . . . during the war, for stores or supplies taken or furnished during the rebellion for the use of the army of the United States in States proclaimed as in insurrection against the United States." A three-member commission was created, to sit in Washington, to adjudicate the claims on the basis of "testimony of witnesses under oath, or from other sufficient evidence." The commissioners were required to keep a journal of their proceedings and a register of claims.[16] These papers are now in the National Archives.[17]

John C. Brawner was quick to file his claim. The statute was approved March 3, 1871. Brawner hired Uriah B. Mitchell, a Washington attorney, and filed his claim on April 27, 1871. Identified in the claim form as a resident of Prince William County with a Gainesville Station post office address, Brawner apparently still lived on the wartime farm or close by. Taken down in longhand by someone acting for the Commission, the testimony of Brawner, his daughter Mary, and two witnesses in his behalf, Richard Graham and John Crop, are in the claim file. Also included in the file is the statement of one Jackson Tippins.

Sworn before Justice of the Peace G. A. Simpson, Brawner asserted that he had supplied corn, hay, wheat, bacon, oats, salt, and flour to the soldiers of General King's Division. These men, he said, had also killed and eaten a cow and twenty-two hogs and taken $23.00 worth of fowls. His horse was shot and died from wounds. Some of his household and kitchen furniture was taken for use by wounded men. His vegetable garden was destroyed. Finally, axes, hoes, spades, and other farm tools were appropriated. The total claim was for $1,153.75. The claim concluded with Brawner's certification that he did not "voluntarily serve in the Confederate army or navy . . . that he never voluntarily furnished any stores, supplies or other material aid to said Confederate army or navy, or to the Confederate government . . . or yielded voluntary support to the said Confederate government."

In support of his claim, Brawner testified that he was a native of Maryland and had moved to Virginia at seven years of age. He had witnessed the

D

TO THE COMMISSIONERS OF CLAIMS,
Under Act of 3d March, 1871,
Washington, D. C.

The petition of John C. Brawner, respectfully represents:

That your petitioner is a resident of the county of Prince William in the State of Virginia; that his post office address is Gainesville Station in said county and State; and that at the time his claim and each item thereof as herein set forth accrued, he was a resident of the County of Prince William and State of Virginia; that he is the original owner of said claim; that he has never sold, assigned or transferred the same or any part thereof to any person; that no mortgage, bill of sale or other lien of like nature has at any time rested upon it, or any part thereof, nor has it been attached or taken in execution; that the same has not been paid by the United States or any of their officers or agents, nor have the United States any legal offset against the same or any part thereof; that he is the sole owner of the said claim, no other person being interested therein; that said claim does not contain any charge for property which was destroyed or stolen by the troops or other persons; that the rates or prices charged are reasonable and just, and do not exceed the market rate or price of like stores or property at the time and place stated; all of which your petitioner states of his own knowledge.

Your petitioner further states that he is now and was at the time the several items of his said claim accrued; as stated herein, a citizen of the United States; that he remained a loyal adherent to the cause and Government of the United States, during the war of 1861, &c.; and was so loyal before and at the time of the taking or furnishing of the property for which this claim is made.

And your petitioner further represents, and of *his own knowledge states*, that on the 28th day of August, A. D. 1862, at His Residence in the State of Virginia the following property or stores were *taken from* him *furnished by* your petitioner for the use of the army of the United States, and for which payment is claimed, viz:

	1862		$	Cts.
1	Aug 28	33 Bushels new corn @ 1.00	33	00
2	" "	75 " Old " @ 1.30	97	50
3	" "	13000 lbs Hay @ 1c	130	00
4	" "	25 Bushels wheat @ 2.00	50	00
5	" "	100 lbs Bacon @ 35	35	00
6	" "	25 Bushels Oats @ 75	18	75
7	" "	3 " " Salt @ 2.00	6	00
8.	" "	100 lbs Flour @ 4	4	00
9	" "	1 Cow Killed & eaten	50	00
10	" "	22 Hogs Killed & eaten	180	00
11	" "	1 Horse Shot (died from wound)	75	00
	" "	Household & Kitchen furniture		
12	" "	taken & destroyed (part for wounded)	200	00
13	"	Garden destroyed	30	00
	"	Value of axes hoes spades and		
14	"	farm tools generally taken	17	50
15	" "	Value of Foods taken	25	00
16		And on or about the 1st day of		
		September 1862 one No 1 3 yrs		
		Old Colt was taken by a scouting		
		Party from Genl F. Sigels Corps		
		Value of Colt	200	00
		Balance	$1153	75

Page from the original John C. Brawner Damage Claim.
Courtesy of the National Archives.

First Battle of Bull Run in July of 1861. When the Confederate army had fallen back toward the Rappahannock in March of 1862, Brawner had remained on the farm although his neighbors in the area had left. When the Federals moved in during the spring of 1862, officers had visited Brawner and had asked him why he had remained. According to his testimony, he had explained that he was crippled and could not leave and that he did not believe that the Union soldiers were "barbarians." The officers, he said, had then given him "protection papers."

Brawner also stated that he had stayed inside during the August 28 battle on his farm, although bullets had crashed through the house. His home and farm were "broken up" by the battle of August 28 and he and his family were "driven away." They left the morning after the battle and went to a neighbor's house to the north of the combat area.

To perfect his claim, Brawner needed to establish three things: the identification and value of the goods furnished by him, that *Federal* troops had taken those goods, and that he had been loyal to the United States. Having listed the goods, Brawner's statements were principally directed to two issues, presumably reflecting the questions with which the claims commissioners were concerned: whether the Federals or Confederates were responsible for his losses and whether or not he met the statute's loyalty requirement.

On the issue of which army was responsible, Brawner asserted that "General King sent to my house and officers came for supplies." Regarding the loss of the hogs included in his claim, these, he said, were butchered by the soldiers and then carried off. When he left the farm on August 29, the day after the Iron Brigade's fight, Union soldiers were in his house. When he returned, they were still there, but the furniture was gone or "used up." Among the soldiers were Union wounded. Brawner and his daughter waited on them, he said. The farm tools, presumably the spades, were used by the soldiers to dig graves.

Regarding his allegiance to the Union, despite his certification Brawner admitted a number of incriminating facts. He was uncertain whether he had voted in the election of delegates to the Virginia Convention that had ultimately voted to secede. He did not think he had voted "on the adoption of the Constitution," presumably a reference to the balloting of May 23, 1861, when Virginia voters had approved the earlier secession ordinance.[18] But Brawner's sons were a major problem. He said they had left the farm in March of 1862, when the Confederate army had fallen back toward the Rappahannock, and had then entered the rebel army. Brawner said that they had been drafted and he was questioned about them at length. He had, he said, advised them against enlisting. Although they had reached their majority and he had no control over them, they had listened to him and had not volunteered. He and his sons "agreed about the war and did not want the government broken up." He had not heard from them and did nothing for them while they were in the army. The younger son had been captured and imprisoned for approximately two years. Having been exchanged, the son "came home from prison," returned to the army, and was again captured by the Federals.

Pursuing the loyalty issue, the examiners questioned Brawner about his neighbors. Although he identified Philip Smith, with whom he had taken refuge after the battle on the farm, as "with the South," others whom he named were "all Union men," including his witness, Richard Graham. Returning to questions about his own views, Brawner said that his "sentiments were peace," "let the Union stand as it was and have no war." Apparently pressed about his feelings, he made this answer:

> I had no sympathy for either side when the battle was going on. I suppose my feelings naturally were with my sons when in battle and I suppose I wanted them to whip. But I had no sympathy with either side, for they brought it on themselves.

Mary B. Brawner, John C. Brawner's daughter, had moved away from the farm sometime prior to the hearing. Her statement essentially conformed with her father's but she also added some interesting details. Part of the time the farm was within the Confederate lines and part of the time within the Union lines, "the Union army was passing backward and forward all the time after the Southern army left" in March of 1862. At times when the rebel army was nearby, Confederate officers came to the farm and either purchased or took such things as milk and butter. Her brothers had indeed been drafted into the Confederate army. One was a cavalryman and the other an infantry soldier. Her father had not furnished either of them a horse or anything else. They had come home occasionally during the war.

With reference to which army had supplied itself on the farm at the time of the "the battle . . . all around my father's house," the daughter testified that a quartermaster and soldiers who came for supplies said that they were from General Rufus King, the Federal, and that they would bring receipts for what was taken. "But then," she said, referring to August 28, "the battle came on, and we did not get any receipt." She generally verified her father's statements as to what goods had been taken and said that she had seen the soldiers who took some of the goods.

Brawner's remaining witnesses were two men who purported to testify as to his loyalty. Neither was particularly helpful to him. Richard Graham's nearby store was the prewar post office, presumably the Gainesville Station site. He testified that Brawner was often in the store and in the discussion there "he always took a stand against it," an apparent reference to secession. Graham and Brawner were in agreement on this point. Graham further testified that he himself had "hesitantly" voted for secession in the Virginia referendum and "went with the state" after it seceded. He did not know Brawner's feelings after Virginia seceded. When the Confederate army withdrew from northern Virginia in March of 1862, Graham left the area and moved to Richmond. John Crop, an acquaintance of Brawner for twenty years, corroborated Graham regarding Brawner's prewar opposition to secession. "He said he was in favor of U.S. Govt.," before the war. Concluding his statement, Crop added what one suspects was a touch of realism. "Nobody could talk in favor of the Union after the state seceded."

The most interesting testimony in the Brawner file is that of Jackson Tippins, identified in the record as a "colored employee of the Commission." He had lived, he said, in Stafford County, the county immediately south of Brawner's Prince William County. Nothing in the record tells whether Tippins had been a free black or a slave before the war, or whether he was called to the hearing or simply happened to be on hand in Washington at the time. His testimony, however, was plainly damaging to Brawner: "I know Brawner. . . . I know he was no Union man. I heard him talk. . . . His reputation was that of a rebel." And Tippins testified to an overt act. At some unstated time, he said, a man named Underwood had "put up a Union flag in Occaquan," a Virginia village that has since disappeared from the map. According to Tippins, "Brawner was with the men who cut it down."

The claim file ends with the Commission's brief decision. The issue of which army had taken or destroyed Brawner's property was not addressed or resolved by the Commission. Although the record of the proceedings does not say so, in view of the logistics of the battle on the farm, there is reason to doubt that Federal troops were responsible for the losses. When attacked, the Iron Brigade was marching on the turnpike that ran past the farm. It fought on the part of the farm around the house and east of it, and retreated then toward Manassas Junction. At no time had it been encamped on the farm. It is much more likely that Confederate troops, who had encamped nearby before and occupied the farm after the battle, were the takers.

Concerned entirely with the loyalty issue, the decision noted the two sons in the Confederate army, recited Brawner's statement that they were of age and beyond his control, acknowledged that he had opposed their entering the army, but quoted his admission that he wanted them to "whip" in battle. The decision then set forth the substance of Tippins's testimony and concluded: "This claimant fails to establish his loyalty. . . . We reject the claim." A reading of the decision suggests that the word of the lowly and disenfranchised black man was a material factor in the deliberations.

Brawner's file contains two later entries that were not before the Commission that denied his claim. Dated November 30, 1875, and March 31, 1879, respectively, these facts were apparently turned up during the War Department's early work in assembling for publication the 127 volumes of *The War of the Rebellion: Official Records of the Union and Confederate Armies*. The first entry closely paraphrased a First Bull Run battle report of General P. G. T. Beauregard, the victorious Confederate commander, which stated: "Messrs. McLean, Wilcoxen, Kinchelo, and Brawner, citizens of the immediate vicinity . . . have placed me and the country under great obligations for the information relative to this region, which has enabled me to avail myself of its defensive features and resources. They were found ever ready to give me their time without stint or reward." The second reported that "Mr. Brawner sold to the Confederate States 3000 lbs Hay at 75 Cts, amt $22 50/100. Paid at Centreville, Va. Dec. 9th, 1861." The document recording this transaction, presumably a receipt, was signed by Captain John Page, a quartermaster of the Confederate States of America.

Whether these documents referred to John C. Brawner or one of his sons will now never be known. Brawner is in fact a relatively common name in northern Virginia. But the incidents took place very close to the Brawner Farm and would surely have interested the claims Commission.

The Significance of the Claim

The claim file provides dramatic insight into what happened when Civil War armies met on one's property. It also suggests the complicated circumstances of life and loyalty in a Civil War marchland. The crediting of the black man's word is a specific example of the social revolution wrought by the war.

And the file does more. The evidence verifies the precise location of the battle of August 28, 1862. It did take place on John C. Brawner's farm. This, in turn, validates the naming of the battle as the Battle of Brawner Farm, the unique name I gave it in 1961 when my military history, *The Iron Brigade*,[19] was first published. Prior to 1961, there was widespread confusion about the name of the Brawner Farm fight. Federal writers at the time of the war, like Rufus R. Dawes of the Sixth Wisconsin Volunteers, called it the "Battle of Gainesville," as did the *Official Records*.[20] This was not apt because the battle did not in fact take place at Gainesville. Modern authorities like Kenneth P. Williams called it "Groveton,"[21] which was also inappropriate from a location standpoint and tended to confuse it with the larger and foreshadowing engagements of the next two days. Other modern authorities, including Douglas Southall Freeman, avoided the name problem entirely by leaving the battle unnamed. I believe that in a history of the Iron Brigade, the event on August 28, 1862, simply has to have a meaningful name.

I selected the Brawner name because it was distinctive, and thus confusion with other days' events were avoided, and because it was geographically accurate. For identification of the Brawner ownership prior to the finding of the National Archives claims file, there were two widely different authorities. The first of these was Stonewall Jackson, whose report of the affair, written April 23, 1863, accurately set forth the name of Brawner.[22] The second was Joseph Mills Hanson, former superintendent of the Manassas National Battlefield Park. An unpublished manuscript in the park's files contained an excerpt from a letter written under date of December 21, 1946, by Hanson to the author of the manuscript, Fred W. Cross. Hanson said: "I believe . . . investigation would show the name of the place should be Brawner's. . . . Brawner is a common name around Manassas; there are many here today."[23] The only published Federal source that attempted to identify the property called it by the name of the owner rather than the tenant of the farm. In his *Personal Recollections of the Civil War*, John Gibbon included a rough map at page 53 which set forth the farmhouse, and called it "Douglass House." On the following page, this name is spelled "Douglas."[24] But the name applied by Stonewall Jackson at the time, and approved by Mr. Hanson, seemed to me to be preferable. The only other Confederate participant who tried to name the farm was not so successful. Captain J. B. Evans's report for the Fourth Virginia in the Stonewall Brigade refers to the name as "Brown," incorrect but not unlikely.[25] Since my application of the name Brawner Farm to the battle, other historians have adopted the Brawner Farm name. Among these other historians are Alan D. Gaff, Lance Herdegen, William J. K. Beaudot, and John J. Hennessy. The battle is now aptly identified with the Iron Brigade.

"They Must Be Made of Iron"

The Ascent of South Mountain

KENT GRAMM

The sun rose bright in the clear sky this September Sunday morning, and the church bells of Frederick, Maryland, gleamed gold as they rang for the boys in blue. Things were different here. No more the parched and trampled acres of Virginia; here the rolling fields were lush green. Here women along the line of march did not jeer or watch in cold, sullen defiance; since crossing the Potomac these soldiers had been welcomed, cheered, refreshed with bread, milk, pie, cold water, even flowers and kisses. And this morning, long before church services began, the bells of Frederick City were ringing welcome to the deliverers—for that is how most of the civilians up here seemed to think of the soldiers of the Army of the Potomac.

These were the boys of '61. In John Gibbon's black-hatted brigade, the boys had joined up in large part for reasons that late-twentieth-century Americans might find naive or sentimental. It was the flag; it was for freedom and the best government on earth; it was to preserve representative government in a world ruled by kings, princes, tyrants; some few wanted the slave aristocracy overthrown and with it, the evil of slavery. So among the usual motivations of adventure-seeking, avoidance of boredom, need to prove their manhood, group enthusiasm, fear of being thought a coward, the core of selfless idealism shone through:

> The World shall burn, and from her ashes spring
> New Heav'n and Earth, wherein the just shall dwell
> And after all their tribulations long
> See golden days, fruitful of golden deeds,
> With Joy and Love triumphing, and fair Truth.
> (Milton, *Paradise Lost* III. 334–38)

This morning opened the last push in a campaign that would indeed change the nature of the war, and in so doing change the country. But to the Black Hats filing into the National Pike east of Frederick, the bells did not signal anything that felt new. They were in the midst of three weeks of fighting, marching, dying, hungering, thirsting—weeks the likes of which the North American continent had not seen before and would not see again until the dark days in Virginia two years hence.

On the 28th of August these "Western" soldiers had fought their first battle and lost one-third of the brigade.[1] That night's march, little more than two weeks ago, left a lasting impression: "Many times since then I have been tired, footsore and weary, but I cannot recall one instance where the feeling of fatigue was so great as on this night's march from Gainesville."[2]

A couple of days later Gibbon's boys were fighting the losing battle of Second Bull Run, impressing the high command, being chosen by Irvin McDowell to act as the army's rearguard. More men dead on the field. Three days after that, the brigade was back in camp across the river from Washington City, "defeated, disgusted, dispirited, but not despairing,"[3] wrote a soldier in the Sixth Wisconsin. The scene at first "baffled description":

> On the heights of Centerville were generals, colonels, captains, and all other rank officers of all the branches of the service, looking for their commands and mobs of men looking for their organizations. Infantry, artillery, cavalry, ambulances, wagons and all the impediments used in an army all mixed up in dire confusion. Our brigade [remained] in regular form and no confusion. . . .[4]

The army was to receive little time to rest and restore spirits. Some cheering news helped, however: General George B. McClellan was now in command of the whole unified army. The blustering John Pope had been relieved and his Army of Virginia had been officially absorbed into the Army of the Potomac. Gibbon's brigade was now part of Joseph Hooker's First Corps. (The division was still Rufus King's, but that unpopular general would be replaced in a few more days.) These things had to be done quickly. In Gibbon's brigade, the losses of August 28th necessitated some prompt and significant assignments. William W. Dudley became acting major of the Nineteenth Indiana. George H. Stevens, who would ask to be buried with his men at Gettysburg, rose to the rank of major as Lucius Fairchild, a future governor of Wisconsin, was promoted colonel of the Second Wisconsin. John B. Callis, a transplanted North Carolinian like General Gibbon himself, rose to command of the Seventh Wisconsin. These were very good officers, as subsequent events would prove.[5]

On September 5, the brigade was marching again. Filing through the capital, Gibbon's men experienced the fatiguing and annoying halt-and-move-and-halt progress one would expect in a city crowded with elements of the nation's principal army. One of the halts was on Pennsylvania Avenue. A Wisconsin man recalled,

> While on the sidewalk we could look over on the lawn in front of the White House. It was as thickly strewn with played-out soldiers as was possible for them to lie. We could see the tall form of the President ("Old Abe," as we called him) in shirt sleeves, water pail and dipper in hand, stepping over and among the boys lying around all over the grounds, giving them water to drink.[6]

A series of short but apparently fatiguing marches followed. Clearly, the men had not recovered from their exertions under the hot Virginia sun. Straggling in Gibbon's disciplined brigade must have been unusually high. A veteran of the Sixth Wisconsin recalled catching up with the regiment after having fallen behind the night before: "It had halted for the simple reason that there was no longer anyone there to march."[7]

General Gibbon, showing his understanding of volunteer soldiers, coped with the situation effectively. He had visited the commanding general's tent to request an additional regiment for his brigade, to make up the recent losses. McClellan, hearing Gibbon describe the unique composition of the Black Hats, promised him the first "Western" regiment he got. He also showed Gibbon a folded paper and declared, "Here is a paper with which if I cannot whip 'Bobby Lee,' I will be willing to go home. . . . it gives the movement of every division of Lee's army." It was a copy of Lee's Special Order No. 191, which had been discovered by some infantrymen looking for a place to make a fire. The order revealed that Lee's divisions were widely scattered. The commanding general told Gibbon, ". . . if you people will only do two good, hard days' marching I will put Lee in a position he will find hard to get out of."

The prediction was right, as far as it went. It was pure McClellan: "hard marching," not *hard fighting*. Nevertheless, it made an impression upon Gibbon, and he returned to his men with a speech about some of what he had seen and heard in McClellan's tent. The news of a new *Western* regiment coming to them elicited cheers—Gibbon's embellishing things with a comment about McClellan knowing where a new regiment would best learn how to fight was an effective ploy—and they took seriously the idea that a couple of days' hard marching would make a difference. Gibbon brilliantly suggested that the boys commence "hooting and jeering at every man they saw along the road straggling from his command." The Black Hats responded.

> Very soon, news of what we were doing spread and the stragglers began to disappear from the sides of the road in our vicinity. What was of more importance to my command, a strong spirit of opposition to straggling was created and it became an honorable ambition to remain in the ranks, instead of constantly inventing pretexts to fall out.

Gibbon's brigade had regained its exemplary, disciplined style.[8]

On the morning of the 14th of September, Gibbon's brigade passed through Frederick, with its ringing bells, pretty girls, and appreciative citizenry:

> Our entry into the city was triumphal. The stars and stripes floated from every building and hung from every window. The joyful people ran through the streets to greet and cheer the veterans of the Army of the Potomac. Little children stood at nearly every door, freely offering cool water, cakes, pies and dainties. The jibes and insults of the women of Virginia, to which our men had become accustomed, had here a striking contrast in a generous and enthusiastic welcome by the ladies of Frederick City.[9]

West of town the orchards were laden. Corn stood man high, awaiting the impending harvest. Many soldiers noted the exhilarating spectacle of the Army of the Potomac on the march. From high points on the undulating road, the Wisconsin and Indiana men saw not only their own companions but, moving steadily westward, long lines and masses of blue, rank on rank of sloping steel—a converging river of power, silver and glittery, gleaming in the noonday sun as thousands of rifle barrels caught and split the light.

The Western men had confidence in the officers closest to them, the captains. The oldest regiment, the Second Wisconsin, had "Allen, Bouck, Colwell, McKee, Stevens and others," one veteran wrote, who were "the very best material."[10] In Wilson Colwell, for example, "all recognized fatherly attainments, an excellent adviser, a true gentleman, a thorough disciplinarian and a brave soldier."[11] The companies all marched well this day, heading toward the dark shape of South Mountain.

The name covered a line of low mountains rather than a single eminence—an extension of the Blue Ridge. There were three nearby gaps in the South Mountain chain, and the Army of the Potomac was marching toward all three. Behind those passes, the scattered and vulnerable elements of the rebel army were desperately attempting to concentrate. Lee had by now learned that his army's dispositions had been discovered by the Federals, and had posted Major General D. H. Hill's division—a thin line, to be sure—to cover the two upper passes and buy time.

John Gibbon did not know that the Confederate division toward which his wing of the Army of the Potomac was marching was under the command of his old friend Hill, at whose wedding Gibbon had served as best man. But before long he learned that his Black Hats were to move on the northernmost pass, the one called Turner's Gap. He could plainly see Federal divisions fighting their way forward and upward, off to the right and left of the Pike. One soldier recalled,

> . . . a splendid view was spread before us, in the valley of Middleton [*sic*]. Over beyond the valley, eight miles away, from along the slopes of the South

> Mountain, we could see arising the smoke of battle. We hurried along down the road toward the scene of action, every gun of which we could see and hear. . . . on our right, long lines and heavy columns of dark blue infantry could be seen pressing up the green slopes of the mountain, their bayonets flashing like silver in the rays of the setting sun, and their banners waving in beautiful relief against the background of green.[12]

A little after noon, the brigade halted. Men fell out of the ranks and went right to one of the main occupations of soldiers on the march: making coffee. Small bundles of fuel appeared on both sides of the road. Men dropped to the ground in relief, lounged, slept, or gathered branches and rails in the warm midday sun. They may well have thought back on the last days, a compressed eternity of terror, smoke, heat, and fatigue, and wondered whether they would meet the rebels again today or tomorrow. George Miles, one of the more ebullient boys in Company A of the Sixth Wisconsin, the Sauk County Riflemen, was quiet this afternoon. His friends noticed. "You fellows would be quiet too," he told them, "if you knew you would be killed tonight."[13]

The season had imperceptibly changed. It was still hot, but harvest time was coming. One could see it in the fields and orchards and in the longer slant of sunlight. These boys had also changed since high summer. They joked but they were not easily amused; they could be cool but casualness was not their cause. Present-day studies and battlefield tours cannot contain that certain, still fire in their eyes, or the subtle fury of their devotion. The times were alive in a terrible way. Peaceful hearths had poured forth the boys of '61—alight with silly glory but on the march of terrible events with towering and mysterious importance. Grim they had become in the bantering way of old soldiers, indifferent to the shows of glory now, and indomitable. They had kept at it these endless days past as though the hand of history was upon them: joking, cursing, marching, writing letters home, playing cards, coughing as they passed young ladies standing in their doorways, biting cartridges, bleeding on the ground at Brawner Farm and Manassas, singing patriotic songs and sweet old songs, and killing.[14] Frightening men they had become, lonesome sons and brothers, the face of humankind and history. Their golden youth was gone now, dispelled in the silvery set of the bayonet—boys becoming what men have always become, looking up the dusty road to the mountain.

The men were ordered up before they could boil their coffee.

Turner's Gap defies belief as a place where men actually fought a battle. The National Road, going west from Frederick through Middletown, ascends Turner's Gap up a narrowing defile that quickly becomes steep. At first there are farms and fields, but the last half mile is very rough. Hills rise abruptly alongside the road. Woods crowd close on the north side; to the south, the ground falls away abruptly, descending into a narrow ravine of secondary growth and rocks, before rising steeply again. The road itself is not straight. Within a half mile of the top, it bends sharply to the left, continuing southwesterly for about 200 yards, then bends to the right, west again, for the last hundred yards or so to the top. In 1862 Mountain House stood alongside the road at the highest point. Back then, before entering the defile one passed farms and fields. Stone fences divided the fields, some at right angles to the road. At the lower bend, a stone fence made a line perpendicular to the pike, extending from the road to the woods about two hundred yards away. Part of Colonel Alfred Colquitt's brigade, the Twenty-third and Twenty-eighth Georgia, used this as an advanced line on the afternoon of September 14. The main line was at the bend near Mountain House.

This brigade contained little more than 1,100 men, according to General D. H. Hill, about 200 fewer than the number in Gibbon's brigade.[15] Colquitt's five regiments were, from the Union left to right, Thirteenth Alabama, Twenty-seventh Georgia, and Sixth Georgia south of the road, and the other two Georgia regiments extending the line north of it. Their position was virtually ideal. Behind them a battery was posted at the summit. Looking down the road and ravine, their infantry line extending from the south side of the gorge into the woods on the north side, these Southerners probably understood that under normal circumstances they should be able to hold off three times or more their number. Here the old boast might have been made good, that one Southerner could whip two or five or however many Yankees you please. To be attacked by only one brigade might have appeared to be indecently good fortune.

Pressure was being applied on both sides of Turner's Gap, however, and if either of these quite large attacks should succeed, Colquitt's men would become a bony sandwich. The fight for Fox's Gap to the south had been going on, in fact, since about 9:00 A.M. By 4:00 in the afternoon the battle had involved four Union divisions (eight brigades) and three Confederate brigades. The Confederates were engaged in a desperate fight. General D. H. Hill wrote later that he had never "experienced a feeling of greater *loneliness.* It seemed as though we were deserted 'by all the world and the rest of mankind.'"[16] Nevertheless, the outnumbered Southerners were not driven back until late evening.

To the north, four Confederate brigades held off three Union divisions attacking up the steep, wooded terrain. Though gradually pressed back, those Southerners did not retire until 11 P.M. Gibbon's men were ordered to halt on the National Road, out of range of the artillery at the top of Turner's Gap. They waited in the fields as the afternoon went by, listening to the battles raging ahead on the right and left.

Although the fighting was occurring to the northeast and south of Turner's Gap, a lot of high-ranking attention was focused on this central point. D. H. Hill had been with Colquitt, personally overseeing the placement of the Georgia and Alabama troops, their artillery, and their skirmishers down front in

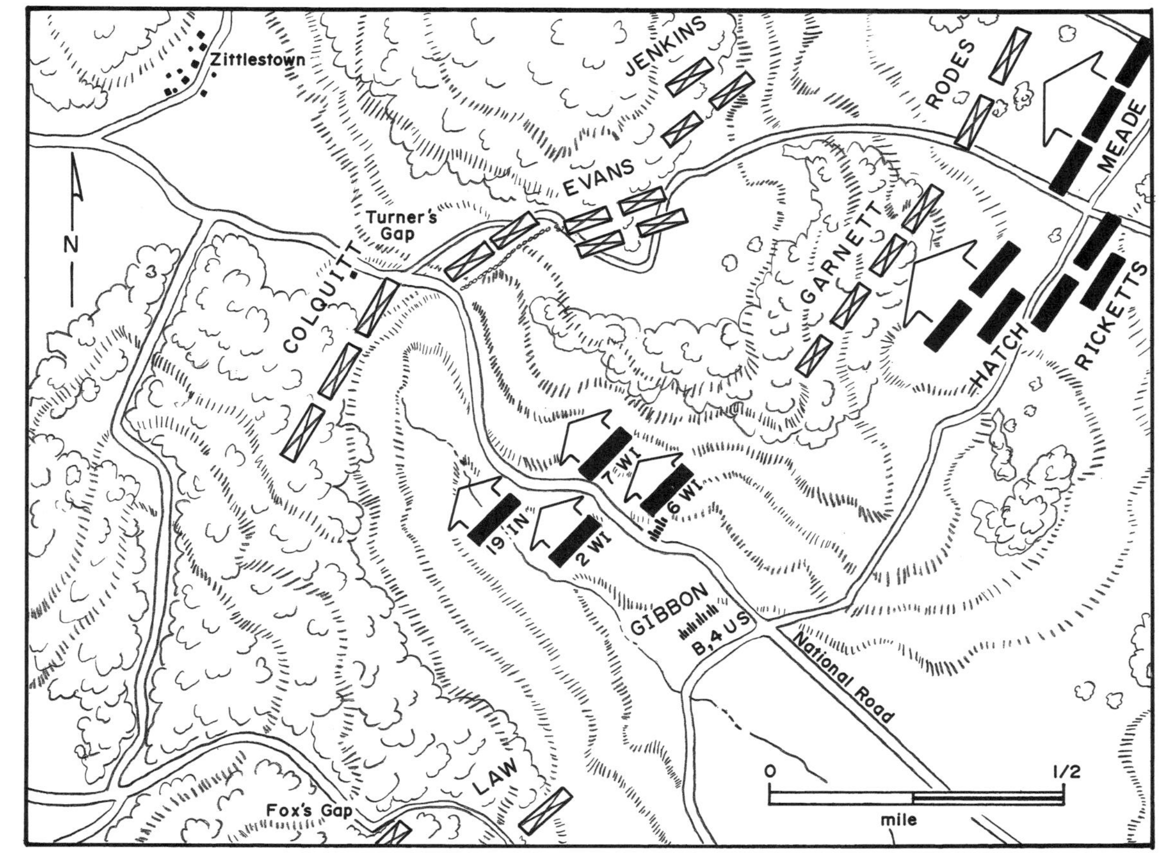

National Pike Gorge, South Mountain Battlefield, Virginia. Source: *Battles and Leaders*.

the fields and buildings.[17] Longstreet must have inspected the position as well. A few miles to the east, George McClellan, the Young Napoleon, had arrived with his escort and staff. This surely meant that combat was imminent. The main attacks were slowly advancing right and left of the road; the sun descended toward the tops of the trees along South Mountain. A demonstration, meant to fix the rebel center, would have to be made soon if it were to be made at all. As Gibbon's Black Hats looked back down the pike, a rider came galloping toward them.

Orders were passed quickly. The brigade was to go forward on both sides of the National Road. Gibbon deployed the Seventh Wisconsin to the right in line of battle. Behind them, alongside the road, the Sixth Wisconsin was to advance in double column as support. The same formation was made on the left: Nineteenth Indiana in line of battle in front, Second Wisconsin in column behind. One section of Battery B, Fourth United States Artillery, under the command of Lieutenant James Stewart, took position in the road itself. Skirmishers were sent out to protect the flanks. On the far right, Companies B and K of the Sixth Wisconsin ran ahead of their regiment and fanned out to the right of the Seventh Wisconsin. Similarly, Companies B and E of the Second Wisconsin, both commanded by Captain Colwell, plunged ahead to protect the Nineteenth Indiana's left.[18] Gibbon rode alongside on higher ground and began calling, loudly and clearly, "Forward! Forward!"

It was about two miles through open fields of fire to Colquitt's line at the top. The Western brigade, a wide line of Black Hats with two support columns behind, skirmishers on the flanks, two guns now discharging from the road, moved forward. Their tanned faces were burnished bronze by the setting sun.

The Wisconsin and Indiana men went forward with a cheer. Where they began, sunshine still spread across the fields and buildings. But the sun was going down, and not far ahead long shadows became engulfed by the one great shadow of the mountain. Soon came the *pop* and *wzzt* of skirmish fire from a long cornfield in front on the right. Then from the left, too, where rebels were waiting behind trees and rocks and fences, and in a two-story house. Dull, distant reports sounded from the summit of the gap: one, two, three puffs of smoke. The airy rush of a shell, *flash!* Seven Wisconsin men left of the road were down, four still and mangled, three severely wounded.[19] "Forward! Forward! Forward!" Gibbon shouted from his horse, and the regiments pushed on.

The two companies of skirmishers on the far right, Rollin Converse's Prescott Guards (Company B) and John Ticknor's Lemonweir Minute Men (Company K), moved forward carefully but intrepidly, inexorably pushing outward and upward, engaging the meticulously firing Confederates. "Nothing could be finer than the conduct of these two companies," Rufus Dawes wrote, "or more gallant than the bearing of their young leaders." It was "a deadly game of 'Bo-peep,' hiding behind logs, fences, rocks and bushes."[20]

Wilson B. Colwell, Second Wisconsin Volunteer Infantry Regiment.
Courtesy of the Wisconsin Veterans Museum.

On the left, Company B of the Second Wisconsin was also playing this deadly game. Its admired captain, Wilson Colwell, led them forward with even more than his customary boldness. This twilight skirmishing had acquired a particular significance. The captain stood and waved his crouching men forward, watching for the rebels' puffs of smoke. Colwell had been popular and respected at home; just before the war began he had been elected mayor of La Crosse. When the La Crosse Light Guard (now Company B) was formed, Colwell had been chosen for its captain. However, someone had written a letter to the governor casting aspersions upon Colwell's bravery. Whether written in envy, in hopes of his own advancement—or in fact by whom—is not known, but all soldiers writing of Colwell attested to his courage. Veterans of the Second remembered Colwell coolly "sitting down where the shell struck his company at Blackburn's Ford, July 18, 1861, which killed Gardner and wounded several others, and taking out his pipe, deliberately filled it and commenced smoking, saying at the same time, that 'lightning never strikes twice in the same place.'"[21] However, "Colwell was naturally very sensitive, and this [false accusation] affected him so much that he went into battle determined to die. . . . He even stated that he had no desire to survive the fight."[22] Standing in the field, directing his men with "bravery and desperation," the captain could not be ignored by the steady shooters from Georgia. When he went down, Colwell was carried to the rear by his stricken men. He died within the hour. "His place can hardly be filled," wrote the dismayed colonel of the Second. "He was a fine officer and beloved by the whole regiment."[23]

The single section of Battery B was unusually effective as support for the skirmishers. When shots began coming from the house ahead of the Nineteenth Indiana, Stewart directed his guns to hit the structure. The first shot went through the second story, where the Southerners were ensconced, sending them "stampeding," Colonel Meredith reported. Here was a battery that could hunt rabbits. The Nineteenth went forward "cheering all the time." Some twenty-pound Parrotts on a rise well behind the Black Hats, together with the rest of Battery B, were directing their attention to the Confederate battery at the top of the gap.[24]

Those guns were having an unsuccessful time of it. Perhaps the best testimony to the steepness of the grade at Turner's Gap is the failure of the Confederate artillery to hit their targets after Gibbon's men closed to within the last mile. Accounts do not speak of these Confederate guns as a factor, though more than one mention that after the first destruction dealt by these guns, they always fired over the Western men's heads. They could not depress their tubes enough. Meanwhile, Federal artillery was eating them up.

Setting their faces toward the backlit summit, the Indiana and Wisconsin men moved forward in earnest, the light of battle in their eyes answering the twilight flashes from skirmishers ahead and on the flanks. Colonel Solomon Meredith ordered his Company G to move around left of the regiment and try to sweep the persistent rebels. Meanwhile the Nineteenth Indiana filed to the left, broadening the brigade's front south of the road, and the Second Wisconsin stepped out of column into line of battle, filling in the newly opened space between the Nineteenth's right and the pike. The first mile had been covered. Now the shadows fell and the way tilted against them. The ascent began.

The Confederate line crouched up ahead somewhere holding their fire, but the woods were thick with skirmishers. The Western men were thirsty.

> . . . climbing of the rocky sides and firing as we went was hard work. After a while the water in the canteens was gone, the mouth parched, the lips and tongue swollen and cracked caused by the powder taken in the mouth while biting off the end of the cartridges. . . .[25]

Over on the right, skirmishers of the Sixth went forward with "utmost enthusiasm" though the "fellows were as cool and collected as if at target practice, and, in fact, on more than one occasion when gathered behind a boulder, one would ask the other to watch his shot and see where he hit."[26] But they were getting close to the line of the Twenty-third Georgia and Twenty-eighth Georgia, waiting behind the stone fence.

> It was now sundown and being in the shadow of the mountain it was getting dark very fast, and our fellows pushed the rebel skirmishers up to their line of battle, and our squad took shelter behind a big boulder and two of us fired from each side of it. The Seventh, which was in line of battle behind us, opened fire and the skirmishers who had gradually moved to the right toward the woods had uncovered their front and were fighting the rebel skirmishers at close quarters, when a heavy line of battle rose up and advanced towards the right flank of the Seventh, and then came the crash of their volley by regiment.[27]

Anyone who has witnessed even part of a company of reenactors demonstrating a unison volley can imagine the stunning, deafening bang of regimental fire in this manner. It was a punishing, lethal explosion, striking men off their feet all along the Wisconsin line:

> . . . a most terrific fire was poured into the gallant old Seventh, until even the colors were dropped and picked up many times, so severe was the fire, killing off the men, that it seemed that no one could survive.[28]

This fire was all the deadlier for coming obliquely from the Seventh's right; the Georgia line extended far beyond its flank. With desperate haste the Sixth Wisconsin jogged out of column by the right and left flanks and came up in line of battle, Gibbon having fired off the order even as an officer of the Seventh ran back to the Sixth shouting, "Come forward, Sixth!"[29]

Colonel Bragg of the Sixth took his regiment obliquely to the right, coming up behind the Seventh and extending across their flank through the field behind them. Gibbon's brigade was not one of the best-drilled and best-led organizations in the Army of the Potomac for nothing! Despite the dark, the Wisconsin men held formation crisply, clasping hands when necessary, extending their line neatly toward the woods on the field's right. Bragg shouted to Rufus Dawes: "Major, take command of the right wing and fire on the woods!"

Dawes's men loosed a volley at the Georgians, cutting a killing fire through the trees. "Have your men lie down on the ground," Bragg shouted. "I am going over you."[30] Here the Wisconsin regiment improvised and precisely executed a sophisticated maneuver, on the spur of the moment. One wing fired and advanced with a rush while the other group covered them. Bragg then had his wing dash over Dawes's prone, reloading men. Bragg unloosed a volley, then Dawes's men were up and running. Bragg ordered his men down; Dawes leapt over them and fired a volley.

The Seventh cheered and poured their fire into the gray line ahead. An officer of the Nineteenth Indiana, lying wounded across the road, cried with relief when he heard the Wisconsin volleys, for he knew then that he would not fall into enemy hands.[31]

Three times the Sixth Wisconsin repeated Bragg's maneuver, getting into the woods on the Twenty-eighth Georgia's front and flank, and in the sparking, flashing dark the whole Indiana and Wisconsin line was moving forward, up the rocky ascent. The Georgia men began giving ground slowly, moving back toward the line up at the last turn in the road.

The battle on the mountain was being watched. On a hilltop several miles to the east, McClellan observed the wide battle all along South Mountain. General Hooker rode up for orders and McClellan called to him, "What troops are those fighting in the Pike?"

"Gibbon's Brigade of Western men," Hooker replied.

"They must be made of iron!" The two generals saw the line of fire slowly rise along the steep, rocky mountainside. "They fight equal to the best troops in the world," McClellan said. So electrified that he forgot to get his orders, Hooker galloped off toward the front.

The next morning, Hooker asked McClellan, "What do you think now of my iron brigade?" The name was first used outside the army several days later by a newspaper correspondent. At least two other units tried to adopt the name. Only this one kept it.[32]

The new description of the brigade had been bought dearly. "By gaining the name," a soldier wrote twelve days later, after the fight along the banks of the Antietam, "we have lost from the brigade seventeen hundred and fifty men."[33] Here at South Mountain, the deadly fire seemed at times to be even heavier than it had been at Brawner Farm. Colonel Colquitt wrote in his report that his two left regiments must have been engaged against "at least five, perhaps ten, times their numbers."[34]

The Seventh Wisconsin was having the worst of it. Directly ahead of them was the stone wall. The rebels on the left of the road were in position back up at their main line, with only skirmishers immediately in front of the Nineteenth Indiana and Second Wisconsin, but the Twenty-third Georgia and Twenty-eighth Georgia were present in force at the stone wall. "All we could see of the enemy," wrote a member of the Seventh Wisconsin, "was a streak of fire as their guns were discharged."[35]

To their right, the Sixth was also heavily engaged. One man, wounded and hobbling to the rear using his rifle as a crutch, looked back and saw that "the sides of the mountain seemed in a blaze of flame and the lines of the combatants did not appear more than three or four rods apart." He added that "the angry 'Zip, zip, Whing' of the bullets" prevented him from "dwelling long on the sight." He made his way down to the road, a goal made highly visible, "lit up by the flashes of a couple of Battery B's guns which were firing as guns never fired before. The two pieces made an almost continual roar and they were being pushed forward by hand at every discharge. The gap in the mountain seemed all aflame and the noise and uproar and cheers and yells were terrific." The Sixth and Seventh, as another man observed with satisfaction, were "giving them Wisconsin hell."[36]

There was plenty of hell to go around. Writing of both sides, General Hill observed that Gibbon "had brave men and . . . he encountered brave men." Dawes wrote that some rebels shouted, "You damned Yanks, we gave you hell again at Bull Run!" The Wisconsin boys answered, "Never mind Johnny, it's no McDowell after you now. . . . "[37]

Both sides were beginning to run out of ammunition. The Sixth had worked its way around the Confederate left, extending in a deadly semicircle up through the woods. But this advantage was almost nullified. "Just as crippling" as the shortage, "the rifles of the Sixth were now too hot for loading and too full of carbon for safe use."

> We had to wait until they cooled and we wish to remark that this is about as trying a place to be in as you could imagine with the enemy peppering you and you cannot shoot back. . . .

Soldiers were scavenging the wounded and dead for cartridges, and firing very carefully. They "would kneel down and look under the smoke to see the flash of the rebel muskets not to waste our ammunition." This same soldier wrote that his barrel became so hot that he could load only by using his haversack to cradle the weapon.[38]

Gibbon's men had been issued eighty rounds. The unusually fast fire of the Western men was slacking off, but the Southerners were also running low. The Georgians carefully fell back from their advanced position, and the Wisconsin and Indiana men on both sides of the road continued their ascent to the main line. There the firing gradually ceased. Gibbon, told of the ammunition shortage, sent word to hold the ground they had won as long as there was "an inch of our bayonets left." The Southerners, close enough to hear Wisconsin boys calling for ammunition, advanced toward the Seventh, but Callis's men loaded their last rounds, rose up, advanced, fired, and broke the Confederate reconnaissance.[39]

Colonel Bragg of the Sixth said that his men were so exhausted that some "fell fast asleep . . . without a cartridge in their boxes. . . . " The ones awake were not in much better condition. One remembered being "so wet from perspiration that running my hand down my wool sleeve the water would run down in front of it." Word arrived, however, that South Mountain was being carried. The divisions to the right had made it to the crest, and now the defenders of Turner's Gap were flanked. Colonel Bragg began to think he heard the rebels withdrawing. He called out, "Three cheers for the Badger State!" With what energy they could still muster, his regiment shouted huzzahs into the dark. A defiant answer came, but it came from the other side of the summit. The men collapsed to the ground and slept, "with their commanding officer and a captain as their pickets."[40]

General Edwin Sumner's Second Corps had been moving up within supporting distance, and at midnight, three of Gibbon's regiments were relieved by regiments of Brigadier General Willis Gorman's brigade and made their way back down the National Road—except for the Sixth Wisconsin. Gorman refused to send any of his regiments up into the woods where Bragg's men were lying. "I can't send men into that woods to-night. All men are cowards in the dark."[41] Not all. The Sixth Wisconsin remained where they were in the chilling mountain air.

> . . . we lay that night where we were when the fight stopped and the ground was so rough and rocky that more than one of the boys had to use his dead comrade for a pillow.[42]

In his official report, General Hooker says of Gibbon's brigade, "I can only call your attention to their list of casualties; it speaks for itself."[43] The Wisconsin and Indiana men had lost twice as severely as had any other First Corps brigade: 318 officers and men, or 25 percent. The Seventh Wisconsin, facing the stone wall, had suffered the worst casualties with 147 men shot. Dawes wrote:

> The night was chilly, and in the woods intensely dark. Our wounded were scattered over a great distance up and down the mountain, and were suffering untold agonies. Owing to the difficulties of the ground and the night, no stretcher bearers had come upon the field. Several dying men were pleading piteously for water, of which there was not a drop in the regiment, nor was there any liquor. Captain Kellogg and I searched in vain for a swallow for one noble fellow who was dying in great agony from a wound in his bowels. He recognized us and appreciated our efforts, but was unable to speak. The dread reality of war was before us in this frightful death, upon the cold, hard stones.[44]

The Western men had given a demonstration of military effectiveness. Their discipline held them firm and cohesive in the dark, in the woods, and on a difficult ascent under fire which would have broken up and demoralized less perfected organizations. Discipline also enabled them—the Sixth Wisconsin in particular—to respond effectively to novel orders requiring courage and precision. Leadership was also a strength of Gibbon's brigade. The general himself had shown his excellence simply by bringing to this field a brigade with such discipline and high morale. But the regimental commanders and captains, mentioned time and again in soldiers' accounts of the battle at South Mountain, proved themselves worthy of their men's confidence, obedience, and admiration. The brigade also excelled in basic military skills and in physical stamina. This is, of course, a result of effective leadership, but it also reflects the men's intelligence, attitude, and backgrounds. General D. H. Hill referred to "the North-west, where habitually good fighters are reared."[45] No ordinary unit could have successfully ascended that mountain under fire, or done such effective work with two Napoleons, or have given the veteran Southerners the impression that the black-hatted attackers outnumbered them five or ten to one. Involved in all this is the intangible essential, *morale*, which makes itself felt in tangible and decisive ways. The men from Indiana and Wisconsin were well-disciplined, skilled, efficiently and intelligently led, respected, and well taken care of by their officers. But they also believed in their cause. These were volunteers. And the story of this brigade is the story of a group of men who steadily gained an identity.

Ascent is an age-old metaphor for becoming who and what human beings have most aspired to be. At the summit of Mount Carmel, or of South Mountain, waits in some form or other the new man or woman, the higher human being which the Greeks characterized by *arete*, or excellence. Excellence describes the hero, called by many names. It is the quest of each hero to find his or her own particular identity. At the top of the mountain the hero finds his name.

The next morning, General Sumner and his staff had ridden up the National Road, up past the fields and walls and woods. The tough regular had watched Gibbon's men pass the night before. Old "Bull" Sumner was known to detest the shows of military pomp and glory favored by the less hardheaded—by McClellan, for example. But today he did something utterly different, and unforgettable. He ordered his men to *cheer* the Black Hats from Wisconsin and Indiana. As Bruce Catton wrote of another salute this brigade would receive some months hence, it was "the Army of the Potomac, giving and receiving the only accolade it would ever know or care for."[46]

As it was, perhaps appropriately, the Black Hats had already passed the Second Corps troops before Sumner's directive reached his men.[47] For if these Western men had given a demonstration in military excellence, the rough mountain and the stubborn Georgians and Alabamians had given a lesson in futility. Due primarily to their excellent position, D. H. Hill pointed out,

Colquitt's brigade lost only about 100 men and never lost one foot of ground from their main defensive line. "The Western men had met in the Twenty-third Georgia and Twenty-eighth Georgia regiments men as brave as themselves and far more advantageously posted."[48] In larger terms,

> If the battle of South Mountain was fought to prevent the advance of McClellan, it was a failure on the part of the Confederates. If it was fought to save Lee's trains and artillery, and to reunite his scattered forces, it was a Confederate success.[49]

The North took the former view; the South, the latter.

Narratives of battle, one must conclude, are only partial narratives, and our "analyses" are merely attempts to handle the small fragments we see. "Our poor power to add or detract" must be understood for the small thing it is, and the great forces at work in battle always must be acknowledged as being far above the force of bullets or the force of argument. In this way only can we begin to appreciate the experience of battle.

Human affairs and efforts are mixed. Things gained are paid for, and the full nature of what is gained must be sought in "the foul rag and bone shop of the human heart." Ultimately, the men of Gibbon's command had to achieve something other than military advantage, or else the great name was surely won in vain. Coming down on the west side from South Mountain, the Black Hats were met by a group of old men, one of whom cried out, "We have watched for you, Sir, and we have prayed for you and now thank God you have come."[50] These young men in dirty blue had come a long way from the golden bells of Sunday morning. In their way, they had ascended and descended the strange mountain of human history, had marched through the world's four ages, and now these soldiers in the shadow of the rising sun had new and different faces. "What do you think of my iron brigade now?"

One of them wrote home,

> well you want to know wether [*sic*] I took aim at any particular Rebbel [*sic*] or not. I took aim at one several times but they always fell before I could fire. some times when I would get a good aim at one rebbel there would be another rebbel come up before him so I could not hit the one that I aimed at. but to tell the truth I could not tell wether I killed any or not as they fell so fast. but I know I tryed as hard as I could to kill some of them.[51]

Such was their nature—to climb and to kill, to die giving their country a new birth of freedom and to take the lives of their enemies. They dedicated themselves to one of the best causes ever fought for, and won victory for it by suffering and inflicting suffering, and by mangling opponents who were trying to mangle them. They were men at war. They were sentimental and hard-handed, beautiful and tragic, leaving widows and sisters and bereft parents at home, and making widows of the wives of their enemies. In the midst of deadly struggle—from the stand-up killing and dying in a Northern

Virginia twilight, through the confused alarms of fight and retreat on the twice-lost field of Manassas, toward the most terrible day in American history—in the midst of life and death this brave band of men had climbed. Brave by day, brave by night, they became an image of what is always best in charred and senseless human conflict: real heroes, living and dying not for themselves but for others, inspiring and enabling a genuinely noble hope and winning a cause worth winning. Up through the twilight, sometimes clasping hands to stay aligned in the dark, up amid crashing sulphurous chaos, scrambling through brush and up a steep, steep slope, dry and cracked with thirst and low on ammunition, still they went on and up, carrying the weight of their time and so becoming men for all time. Plain boys from nowhere, they started in the sun at the foot of a rough mountain with names like any other names, and in the shadow of death they became the Iron Brigade.

3

"I Dread the Thought of the Place"

The Iron Brigade at Antietam

D. SCOTT HARTWIG

Near Sharpsburg, Maryland. September 16, 1862. It was the eve of the Battle of Antietam, the bloodiest single day in America's Civil War. Major Rufus R. Dawes, of the Sixth Wisconsin Infantry, recalled it:

> It was nine o'clock at night when our brigade reached the position assigned it. The men laid down upon the ground, formed in close column, muskets loaded and lines parallel with the turnpike. Once or twice during the night, heavy volleys of musketry crashed in the dark woods on our left. There was a drizzling rain, and with the certain prospect of deadly conflict on the morrow, the night was dismal. Nothing can be more solemn than a period of silent waiting for the summons to battle, known to be impending.[1]

A short distance from Dawes that night lay Sergeant William Harries, in the ranks of the Second Wisconsin Infantry. He shared Dawes's dark mood and thoughts. "I slept very little," he wrote; "I felt certain that there would be desperate fighting in the morning and that many of my comrades would fail to answer at roll call when the morning sun had again set behind the western hills. I realized that I might be among the killed." Harries's and Dawes's brooding reflections were undoubtedly shared by every man in the Western brigade of Brigadier General John Gibbon as they shivered through that damp September night. They faced battle in the morning. The enemy were so near, Harries wrote that, "we could hear the commands given by the officer's [*sic*]of the enemy's troops." Since August 28, 1862, only twenty days earlier, Gibbon's brigade, consisting of the Second, Sixth, and Seventh Wisconsin, and Nineteenth Indiana, had passed through a fiery baptism. At Brawner Farm on August 28th, and Second Manassas on August 30th and 31st, they had lost 894 men, including 148 killed in action. Two weeks later, on September 14th, they lost 318 more men, including thirty-seven killed, at South Mountain. Few units of the Army of the Potomac, including those that had fought through the Seven Days battles, had incurred such heavy casualties. The 2,100 men Gibbon had taken into action at Brawner Farm had been reduced to 800.[2]

The arithmetic of these casualties is instructive. There had been 1,212 battle casualties from Brawner Farm to South Mountain. If there were 800 men present in the ranks at Antietam, then there were less than 100 men who were absent from the ranks due to nonbattle causes. Considering the carnage the survivors had witnessed, and hard campaigning they had endured, this is a remarkably low figure.[3] The odds were clearly against those who remained in the ranks, but the overwhelming majority did so. They did largely because of loyalty to their comrades and a fierce determination to do their duty. Everyone suffered from exhaustion. The regimental commanders of the Second Wisconsin and Nineteenth Indiana, Colonel Lucius Fairchild and Colonel Solomon Meredith, were both forced to relinquish command following South Mountain, the former due to severe diarrhea, and the latter due to wounds. In the Second Wisconsin, Sidney Meade reported in his diary that one officer and forty-one enlisted men fell out of the ranks on the fourteen-mile march from South Mountain to Antietam because of extreme fatigue. But, nearly all of these men were apparently back in the ranks by September 17th. Lieutenant Henry B. Young of the Seventh Wisconsin wrote his wife on September 13th that in battle "we forget home[,] friends[,] in fact[,] everything but our duties as soldiers." To cope with the risks of combat the men confronted the possibility of their death with a matter-of-factness that likely did not sit well with the family at home. Colonel Edward Bragg, commanding the Sixth Wisconsin, passed through two major engagements safely and evaluated his chances of surviving the probable upcoming battle in a letter to his wife on September 13th. He wrote, "But I am hopeful—and have been so lucky that I do not think I shall suffer except it may be a slight wound—No one can tell if it be my fate to fall—My body will be sent to you." Lieutenant Young of the Seventh Wisconsin was equally candid and practical with his wife, Delia, in his letter on the 13th. Addressing the prospects of his death he wrote, "You ask what you should do if I should be killed. It is a hard question, but I have seen so many men killed and die in the last few weeks that I will give you the best advice I can. If I should be killed in battle or die while in the service, you as the wife of a 1st Lieut will draw from the government, seventeen dollars per month for five years." The wife of a private, Young explained, would draw "but four dollars a month." Religion also helped the men cope with the perils of combat. Gibbon's aide-de-camp, Lieutenant Frank A. Haskell, very likely spoke for many men in the brigade when he wrote his family, "I have the belief that He who controls the destinies of nations and men, has saved me, and will, unharmed, in many more battles." No doubt there were many prayers offered up to God that somber night from Gibbon's soldiers.[4]

The 800 officers and men of Wisconsin and Indiana who constituted Gibbon's brigade crossed Antietam Creek late on the afternoon of the 16th with the rest of Major General Joseph Hooker's First Corps. Hooker's mission was to locate the left flank of General Robert E. Lee's Army of Northern Virginia and strike it on the morning of the 17th. As they groped forward in the fading light of day, the Federals collided with elements of Confederate General John B. Hood's division in a woodlot that became known as the East Woods. Sharp skirmishing ensued, but Hooker was only sparring. He would wait to land heavier blows on the 17th. The main body of the corps bivouacked for the night several hundred yards north of the North and East Woods on the farm of Joseph Poffenberger. Gibbon's brigade halted after dark in a pasture on the northern edge of an orchard surrounding the Poffenberger farm buildings. Each regiment of the brigade formed in column of divisions (two companies wide and five companies deep) facing south. In formation from left to right was the Sixth Wisconsin, Second Wisconsin, Seventh Wisconsin, and Nineteenth Indiana. The brigade lay on the southwestern slope of a hill, but in the pitch darkness no one could determine whether the position was sheltered or exposed. The troops bedded down in Poffenberger's wet pasture in their company lines with their equipment on and muskets beside them, ready for the call to action.[5]

Gibbon and his regimental officers were completely ignorant of the enemy position and the ground that would become their battlefield. Their arrival after dark at their bivouac site precluded any opportunity of reconnoitering the ground, or of gathering information on enemy dispositions. Constant outbursts of musketry throughout the night provided a vague idea of the Confederate position, but Gibbon was nonetheless disturbed by what he described as the "very confused and huddled up condition" in which the First Corps hunkered down to pass the night of the 16th.[6]

Despite the excitement of impending action, fatigue eventually overcame many in the brigade and they fell into a "heavy slumber," despite the misty rain that added to the general misery of the night. The first streaks of daylight came around 4:45 A.M. on September 17. Colonel Edward Bragg recalled it "was misty and foggy." But as the early morning light revealed more of the landscape, it became clear that a Confederate battery (probably on Nicodemus Heights, about 800 yards southeast of the Poffenberger farm) had a clear line of fire on Gibbon's brigade. The First Division commander, Brigadier General Abner Doubleday, mounted his horse and galloped up to the Western brigade commanding, "Move these troops out of here at once. You're in open range of a battery." Officers shook or kicked their sleeping men awake and formed them into line in column of division.[7]

Gibbon ordered the brigade to march east, over the high ground toward the shelter of the reverse slope and the Poffenberger farm buildings. Major Dawes thought that "too much noise was probably made" in forming up the brigade, for before they had marched sixty yards, "whiz-z-z! bang! burst a shell over our heads." Sergeant William Harries had earlier seen the battery

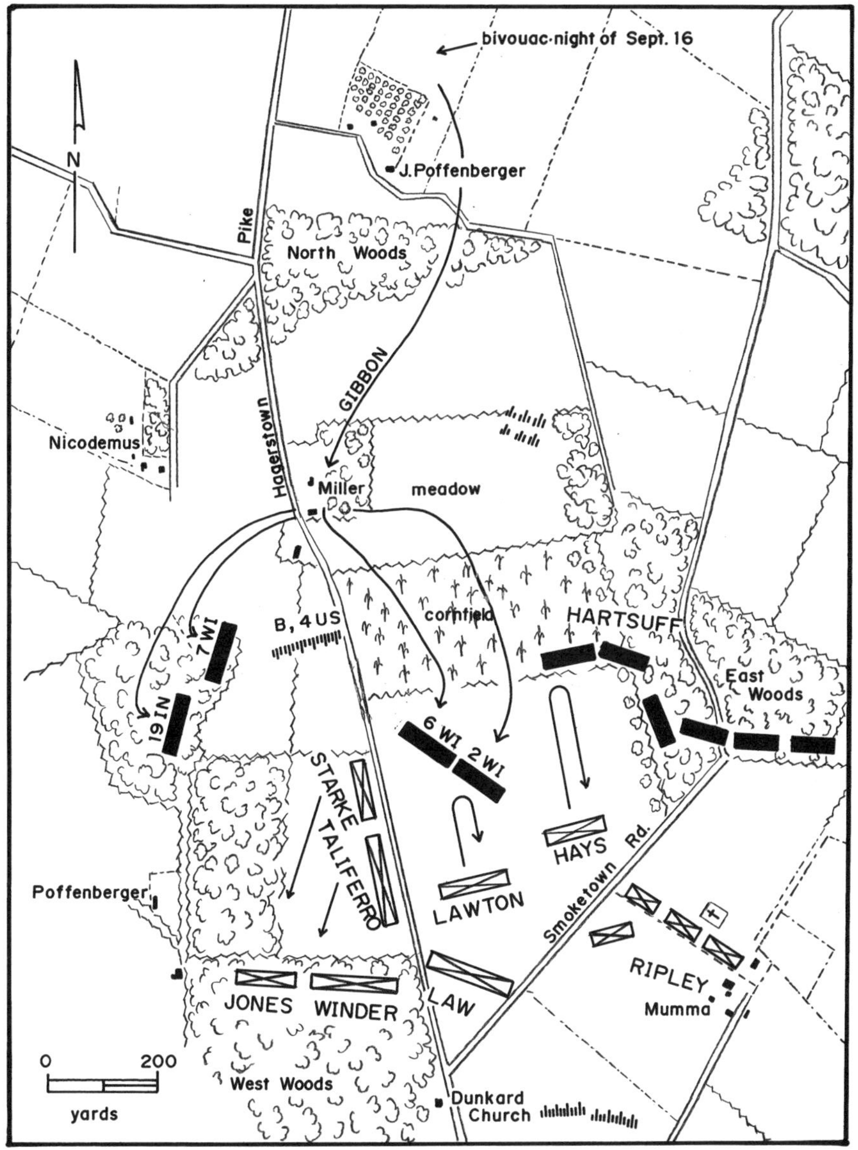

Antietam Battlefield, Sharpsburg, Maryland

that fired this shell move into position, and such was the disorientation of infantrymen in the brigade, that he believed these were friendly guns. A second shell burst over the column—which had probably shaken off its slumber very quickly—but caused no damage. The third shell sent toward the hurrying column was a percussion shell. It struck in the rear of the Sixth Wisconsin's dense formation and exploded in the ranks of Company A. The company commander, Captain David K. Noyes, had his right foot mangled by the explosion, and another man in Noyes's company had both arms severed. In all, two men were killed and eleven wounded.[8]

The horror of that moment must have been profound for everyone who witnessed it. Even Gibbon, a professional soldier, was shocked. He recalled in 1880, "Even the eighteen years which have elapsed have failed to obliterate the recollection of the thrill of horror [with] which I witnessed the sight, nor the apprehension I felt lest the shock should scatter the regiment like a flock of frightened sheep. I had not yet learned all the powers of discipline in that brigade, nor what the extent of the tests it could successfully pass through."[9] A simple command from Colonel Bragg, "Steady, Sixth; Close up!" restored order in the regiment, and they swept onward, leaving the bloody, mangled forms of their comrades behind. "Thus opened the great battle of Antietam on the morning of the 17th," wrote Major Dawes.[10]

Gibbon's column finally gained shelter on the hill's reverse slope and near the Poffenberger farm buildings. Directly in front of the brigade lay a thin belt of woods, later named the North Woods. Gibbon found First Corps Commander Hooker near this point in conference with Brigadier General George G. Meade, commanding the division of Pennsylvania Reserves, and stopped for orders. "Hooker's instructions were short and to the point. . . . I was to advance directly to the front and attack," recalled Gibbon.[11]

When the head of the column reached the North Woods, Gibbon ordered Colonel Bragg to deploy two companies as skirmishers and form the balance of his regiment in support in line of battle. Bragg ordered Captain Alexander S. Hooe's Company C and Captain John A. Kellogg's Company I forward. Kellogg was a gifted leader and man of great personal courage. Hooe's father had been a regular army major, from whom he had learned proficiency in tactics and drill, but the dangers of the battlefield paralyzed him. Skirmish duty was dangerous work, particularly for officers, who had to expose themselves constantly in supervising the extended line. Skirmishers were the extreme forward elements of an attack and, as such, bore the unpleasant duty of finding the enemy and drawing his fire.[12]

While Kellogg and Hooe deployed their companies as skirmishers, the remaining eight companies of the Sixth Wisconsin formed into line of battle in their rear. "The artillery fire had now increased to the roar of a hundred cannon," wrote Major Dawes, as more guns on both sides joined in the combat. A plowed field dotted with numerous limestone rock outcroppings extended from the front of the North Woods for nearly 250 yards, to where it met a grass field. At the northern edge of the grass field, adjacent to the Hagerstown Turnpike, were the house and outbuildings of David Miller's farm, which were surrounded by an orchard of peach and apple trees and a large garden on the northern side of the house. Nearly 100 yards south of Miller's house was a thirty-acre field he had planted in corn. Fences crisscrossed the landscape, separating the fields. Despite the heavy shelling, Gibbon recalled "no enemy was in sight." The Confederates lay concealed, waiting.[13]

The instant Hooe's and Kellogg's men appeared at the southern edge of the North Woods, Confederate skirmishers of Colonel Marcellus Douglass's brigade of Georgians, positioned around Miller's farm building and orchard, opened a "vigorous fire." Captain Kellogg and Company I "dashed across the [plowed] field at a run," and by a "rapid flank movement very handsomely executed," drove the Georgia skirmishers from the Miller farm. In sharp contrast to Kellogg, Captain Hooe shrank from the danger before him. Possibly the percussion shell that had sown carnage in the ranks during the advance had sapped Hooe's courage. Bragg wrote years later that "he showed the white feather that morning, dodged behind a tree and grew there, letting his line go helter skelter without direction." Bragg several times commanded, "move forward that line on the right," but without leadership Company C did not respond, "and we saw no more of them for some time," recalled Dawes.[14]

The main body of the regiment obliqued to the right to follow the skirmishers of Company I, who also inclined to the right, until the right of the regimental line rested upon the Hagerstown Turnpike. As the regiment reached the Miller farmyard they struck the farmer's fencing that neatly enclosed his garden, orchard, farmhouse, and outbuildings. Lieutenant Colonel Bragg recalled a board paling fence around Miller's house that "was knocked down in the rush." The left companies of the regiment under the immediate supervision of Major Dawes came up against a picket fence that bordered Miller's garden. Dawes reported that "I ordered the men of the left wing to take hold all together and pull down the fence." Miller's fence prevailed and Dawes was forced to order the left wing to move by the flank through a gate in the fence "with the utmost haste," in order to catch up with the right wing of the regiment which had moved ahead through Miller's farmyard. Captain Edwin A. Brown, of Company E, Dawes's "best friend in the regiment," raised his sword and shouted "in a loud, nervous voice, 'Company E, on the right by file into line'." An instant later a bullet struck Brown in the face and killed him. The poor captain, according to one of his men, had been "almost worn out, and so lame that he could scarcely walk."[15]

Dawes left his friend lying next to Miller's picket fence and led the left wing through briers and flowerbeds in Miller's garden into the farmer's peach orchard. The companies swept through this to a rail fence along the southern face of the orchard. Here Dawes's left wing caught up with the right wing and redeployed into line. Some Georgia skirmishers had been lying behind this fence and Bragg recalled, "they gave us a hot reception, but it was unavailing to check the bullet like force of the command," and the Confederates dashed back for the cover of Miller's cornfield. "Before us was a strip of open field, beyond which, on the left-hand side of the turnpike, was rising ground, covered by a large cornfield," observed Dawes. The southwesterly angle of the regiment's advance had caused the right three companies to be crowded out of the cover of Miller's orchard and farmyard, into an open pasture on the west side of the turnpike, in front of Miller's barnyard. Beyond their unsupported right flank were the West Woods. The rapid movement of the regiment had also caused it to move in advance of the rest of the brigade so that its left flank also had no direct support. Little had been seen of the enemy to this point apart from rebel skirmishers. Despite the cultivated nature of the Antietam battlefield, the crop fields, woods, and highly undulating terrain offered numerous places of concealment for large bodies of troops. The steady stream of friendly and hostile artillery shells that passed overhead gave warning that there were plenty of enemy soldiers ahead. Without waiting for his supports to come up, Lieutenant Colonel Bragg, "with his usual battle ardor," ordered the regiment to advance.[16]

"We climbed the fence, moved across the open space, and pushed into the corn-field," wrote Dawes. Entering the cornfield tested the mettle of every man and officer who ventured into it. The cornstalks stood seven to eight feet in height. "We could neither see or be seen," recalled Dawes. The enemy were very close but their precise position was still unknown. The air fairly shook with the crash and bang of exploding artillery shells and the screech of shells arcing across the sky. Bullets, fired by an unseen foe, whined overhead, or clipped through the corn.[17]

While Dawes led the left of the regiment into the corn, the three right companies moved cautiously over open ground, advancing past Miller's barn and several strawstacks south of it to rising ground. Less than 200 yards west of the barn stood the northern end of the West Woods, looming dark and forbidding in the gloomy early morning light. Along its eastern edge and squarely on the flank of Bragg's right companies, lying undetected, were skirmishers of Colonel Bradley T. Johnson's brigade under Captain A. C. Page. They had not been discovered because Captain Hooe's Company C, with no direction or leadership, had not kept its place on the skirmish line.[18]

Moments before the Virginians revealed themselves, Bragg observed a limbered Confederate battery move from its position beyond the cornfield and swing onto the Hagerstown Pike traveling south. Bragg ordered Captain Werner Von Bachelle, commanding Company F, astride the turnpike, to advance to a ridge line running south from the cornfield [where the present-day parking area for the cornfield stop is located] and attempt to shoot the horses on the limbers. Von Bachelle was possibly the most experienced soldier in the Sixth, having served as a staff officer with the French army in Algiers. Dawes remembered him as a gallant man and model soldier. He was accompanied in battle by "his faithful dog," a black and white Newfoundland. Von Bachelle led his company forward and Companies G and K, on his right, likewise advanced.[19]

Company F advanced to a "small knoll" when they were suddenly confronted with Colonel Andrew J. Grigsby's and Brigadier General John R. Jones's Confederate brigades lying down in line of battle perpendicular to the turnpike. The Confederates opened fire upon Von Bachelle's company and at the same time Captain Page's gray skirmishers, positioned along the edge of the West Woods, poured lead into the flank of Companies G and K. Von Bachelle was riddled with bullets and killed ("I think I counted twelve," wrote Bragg in 1894), and his company's advance checked. A bullet from the direction of the West Woods also struck Bragg, who was standing in the turnpike, in the arm. "I thought my elbow fractured," he wrote after the battle. With quick presence of mind, and despite his painful wound, he ordered the three right companies to fall back to the turnpike where they lay down behind the turnpike fences and returned the fire from the woods. "There I must confess, things began to look pretty dark, & I felt faint," Bragg recalled. He sent regimental Sergeant Major Howard J. Huntington dashing into the corn to find Dawes and bring him over to the turnpike.[20]

While the right companies of the Sixth Wisconsin were driven back to the turnpike by an enfilading fire, Dawes and the left wing of the regiment were suffering their own ordeal. Bullets were clipping through the corn "thick, almost, as hail," and although the men were hugging mother earth, people were being struck. But the most serious hazard at this moment was Union artillery, which was firing short and bursting shells "all around us," according to Dawes. A fragment from one shell went through the body of Lieutenant Edward Bode of Company F and killed him instantly, the second officer of that company to die in a matter of minutes. Another shell burst over the pike and wounded Lieutenant John Ticknor of Company K. The terror of these moments must have been extreme. But Dawes observed in his journal that—from the perspective of someone who understood the perils of an infantryman—"this has happened often in the war." To be fired upon by the enemy and your own men was not uncommon.[21]

Sergeant Major Huntington, meanwhile, dashed through the corn until he found Dawes. "Colonel Bragg wants to see you," he told the major. The two men ran to the turnpike, where Dawes found Bragg. The lieutenant colonel, who remained on his feet only through sheer will, said to Dawes, "Major I am wounded take command." He then fainted. Dawes and the others around their commander saw a tear in his overcoat (the lining of which was red) and in the excitement of the moment believed he had been shot through the body. Dawes called for two men nearby to evacuate Bragg on a shelter tent.[22]

"I felt a great sense of responsibility, when thrown thus suddenly in command of the regiment in the face of a terrible battle," recalled Dawes of the moment Bragg informed him he had been wounded. The major was twenty-three years old. Besides the loss of Bragg, two company commanders were dead, one cowered in the rear, and two lieutenants were down, one killed, the other wounded. Around the young major and his regiment the battle raged and roared with incredible violence. But Dawes and his men were sustained in this trying moment by the discipline and drill that John Gibbon had subjected them to for so many months in the spring and summer, and by their experience in the battles of Second Manassas and South Mountain. They had "faced the elephant" before and knew their duty. Yet, there was more to it than drill and discipline. Captain Hooe had excelled in this aspect of soldiering. In the face of the enemy and death, plain, simple courage was necessary. The courage to lead men through eight-foot corn against an unseen enemy. The courage to conquer your fears and do your duty when friendly artillery killed comrades around you and hostile bullets snapped over your head. Anger, too, helped propel men forward. Dawes recalled that after Bragg had been carried off he remained at the fence along the Hagerstown Turnpike, where the men of Companies F, G, and K were trading fire with the Virginians in the West Woods. Standing there, Dawes observed a group of mounted Confederate officers. He asked one of the men for his musket and rested it on the turnpike fence and fired. He repeated this five more times until he had the satisfaction of seeing the group scatter.[23]

From the perspective of Lyman Holford of Company C, the enemy had "began to get pretty thick." Help was approaching to support Holford and his comrades. Gibbon sent Lieutenant Colonel Thomas S. Allen's Second Wisconsin Infantry forward in line of battle into the cornfield on the Sixth's left. To counter the threat to Dawes's right flank, Gibbon ordered Lieutenant James Stewart to take his section of Captain Joseph B. Campbell's Battery B, Fourth U. S. Artillery—Gibbon's old battery in the regular army—forward and unlimber in front of Miller's barn, west of the turnpike. Stewart commanded what was called the "Gray horse" section, because of the color of the horses that pulled his limbers and caissons. He unlimbered his two Napoleons "alongside of the straw stacks [at Miller's barn] or a little in front of them," and placed his limbers behind the stacks where they might have some cover, then ordered his gun crews to open on the enemy with spherical case shot.[24]

The Seventh Wisconsin and Nineteenth Indiana, still in column of division, had halted during the brigade advance at the edge of the cornfield, where they were ordered to lie down. After Stewart's section had unlimbered at the straw stacks, Gibbon ordered both regiments to move across the turnpike, deploy into line and to "push forward rapidly" into the West Woods, to relieve the flank fire upon Dawes's regiment.[25]

Back in Miller's cornfield, Allen's Second Wisconsin, only 150 strong, came sweeping through the corn in the Sixth Wisconsin's left. The Second had supported the advance of the Sixth to the Miller Farm and followed

Bragg's regiment through Miller's orchard and into the cornfield. In the corn, Allen ordered his regiment to move by the left oblique until they came up on the left of the Sixth. Allen had been shot in the neck and wrist at the Battle of Brawner Farm on August 28th. He carried his wounded arm in a sling and held his sword with his other arm. When he encountered Dawes in the corn he simply pointed his sword forward and told the major to advance his regiment. Dawes commanded, "Attention battalion, forward, guide left, march." At the same time he ordered Sergeant Major Huntington to find Captain Philip W. Plummer, commanding Company G on the turnpike, and tell him "if it is practicable," to move the right companies on the pike forward in alignment with the rest of the regiment. Huntington discovered that Captain Kellogg had replaced Plummer in command of the companies on the turnpike. Kellogg sent Huntington dashing back through the corn with the response, "Please give Major Dawes my compliments, and say it is impracticable, the fire being murderous."[26]

Dawes's orders to his regiment to "guide left" on the Second Wisconsin, caused the six companies in the corn to swing away from the turnpike and break contact with Captain Kellogg's companies. The major again sent Sergeant Major Huntington, who must have been breathless by this time, back to tell Kellogg that he could find cover in the corn and that "if it is possible," to move his companies forward and join the rest of the regiment. Huntington was struck by a bullet during his perilous journey. He managed to reach Kellogg and deliver Dawes's orders, but he failed to add that the major had given Kellogg the discretion to determine whether or not he could safely execute his instructions. Kellogg did not think he could, but he tried. He ordered his men up but "so many were shot in their tracks that he immediately ordered them down again." The right companies were pinned down.[27]

The main body of Dawes's regiment, together with the Second Wisconsin, shouldered their way through Miller's corn and continued on until they reached the southern edge of the field, enclosed by a Virginia rail fence. South of the corn were pastures and meadows. Here, at the edge of Miller's cornfield, the Second and Sixth Wisconsin encountered the main Confederate line. Less than two hundred yards south of the corn, the Georgia brigade of Colonel Marcellus Douglass had torn down the rail fencing nearby, piled the rails for protection, and lay down behind their slight shelter. When the Wisconsin regiments appeared at the edge of the corn the Georgians rose up from their cover.[28] In one of the more memorable passages from the war, Dawes described the lethal encounter that ensued:

> Simultaneously, the hostile battle lines opened a tremendous fire upon each other. Men, I can not say fell; they were knocked out of the ranks by dozens. But we jumped over the fence, and pushed on, loading, firing, and shouting as we advanced. There was, on the part of the men, great hysterical excitement, eagerness to go forward, and a reckless disregard of life, or every thing but victory.[29]

"Every body tears cartridges, loads, passes guns, or shoots," wrote Dawes, in the furious effort to fire as fast as possible. Captain Kellogg came up in the road with the three right companies, who had been relieved from the murderous enfilade fire by the Nineteenth Indiana and Seventh Wisconsin. Slowly the line advanced until it was nearly twenty yards south of the corn. The storm of bullets from the Sixth and Second regiments, combined with an enfilading artillery fire from the Union heavy batteries positioned east of Antietam Creek, finally proved too much for Douglass's Georgians, and they fell back in the direction of the Dunker (or Dunkard) Church. But as they did the Federals observed a powerful Confederate force come pouring out of the West Woods threatening the right flank of the Sixth Wisconsin. It was Brigadier General William Starke's Louisiana brigade and Taliaferro's Alabama-Virginia brigade, commanded by Colonel E. T. H. Warren, a combined force nearly 1,100 strong. Lieutenant Colonel Allen saw them coming and ordered his regiment to change front to face them. He also ordered his men to hastily throw up a rail barricade—probably with the same rails Douglass's men had used for protection. "In this position the regiment opened a rapid and telling fire upon the enemy," wrote the regiment's acting adjutant, James D. Wood.[30]

The Louisianians, Alabamians, and Virginians pressed forward despite the fire of the Second and Sixth, right up to the fences along the western edge of the Hagerstown Turnpike. The range between the two lines was a mere thirty to seventy-five yards. "Their volleys are tremendous," reported Dawes. Allen received a wound in the arm and command of the Second Wisconsin fell to Captain George D. Ely of Company D. The change of front by the Second had exposed them to flank fire on their left from Confederates of Douglass's brigade, who were lying concealed behind a ledge. Colonel Walter Phelps's brigade rushed out of the corn to bolster the rapidly thinning ranks of the Sixth. "Now is the pinch," wrote Dawes. "Men and officers of New York and Wisconsin are fused into a common mass, in the frantic struggle to shoot fast. Men are falling in their places or running back into the corn." Despite the support of Phelps's New Yorkers and Second U. S. Sharpshooters, the Federal line began to "sag, slowly, stubbornly back to the edge of the corn and down on our faces again." The Second Wisconsin "nobly stood their ground until fully two-thirds of their number had been killed or wounded," and they too fell back. As the Federals gave way, some of Starke's and Warren's Confederates began to climb the fence along the pike. This proved to be the limit of Starke's counterattack, for trouble suddenly reared its head upon the exposed left flank of his line.[31]

Gibbon's deployment of the Nineteenth Indiana and Seventh Wisconsin on the west side of the turnpike now paid dividends against Starke's counterattack. The two regiments crossed the turnpike between Miller's house and barn in rear of Stewart's section of Battery B and formed into line. The Nineteenth Indiana under twenty-three-year-old Lieutenant Colonel Alois

Alois O. Bachman, Nineteenth Indiana Volunteer Infantry Regiment. From the collection of Alan T. Nolan.

O. Bachman formed on the right and the Seventh Wisconsin under Captain John B. Callis on the left. The northern end of the West Woods lay south of the two regiments. Bachman ordered Company B under nineteen-year-old Captain William W. Dudley forward as skirmishers. Dudley's advance threatened the flank of Captain A. C. Page's Virginia skirmishers, who withdrew into the woods. It was this development that helped relieve the pressure upon the right of the Sixth Wisconsin. The Hoosier skirmishers entered the West Woods, which were open and free from undergrowth. They pressed forward for nearly 120 yards until the resistance in their front stiffened and Callis sent a company forward from his regiment to reinforce Dudley. The main body of both regiments advanced into the woods to the support of the skirmish line. The Confederate skirmishers were forced back, and the remnants of Grigsby's and Jones's small brigades retired to the woods in rear of Starke's and Taliaferro's (Warren) brigades. This relieved the Sixth Wisconsin companies under Kellogg along the turnpike and allowed them to move forward to the aid of the main body of the regiment, which was then shooting it out with Douglass's brigade.[32]

When Starke's and Warren's brigades came swarming out of the West Woods to strike the flank of the Sixth and Second Wisconsin, Gibbon sent his aide, Lieutenant Frank Haskell, forward with orders for Lieutenant Stewart to move his section of Battery B forward to gain the field of fire offered by a slight ridge that ran across Stewart's front in a southwest-northeast orientation. "I could see large bodies of the enemy coming out of the [West] woods," wrote Stewart, and he questioned the wisdom of an order that would leave his guns and limbers greatly exposed to small arms fire. He appealed to Lieutenant Haskell that moving forward would not make any difference in the effectiveness of his artillery. Haskell apparently did not lend a sympathetic ear, for Stewart soon ordered his guns limbered up and moved forward approximately fifty yards, where he opened upon the exposed flank of Starke's brigade with shrapnel.[33]

Meanwhile, in the West Woods, Captain Callis also observed the masses of Confederates moving up to the Hagerstown Turnpike. He ordered his regiment to change front to the left so that it could deliver its fire into the left and rear of Starke's brigade. "We were brought up in rear of a brigade of Rebels," wrote Hugh Perkins of Company I, nine days after the battle, "and laid in the woods and fired 20 rounds before we was discovered." Under a converging fire from front, left flank, and rear, Starke's brigade could not maintain its position and withdrew, followed immediately by Warren's brigade, back to its jump-off point in the West Woods.[34] Hugh Perkins, from the perspective of a front-line infantryman who understood the ugly reality of battle, described the ghastly toll he and his comrades took of the retreating Louisianians:

> After they discovered our position they threw down their arms and broke for the woods (what was left of them). Then we had fun picking them off. We might have taken them all prisoners, but we wasn't in for that. We killed every one of them; even a wounded man could not be seen creeping off without being plugged by a minie. They refused to surrender to us, but they had to our minie balls.[35]

In Miller's cornfield, the men of the Sixth and Second Wisconsin, and Phelps's brigade, heard a "rattling fusillade" and "*three* cheers" from their right, and saw the Confederate line starting to fall back in disorder. Dawes recalled the shout, "Bully, Bully, Up and at them again. Our men are giving them hell on the flank." He did not record who shouted this—it may have been he—but it nevertheless brought the prone line to its feet. The men rushed out of the cover of the corn, jumped the rail fence, and advanced into the open field where so many of their comrades littered the ground. Dawes wrote, "the men are loading and firing with demoniacal fury and shouting and laughing hysterically, and the whole field before us is covered with rebels fleeing for life, into the woods." Dawes provides a glimpse of the absolute ferocity and tension of the battle in front of Miller's cornfield, of men seemingly driven half out of their minds with the violence and excitement of the combat. Frank Holsinger, who served in the Pennsylvania Reserves during the battle, and experienced combat nearly as fierce as that of Gibbon's brigade, wrote that when his regiment broke the Confederates in his front, "We cheer; we are in ecstasies. While shells and canister are still resonant and minies sizzling spitefully, yet I think this one of the supreme moments of my existence." There was something euphoric and heady about seeing the backs of the enemy that, even with death or wounds lurking about, would cause men to shout and laugh hysterically, or describe it as the supreme moment of their existence. Others, like Hugh Perkins of the Seventh Wisconsin, reacted coolly to the desperate combat. "I have had over one hundred good fair shots at the gray back," he wrote to a friend, "and I have got so that I can shoot just as cool and deliberate at them as I can at a prairie chicken. . . . It has got so that it does not excight [*sic*] me any more to be in action than to be in a corn field hoeing, or digging potatoes."[36]

Another vital factor that caused the men of the Sixth and Second Wisconsin to leave the relative cover of the corn for the dangers of an advance over open ground was leadership. "Captains P. W. Plummer and Rollin P. Converse, Lieutenants Charles P. Hyatt, Lyman B. Upham and Howard V. Pruyn were always in the lead," wrote Dawes. He added to this statement the comment that "whoever stood in front of the corn field at Antietam needs no praise." The same could be said for the Second Wisconsin. But not only the officers provided leadership. Non-commissioned officers and enlisted men also set examples of courage for their comrades to follow. Colonel Bragg wrote with pride over thirty years after the battle that "every man of the Sixth acted as if he thought *he was the Sixth Wis. and had its honor in his keeping* [italics added]." Dawes recalled Corporal Reuben Sherman, of Company D, who brought down a Confederate color after firing six or eight shots at its bearer, suddenly received a wound through his arm. He announced to those around him that he had "fetched it," and went to the rear "apparently perfectly happy." When Dawes ordered the retreat back into the corn during Starke's counterattack, another enlisted man, Robert Tomlinson of Company B, "with disappointment in every feature," shouted, "God, You ain't going back are you? Not yet. I still have a few more cartridges left."[37]

Smelling victory, the Second and Sixth Wisconsin, and Phelps's brigade advanced over the open ground east of the Hagerstown Road toward the Dunker Church, the men "firing and yelling" at the retreating enemy as they moved forward. Everyone had fired a great deal of ammunition, which had fouled the muskets, and only by hard pounding with their ramrods could the weapons be loaded. This reduced the firepower of the line. So too did the inevitable confusion and disorder in the ranks the hard fighting on the edge of Miller's corn had wrought. Dawes wrote that his regiment and the Fourteenth Brooklyn of Phelps's Brigade were mingled together. But there was no time to sort things out. The advance continued to nearly one-half way to the church from Miller's cornfield. At this moment "long gray lines of men emerged from the West Woods in rear of the Dunkard Church," and "double quicked out to the right and left of the turnpike, fronted their lines and moved forward." This was the division of Confederate Brigadier General John B. Hood, nearly 2,000 strong.[38]

The fresh Confederate line bearing down upon the ragged Federal line raised the rebel yell and opened fire. "It was almost like a scythe running through the line," recorded Dawes in his journal. "Two out of every three of the men who went to the front of the line were shot." The veterans of Wisconsin and New York knew that they did not stand a shadow of a chance of stopping the long lines of tough Confederate infantrymen who moved steadily toward them. The Federal line broke and the men dashed in a "race for life" for the cover of Miller's cornfield. But this time they did not halt after climbing the rail fence on the southern border of the cornfield. Instead, they continued their retreat through the corn. When they emerged from the corn, into the low, open ground opposite Miller's barn, Dawes took the blue state color from its bearer, and waving it called out for his men to rally to the colors. The Sixth and Second Wisconsin were so scattered that only "a dozen or two men" rallied to Dawes's call. Suddenly, John Gibbon appeared, begrimed with powder smoke, and ordered Dawes to move his small band across the turnpike to support Stewart's section of Battery B, which was under heavy attack by Hood's men. In as loud a voice as he could muster, Dawes shouted, "Let every man from Wisconsin follow me." He recorded with evident pride in his journal that he thought every Black Hat within sight of their state color gathered around the flag until he had some sixty men. He led them across the pike to the haystacks in rear of Battery B, whose own harrowing battle was nearly over.[39]

The moment Hood's men came into view of his section, Lieutenant Stewart had his two guns open upon them with canister. Stewart's principal targets were the Eighteenth Georgia and Hampton Legion, whose left flank rested on the turnpike and who were driving the Sixth Wisconsin and elements of Phelps's brigade before them. They were joined by elements of Starke's brigade, who worked their way forward along the turnpike and the fence on its west side. From the cover of the turnpike fencing and Miller's corn, battle-hardened Georgians and Louisianians, seemingly unfazed by the terrible storm of canister the Federal gunners were pouring into them, kept creeping closer, returning an equally deadly fire of small arms. In ten minutes they shot down fourteen of Stewart's seventeen gunners, and killed the lieutenant's horse. Stewart took the horse of his bugler, but it too was killed. He ordered his three remaining gunners to lie down, then ran back to his limbers and ordered the drivers to dismount and go forward to serve the now silent guns. "The drivers did not want to leave the horses," Stewart recalled, but he gave them no choice and they obeyed his orders.[40]

By this time Gibbon had taken notice of Stewart's peril and ordered Captain Campbell to bring forward the remaining two sections of Battery B from their position north of Miller's house. Campbell brought the guns down the Hagerstown Road at a gallop. They swung into battery on the left of

Stewart's section, with the far left gun resting in the turnpike. Campbell gave the command, "Action front," and ordered canister. The crews thumped the deadly loads down the gun tubes and blasted away at the Georgians and Louisianians in the corn and along the turnpike. The return fire back toward the Federal gunners was terrific and Campbell, fearing the enemy might overrun his left guns, gave orders for the two left pieces to be withdrawn. In the intense excitement the order was misunderstood and the entire battery thought they were to limber to the rear. "Such a movement under fire would have been out of the question," wrote Gibbon. Fortunately, the order was canceled and the men ordered to fire faster. Soon after, Campbell took a bullet in the shoulder and was carried to the rear. Command in this moment of crisis fell to Lieutenant Stewart.[41]

Gibbon, meanwhile had ridden forward along the turnpike to a point near the left gun of the battery. He wrote later that:

> We knew but little of what was going on beyond our immediate vicinity. We were in the hottest of hornet's nests and had all we could do to attend to what was in our front whilst the sounds of a severe battle reached our ears from all directions. Bullets, shot and shell whistled and screamed around us, wounded men came to the rear in large numbers, and the six Napoleon guns of Battery "B" hurled forth destruction in double rounds of canister as the enemy in increased numbers rushed forward to capture the guns.[42]

It became evident to Gibbon that the battery could not hold on alone, and he sent to division commander Doubleday a request for infantry supports. Doubleday sent the small Twentieth New York State Militia, only about 150 strong, and it formed near the straw stacks in rear of the battery. In the battery, men and horses were falling right and left under the deadly musketry of the Georgians and Louisianians. The fire from the cornfield was particularly galling, for there the Confederates had cover that allowed them to get within thirty feet of the battery. It was the particular duty of the left gun of the battery to deal with this threat. But the gun was positioned on a slope in the turnpike and every time it was fired it recoiled "a great distance" down the slope. Gibbon observed the crew at work and noticed that in their excitement to load and fire as rapidly as possible, they had allowed the elevation screw to run down so that the muzzle pointed up in the air and sent each discharge of canister harmlessly over the heads of the enemy. Gibbon shouted to the gunner to run up the elevating screw, but the noise was so great he could not be heard. He jumped from his horse, ran to the gun, quickly ran the elevating screw up "until the nozzle pointed almost into the ground in front," then stepped back and nodded to the gunner. The gunner jerked the lanyard and the blast "carried away most of the fence in front of it and produced great destruction in the enemy's ranks."[43]

Moments after Gibbon corrected the elevating screw on the left gun, Dawes appeared at the south edge of Miller's corn waving the state color of the Sixth Wisconsin. By the time he led his band of Black Hats across the turnpike to support the hard-pressed battery, the Confederate effort to capture the guns had begun to recede, and only scattered rebels continued to send a sharp fire in their direction. The veritable storm of canister from Battery B's Napoleons had sown devastation. But it alone had not checked the effort to capture the battery. A flank fire, delivered by the Nineteenth Indiana and Seventh Wisconsin, and the Twenty-first and Thirty-fifth New York of Brigadier General Marsena Patrick's brigade, had played a critical role in taking the steam out of the Confederate attack.

When Hood's counterattack came sweeping up from the south, the skirmishers of the Nineteenth Indiana observed the Southern lines moving across their front, east of the turnpike, and sent word into the West Woods to Lieutenant Colonel Bachman and the main body of the regiment. Bachman immediately ordered his regiment to change front to the east and marched out of the woods to a limestone ledge running parallel with and about 150 yards from the turnpike. At nearly the same time, on Bachman's left, Captain Callis also observed Hood's and Starke's men advancing and he moved the Seventh Wisconsin up to the same ledge. From nature's breastwork both regiments opened fire upon Starke's Louisianians and Hood's Georgians. George S. Hoyt, of the Seventh, recalled that the musketry of the two regiments "broke the advancing column, some of them going back, and others halted where protection could be found, and kept up a heavy fire, and others pressed forward and attempted to capture the guns of Battery B, but were foiled in all of these attempts."[44]

The front fire of the battery and flank fire of infantry eventually caused Hood's and Starke's men to give ground. Seeing the enemy falling back, men in the Nineteenth Indiana appealed to Bachman to order a charge. The young lieutenant colonel pushed his way through the ranks of his regiment, drew his sword and, recalled a member of the regiment, in his deep bass voice called out, "Boys, the command is no longer forward, but now it is follow me." He ordered the advance at the double-quick, and with his hat in one hand and sword in the other, led the charge. "I shall never forget following his young, tall athletic form as he ascended the slope of the hill," wrote Bob Patterson. The regiment advanced in a southeasterly direction, toward the bloody ground south of Miller's cornfield. Although some of Hood's men fired upon them, the Nineteenth steadily advanced to the turnpike, climbed the fences and pushed into the grass field where the Sixth and Second Wisconsin had seen such terrible fighting earlier. As they crested the ridge south of the corn, however, they were suddenly confronted by Brigadier General Roswell Ripley's fresh brigade which had been sent forward to relieve Hood's troops. The Confederate line blazed away. Bachman fell, "his body being pierced by many minie balls," as did many others. Captain William W. Dudley assumed command of the regiment upon Bachman's death. With no support on either flank and a large force in front, Dudley had no choice but to order the regiment to retire. Despite his youth, Dudley was a cool-headed fellow. He ordered the bodies of Bachman and others who had fallen to be picked up and carried back. During the retreat the regimental colors went down three times. The last time they fell, Lieutenant D. S. Holloway, of Company D, saw the flag go down and ran back, "amidst the fire of almost a whole secesh Brigade," retrieved it and carried it off unharmed.[45]

When the Nineteenth reached the turnpike they found the Twenty-first and Thirty-fifth New York of Patrick's brigade, who had come up in rear of the Seventh Wisconsin and charged soon after Bachman led the Nineteenth forward. The Thirty-fifth halted upon reaching the road, but the Twenty-first had advanced across the road into the grass field immediately south of Miller's corn, on the left of the Nineteenth. When the Nineteenth started back, the Twenty-first fell back to the road on the right of the Thirty-fifth. The stand on the turnpike did not last long, for Starke's seemingly indefatigable brigade, using the cover of the West Woods, advanced unseen to within 100 yards of the Nineteenth and opened fire upon the flank of the Indianians. Dudley ordered the regiment out of their exposed position in the road, back over the line of their advance to the shelter of the West Woods, followed soon after by Patrick's regiments.[46]

The withdrawal of the Nineteenth Indiana and Seventh Wisconsin to the West Woods marked the end of Gibbon's brigade's offensive operations. Gibbon took the reprieve offered by Bachman's impetuous charge to limber Battery B and send it limping to the rear, leaving, the general wrote later, "the corner of the field thickly strewn with its dead men and horses." While the brigade commander attended to his old battery, Dawes observed division commander Abner Doubleday near the Miller farm and asked him for orders. Doubleday told him to remain where he was, but several minutes later Gibbon ordered Dawes to return to the North Woods and await further orders. The major led his sixty men up the Hagerstown Turnpike. When he reached the North Woods he met Captain Ely and what remained of the Second Wisconsin in the form of "the colors and perhaps fifteen men." Although the North Woods was technically "the rear," Dawes recalled that "bullets, shot, and shell fired by the enemy in the corn-field were still flying thickly around us, striking the trees in this woods, and cutting off the limbs." Dawes placed the two regiments in the best shelter he could find, then set to assessing the damage his regiment had sustained. It must have been a depressing duty. They had carried 314 officers and men into action that morning. Dawes had returned with sixty. Men who had been jarred loose from the regiment in the savage fighting in the cornfield trickled in and gradually raised the strength, but the losses had been frightful. From what Dawes could assess they had lost 152 officers and men killed and wounded. Since Company A, under Captain Hooe thirty-five strong, had drifted out of the fight, losing only two men wounded, the remaining nine companies, consisting of 279 effectives, had absorbed the 150 casualties. "This was the most dreadful slaughter to which our regiment was subjected in the war," wrote Dawes.[47]

Captain Ely was unable to tally the losses in the Second because he received a painful wound in the arm from a spent cannon ball that led to his discharge from the army three months later. His replacement, Captain John Stahel, found that out of 150 men taken into action, eighteen enlisted men had been killed, six officers and sixty-one enlisted men wounded, and six enlisted men were missing—a percentage loss as terrible as that suffered by the companies of the Sixth Wisconsin that had shared the dreadful experience of Miller's cornfield. Sydney Meade, a member of the Second, concluded his journal entry on September 17th with the gloomy statement, "the casualties of the regiment were as usual very heavy."[48]

The Nineteenth Indiana and Seventh Wisconsin remained in the West Woods for a short while under a severe artillery fire until orders from Gibbon reached them, ordering them back to the North Woods. The time was probably about 8 A.M. The brigade had been under fire for nearly two hours. Having fought principally in the West Woods, or from behind the limestone ledge east of the woods, the Seventh Wisconsin had suffered the fewest losses in the brigade, ten dead, twenty-three wounded, and five missing. The Nineteenth Indiana might have escaped with similar losses, but their charge across the Hagerstown Turnpike had exposed them to heavy fire. They counted one officer and twelve men dead, and one officer and fifty-eight men wounded.[49]

While the brigade reorganized in the North Woods, the roar of battle continued unabated in the direction of the cornfield and West Woods. Large numbers of stragglers began streaming to the rear, and Gibbon ordered Dawes, who was the ranking field officer left in the brigade, to deploy the entire brigade—only about 500 men—in a skirmish line along the edge of the woods to stop any able-bodied men from going to the rear. While engaged in this duty, Captain Kellogg managed to gather a large number of stragglers whom he formed behind a stone wall. Observing this group of men, General Doubleday rode up. The exchange that ensued was recorded by Dawes in his journal.[50]

> "What regiment is this?" asked Gen. Doubleday. "A Regt of stragglers," says the Captain. "What regiment do you belong to?" "The Sixth Wis., Sir." "Are these Wisconsin men?" "*No* Sir, Wisconsin men never run."[51]

Dawes added in his journal that Kellogg's "rallying of stragglers was one of the most creditable affairs of the battle." Within this story of the captain and the stragglers can be found the reasons that Gibbon's Black Hat Brigade fought as effectively as they did at Antietam. First and foremost was leadership. Apart from Captain Hooe, at nearly every point the regimental officers *led* their men forward; Bachman leading the charge of the Nineteenth Indiana; Bragg refusing his line after being shot; Lieutenant Holloway braving a murderous fire to rescue his regiment's colors; Dawes rallying his regiment after their ordeal in the cornfield; Lieutenant Colonel Allen leading his men forward despite the effects of his two Brawner Farm wounds; and Kellogg, by sheer will and leadership, rallying stragglers. These men inspired the soldiers under their command to do things they probably would not have done without such examples. Second, was élan and pride. Kellogg undoubtedly firmly believed what he said to Doubleday, and because he believed it, his men did too. Strong leadership is infectious. These Western soldiers believed they were the best soldiers in the army—Gibbon and his regimental officers had imbued that in them—and they fought tenaciously and aggressively because of it. The officers of every other regiment could have echoed Edward Bragg's statement that every man "acted as if he thought *he was the Sixth Wis., and had its honor in his keeping* [italics added]." Finally, simple discipline and drill held the men together under the most desperate circumstances. Sergeant George Hoyt, of the Seventh Wisconsin, wrote that "every move of the Regiment on this day was with precision and in order, not withstanding the front and sometimes the flank fire it was under almost continuously for several hours." Discipline, too, held the Sixth Wisconsin together when the Confederate shell burst in their ranks with horrible effect early in the battle, and when they and the Second Wisconsin suffered the punishment of their own artillery in the cornfield, and in the terrible fighting south of the corn, where every man faced death or wounds by going forward but, nevertheless, did.[52]

Not everyone went forward, though. Captain Hooe did not. Captain Dudley, in his report of the action, wrote that all the men of the Nineteenth Indiana were brave, "if we except the few who found their way to the rear when danger approached." Every regiment had its share of men who shirked duty, but evidence indicates that their numbers were few. The majority remained in the ranks, and even if jarred loose by the shock of combat, rejoined their unit quickly. This was not the case in many regiments of Hooker's corps, where large numbers of able-bodied men straggled during the battle and made no haste to return to their units.[53]

Antietam was a shockingly violent battle that took place on a scale no one in either army had yet seen to that date in the war. Although the 348 casualties Gibbon's brigade had suffered exceeded the losses at South Mountain by only thirty-five men, and were only about half that suffered at Brawner Farm, the battle nevertheless left an indelible impression upon the men of the brigade, particularly in the Second and Sixth Wisconsin. After the battle of Fredericksburg in December of 1862, Major Dawes wrote, "Another great battle fought. Terrible as it was to some, to us it was really almost nothing compared with Antietam."[54]

It was not only the terrible ferocity of the combat of Antietam that left its mark upon Gibbon's men. It was the aftermath of the combat, too. No one had seen slaughter such as occurred in Miller's cornfield, along the Hagerstown

Pike, and in the East and West Woods. Over 10,000 men had been killed or wounded in this relatively small area. It horrified and shocked all who looked upon it, and left a scar upon their memory that nothing could erase. Dawes recalled when he rode down the Hagerstown Pike on September 19th, past hundreds of torn and bloated human bodies, his horse "trembled in every limb with fright and was wet with perspiration." The carnage was, he wrote, "indescribably horrible." Later, he mentally compared the carnage he observed at Fredericksburg, Spotsylvania Court House, and at Cold Harbor. "My feeling was that the Antietam Turnpike surpassed all in manifest evidence of slaughter," he wrote. Lieutenant Colonel Bragg wrote to his wife, "the battlefield was too terrible to behold without a shock—I never want to see another such." No one can see such sights and not be deeply affected for life.[55]

On September 18th the brigade waited anxiously for the renewal of fighting. "I expect another big fight to day what is left of us feel in good spirits for we have got the Rebbles [*sic*] in close quarters," wrote Lieutenant Young of the Seventh Wisconsin to his wife. But the expected clash did not occur and during the night the Confederate army withdrew across the Potomac. The brigade was formed up and marched down the Hagerstown Pike, passing by carnage that no man ever forgot, and continuing to a point one mile west of Sharpsburg where they bivouacked. Details were left behind to find and bury the dead. Hugh Perkins, of the Seventh Wisconsin, was selected for this unpleasant duty. He wrote to a friend, "I was on detail to bury the dead for three days. It was an awful job. It made me feel bad to see our poor boys laying dead, but the Rebs didn't have no more effect on me than so many sheep." Captain Von Bachelle, of the Sixth Wisconsin, was found lying on the turnpike, "his cap drawn forward over his eyes, his body riddled with bullets, his field glass across his shoulder shattered into innumerable pieces, and his faithful dog, a black and white Spaniel [Newfoundland], lying across his body dead." Others were probably more difficult to identify among the windrows of dead bodies. James Perry, of the Sixth Wisconsin, wrote, "the dead [have] been robbed of all valuables that they possessed," which often meant their identification had been stolen or cast aside in the search for more valuable items. The dead of the Sixth Wisconsin were buried in a long trench dug with a hoe from an artillery battery, under a locust tree west of the Hagerstown Pike, near where they fell. The other regiments likewise collected their dead and buried them together. "Neat headboards are placed at the head of each grave, giving the name and company of each," wrote a member of the Third Wisconsin. It was such a sad and depressing duty that most soldiers said little of it.[56]

The 275 wounded officers and men of the brigade were gradually moved from the Miller and Poffenberger farms and other collection points to general field hospitals established at Smoketown (about three miles north of Sharpsburg) and Keedysville (about three miles north and east of Sharpsburg). From here those capable of travel by ambulance were transported to Frederick, Maryland. Compared with the collection and treatment of the wounded on the Peninsula and at Second Manassas, the wounded of Antietam received swift and reasonably good care because of an efficient system established by the Medical Director of the Army of the Potomac, Jonathan Letterman. Nevertheless, there was much suffering. Many eventually recovered and returned to their units. Some would die from their wounds. Others would be crippled for life, such as Aries A. Young of Company A, Sixth Wisconsin, who would suffer the amputation of both arms as a result of the early morning shell that burst in the ranks of his regiment on September 17.[57]

There was one other group of casualties not represented on the battlefield: the families of the dead and maimed. Captain Edwin Brown's wife and three children would be without a husband and father. Their story was particularly heartrending, because immediately after the battle a sergeant from the Sixth Wisconsin telegraphed Fond du Lac, Wisconsin, with the report that Lieutenant Colonel Bragg had been killed and his body was being sent home. Bragg's family was plunged into grief. The city council appointed a committee to travel to Chicago to escort Bragg's body home for the funeral and burial. But when the committee reached Chicago they found the body was that of Captain Brown, not Bragg. "The results were sensational and very sad," commented Major Dawes. In another similar incident, Bob Patterson of the Nineteenth Indiana, who had been wounded by the bursting of a shell on September 17th, found when he returned to his regiment after the battle that his company commander had already written his family and reported their son killed. Although families whose loved ones had been wounded were spared the utter grief and sense of loss experienced by those whose sons or husbands had been killed, many would find that Antietam had permanently scarred their lives. When Aries Young came home without his arms, or David Noyes returned without a foot, and others reentered their homes with their health broken, unable to earn a living, their families would inherit the painful and depressing legacy of Antietam.[58]

Considering the hard service they had endured and their heavy losses, it might be imagined that morale in Gibbon's Black Hat Brigade dipped to a low ebb. For a few individuals it did. Everyone exposed to the stress of combat has a point beyond which he cannot endure. James C. Leach, of Company B, Second Wisconsin, was apparently one of them. He was promoted to corporal on September 25. The next day he deserted. In Company D, a twenty-one-year-old laborer from New York named John Donovan shot himself in the hand on September 23rd. One man, Amos Albert, deserted from the Sixth Wisconsin seven days after the battle, and the Seventh Wisconsin likewise lost a single deserter, David Beeke, who departed on September 17th.

After the arduous and bloody service of the weeks leading up to Antietam and in the backwash of the most violent battle yet fought in the war, the fact that Gibbon's brigade had only four deserters from three regiments was a clear statement that morale in the brigade remained strong. The surviving letters and diaries from this period bear this out and testify to the magnificent fighting spirit that Gibbon had developed and nurtured in the brigade. Henry Young wrote to his wife on September 18th that his company was almost all killed, wounded, or sick, but "what is left of us feel in good spirits." On October 4th, he wrote, "we feel in good spirits and are ready for another fight when ever called on." In a letter to his father on September 20th, Henry Marsh of the Nineteenth Indiana wrote, "I still think and know that our brigade is the best in the service." Lieutenant Frank Haskell struck upon an important reason for the high morale. "But amid such scenes we are all cheerful," he wrote; "the men were never more so, victory in two hard, great battles [South Mountain and Antietam], and the rebels out of Maryland make us glad." The attitude of Hugh Perkins of the Seventh Wisconsin was likely shared by many veterans in the brigade. He wrote his friend on September 26th, "I have seen some hard times and run some narrow chances on my life, but I hope I shall always come out as well as I have so far." Perkins and his comrades remained in the land of the living and despite the sorrow for comrades lost, they did not dwell upon those deaths. They had won a victory at South Mountain and Antietam and remained optimistic about the future, hoping for the best, and willing to do their duty when called upon.[59]

The call would come again at Fredericksburg and Chancellorsville, and then again in June of 1863 when Lee's army moved north to invade Pennsylvania. On June 18, 1863, while bivouacked near Leesburg, Maryland, and preparing to reenter that state in pursuit of Lee's army, a newsboy found his way into the camp of the Sixth Wisconsin to deliver his papers. Now a lieutenant colonel, Rufus Dawes scanned the headlines: "Rebels in Pennsylvania—Another battle at Antietam on the tapis." The news stirred troubled memories for Dawes and he revealed them to Mary Beman Gates, who would be his wife in less than one year: "I hope not. I never want to fight there again. The flower of our regiment was slaughtered in that terrible corn-field. I dread the thought of the place."[60]

4

John Gibbon and the Black Hat Brigade

STEVEN J. WRIGHT

Captain John Gibbon, Battery B, Fourth United States Artillery, had developed little respect for *volunteer* soldiers in his years as an officer in the United States Army. However, the outbreak of the American Civil War gave him an opportunity to work with a unique group of *Western volunteers* and from this association came a deep and abiding respect for the men from small towns and farms who had enlisted to serve and die for their country.

When Fort Sumter was attacked in April 1861 Gibbon and his battery were posted at lonely, desolate Camp Floyd in the Utah Territory. The subsequent outbreak of hostilities was cause for Gibbon, his men, and their twelve-pounder Napoleons to be brought back east. Soon after arriving in Washington, D.C., in the early summer of 1861, Gibbon was appointed Chief of Artillery for Brigadier General Irvin McDowell's division.

Gibbon was a professional soldier in every sense of the word. He had graduated twentieth in a class of thirty-eight from the United States Military Academy in 1847. After graduation he served in Mexico, arriving too late to see any battle action, and later in Florida during the seemingly endless "Seminole Wars." Gibbon returned to the Military Academy at West Point in 1854 as an assistant instructor of artillery and later as post quartermaster. In 1859 he published *The Artillerist's Manual* which was never officially approved by the War Department, despite its widespread use by Federal, and later Confederate, gunners.[1]

When the clouds of war were gathering, Gibbon was perhaps more concerned than most. He was born in the Holmesburg section of Philadelphia on April 20, 1827, but his family had moved to North Carolina when John was about ten. Although he never wrote of it, the decision to remain with the Union must have been difficult. Having grown up in the South, he was undoubtedly familiar with Southern views, but not sympathetic to the Southern cause. In his extensive wartime letters to his wife, Frances, he wrote at length of his devotion to the preservation of the Union, with the full knowledge that three brothers and two brothers-in-law had cast their lot with the Confederacy. An appointee to the Military Academy from North Carolina, Gibbon did speculate throughout the war that he was slow to receive promotion because there was no one in Congress from his home state to champion his cause. In a paper read before the Minnesota Commandery of the Military Order of the Loyal Legion of the United States in 1904, William Harries, formerly of the Second Wisconsin, recalled a conversation with Gibbon that had occurred while visiting the battlefield of Second Bull Run:

> One evening as Gen. Gibbon and I were retiring at the Dogan farm in 1892, I said "General, so you think that because you had two brothers in the Confederate Army that fact had anything to do with retarding your promotion during the war," and he replied, "Possibly, possibly" and as he showed no inclination to continue the conversation on that subject, it was dropped. He never complained of his treatment.[2]

Upon being appointed McDowell's Chief of Artillery, one of Gibbon's first tasks was to fill the depleted ranks of his former battery. For this he examined the men of McDowell's division, took some New York volunteers, but decided that the best candidates came from a brigade of Wisconsin and Indiana troops that had been organized by Brigadier General Rufus King. In his *Personal Recollections of the Civil War*, written in 1885 but not published until thirty-two years after his death, Gibbon recalled:

> It is scarcely to be expected that, with the popular ideas existing in regard to the Regular Army, men could be induced voluntarily to leave the free and easy life of amongst the volunteers to submit to the rigid discipline and, presumably, hard life of the Regular. But fortune and time of the call favored me. I was more than amazed at the number of the men who stepped forward.
>
> Gibbon continued:
>
> Many times the number I wanted volunteered, frequently amid the jeers of their comrades. As they paraded in front of their regiments, I passed down along the line and selected men such as I wanted. I could generally tell from their bearing and appearance whether or not they were suitable for artillery service. If in doubt, a simple question or two settled the matter. In this way not taking too many men from one regiment, I obtained 150 of the finest material for soldiers I ever saw and it is a remarkable fact that, of this 150, but one single man was returned to his regiment as unsuitable. Here then was an excellent opportunity for learning the difficult problem of how to discipline and instruct the volunteer element.[3]

Having served as a professional soldier for more than fifteen years, Gibbon believed that pride and discipline were of the utmost importance in the making of a solid, dependable soldier—whether the soldier was of the regular army or a volunteer. Soon after the selection of volunteers to serve in Battery B, Gibbon marked each of the six artillery pieces with small American flags, upon which were printed the names of the states from which the gunners hailed. In doing so, he told the artillerists, "These guns belong to your states, it is your duty to defend them."[4]

Throughout the fall and winter of 1861 Gibbon performed the duties of Chief of Artillery, all the while quietly fretting when comrades of equal rank received higher promotions and larger commands. Finally, on May 2, 1862, he was promoted to Brigadier General of Volunteers. Six days later he was given command of Rufus King's brigade, composed of the Second, Sixth, and Seventh Wisconsin, and the Nineteenth Indiana Regiments. These were the same units from which Gibbon had selected his replacement artillerymen. It was this brigade to which he had hoped to be assigned.

A week after taking command of the brigade, Gibbon wrote his wife from camp near Falmouth, Virginia, "I am right now down on the banks of the river opposite Fredericksburg with my brigade, and hard at work trying to knock the *kinks* [Gibbon's emphasis] out of it and indoctrinate the officers and men into the ways of the regulars. It is sometimes pretty hard work but I am getting along as well as can be expected, and I think I have a very fine brigade."[5]

Among the "kinks" that Gibbon was trying to work out was a lack of discipline, although it was probably no worse than that of many volunteer units. Gibbon shortly instituted a number of policies which officers and men alike undoubtedly found annoying: The regiment closest to a fence that was torn down for firewood was required to replace the fence, regardless of whether its soldiers were responsible for the destruction. Company commanders became responsible for carefully charging their men for lost or discarded uniforms and equipment, and sentinels were required to stand their posts and salute all officers. Although there was grumbling within the ranks, Gibbon was pleased that the new policies had a positive effect.[6]

For Gibbon, the matter of discipline was not reserved for enlisted men. In his postwar memoirs, he recalled:

> It was not long before I discovered that reveille was a mere farce which none of the officers attended. An order was issued requiring the whole command to turn out under arms and as soon as reveille ceased beating companies were to move out at a double quick, form on the colors and remain until dismissed by me. The horses of myself and staff were brought up and saddled and as the drums ceased beating I started at a gallop round through camp, saw that each regiment was promptly formed and dismissed it. They soon learned to form promptly and regiments vied with each other to see which could be most promptly in line. The privates were delighted with the order and remarks were heard to the effect that "now the officers had to turn out just as the men and had no advantages over them."[7]

Gibbon also learned from the experience of working with volunteers. During one of his first guard mount inspections he was shocked at the unsoldierly appearance of the sentries. Noticing one particular soldier who was especially well turned out, he relieved the man of guard duty, marched him past three disheveled comrades, and rewarded the man with a twenty-four-hour pass—an especially significant matter since blackberries were in season. He soon made this a standard practice. Years later he recalled, "I made a discovery which was of infinite value to me thereafter. With these men 'the hope of reward was far more powerful than the fear of punishment' and thenceforward I acted on that principle."[8]

Turning to the appearance of the brigade, within a week of taking command, Gibbon had black felt Hardee hats issued with ostrich plumes, and soon after the regiments were issued frock coats, and white leggings—the same uniform worn by regulars. Lieutenant Colonel Rufus Dawes of the Sixth Wisconsin noted in his journal on May 17, 1862: "General Gibbon attended our dress parade to-day, and the regiment was in 'fine feather.'"[9] One member of the Second Wisconsin wrote to his hometown newspaper of the new uniforms, "We have a full blue suit, a fine black hat nicely trimmed with a bugle and plate and ostrich feathers; and you can only distinguish our boys from the regulars, by their [our] good looks."[10]

The change in uniform seemed to have been met positively except for the white leggings, which were impossible to keep clean. One day before a brigade drill, Gibbon's mount was brought to him with its legs encased in the much-hated white gaiters. Years later, while traveling though Wisconsin, Gibbon stopped at a veterans' reunion and immediately inquired if any former Iron Brigade members were present. One old fighter was brought forward and introduced to the general. After a few brief words, Gibbon reminded the soldier of the incident and asked the identity of the prankster, but he remained anonymous.[11]

Instituting daily and rigorous drills was chief among Gibbon's efforts to transform his volunteers into soldiers who marched and fought like U.S. Regulars. One day he rode into camp and discovered one of the other brigades being put through the brigade drill by an old officer of the Regulars. Gibbon wondered why he shouldn't drill his brigade the same way and was even more challenged when he overheard one of the field officers in his brigade comment, "Why, Gen. Gibbon was only an artillery officer and did not know anything about infantry drill." Gibbon acquired a copy of Professor Henry Coppee's brigade drill manual and discovered it very similar to the Light Artillery drill, with which he was intimately familiar. On Saturday, July 19, 1862, Gibbon wrote his wife:

> I have lately taken to having brigade drills in the morning. Never having had them since I took command they got sort of an idea that I was only an *art.* officer and could not drill at Infty. I let it run on for some time, and

> then brushing up a little on tactics took them out. After drilling two hours one of the men was overheard saying "I thought you said our Genl. could not drill us, and new nothing but arty.?" They have now pretty much concluded that if they are able to perform all the movements I can put them thru' they will do pretty well![12]

Within a few days he had the brigade maneuvering "with clock-like regularity, until finally I began to perform them at the double quick."[13]

The process of drilling the volunteers continued to develop Gibbon's respect for these citizen soldiers and any doubt he had in their ability disappeared. Twenty years after the end of the war he fondly wrote:

> School teaching of any kind is at best a laborious business but when the scholars number several thousand and the head teacher has to assist him but few who know even the A.B.C. of the subject to be taught, the task becomes Herculean. In this case, however, the quick intelligence of the scholars (the volunteers) smoothed over many of the rough places and served to nullify even the strong opposition exhibited to a Regular officer being in command. Regular drills were instituted and where the regimental commander knew nothing of the drill, I sometimes took command myself, and then it was wonderful to see the transformation; how eagerly my explanations were listened to by both officers and men, and how intelligently the commands were executed.[14]

The ultimate purpose of training and drill is to prepare a soldier to fight. While Gibbon was training his brigade, Major General George McClellan and his army were fighting their way up the Virginia peninsula in an attempt to capture Richmond. All throughout the campaign Gibbon hoped that he and his brigade might be reassigned to McClellan's command, and used effectively in combat. Gibbon's chance finally came on July 24, when he led a reconnaissance toward Gordonsville, Virginia. The Second Wisconsin, the only regiment of Gibbon's brigade to have already seen action, was detached with Battery B; they were joined by two regiments of infantry from brigades other than Gibbon's, a squadron of cavalry, and sixty sharpshooters. The reconnaissance was successful in that it did determine that a Confederate concentration was taking place near Orange Court House and Gordonsville. The whole expeditionary force returned to its camp at Fredericksburg, having captured one prisoner and lost one horse.[15]

Gibbon and his brigade were sent on another reconnaissance on August 5 for the purpose of destroying the Virginia Central Railroad. The railroad line was cut and although the operation was not totally successful, it proved auspicious as it was the first time the brigade as a whole served together in field operations.[16]

The brigade, as part of King's division, remained on the move. On August 18, they camped on the Cedar Mountain battlefield, giving Gibbon occasion to write his wife that evening:

> I wrote you on Saturday that we were to march about 5 miles, we only came about 2 on account of there being no water at the other place. This brought us exactly on the Battle ground where we still remain. My tent is just in front of where the rebels had a battery and as they left several of their dead horses on the ground the first thing we had to do was to go to work and *burn* them up, and they did not smell *exactly* like roast beef. I rode all over the field yesterday with Maj. Holabird and Maj. Perkins, who were both in the battle, and got a very good idea of the fight. There has been a great expenditure of life with very little practical good except that their great General, Jackson, has been made to retreat.[17]

At the time, of course, it was impossible for Gibbon or his men to have known that ten days later, they would encounter the great Confederate General Thomas J. "Stonewall" Jackson. While marching up the Warrenton Turnpike behind Brigadier General John Porter Hatch's brigade on August 28, Gibbon noticed a battery of Confederate artillery coming into line on high ground to the north and east of his position in front of the Brawner Farm. Ordering his men to lie down on the road, Gibbon brought up Captain Joseph B. Campbell's Battery B to return the enemy's fire, which quickly silenced the Confederate battery. In his history of the Second Wisconsin, George H. Otis recalled:

> At about 6 o'clock P.M., and two miles from Gainesville, while marching by the flank, a rebel battery, posted on a wooded eminence to the left of the road, opened fire on our marching column. The Second Regiment, promptly faced to the front, and soon met the enemy's infantry emerging from the woods. Here for twenty minutes this regiment alone checked and sustained one of the most intensely concentrated fires of musketry ever experienced by any troops in this or any other war.[18]

What ensued was some of the most devastating fighting that Gibbon or his men would encounter during their entire term of service. In his official report, Gibbon simply stated, "Of the conduct of my brigade it is only necessary for me to state that it nobly maintained its position against heavy odds. The fearful list of killed and wounded tells the rest. The troops fought most of the time not more than 75 yards apart."[19] "My command exhibited in the highest degree the effects of discipline and drill," Gibbon wrote in his postwar memoirs, "the officers and men standing up to their work like old soldiers. Going over the ground the following year I could clearly trace out the line of battle they had occupied by the half-buried bodies and cartridge papers."[20]

Two days later the brigade was supporting Major General Fitz John Porter's assault against the Confederate line which was well entrenched along an unfinished railroad embankment west of the Warrenton Turnpike. The fighting in the thick woods was furious. In a letter to his wife two days after these events, Gibbon reported, "It was my first great battle. The shot & shell tore thro' the air, and the bullets whistled around our ears, in a most astonishing way, but the feeling of personal fear seemed to be almost swallowed up by one of anxiety for the result of the battle. My men behaved splendidly & by their coolness & courage set a good example to some less inclined to be steady."[21]

The Union line began to fall apart on August 30, but Gibbon's brigade remained steadfast. Then, as Rufus Dawes recalled, Gibbon ran up to the Sixth Wisconsin with his revolver drawn, shouting, "Stop those stragglers!—Make them fall in!—Shoot them if they don't!"[22] Dawes continued:

> All the troops that had been in the woods, except the Sixth Wisconsin, had now retreated and gone to the rear. Brigadier General Gibbon, be it ever remembered to his honor, remained with our regiment. He said he had received no orders to retreat and he should stay until he got them.[23]

Not believing two later, separate orders to withdraw, Gibbon finally retired and met General McDowell, who had been told by Fitz John Porter that Gibbon had been killed. Because of their determined fighting, Gibbon's troops were selected to serve as the rear guard for the Federal retreat. In their action between August 21 and 30, the brigade reported losses totaling 894 men. Gibbon concluded his official report of the action by saying, "I have great cause to be proud of the brigade I have the honor to command."[24] The Westerners also received the attention of Major General John Pope, former commander of the Army of Virginia, who wrote in his final report, "Gibbon's brigade consisted of some of the finest troops in the service, and the conduct of both men and officers was gallant and distinguished."[25]

The men of his brigade now developed a sincere respect for Gibbon, largely because of his actions in the heat of battle. One veteran recalled: "Many a time, by day and by night, I have heard some old soldier in the ranks say when the general was making his way to the front while we were on the march, 'There's business ahead, here comes Johny [*sic*] the War Horse'; and his name stuck to him with the men of his old command."[26]

With the defeat at Second Bull Run, the Army of Virginia was disbanded and was reorganized into the Army of the Potomac, under the command of the flamboyant Major General George B. McClellan. On September 3, 1862, Gibbon wrote his wife:

> . . . it did my heart good to hear my brigade cheer when I told them he [McClellan] was in command. They were perfectly wild with delight hurled their caps in the air and showed the great enthusiasm, right within hearing, too, of Genl. Pope who has turned out a complete failure. . . . My poor Brig. is sadly cut having lost more than 900 men, but what remains is in excellent condition & ready for the coming struggle which will probably be decided in a few days, & I have every confidence in our favor.[27]

McClellan and his newly reorganized army were soon on the march, in pursuit of Robert E. Lee's Army of Northern Virginia which had moved into Maryland. Perhaps the most significant occurrence of the campaign was the discovery by Union troops of Lee's Special Order #191, which outlined the Confederate commander's troop dispositions and plans. Shortly after the order had been discovered, Gibbon happened to be at "Little Mac's" headquarters and was shown the lost missive. Gibbon took the occasion to note that his brigade had suffered terribly at Second Bull Run, and noted that he would like to have a fresh, new regiment assigned to it. Gibbon, however, did not want just any regiment, but rather one from the West. McClellan agreed that the next Western regiment to reach the Army of the Potomac would be assigned to serve with the Black Hats, and thus another of Gibbon's marks was put on the brigade.[28]

The brigade's next great test came on the slopes of South Mountain, at Turner's Gap, on the afternoon of September 14, 1862. Upon encountering enemy resistance while moving up the National Road, the brigade split and advanced up the steep wooded hillside on either side of the road. In his history of the Sixth Wisconsin, Rufus Dawes recalled Gibbon in the heat of battle: "General Gibbon mounted upon his horse and riding upon high ground where he could see his whole line, shouted orders in a voice loud and clear as a bell and distinctly heard throughout the brigade. It was always, 'Forward! Forward!'"[29]

The battle continued long after dark, finally ending with the men of Gibbon's brigade holding their ground, their ammunition nearly exhausted. In his official report, Gibbon noted, "The conduct of the officers and men was during the engagement everything that could be desired, and they maintained their well-earned reputation for gallantry and discipline acquired in the engagements of the 28th and 30th of August."[30]

The actions of the brigade drew attention from many within the Federal army. The day after the battle Gibbon wrote his wife, "Every one, from Gen. McClellan down, speaks in the highest terms of my gallant Brigade and I of course am proud." In his numerous reports on the Maryland campaign McClellan touted Gibbon and his troops on several occasions, noting, "General Gibbon, in this delicate movement, handled his brigade with as much precision and coolness as if upon parade, and the bravery of his troops could not be excelled."[31] As described elsewhere in this book, the name of "Iron Brigade" was attached to Gibbon's brigade at South Mountain.

The next day the Army of the Potomac continued its pursuit of the Army of Northern Virginia toward the tiny borough of Sharpsburg. Gibbon wrote:

> We marched through the ranks of the 2nd Corps and on reaching the Mountain House at the summit, found Gen. [Edwin Vose] Sumner there. I stopped to speak to him when his Adjutant General [J.H. Taylor] quietly told me that he was sorry I had arrived so soon, as he had just sent directions from

> Gen. Sumner to his troops to cheer my brigade as it came through, as a testimonial of the gallantry it had exhibited the night before in the fight which he had seen from the hill behind us. This action, on the part of Gen. Sumner, was all the more gratifying from the fact that it was well known in the army that he was very much opposed to such demonstrations as not being proper for disciplined troops.[32]

Three days after the battle of South Mountain the two armies again clashed, this time along the banks of Antietam Creek in what would become the bloodiest single day in American military history. As part of Major General Joseph Hooker's First Army Corps, Gibbon, his brigade, and former battery were involved in the desperate fight at David Miller's cornfield in the early morning action of the opening phase of the battle. As Gibbon reported:

> The whole line soon became hotly engaged, and the enemy, heavily reinforced from the woods, made a dash upon the battery. This attack, however, was successfully repelled by heavy discharges of canister from the guns, the fire of the few remaining men of the Second and Sixth Wisconsin, and the flank fire poured in by the Seventh Wisconsin and Nineteenth Indiana, which had been brought around to sweep the front of the battery with their fire, Captain Campbell having in the mean time joined Stewart's with the other four pieces of the battery.[33]

What Gibbon failed to report was that in the hottest part of the battle, when the guns of Battery B were threatened with being overrun, he dismounted and personally manned a piece. In his official report Lieutenant James Stewart of Battery B noted, "General Gibbon was in the battery, and, seeing the advantage which the enemy had, ordered one of the guns which was placed on the turnpike to be used against the enemy's infantry in the cornfield, General Gibbon acting as both cannoneer and gunner at this piece."[34]

The action of leaving his brigade and serving the guns of his former battery said a great deal about Gibbon's confidence in his men. In a paper read before the Minnesota Commandery of the Military Order of the Loyal Legion of the United States, William Henry Harries, recalled:

> I told this incident a few years before the death of General Gibbon to General Harry Heth, who was a classmate of Gibbon, while we were sitting at a table together at the Army and Navy Club room at Washington. General Heth, after I had finished, said to Gibbon, "John, did you leave your brigade during the fight and act as gunner of your old battery? Why, you should have been courtmartialed [*sic*] for it." Gibbon replied, "Yes, I did do that. I knew the men of my old brigade would fight without me and just at that particular moment that gun needed looking after to make its fire effective."[35]

Following the battle the Army of the Potomac remained at Sharpsburg. In a letter to his wife, dated October 5, 1862, Gibbon wrote:

> I was so glad to receive today your letter of the 28th, altho' it was a week old, and was considerably amused at the mutual admiration society you had formed with some of my poor fellows in the hospitals [in Baltimore]. I hope you will keep up your good intentions of visiting them often. Money spent in buying them little delicacies is well laid out, and I hope you will not spare it. They are as brave a set of fellows as ever lived or died. I paid a visit to my Brigade Hospital here the day after the battle, and was much gratified at the spirit displayed by the wounded. Very few were desponding, and the general feeling seemed to be to get well, get back to the Regt. and try it again. After the battle of South Mountain I met a man with one arm in a sling on his way back to join his Regt. I said "My man where are you going[?]" "Back to my Regt. sir," "But you can't handle your musket in that fix." "Yes I can sir" he said in such a decided tone that I had nothing more to say. To show you that my estimate of the Brigade is not an imaginary one I will mention one fact. After the battle of the 17th it was found that there were an unusual number of stragglers many of whom had no doubt ran [*sic*] away from the battle field. A return was called for on the 18th & again on the 22nd and it was found that our corps had nearly doubled its numbers in those four days. I required a comparative statement to be made and all increase to be accounted for. It was found that my Brigade had increased about 80 men and *every one* [Gibbon's emphasis] of these were men who were returned from detached service and hospitals, so that I had *no stragglers.* I felt as proud as a turkey cock! and forwarded the statement to Genl. McClellan.[36]

The strength of Gibbon's decimated brigade was nearly doubled on October 8, when the Twenty-fourth Michigan was assigned to it. As he had with all of his Western troops, Gibbon quickly turned to the task of transforming the raw volunteers, some of whom did not even have complete uniforms, into well-trained, highly disciplined soldiers. In the meantime, the Army of the Potomac licked its wounds following the battle of Antietam while Gibbon hoped for promotion and a larger command.

Finally, on November 4, Gibbon's wish was granted, but was met with mixed emotions from the general. That day he wrote his wife from camp near Bloomfield, Virginia:

> I was sent for this morning by Gen. [John F.] Reynolds who commands our corps & offered the command of a *Division* [Gibbon's emphasis]. I hated to leave the old Brig. but could not refuse a higher command & have just finished my farewell order to the Black Hatted Brigade *almost* with tears in my eyes. I would rather take them into action than any Division I know of but cannot expect to keep them always, & so may as well give them up now, tho' I think they might let me have them as part of my new command. I have been much gratified at the regrets expressed in the Brigade at the idea of my leaving and the desire to go with me. I take all my old staff with me, but leave old Co. B [Fourth U.S. Artillery] behind.[37]

While not everyone in the brigade was a supporter of Gibbon, the majority undoubtedly recognized his dedication to his men and skill as a soldier. Less than a week after Gibbon received news of being moved to divisional command, Rufus Dawes of the Sixth Wisconsin wrote: "We have just learned that General Gibbon has been promoted to Major General. His honors are fairly won. He is one of the bravest of men. He was with us on every battle field."[38]

In moving to higher command, Gibbon was not concerned with the quality of the soldiers he left behind. They had been thoroughly tested in battle and proven themselves as capable as any in the Army of the Potomac. Discipline was keen and the unit had a unique esprit de corps that was akin to that of his beloved Regulars. He was worried, however, about the caliber of commander who would replace him.

Gibbon hoped that one of the battle-hardened regimental commanders, preferably Lucius Fairchild of the Second Wisconsin, would be his replacement. Instead, Colonel Henry Morrow was given temporary command of the brigade until newly appointed Brigadier General Solomon Meredith, of the Nineteenth Indiana, was chosen to become the unit's commander. More than twenty years after the incident, Gibbon was still incensed at how he perceived the selection of his replacement had been made. Never being one to have respect for those who pulled strings to gain favor, Gibbon wrote, without mentioning Meredith by name:

> After the battle of Antietam, one of my colonels who had not been with his regiment there, went to Washington where he succeeded, as I supposed, by purely political influence in getting himself appointed a Brigadier General of Volunteers, a position he was in no way fitted to fill. I felt outraged at this way of making military promotions, especially when I was told that this appointment was made for distinguished services in the battle of Antietam, where the Lt. Colonel of this regiment [Alois O. Bachman] was killed commanding the regiment. I had at least two colonels in the brigade, who had richly won promotion. I afterwards learned, however, that the appointment referred to, had been made on the special recommendation of *General Hooker!* [Gibbon's emphasis.][39]

If Gibbon was upset about the selection of his successor, he was pleased that he was able to keep his personal staff intact, which included Frank Aretas Haskell.

Haskell was born in Tunbridge, Vermont, on July 13, 1828. After graduating from Dartmouth College with distinguished honors in the class of 1854, he moved to Madison where he joined the law firm of Orton, Atwood & Orton. Haskell was commissioned a first lieutenant of Company I, Sixth Wisconsin, on June 20, 1861, and served on Gibbon's staff from Gibbon's assumption as brigade commander until Haskell was promoted to colonel of the Thirty-sixth Wisconsin on February 9, 1864. The two became close friends and Gibbon named Haskell in a number of reports for his gallant action in battle. It is also obvious that Gibbon relied on Haskell to assist in the transformation of the brigade of rough-hewn Western volunteers into the elite soldiers they became. In a tribute to Haskell, Jerome A. Watrous, formerly a first lieutenant in the Sixth Wisconsin, wrote:

> Adjutant Haskell did more, by far, than any officer to make the Sixth the kind of regiment it was. Haskell had belonged to a college military company, and led in the first and in many subsequent lessons to all of the earlier officers. Haskell first knew and could impart intelligent instructions in all of the drill, parades, and reviews, and made known what must be done in all of the situations imaginable in battle. Haskell's orderly bearing—I never saw a finer appearing soldier—gave birth to ambition in rank and file to become soldiers in the fullest sense of the word. Haskell's fire of criticism and emphatic, plain instruction to individuals and companies as a whole, in Sunday morning inspections, gave the men information on scores of subjects, of which they availed themselves—information without which no regiment can become thoroughly competent in either war or peace. Though others became Adjutant of the Sixth, Frank A. Haskell never had a successor.[40]

Of course Haskell's supreme moment came on July 3, 1863, when during the battle of Gettysburg and while serving as Gibbon's aide, he played a pivotal role in the repulse of Pickett's Charge. He recounted his exploits in a letter written to his brother which has since become a classic of Civil War scholarship. Years later Gibbon fondly wrote of Haskell, "There was a young man on my staff who had been in every battle with me and who did more than any other one man to repulse Pickett's assault at Gettysburg and he did the part of a general there."[41] History suggests that Haskell's role at Gettysburg has been exaggerated, but Gibbon's statement about Haskell shows that he could be generous in praise, as well as sometimes critical, of subordinate officers.[42]

Haskell was promoted to colonel of the Thirty-sixth Wisconsin on February 9, 1864, although he was not mustered into service as such until March 23. He returned to Wisconsin to recruit and organize the unit and upon joining the Army of the Potomac, the regiment was assigned to the First Brigade of Gibbon's Second Division, Second Army Corps.

On June 3, 1864, Haskell assumed command of the brigade when Colonel H. Boyd McKean was killed in the assault against the heavily entrenched Confederates at Cold Harbor. As the Wisconsin Adjutant General's Report for 1865 noted:

> After a moment's rest, Colonel Haskell, by command of General Gibbon, ordered the brigade forward. The men rose to obey, and were met by a shower of bullets, when the other parts of the line halted. Colonel Haskell surveyed the situation for a moment, as if irresolute; he finally gave the

> order, "Lie down, men," which was at once obeyed. An instant afterwards, he was struck in the head by a rebel bullet, and instantly killed. Thus fell one of Wisconsin's most gallant soldiers, a thorough disciplinarian, and an accomplished scholar.[43]

Upon hearing of Haskell's death, Gibbon was reported to have cried, "My God! I have lost my best friend, and one of the best soldiers in the Army of the Potomac has fallen!"[44]

The promotion Gibbon received which took him away from his brigade advanced him to command of the Second Division of Major John F. Reynolds's First Corps. A month later he was wounded at the battle of Fredericksburg. Following a three-month convalescence he returned to the Army of the Potomac to command the Second Division of the Second Army Corps. Gibbon received his second wound at the battle of Gettysburg, during the repulse of Pickett's Charge. While recovering from this wound he commanded draft depots at Philadelphia and Cleveland before returning once again to "Mr. Lincoln's Army." He was finally appointed Major General of Volunteers on June 7, 1864, and the following January was given command of the newly created Twenty-fourth Army Corps of the Army of the James. At Appomattox he was appointed one of three Federal commissioners to oversee the surrender of the Army of Northern Virginia.

Honorably mustered out of volunteer service on January 1, 1866, Gibbon remained with the Regulars, and was promoted to Colonel of the Thirty-sixth Infantry on July 28, 1866. Three years later, on March 15, 1869, he was transferred to command the Seventh Infantry, and saw service during the ill-fated "Centennial Campaign" of 1876, arriving at the Little Big Horn battlefield in time to rescue the remnants of George Armstrong Custer's command. The following year Gibbon was wounded a third time at the battle of the Big Hole during a campaign against Chief Joseph and the Nez Perce. Ironically, Gibbon and the Chief afterwards became close friends. He was promoted to brigadier general in the regular army on July 10, 1885, and was placed on the retired rolls on April 20, 1891, his sixty-fourth birthday.

With retirement Gibbon became active in writing, visiting battlefields, and speaking before veterans' groups, especially the Military Order of the Loyal Legion of the United States, a group consisting of honorably discharged Army, Navy, and Marine Corps officers, of which he was elected commander-in-chief. This was a time which he relished, and during which he became particularly close to the men of his former commands, especially the Iron Brigade. When traveling to the Midwest Gibbon made it a point to stop in Wisconsin and Indiana to visit many old friends, and there was even an effort to have the general choose Wisconsin as his final resting place.[45]

In February 1896 Gibbon was planning to travel from his home in Baltimore to St. Paul, to address the Minnesota Commandery of The Military Order of the Loyal Legion in celebration of Lincoln's birthday. During his return home the itinerary called for a stop in Wisconsin to address that commandery, and specifically to visit with Iron Brigade veterans. But the hoped-for meetings were not to take place. On February 7 it was announced that Gibbon had died at 3:30 P.M. the day before at his home in Baltimore, of pneumonia he had contracted the previous Sunday. The old soldier was dead at the age of sixty-eight. Just five days before his death, *The Milwaukee Telegraph* wrote of Gibbon in preparation of his anticipated visit, "General Gibbon is in no sense a paper soldier: he is a man of iron."[46]

Gibbon was not buried in Wisconsin but rather at Arlington National Cemetery, just a few yards from the home of Robert E. Lee, who had served as Superintendent of the Military Academy at West Point when Gibbon was assistant instructor of artillery. On his headstone were engraved the symbols of his two favorite commands, the trefoil of the Second Army Corps and the emblem of the Iron Brigade.

The association between Gibbon and the Westerners was quite unique, and in many ways symbiotic. From these rough-hewn, independent Westerners he learned that reward and mutual respect were as important as drill and discipline. Just as the brigade would remain Gibbon's for its entire term of service, he, too, proudly bore the influence of these volunteers. The love and respect between Gibbon and the Westerners was mutual and lasted a lifetime. Brigadier General Edward S. Bragg, formerly of the Sixth Wisconsin, recalled the brigade's first great battle under Gibbon at Brawner Farm: "General Gibbon stood up with his command, face to face, against the flower of Jackson's corps—and strong and chivalrous was the foe! hand-to-hand, almost, was the battle of that night. And then there it was that Jackson's stubborn fighters learned that iron was as enduring and immovable as stone."[47]

"The Dread Reality of War"

Gibbon's Brigade, August 28–September 17, 1862

ALAN D. GAFF AND MAUREEN GAFF

Men who fought in our Civil War grew up in the literary shadows cast by the American Revolution, when every soldier, save for Benedict Arnold, was portrayed as courageous, patriotic, and noble. Hero worship was in vogue. Historians and novelists alike catered to readers, who, according to one writer, "want to hear of people utterly unlike themselves, more noble, and able, and just, and sweet, and pure; who long to hear of heroism, and to converse with heroes."[1] The Mexican War also furnished the country with a new group of heroes to admire after they had successfully vanquished a foreign foe. Schoolteachers perpetuated this hero worship in daily lessons conducted in classrooms across the country, and young boys were raised to believe that soldiers emerged from battle covered with glory and that good always triumphed over evil. When these young men marched off to their own war in 1861, they quickly discovered "much that they encountered was at odds with their expectations."[2]

When General John Gibbon assumed brigade command in May of 1862, he urged the soldiers in his four Western regiments to "emulate the gallant deeds of their brave Statesmen in the West, and prove to them that the heroism displayed at Fort Donelson and Pittsburg Landing, can be rivaled by their brothers, who have come East, to fight the cause of the 'Union.'"[3] The boys from Wisconsin and Indiana were eager to do just that. Expressing the frustration built up in almost a year of training and preparation, one man in the Seventh Wisconsin exclaimed, "For God's sake kill us off in battle, and don't do us to death as jack mules."[4] Henry Marsh, Nineteenth Indiana, wrote that the brigade was "spoiling for a fight," then later confessed, "Father if I had a thousand lives I would rather lose them all than for our cause to be lost."[5] Robert K. Beecham, Second Wisconsin, admitted that "of course there is danger in war," but he insisted that indeed "it is sweet to die for one's country."[6] Captain Joseph Bird, Seventh Wisconsin, would later assert, "All were eager for the day when we might try our metal," although he did admit that "most of us then knew little of grim-visaged war."[7] All this silliness about wanting to fight a battle was typical of untried troops. As early as the fourth century A.D., Publius Flavius Vegetius Renatus had cautioned Roman commanders that "war is sweet to the inexperienced."[8]

Any such yearning for battle would quickly evaporate during that horrid summer of 1862 when Gibbon's brigade fought four major engagements in three weeks' time, sustaining casualties of over 75 percent during that brief period. What was it like during those battles? How did soldiers feel as they marched into combat? How did they react under fire? How had combat changed them? If only someone had been there to interview survivors and record their thoughts while emotions and actions were still fresh in their minds, we might know the answers to these questions. But S. L. A. Marshall and other "combat historians" would not begin their work with front-line troops for many generations, so we are left with but a few tantalizing snippets of anecdotal information gleaned from diaries, letters, and memoirs. Of those types of sources, the first two are most preferred. Memoirs have the advantage of mature reflection, but they also suffer from the human tendency to repress or block out the most terrible of memories. Immediacy makes for better history.

Combat involved more than simply shooting at the enemy. Medical men of the twentieth century would eventually identify the types of stress which occur under combat situations and every one of these is applicable to men who served in Gibbon's brigade during 1862. These elements of stress, in no particular order, are:

1) Threats to life, limb, and health
2) Physical discomfort
3) Deprivation of social and sexual satisfaction
4) Isolation from typical sources of affection
5) Loss of comrades, along with sights and sounds of wounded and dying men
6) Restriction of personal movement
7) Continual uncertainty
8) Conflict between military duty and individual safety, family obligations, loyalty to comrades, and moral code of conduct
9) Arbitrary demands of authority
10) Lack of privacy
11) Boredom and anxiety between periods of action
12) Lack of individual goals

As will be readily observed, many of these stressful factors often occurred simultaneously, compounding the pressure upon individual soldiers. Although this chapter will not touch on every type of stress listed above, they should all be considered as important factors in the overall effect on soldiers' attitudes.[9]

In an attempt to counter combat-induced stress and to ensure that soldiers followed orders, military commanders have always relied upon drill and discipline, both of which serve to reinforce a system of mutual dependence where the success of a regiment depends upon the actions of each man. For three months Gibbon drove his Western troops with the intensive training and rigid discipline characteristic of the regular army, thereby increasing their ability to withstand hardship and their willingness to follow commands. His efforts, although unpopular at the time, proved to be remarkably effective. General Edward S. Bragg, then lieutenant colonel of the Sixth Wisconsin, remembered, "The men were growing steadier as we pushed them harder."[10] Captain John Marsh, one of Bragg's officers, thought that every soldier in the brigade began to show "a feeling of personal responsibility, each man for the man whose elbow he touched in the ranks, and the responsive thought, 'I must not fail myself in the duty I demand of my comrade.'"[11]

William W. Macy, Nineteenth Indiana, recalled that he, as well as everyone else, "was worked up to the battle-fever" before his first battle and that the brigade was "rather looking for trouble" when it suddenly encountered Stonewall Jackson's command on the night of August 28, 1862.[12] General Gibbon noticed that the sun was shining and the birds were singing when a rebel battery suddenly opened fire on his column as it approached the village of Groveton. The general later confessed that "there was no worse scared man in that brigade than I was" as the enemy shells began to explode and he remembered "a wonderful disposition when you hear a shell coming along to lie down." Overcoming his fright, Gibbon quickly put his own battery into position, then ordered the Second Wisconsin forward to drive off a second rebel battery, riding along behind to oversee the maneuver himself. When the Badgers encountered rebel infantry, the general was "more afraid than ever" and worried that the Wisconsin boys were also frightened and might not hold their ground.[13]

Gibbon need not have worried. The sight of an advancing rebel battleline did not scare these proud Badger soldiers, "the men grasping their pieces with a tighter grasp and expressing their impatience in low mutterings in such honest, if not classic phrases, as, 'come on, God damn you.'"[14] Firing with frantic energy, the Second Wisconsin held the crest of a hill east of the John Brawner farmhouse until the remainder of Gibbon's brigade could hasten forward to extend the Federal line.[15] Some thought the Second Wisconsin maintained the line alone for about ten minutes, while others thought it longer, but whatever the duration, Gilbert M. Woodward termed those few minutes an "opportunity for development and display of character more ample than a life-time of ordinary existence."[16]

As Gibbon's other regiments advanced to support the Second Wisconsin, some men were as frightened as their general had been. Albert V. Young, Sixth Wisconsin, tried to explain the varied sensations that overwhelmed him:

> I must have been very pale. It seemed as if my blood had stopped circulating. Waves of intense heat flashed in quick succession through my entire being. I trembled so I could with difficulty keep from dropping my musket, but I hung on to it because I realized I should soon have need of it if I were not knocked out very early by a rebel bullet. My legs quaked so they would scarcely support my weight, slight though it was. . . . My mouth in an instant, as it seemed, become [*sic*] dry and parched. I was suffering a terrible thirst. With trembling fingers I managed to get my canteen to my lips, and took a long draught. It did not quench the thirst by which I was consumed.

Young then realized that, no matter how frightened he was, he was too much of a coward to run away, since he was more afraid of being tagged a coward by his comrades if he happened to come back alive! The commands "Ready! Aim! Fire!" brought Young to his senses and he recalled that after firing a few rounds, "My nerves became steady and I grew cool."[17]

Mickey Sullivan, another Sixth Wisconsin soldier, confessed to having "a queer choking sensation about the throat," but he was distracted before his fear reached the magnitude of Albert Young's. As the regiment started forward, someone behind Sullivan stepped on the heel of his shoe and he turned around angrily to inquire if the rear rank man did not have enough room to march without walking on the feet of those in front. The two men argued back and forth all during the advance, Sullivan completely forgetting his choking sensation until after the battle.[18]

Participants tried to describe the battle for friends and family members, but could do little more than offer some personal experiences. The intense concentration necessary for a strict adherence to duty had suddenly narrowed their focus of attention to what they could see to the front and a few yards on either side. Lieutenant Alexander Hill, Second Wisconsin, wrote, "I had two men shot in front of me, which must otherwise have hit me; but all the mark I have of the fight, is a bullet-hole in my hat."[19] Captain Marsh recalled, "Every man in my company seems a hero, and when a Corporal whom I had disliked quietly says during the hottest of the battle, 'Captain, my gun's so foul I can't get the cartridge down; can you find me another?' I felt like embracing him."[20]

Lieutenant Frank Haskell, one of Gibbon's staff officers, saw that the opposing battlelines were "nowhere a hundred yards distant, and in some places not more than twenty."[21] As the sun set and darkness gradually settled over the battlefield, Major Rufus Dawes, Sixth Wisconsin, watched the fighting to his left:

> Our men on the left loaded and fired with the energy of madmen, and a recklessness of death truly wonderful, but human nature could not long

> stand such a terribly wasting fire. It literally mowed out great gaps in the line, but the isolated squads would rally together and rush up right into the face of Death.[22]

Sometimes as the crowds of men surged forward, the fighting was almost hand-to-hand. Once when this happened in front of Company A of the Second Wisconsin, Lieutenant Henry Converse watched in amazement as Gustavus Horn suddenly charged the enemy and triumphantly brought back a prisoner at the point of his bayonet.[23] A Seventh Wisconsin soldier bragged, "My person did not receive a scratch, though a buckshot passed through my coat. I stood square and threw cold lead without a shake of nerve."[24] Everyone threw cold lead as fast as they could. Although he had received a slight wound in his right leg, John St. Clair, Sixth Wisconsin, boasted, "I shot 45 times at the Devils in the first fight."[25] Soldiers in the other regiments, which had been under fire for longer periods, fired away all their cartridges, including those of the dead and wounded, leaving many to hold their line with only the bayonet. One-half of the men in the Nineteenth Indiana had been shot down, but orders to fall back had to be given three times before the survivors would relinquish the field. Among those were soldiers who were still unhurt, "but very few escaped having their hat or clothes perforated with balls."[26]

Colonel Solomon Meredith, Nineteenth Indiana, exaggerated but slightly when he called the brigade's first battle "one of the most terrific engagements in the history of warfare."[27] Captain John Clark, one of Meredith's officers, said that his company "stood to a man the terrible cross-fire which the regiment was subjected to."[28] Captain George Otis, Second Wisconsin, declared it to be "one of the bloodiest of the war, a clear infantry contest, a fair square stand up face-to-face fight, both sides sufficiently firm to keep each other from gaining ground and position."[29] It was only a "stand up face-to-face fight" for the first few moments, then the relentless musketry forced everyone, Yankee and rebel alike, to take cover behind fences, trees, farm buildings, or any other available shelter. Although the brigade had been trained to fight standing in a line of battle, intelligent officers quickly saw that the men would be exterminated by doing so and tactics were quickly modified to fit the occasion.[30]

Lieutenant Colonel Bragg reported that "there was no confusion, no faltering" in the Sixth Wisconsin, an admission that Gibbon's training had paid off. The mutual dependence of soldiers upon one another was exhibited by three men from that regiment who left sickbeds in the ambulances and rushed up to join their comrades after procuring muskets and ammunition. One of them, Corporal John H. Burns, was so sick that he was afterward sent off to an Alexandria hospital.[31] Dozens of men refused to go to the rear after receiving slight wounds, preferring to remain on the firing line where they were badly needed. W. H. Church, Second Wisconsin, explained that "they shot me three times through the leg[,] tore a piece of bark from my left hand[,] and cut off my shoulder strap near the cartridge box." He then added, "But they didn't do me any serious injury."[32] J. O. Johnson, Sixth Wisconsin, was struck in the left thigh by a ball early in the fight, but stayed at his post until Gibbon's brigade withdrew from the battlefield after dark. Only then did he examine the wound, binding it up with a handkerchief before lying down for a nap.[33]

Individual reactions to the battle varied greatly. On the one hand, Lieutenant Nathaniel Rollins, Second Wisconsin, became so exhausted from heat, physical labor, and mental strain that he fainted and had to be carried from the field.[34] At the other extreme was Captain Wilson Colwell of the same regiment who seemed to enjoy the pressure and excitement. His orderly sergeant remembered, "When the survivors of the Second were no longer under fire, many I know suffered a reaction from the extreme nervous tension of the struggle, and were prostrated." Not so Colwell, who was thought to be "incapable of fear," and appeared virtually unchanged by the experience.[35]

When Gibbon's brigade, along with the remainder of King's division, abandoned its battlefield and started for Manassas Junction, the men were exhausted. George Fairfield, Sixth Wisconsin, wrote of that night march, "I never saw men more in need of sleep. When we would halt for a few minutes one half would go to sleep, each man sitting or laying down upon the spot where he halted."[36] A soldier from Marsena Patrick's brigade said of that march, "Many drank from muddy ruts of the road. Rain on the skin could not quench the burning thirst engendered by the fierce hardships, exposure, and lack of sufficient and proper food."[37]

Mickey Sullivan described his brigade, after it reached Manassas Junction on the morning of August 29th, as "bleeding, angry, hungry, tired, sleepy, foot-sore and cut to pieces."[38] Sullivan later commented on the brigade's emotional and physical state:

> I hardly knew our brigade, it was so reduced in size and the men looked so dirty and powder-stained that I could scarcely tell my own tentmates, and it seemed as if their dispositions changed with their appearance. The intensest feelings of anger were manifested against the commander who allowed one brigade, alone and unaided, to fight the best division in the rebel army.[39]

Captain Otis agreed that the soldiers "were not in a very good humor" and when General Rufus King, their division commander, rode by later that morning he "did not receive that cordial greeting due to one of his rank and station."[40] Lieutenant Hill declared that the Second Wisconsin had been "shot down like sheep" and Major Dawes wrote with unconcealed bitterness, "The best blood of Wisconsin and Indiana was poured out like water, and it was spilled for naught."[41]

After receiving rations and ammunition, the Western men marched north to where General John Pope was assembling his army and, ominously, camped on the battlefield of First Bull Run. Having lost 725 killed, wounded, and missing at the Brawner Farm fight (37 percent of its strength), Gibbon's brigade did not participate in the battle fought by the remainder of King's division on the night of August 29th.[42] That was perfectly fine with the Badgers and Hoosiers, who considered themselves "exceedingly fortunate" to have missed another encounter with the rebels. Rufus Dawes explained, "Our one night's experience at Gainesville [Brawner Farm] had eradicated our yearning for a fight. In our future history we will always be found ready but never again anxious."[43]

While other troops fought and maneuvered, Gibbon's brigade enjoyed its brief period of rest. Food had always been in short supply since the army's retreat from the Rappahannock River and hunger continued to be a problem. Fresh beef had been butchered for the brigade on August 28th, but orders to march had arrived before everyone could cook their meat. Some soldiers had no choice but "cut off chunks and ate them warm and raw."[44] Fresh beef was again issued on August 30th, but as fires were prohibited, the men could not cook it and "had to subsist on that until two days afterward."[45]

At 4 P.M. Gibbon's brigade participated in Pope's grand assault on the rebels, who quickly threw back their attackers and advanced to drive the Yankees from the field. As troops to the front gave way and came running back, Gibbon found his brigade thrust into the front line from its supporting position in the rear. Unable to blunt the rebel attack with his small brigade, he could do little more than slow the pursuing rebels in the thick woods north of Groveton.[46] Gibbon stayed with the Sixth Wisconsin, the last of his regiments to leave the woods, and Lieutenant Haskell described how it "marched slowly out of the woods—faced about, gave three war cry cheers that made the woods ring again, defied the enemy with their flag, and then moved to the place assigned them some five hundred yards in the rear, in the cadenced step, steady, as if an enemy were not within a hundred miles."[47]

As Pope's army began a hasty retreat to Centreville, Gibbon's brigade, despite having lost almost 150 men during the day, was selected to cover the withdrawal.[48] One soldier described the brigade's appearance when it halted at Centreville:

> They had nearly a week with but little sleep, no blankets, no tents, no rations but hard crackers, and had been marching in the dust or mud half of the time, and under fire the other half, and although they were begrimed with dirt and smoke, yet in every man's countenance there could be seen that which seemed to indicate that each one had done his duty.[49]

As long as the men remained together, they were still capable of performing their duties, but they should never have been detailed for picket duty on the night of August 31st. According to Rufus Dawes, his soldiers, "after the privations, labor, and intense excitement of three successive days in battle, were unfitted for such duty." They appeared "haggard and worn out." Sure enough, one Sixth Wisconsin man became confused, got turned around in the darkness, and killed a man from his own regiment coming to relieve him. This singular tragedy could only be attributed to the intense fatigue and exhaustion that affected everyone.[50]

By the time Gibbon's men reached the vicinity of Upton's Hill, they were trying to make sense out of their own personal experience amid the "dark background of blunders, imbecilities, jealousies and disasters in the Pope campaign."[51] Most would have agreed with Henry Rhoten, Second Wisconsin, who could exclaim, "I am no coward!"[52] Others would have concurred with Captain A. S. Hooe, Sixth Wisconsin, who wrote somewhat less enthusiastically, "I am satisfied with my experience. I did my duty and did not disgrace my name or State."[53] William Hayes, a Seventh Wisconsin boy, wrote boldly, "I never liked anything better than to stand right up among the bullets and shells and give it to the rebels." In the case of Hayes, it may have been that the sixteen-year-old was trying to live up to the expectations of his father, who had been an officer in the British Army.[54]

Recruits who joined these regiments in Washington were shocked to find the soldiers "worn out and in poor health."[55] Cases of diarrhea had increased fivefold from July through September, an indication of how their health had eroded during the constant marching and fighting. Doctor D. Cooper Ayres reported that the Seventh Wisconsin had exhibited symptoms of "general lassitude" prior to the Brawner Farm battle, although the excitement of the next few days aroused their spirit and kept their energy levels "buoyant." But that intense excitement subsided at Upton's Hill and "both the physical and mental energies of the men became very much depressed."[56]

This depression was due, in part, to the realization that the brigade's sacrifice had apparently been in vain. From the commanding general down to the lowliest private, everyone expressed the same despondency. Writing to his wife, Gibbon said simply that "my men were literally slaughtered."[57] Captain Patrick Hart, Nineteenth Indiana, bemoaned the "useless slaughter of brave Indianians," then continued, "the men are dissatisfied and denounce the General whose incapacity sent them to that infernal slaughter pen."[58] Henry Rhoten admitted that his regiment had been through "quite enough to satiate the most greedy after military glory."[59]

The depression in Gibbon's brigade was compounded by the fact that its deeds had been largely ignored in the press coverage of Pope's campaign. Lieutenant John Shafer, Nineteenth Indiana, complained, "No mention is made of Gibbon's brigade in any of the Eastern papers."[60] Lieutenant Samuel Birdsall, Sixth Wisconsin, agreed, claiming that "the well drilled, unflinching troops of the West are not the favorites of the Eastern press."[61]

The soldiers themselves were unable to furnish many details to the folks back home because they had been too personally involved in the fighting and did not yet fully comprehend what they had been through. Captain Alexander Gordon confessed to being unable to tell anyone about Pope's campaign, saying simply, "No pen can describe the scene."[62] One unidentified Badger, referring to the "fortnight of marching, fighting, exposure, fatigue, hunger and thirst," said simply, "I am in no mood to discuss these things yet."[63] Lieutenant Frank Haskell admitted to simply being too tired to write about the battles "as the terrible weariness of long fight is upon me."[64] Other soldiers had no intention of telling family members what terrible things they had seen or done. Joshua Jones, Nineteenth Indiana, expressed that feeling in a letter written to his wife: "I would not had you or Mother to of Known Just my Situation for nothing in the world."[65]

While at Upton's Hill, the severely reduced regiments received scanty reinforcements—a few raw recruits, a few convalescents returned from hospitals, and some extra duty men who had been ordered back to the ranks.[66] John Pope's Army of Virginia had been broken up and Gibbon's brigade began the second phase of the 1862 campaign as part of the First Corps, Army of the Potomac. The Western men left their camps near Upton's Hill on September 6th and started north after the victorious rebel army that had invaded Maryland.[67] Doctor Ayres observed the troops on this march and carefully noted their condition, "The men had rested four days at Upton's Hill, but did not recruit physically, and their energy and ambition were so much depressed that they fell out by the wayside in scores, exhibiting the appearance of general exhaustion, without symptoms of corporeal disease." By the end of the first day's march, there were more stragglers than men in the ranks, but Ayres noted that by the time Gibbon's brigade reached Frederick, "the spirits of the men began to assume more buoyancy."[68] Due to the experience gained in their first two battles, Gibbon's men now marched forward knowing full well what to expect in future battles. Their wide-eyed eagerness had disappeared.

After catching up with the rebels at South Mountain, Gibbon's brigade was held in reserve until the afternoon of September 14th when it was ordered forward against the enemy defending Turner's Gap, "an ugly looking place to attack" according to Lieutenant Haskell.[69] Others shared that sense of dread as they began the assault. Jacob Drew, Seventh Wisconsin, remembered, "Something seemed to tell me that I would be killed that night or wounded bad. I prayed for my life, the fear seemed to pass away."[70] Z. B. Russell, of the same regiment, admitted that he "did not feel brave" as the main line followed skirmishers up the mountain.[71] Captain Loyd Harris, Sixth Wisconsin, recalled, "To say I was excited fails to express my condition."[72]

The fighting raged hottest north of the National Road where the Seventh Wisconsin encountered a strongly posted enemy and was quickly reinforced by the Sixth Wisconsin. Captain Harris wondered how he managed to avoid being shot since "the air seemed filled with a sharp, hissing noise as bullets flew by."[73] Jacob Drew had prayed that his life might be spared, and it was, although the bullets did come awfully close: "There was 4 struck in my clothes and traps that night. The 4th hit in the right thigh by going through my pants pocket & tearing the clasp of a pocket book."[74] The musketry continued until after dark and Gibbon's brigade held the battlefield, the men "jubilant and joyous" at their first victory, despite having lost over 300 men.[75]

Except for the Sixth Wisconsin, Gibbon's regiments were relieved shortly after the firing ceased. Those isolated Badgers held their advanced position until daylight, surrounded by dead and wounded comrades whom they tended as well as they could in the dark. Rufus Dawes remembered how he and Captain John Kellogg searched in vain for a sip of water to give to William Lawrence, who was mortally wounded:

> He recognized us and appreciated our efforts, but was unable to speak. The dread reality of war was before us in this frightful death upon the cold, hard stones. The mortal suffering, the fruitless struggle to send a parting message to the far-off home, and the final release by death, all enacted in the darkness, were felt even more deeply than if the scene had been relieved by the light of day.[76]

After a long night spent on the mountainside, the soldiers from the Sixth Wisconsin were overjoyed when other troops marched up to take their place. Major Dawes admitted to feeling the happiness that could be understood only by those "who have experienced the feeling of prostration produced by such scenes and surroundings, after the excitement of a bloody battle."[77]

There was time only to cook breakfast and bury the dead before Gibbon's brigade hastened off after the retreating rebels, who finally took up a defensive position behind Antietam Creek. On the morning of September 17th, the First Corps attacked, Gibbon's brigade moving south along the Hagerstown Turnpike. The left of the brigade, Second and Sixth Wisconsin, charged into a large cornfield south of the D. R. Miller farmhouse, while the Seventh Wisconsin and Nineteenth Indiana prolonged the line into woods across the road. Having fought three battles together, the four Western regiments were ready for yet another bloody challenge.[78] The determination of the men remaining with the colors was demonstrated to General Gibbon on the march from South Mountain. He encountered a soldier tramping along with one arm in a sling and the other carrying his musket, trying to catch up with his regiment. When Gibbon expressed the opinion that he could not handle his musket with such a wound, the man simply responded, "Yes, I can, sir."[79]

Captain Otis described the "awful carnage," standing amid the storm "with the bullets flying all around me and man after man dropping here and there."[80] The cornfield became a living hell as "hungry, ragged and dirty" men repeatedly charged the rebel lines.[81] Rufus Dawes thought that the ground along the turnpike surpassed every other battlefield "in manifest evidence of slaughter," and he stated firmly, "Whoever stood in front of the corn field at Antietam needs no praise."[82] Sergeant Jaspar Chestnut carried the Sixth Wisconsin's regimental color into the cornfield, where five bullets struck the flagstaff and another passed through Chestnut's wrist, the flag itself being "riddled with bullets."[83] Wounded men from Chestnut's regiment were heard to cry out, "Never mind me, fight! hold your position! I will get off if I can, if not never mind! Fight boys, don't give up the ground!"[84] By the time Gibbon withdrew his regiments from the field, he had lost almost 350 men.[85]

Among those killed in the cornfield was Robert Stevenson, a forty-one-year-old private from the Second Wisconsin, who was that regiment's unofficial color-bearer. At First Bull Run, Stevenson had carried the national flag from the field as rebel cavalry harassed the retreating Federals. At Brawner Farm, after every man in the color guard had been killed or wounded, Stevenson again carried the national colors from the field and bore them during the Second Bull Run battle. At South Mountain, although "too unwell for duty," he carried the flag again. At Antietam, Stevenson was sick in a field hospital on the morning of September 17th, but he left his bed and rejoined Company C, saying to its commander, "Captain I am with you to the last." Within an hour Stevenson fell, pierced by five bullets.[86] Another Second Wisconsin man, Gustavus Horn, who had captured a rebel at Brawner Farm, was described as "a true and devoted soldier, one who was always ready and willing for duty, and on that account was loved by all for his daring bravery and willingness to perform every duty, regardless of danger." Horn's right arm was broken by a bullet in the cornfield, and while he was leaving the field another projectile tore through both hips, inflicting a mortal wound.[87]

Two men from the Seventh Wisconsin bore their wounds with unbelievable courage. Gustavus Sargent was wounded by a large shell fragment that broke the thigh and entered his body. A fellow soldier remembered, "He was perfectly conscious of his situation, and bore his pain with heroic fortitude, saying to his friend, Mussey, with almost his last breath, 'I am willing to die.'" Sargent's last message was, "Tell my father and friends I fought and died for my country." James Pattengill had been hit in the arm and struck again by a musket ball that shattered his hip joint. A comrade said that he lived six days, "enduring the most intense pain like a martyr," and died "asking those around him to inform his mother that he did not run from the enemy."[88]

As at South Mountain, the Antietam victory allowed Gibbon's brigade to bury its own dead, but, of necessity, the standard military ceremony was dispensed with. There were no coffins, no ministers, and no volleys of farewell. Soldiers borrowed tools from a battery, hacked out graves, and tenderly buried comrades in their blood-stained uniforms. Men from the different regiments gathered their own dead and buried them together, placing well-marked headboards at each grave.[89] Every effort was made to locate the Western dead. In the case of George Holloway, one of the Second Wisconsin's color guard, the body was identified and buried by his brother William, who served with the Sixth Wisconsin.[90] Soldiers considered it a sacred duty to bury their dead and the Maryland victories allowed them to finally do that. One of Reuben Huntley's friends in the Sixth Wisconsin alluded to the burials in a letter to his widow, writing, "he was burried [*sic*] decently by one of our company, witch [*sic*] is better than some of our poor boys fared."[91]

In comparison to the Maryland burials, very little had been done for those killed at Brawner Farm. Albert Cole, Second Wisconsin, saw his brother, Frank, dead upon the field, but could do no more than compose his limbs and cover his face.[92] After the fighting ended, Ephraim Bartholomew spent several hours crawling over the blackened battlefield in search of his son, John, whom he eventually found lying dead, "a smile on his face, but his soul was with God." All Ephraim could do was crawl back to his regiment, having at least answered the question about his son's fate.[93] Young Anson Linscott, drum major of the Second Wisconsin, wrote his parents a short letter in which he told them of the death of his brother, Archer: "I saw him fall but we could not save him; he died in a few minutes." But, miraculously, Archer still lived, despite a severe wound in the windpipe, although he would die two months later in a hospital.[94] Anson Linscott's confusion over his brother's death points out the fixation that Gibbon's soldiers had regarding the Brawner Farm fight, since it was impossible to discover who had been killed outright, who had been wounded, and how serious the wound.

Abandoning that battlefield left survivors with a sense of guilt over leaving their dead friends unburied, with no chance for a final good-bye. An attempt to rectify that situation was made on the morning of August 30th when Captain Otis started to the Brawner Farm site with a squad of twenty men. Before reaching the field, rebel skirmishers opened fire on the burial party, forcing it to abandon the mission.[95] In November 1862, soldiers returning to the brigade passed by the Brawner Farm battlefield and found Badger and Hoosier remains strewn about the ground or protruding from the dirt that had been carelessly piled on top of them. Colonel Lysander Cutler, then commanding the brigade, sent an urgent appeal to division headquarters: "As a matter of respect to the brave men who there fell, and in justice to the feelings of their living comrades and friends, I ask permission to make a detail of men to proceed to that battlefield and suitably and decently inter the remains of their comrades."[96] Cutler's request was denied, however, because the men could not be spared. It was not until November 1, 1863, that Gibbon's dead could be properly buried. Albert Young offered a eulogy for those who died in the brigade's first battle:

> Theirs was the enviable fate. The quick, sharp agony, as the leaden messenger of death tore its way through the quivering, shrinking flesh, or at most a few days, or weeks, or months of pain and suffering, and then rest—forever rest.

As for those who had survived, Young commented, "The torn and bleeding heart may have been healed by the balm of time, but the scars are there, ever to remain."[97]

The end of the 1862 campaign allowed those who survived to make some sense out of the twenty-one days of marching and fighting. Theodore Calvin, Seventh Wisconsin, whose uniform had been hit five times during that period, remembered having "shot over 80 times in two different battles had dead men fall against me and all around me and blood spirt [*sic*] over me."[98] Experiences such as Calvin's could not leave a man unchanged, and Julius Murray, Sixth Wisconsin, explained the subsequent transformation: "You become callous to those falling around you Dead or wounded in fact we have all become callous and the sights of Dead piled up in every direction on which we would have looked with Horror a few months ago we carefully examine now to see which is friend or foe."[99] In addition to numbing the senses, combat had greatly leveled individuality, at least according to Reverend Samuel Eaton, Seventh Wisconsin, who wrote, "Refinement does not separate itself from rudeness; even the pious and the profane have some heart throbs which are similar." Eaton remembered how men would approach him before a battle and hand over a pocketbook, often "with a word and a tear, or a manner which expresses more than both." He noticed, "At such a moment hearts touch that had hardly recognized their kindred humanity before."[100]

One thing that all these veterans shared was a desire to avoid any such future sacrifice. Captain George Otis admitted, "I have seen so much, passed through such terrible fields of strife, that my heart is sickened against war."[101] Cornelius Wheeler, one of the few men remaining in Captain Otis's company, agreed wholeheartedly: "We have had quite glory enough now, and should all be perfectly well satisfied with a more peace-ful life hereafter, but from present appearances the time has not yet come, tho' I sincerely hope it may not be far distant."[102] Elisha Odle, Nineteenth Indiana, hoped "that the war may soon have an end when the Soldiers can return to loved ones at home." The disheartened Odle then wrote, "when this you see remember me if the bludy [*sic*] grave be first my bed remember me when I am dead."[103] Lieutenant Edward Kellogg, Second Wisconsin, had been mortally wounded at Brawner Farm and composed his last letter while his comrades were fighting at Antietam. He best expressed the bitterness, resentment, and disillusionment that overwhelmed Gibbon's soldiers when he wrote, "We have dared and done all that the most exacting could require, but the stupidity of our leaders has squandered all this wealth of bravery and patriotism, and enthusiasm, and energy, and has made all of no avail."[104]

When he took command of this brigade, John Gibbon's objective was to teach his soldiers three important lessons, "obedience to orders, discipline and military efficiency." He would later write with pride, "The habit of obedience and subjection to the will of another, so difficult to instill into the minds of free and independent men became marked characteristics in the command."[105] Upon entering the Brawner Farm fight, the brigade had fewer than 1,950 officers and men available for the line of battle. In just three weeks the brigade had lost approximately 1,550 men, killed, wounded, and missing.[106] Of twelve field officers who began the campaign, only two—Lieutenant Colonel Lucius Fairchild, Second Wisconsin, and Major Rufus Dawes, Sixth Wisconsin—had escaped death or wounds, although Fairchild had been too sick to command his regiment at Antietam.[107] When a trooper from the Third Indiana Cavalry dropped by to visit friends in the Nineteenth Indiana a week after Antietam, he was shocked by what he found: "The brigade now musters but four hundred effective men, and the Nineteenth less than one hundred. Their loss in commissioned officers has been heavy, three companies at this time being commanded by Corporals."[108] There were only enough men left in Company A of the Sixth Wisconsin to make one stack of muskets and those remaining could not "restrain the bitter emotions of our hearts."[109] The brigade would need a long period of rest and reorganization before it could ever again be effective on a battlefield.

Perhaps the strangest occurrences during this period were those instances when men accurately foretold their own deaths. Most soldiers believed in such premonitions without reservation and both officers and enlisted men experienced these presentiments. The highest-ranking officer to predict his own demise was Colonel Edgar O'Connor of the Second Wisconsin, who said to his lieutenant colonel the day before the Brawner Farm engagement, "Fairchild, prepare yourself to take command of the Second; I shall be killed in the first battle." O'Connor was shot early in the fight and died of his wounds later that night.[110] Even before the brigade started on Pope's campaign, Major A. Garfield, the younger of two brothers in Company E, Sixth Wisconsin, told his friends that "he would be wounded in the first battle he went into and die from the effects of it." Comrades laughed and teased him about his premonition, but he never wavered in his feeling. As the regiment marched into action at Brawner Farm, Garfield said to those around him, "This is my first and last fight, boys, and I shall do my duty." After receiving a flesh wound in the calf of his leg, Garfield fell to the rear, crying out, "I'm hit, good-bye, boys," then added, "Tell my parents I did not shirk my duty." Although his wound was not thought to be serious, he died from its effects on September 3rd.[111]

In the morning hours of August 30th, as Gibbon's brigade lay in reserve, W. G. Monroe Scott, Seventh Wisconsin, took a short walk with Tanner Thomas. Scott startled his friend by announcing, "My time is short on earth, this is my last day." Sergeant Thomas tried to talk sense to Scott, but he persisted, "We will go into battle to-day; and I will fall as soon as we get there." The sergeant saw that he was "contented with his lot and felt satisfied that his time had come," so the two men talked about the prospects of getting to Heaven. Scott professed to believe in "a just and merciful God," who had watched over them since enlistment and would ensure them a place in Heaven. After praying fervently, they walked back to their company, where Scott announced to his mess, "Boys, I am going to eat dinner with you to-day; this is the last meal I shall eat. I shall be killed before night." His friends laughed and tried to cheer him up, but Scott remained adamant: "It's no use, boys; I am no coward, but you will see that what I tell you is true." That afternoon the brigade was ordered forward and Tanner Thomas remembered, "He seemed perfectly cool and firm, he looked several times to see if I was near him; we had been there but a short time when I heard the whistling of a ball, and a crashing sound and Monroe fell." He was dead before he hit the ground, killed by a ball through the head.[112]

When Gibbon halted his brigade at noon on September 14th, George Miles, Sixth Wisconsin, appeared "very serious, not his usual jolly self at all." Everyone noticed this change of demeanor and asked the reason for it. Miles told them, "You fellows would be quiet too, if you knew you would be killed tonight." His friends made fun of his statement, pointing out that they had chased the rebels for a week and had not caught them yet. When Miles persisted in his belief, the company commander detailed him to a safe place. Miles caught on to this plan and declared, "I came here to do my duty and although I know I shall be killed I shall go in." He was shot dead halfway up South Mountain, his premonition being one of five that would occur in Company A during the war.[113]

Before South Mountain, Captain Edwin A. Brown was heard to say, "I shall be killed in the next battle." He escaped injury on September 14th, but was killed instantly at Antietam just three days later.[114] An unidentified soldier from Company B, Sixth Wisconsin, was driving an ambulance as the army neared Antietam Creek. With a battle looming, he insisted on rejoining his company, saying to others in the ambulance corps, "I'm going to my death, boys, but I'm going into the battle, all the same." He was felled by the first rebel volley fired in the cornfield.[115]

It is hard to imagine anyone more courageous than these men, and others with similar premonitions, marching into what they sincerely believed to be certain death. On the other hand, there were some soldiers who did not have the moral courage necessary for the highly stressful combat situations encountered by Gibbon's brigade. Some men were outright cowards. One notorious case was that of Captain Valentine Jacobs, Nineteenth Indiana. On the evening before the Brawner Farm fight, Jacobs concocted a little charade wherein he brewed a cup of boiling coffee, poured it into his shoe, and blamed someone else for the accident. While on furlough back home, he told an unwitting doctor that the burn had been caused by a shell burst, so his obliging friend certified that the wound had been caused in battle. Knowledgeable officers exposed the scheme and Captain Jacobs was dismissed from the service for cowardice and lying.[116]

Despite having performed well at Brawner Farm, Lieutenant Isaac Witemyre of the Hoosier regiment took extraordinary measures to avoid further combat. At Second Bull Run, Lieutenant Haskell found him "skulking behind a tree some four hundred yards in the rear of his regiment." After the battle at South Mountain, he was discovered behind a large rock, "professing to have the 'belly-ache.'" He left the company, which he commanded, shortly afterward and did not reappear until after Antietam. Witemyre was also dismissed from the service.[117]

While at Upton's Hill, Captain Hooe had written that he "did not disgrace my name or State." George Fairfield disagreed, stating bluntly, "I call the Capt a coward." He then explained why: "He will not run but he is so terrified that he can't give a command. At Bull Run he had to go to the front to lead his company forward in line and you would have thought he was trying to sneak up to a wild turkey."[118] After the Antietam battle, Hooe's regimental commander publicly branded him a coward for his performance there.[119]

During this three-week period, a few enlisted men deserted their comrades. At Brawner Farm, three men from Company B, Second Wisconsin, "left their posts in time of need and have not been seen since." All three later returned and two of them served out their term of service.[120] Two men in Company E, Nineteenth Indiana, deserted their company and were called cowards by a comrade. Both quickly returned to the ranks, one of them being killed at Antietam and the other serving out his term.[121] Captain Brown reported three cowards in Company E, Sixth Wisconsin, including one man who "ran away from the Battle field & was taken prisoner." Speaking of the runaway, Brown said, "I dont want him to come back to the Co."[122]

Company G, Sixth Wisconsin, lost two men when they deserted on September 7th on the march into Maryland. Other men had deserted previously, but had "either been apprehended or returned to duty."[123] One soldier from Company B, Seventh Wisconsin, writing of South Mountain, said, "I do not think there was a man in the whole regiment who left his place; but there were some who left their places before we got into line of battle and never showed up to their companies afterward."[124] In his Antietam report, Captain William Dudley praised the officers, noncoms, and privates of the Nineteenth Indiana, "except the few who found their way to the rear when danger approached."[125] Immediately after Antietam, Gibbon found it necessary to issue a general order that, in part, addressed the issue of cowardice: "Any unwounded man therefore found in rear of his Reg't during a battle will be considered and treated as a coward skulking from a duty bravely faced by his comrades." Despite a claim that his brigade had no stragglers at Antietam, Gibbon obviously had a problem with some men who could not stay in the ranks when a fight appeared imminent.[126]

While the loss of men from the ranks before a battle was a distraction to some extent, the brigade's major problem was finding men to fill leadership roles as officers and noncoms were shot down. Casualties, fatigue, and illness almost destroyed the command structure. In the case of officers, the time lag between recommendation for a higher position and actually mustering into a new rank was often many months. In the meantime, officers received temporary promotions, second lieutenants acting as first lieutenants, first lieutenants acting as captains, and captains acting as field officers. When companies had no officers remaining for active duty, the senior sergeants acted as lieutenants. The Nineteenth Indiana had lost so many officers by Antietam that Captain Dudley acted as major during the battle and four companies were commanded by sergeants.[127] The situation in the Seventh Wisconsin was quite similar, Captain John Callis commanding the regiment and at least three companies being led by senior sergeants at Antietam.[128]

Sergeants and corporals presented another problem. As companies decreased in size because of casualties and debility, a full complement of noncommissioned officers, five sergeants and eight corporals, was not necessary. If more noncoms were needed, junior men or privates were appointed to "acting" ranks for the emergency.[129] Date of rank was generally respected, although deserving individuals were sometimes promoted over those ahead. One example of this was Thomas Kerr, who was fourth sergeant in Company D, Sixth Wisconsin. At Second Bull Run, Lieutenant Colonel Bragg ordered Kerr to take command of the company although other sergeants had held their ranks for a longer time. Kerr's later career fully justified Bragg's action.[130] Vacancies were often left unfilled until there was time for a complete reorganization. William Harries fought as a corporal at Antietam, but later received a promotion to first sergeant, effective ten days before that battle.[131] When it came to filling the position of corporal, Captain Alexander Gordon, Seventh Wisconsin, explained how it was done in his company: "The Corporals I have endeavored to appoint from the most intelligent and meritorious of the company, but after there were so many who merited promotion, and among whom there was no choice, I resorted to the method of writing the names upon a separate slip of paper, and throwing them into a hat and the first one drawn out was the lucky man."[132]

There can be no doubt that in 1862 Gibbon's brigade was superbly officered, from the commanding general down to the company officers. A year of training and preparation had sifted out nearly all problem officers, leaving solid commanders at every level. General Gibbon had always emphasized training, but Lieutenant Haskell wrote that "his tendency was strong to get up to the front where the bullets flew very carelessly."[133] He was a hands-on combat commander, whose two war wounds attested to his willingness to direct troops under fire. The brigade's twelve field officers at Brawner Farm had no superiors in any army. Three of them—Colonel Edgar O'Connor, Lieutenant Colonel Alois Bachman, and Major Isaac May—died of wounds. Colonels Lysander Cutler and Solomon Meredith, and Lieutenant Colonels Edward Bragg and Lucius Fairchild all attained the rank of brigadier general. Majors Thomas Allen and Rufus Dawes were made brigadier generals by brevet. Colonel William Robinson, Lieutenant Colonel Charles Hamilton, and Major George Bill left the army because of wounds received at Brawner Farm.[134] With but few exceptions, the captains and lieutenants were good,

Officers of the Nineteenth Indiana Volunteers, Winter of 1863–64, in Washington. Photograph by Alexander Gardner, courtesy of the Mick Kissick Collection.
SEATED: On left, Joseph L. Hartley, Company F, McCordsville; third from left, Col. Samuel J. Williams, Selma; fourth from left, Adjutant George F. Finney, Elizabethtown; fifth from left, Surgeon Jacob Ebersole, Aurora; on right, Assistant Surgeon Abraham B. Haines, North Vernon.
STANDING: Fourth from left, Maj. John M. Lindley, Indianapolis; fifth from left, Chaplain Thomas Barnett, Selma; sixth from left, Capt. William Orr, Company K., Selma; eighth from left, Capt. John W. Shafer, Company G, Elkhart.

solid officers, who, although lacking a military background, learned their craft well and furnished quality leadership.

The men they led had enlisted in 1861 to save their imperiled country. Ill-prepared for war, but exhibiting boundless vigor and exuberance, these soldiers had longed for a chance to prove their worth in battle. Numerous marches across northern Virginia had prepared them to withstand heat, cold, dust, mud, and aching muscles. John Gibbon's regimen of drill and discipline had taught them to respect themselves and their commanders. It prepared them for the day when they would stand on the perilous abyss of combat and then, with bullets whizzing and shells bursting about them, repress all normal human feelings. Those who were struck down could never be replaced and those who emerged unhurt would be changed forever.

Gone was all that precombat nonsense of soldiers being covered with glory, good triumphing over evil, and the belief that it was "sweet to die for one's country." The Badgers and Hoosiers now knew that war was "a horrid thing" which could be defined only as "the killing of men; the hunting to kill men, and being hunted to be killed."[135] For soldiers on Gibbon's battle line, war was a monster that gobbled up friends and foe alike, leaving in its wake a trail of death, crippled bodies, and shattered dreams. No one could stop it and yet everyone must try. Bravery, courage, fortitude, and endurance meant nothing, except to one's immediate comrades. Everyone was expendable. There were no exceptions.

6

"Like So Many Devils"

The Iron Brigade at Fitzhugh's Crossing

MARC STORCH AND BETH STORCH

For the men of the Army of the Potomac, memories of the battle of Chancellorsville would forever be those of missed opportunities and a battle lost. For the men of the Iron Brigade, however, those days in April and May of 1863 would forever be remembered with pride and a special feeling of accomplishment. As one member of the brigade later recalled, it was "the grandest fifteen minutes of our lives."[1]

April 1863 again found the Army of the Potomac on the offensive in Virginia. Commanding General Joseph Hooker had seen the futility of battering Confederate positions at Fredericksburg in December of 1862, followed by demoralization of the army in the "Mud march." Rather than repeat his predecessor's mistakes, Hooker intended to sweep around General Robert E. Lee's army and force it to do battle on ground of his own choosing. To achieve this, he needed to hold Lee's army near Fredericksburg long enough for him to bring the rest of the army into position. Hooker hoped to accomplish this by having the left wing of the army, under the command of Major General John Sedgwick, force a crossing below Fredericksburg.

This grand scheme was unknown to the men in the ranks. Indeed, for the men of the Iron Brigade, orders came on April 28 to simply leave their winter quarters near Belle Plain. The day did not begin on a note foretelling a Union victory. Instead, as the hospital steward in the Twenty-fourth Michigan, Private Elmer Wallace, wrote home:

> Early in the morning, before we moved, the rain began to fall, and the heavy murky clouds that covered the whole sky, indicated an unpleasant day, and plenty of mud.[2]

A mutiny among some of the "two years men" in the Twenty-fourth New York Infantry added to the sour atmosphere. Evidently the men felt that their term was too close to expiring to risk possible death or injury in the upcoming campaign. The insurrection was quickly put down by the Second and Sixth Wisconsin, supported with "a few pointed remarks from General Wadsworth." With this matter taken care of the brigade was formed and the men were ready to move at 11 A.M. Still it was not until noon, after standing in the rain for an hour, that the order to march was given.[3]

After a march of some seven or eight miles, the order to halt was issued at 8 P.M., and the men were told to make camp in the nearby woods. If there had been any doubt as to the purpose of their march, it was now clear to Wallace and the others. Looking about he noted that

> here was evidence sufficient—that we were again to cross the Rappahannock,—in the long train of pontoon boats that stood with horses hitched, ready for a start.

Immediately the men began to pitch tents or construct a shelter of pine boughs, as Wallace and some of his comrades did. When supper was done, the fires were doused "for fear of alarming the rebs, and all hands turned in, expecting a good nights sleep and an early start in the morning."[4]

Sleep was not to be that night though, for the sounds of moving men and equipment filled the air. For some of the men, the rumbling of the pontoons caused more than lack of sleep. Private Elon Brown of the Second Wisconsin had fallen asleep when

> I was awakened by a succession of noises that I at first took for distant artillery. I instantly started up to a listening posture and after listening a few minutes found it was a pontoon train passing over a corduroy road, the hollow distant sound being given by the boats.

Brown reflected with satisfaction that he was not the only one fooled by the sound of the boats passing. Still, the effect was the same as if it were real, for

> the blood is sent coursing through the veins with double its usual velocity. If there is anything that will excite a man it is to be awakened out of a sound sleep by the sound of firearms.[5]

The orders for the crossing of the brigade filtered poorly down to the men in the ranks, if at all. Colonel William W. Robinson of the Seventh Wisconsin remembered that sometime between 11 and 12 P.M., commanders of the various Iron Brigade regiments were gathered at headquarters and informed that that they would cross the river at 2 A.M. the next day.[6] Colonel Edward S. Bragg of the Sixth Wisconsin remembered the events that evening somewhat differently. Bragg later recalled that it was he alone who learned of the desperate nature of the next day's action, and later wrote that

> Genl. Reynolds sent for me at about midnight—the night before [the crossing]—I rode back over the crest to his Head Qrs—His tent was floored with poles to keep him out of the swamp—Col. Bankhead on his staff was an old school mate of mine before he went to West Point—He told me the General was engaged for the moment and entertained me, while I was waiting in the "ante tent" by asking me about my command & telling me the job the General had in store for me—I told him my command were western men and could do the work if any men could; Soon Reynolds received me & in a few words told me what he desired me to do "Cross—Carry the pits—Deploy to the right & cover the Barnard House, to prevent the lodgment of sharpshooters."[7]

Bragg went on to relate that he was told that the Twenty-fourth Michigan would cross and deploy to the Sixth's left, covering a ravine where enemy pickets had been seen. Thus only two regiments were ordered to cross the river defended by an enemy force of unknown size. According to Bragg, Reynolds's orders were not open to interpretation. "No question of possibilities was made—I was told to do it." Many of the men in the ranks had no idea what the morrow would bring, but as one soldier asserted, "Perhaps before another sun would rise half of our now joyous companions would be stricken, cold and lifeless on the bloody field."[8]

In the darkness of the night the order to march was given and the regiments quickly formed, but again they had to wait for the troops ahead of them to move. The brigade finally moved out sometime past midnight. The advance was slowed by the heavy wagons of the pontoon trains, which the men often had to assist to move forward. Dawes of the Sixth felt that there would be little hope of a surprise attack because "so much noise was made by the donkeys of the pontoon train." Regardless, the pontoons continued on through the dense fog toward the river, pulled, dragged, and pushed with the help of the men of the Iron Brigade.[9] One member of the Second Wisconsin recalled the night as being

> dark and cold.—The pontoons were rumbling over the corduroy road, and the troops on either side of us were ready to march. We marched slowly and in silence, now watching for the boats to pass, and then falling out literally to put our shoulders to the wheel. Thus we advanced, the stillness of the night being broken occasionally by the neighing of horses and the rattle of arms. . . .[10]

While the plan might have been to cross the Rappahannock in the early morning, the mud and fog combined to slow the movement to a crawl. Thus it was about daybreak when the Iron Brigade finally reached the river, having covered only about two miles. Some boats were already at the river, brought forward by the First Brigade who were ahead of the Iron Brigade. The Western men were ordered to drag the boats forward without the use of the mules some three-eighths of a mile in an attempt to preserve some element of surprise. This was done and some boats were placed in the water, but it soon became apparent that the possibility of surprise had disappeared.[11]

As the men of the Iron Brigade neared the Rappahannock, heavy fog hid the river from them. The nearness of the enemy was certain though, as shots were soon heard and bullets began to fall amongst the regiments. Elmer Wallace of the Twenty-fourth wrote that "the fog was so heavy that we could see but a short distance. Things were going on in this way, when a musket shot was fired, then another and an other. This announced the presence of the enemy." Wallace and the surgeons of the Twenty-fourth Michigan were at the rear of the regiment, and not aware of their dangerous proximity to the enemy until "bullets were whistling around very briskly, striking the ground in every direction. We made up our minds that our best hold was to lay down which we did without much ceremony."[12]

The position was not the best one for the Union troops. The site of the crossing was about one mile below where the First Corps had crossed only four months before in December 1862. The northern bank of the Rappahannock was lower than the southern side, so the enemy was looking down on the Federal troops. James P. "Mickey" Sullivan of the Sixth Wisconsin remembered that

> the bank of the river on this [the Union] side slopes gradually down to the water, and was entirely bare, if I remember right, a clover field, while the opposite [Confederate] bank rose very steep from the water's edge and was densely covered with a thriving growth of young timber down the side of the hill to the water.

On this higher, overgrown bank, the Confederates had dug their rifle pits.[13]

The enemy's fire was not so much directed at the Iron Brigade as it was at the engineers and other troops attempting to lay the pontoon bridge. The brigade containing the Twenty-second New York, Twenty-fourth New York, Thirtieth New York, and Fourteenth Brooklyn was assigned to accompany the pontoons to the river. There the Twenty-second New York and Twenty-fourth New York were ordered to assist in the unloading of the boats for the engineers. As the Confederates saw the Federals at work, they quickly opened up on them. Amongst the pontoons, horse teams, and men the bullets soon began to fly.[14]

Colonel Walter Phillips commanding the New York brigade commented that a volley "threw the teams into disorder. The stacks of arms of the Twenty-second were run over by them, and two men of the regiment severely injured." Private Henry Matrau of the Sixth Wisconsin wrote simply: "[T]he 22nd just got up & run & left the boat, wagons, & drivers to shift for themselves. The boat that was in the water drifted to the other side."[15]

Others were not so specific as to who participated in the scramble from the river, but many told of the event. Lieutenant Howard J. Huntington of the Sixth Wisconsin commented that the enemy's fire had wounded "some of the horses of the pontoon train, setting them to rearing, plunging, and running." Edward Brooks, the adjutant of the Sixth, was more to the point, commenting that the enemy's fire among the engineers caused

> them to skeddadle, and creating a perfect panic amongst the drivers of the pontoon train. Here was an officer with pistol in hand, threatening to shoot a runaway driver if he did not stop—and there was a team of six horses, one dead, hanging in the harness, while the others dragged him along at their utmost speed.[16]

Through all of this panic and commotion, the Iron Brigade stood fast, and all too soon the order came for the Sixth Wisconsin and the Twenty-fourth Michigan to drive the enemy from their pits. Lieutenant Colonel Dawes learned of these new orders when General James S. Wadsworth rode up and commanded: "Col. Bragg, move your Reg't to the bank and give them some volleys." With those words, the Sixth Wisconsin "double quicked up in face of their bullets, down on our faces, and lit into them in quicker time and better style than any other Reg't in the U.S.A. can."[17]

The position taken by the two regiments was not the best. The men were moved behind a stone wall in the hope that some small protection might be afforded by it. This wall was described in later years by a member of the Fiftieth New York Engineers as "about two feet high, with rails on top, intended for a fence, which was then in dilapidated condition, at right angles with the river." It was the fact that the wall was at an angle to the river that was the problem, since it gave little protection from the enemy. This, combined with the fact that the rebels were in their rifle pits at a higher elevation than the Federals, caused Dawes to note "we could gain nothing that way. . . . it was destruction to lay under their fire."[18]

Faced with the impossible task of driving the enemy from an entrenched position it was decided to retire the two regiments. "After the Twenty-fourth Michigan had fired a volley across the river, which was too random to take effect, both regiments were withdrawn a few rods" back to where the rest of the brigade was. It was fortunate that the regiments were pulled back for in that short space of time Private Joseph Coryell of Company F of the Twenty-fourth Michigan was killed, and Captain Tom Plummer and Private Charles Adams of Company C of the Sixth Wisconsin were wounded. Companies C and G of the Sixth were left behind as skirmishers, with the Fourteenth Brooklyn reinforcing them. The rest of the brigade were moved back to a depression out of rifle range of the Confederates.[19]

Now, as the skirmishers kept up a desultory fire, First Corps batteries were also put into place to try to shell the enemy out of their pits. After having been unable to drive the enemy away themselves, it was with some satisfaction that a member of the brigade wrote that "The fellows who were out in full view till now began to hunt their holes." The men in the brigade were now out of the line of fire, and the sounds of musketry and the booming of cannon gave them little concern. With an exhausting night behind them, and the unknown before them, Henry Matrau remembered that "most of us went to sleep."[20]

As the Federal batteries sent shot and shell into the rifle pits across the river, the Confederate cannons posted on the other side of the river responded in an attempt to silence their fire. Time began to pass and no change in the situation appeared imminent as an hour and then almost two hours passed. Generals Reynolds and Wadsworth with their staffs were on a height overlooking the action, "cogitating, discussing the situation and taking chances on occasional shells sent over." General Henry W. Benham, Chief of Engineers on Hooker's staff, then rode up to Reynolds with an order from Hooker stating that the First Corps should cross the river "at once at all hazards." Reynolds communicated the order to Wadsworth, who turned to his Inspector-General, Lieutenant Colonel John A. Kress and stated, "Colonel, you will go down to General Meredith's brigade and give the proper instructions for crossing the river at once at all hazards." As Kress spurred his horse toward the brigade he formulated how best to relay the orders. Finding Meredith he informed the general to move his command by the right flank to reach the open ground sloping to the river, then face the brigade toward the river with the first regiments entering the boats without firing and the rest of the brigade maintaining a constant fire to prevent the enemy from contesting the crossing.[21]

Down by the river, either in the water or on the bank, were some twenty boats. Ed Brooks of the Sixth described them as "clumsy, flat bottomed, square-bowed institutions, about 25 feet long, 4 feet wide and 3 feet deep." Calling together the regimental commanders, Meredith put forward the plan which had been discussed the night before. The regiments were to move down to the river, two abreast, by their order of march in column that day. Hence the first down would be the Sixth Wisconsin in line with the Twenty-fourth Michigan. The Second and Seventh Wisconsin would follow in the second line, with the Nineteenth Indiana at the rear. He then ordered Colonel Fairchild of the Second Wisconsin to have Companies B, D, and E carry more boats down to the riverbank. Having been given the orders as outlined by Kress, the regimental commanders returned to their regiments to prepare for the assault.[22]

Across the river, the Confederates continued to hold their positions, though with less confidence. The riverbank had been originally held that morning by the Thirteenth Georgia. Private Henry C. Walker of that regiment commented in a letter to a friend that "our regiment was on picket when the yankees crossed, we fought there about two or three hours until our cartridges gave out." With ammunition getting low, they requested to be relieved and so the Sixth Louisiana was sent to take over the Georgians' rifle pits.[23]

The position of the Confederates was in some ways as difficult as that of the Federals. While they had the protection of their rifle pits, if any man put

The Sixth Wisconsin Regiment Forcing Passage of the Rappahannock Near Fredericksburg—April 29, 1863. There is a handwritten note behind the one pasted on the front of the photograph that says:

> This was sketched by a newspaper correspondent who saw the troops crossing. It was painted, and this is a photo from painting. I was told the painting was in Brooklyn. You will note the boats on right, Co. I Six Wis. Lieut. E. M. Rogers commanding. The colors in fifth boat from left. Gen'l Wadsworth is on horse at right, with uplifted arm, pointing. The tide was going out & the mud delayed on the left. The colors are the Second Wis., Col. Fairchild with whom the General rode. E. M. Rogers

Courtesy of the Vernon County (Wisconsin) Historical Society.

his head above the top of the entrenchment, any number of rifles would "take a crack at him." Indeed, Henry Walker of the Thirteenth Georgia noted that "we never lost but one man while we was in the rifle pits but when we went to leave they swept our boys down like they was chaff." The slope behind the rifle pits leading to the main Confederate line was also open, and the Federal fire played upon the rebel troops advancing toward the river. Indeed, Elmer Wallace of the Twenty-fourth Michigan recalled that "One large party of perhaps a hundred started across the plain. They had not gone more than half way before a shell exploded right in their midst, scattering them in every direction." Regardless, the Sixth Louisiana moved into the Georgians' vacated positions and now found itself defending the river, while the Fifth Louisiana was moved to the left rear, near the plantation house known as "Smithfield."[24]

Among the troops of the Iron Brigade, the order to cross the river caused little joy. Lieutenant Colonel Dawes wrote home that when the order came "Such a feeling of horror came over us—to be shot like sheep in a huddle and drown in the Rappahannock was the certain fate of all if we failed, of many if we succeeded." Colonel Bragg, commanding the Sixth, candidly wrote his wife that he expected to lose half of his regiment in the attempt. Still there was nothing to do but carry out the order. Men crowded around the surgeons and others who would stay behind, asking them to hold letters and money should the worst occur. The men were ordered to strip off blankets or knapsacks; and in some cases even haversacks and canteens were discarded to speed their movements.[25]

Colonel Bragg had to position the Sixth Wisconsin in a line parallel with the river and then move toward the boats. While easily accomplished by one man, positioning and moving an entire regiment with some semblance of order was no easy task. He later wrote to Dawes:

> While I was slowly composing my plan—Genl Wadsworth sent another aide with his compliment—"You are slow, Sir." "My compliments in return, as soon as the right of my line reaches the line of that tree—(that was the outside limit for the pontoons up the river)—The movement will be executed." As we snailed along—so as not to arouse suspicion—our skirmish com[pany] dropped out and the men to go consolidated themselves—as the order & explanations were quietly given—when the proper point was reached came the order "by the right of companies &c."[26]

As the head of the Sixth Wisconsin reached the open plain, the enemy opened fire upon them. Though the Federal batteries did all they could to keep the Confederates' heads down, the bullets began to fly past the running men. Moving quickly over the skirmishers of the Fourteenth Brooklyn, the Wisconsin men ran toward the river. Mickey Sullivan of Company K saw Bragg at the head of the Sixth Wisconsin as it moved forward and

> noticed that our company [K], which was third in line, overtook Bragg, who being small and short-legged, and having an immense pair of military boots and spurs on, was not able to keep ahead, but he reached the river with us and went over in our boat. . . .[27]

As the Sixth Wisconsin and Twenty-fourth Michigan ran to the river, the three companies of the Second Wisconsin dragged and carried their boats to the river. The men in these three companies had not been expecting to carry the boats down; when the order came they quickly stacked arms and went over to the pontoons still loaded on their wagons. There they "seized the pontoon wagons by ropes attached and every other available hold. Having had no previous instructions, the boys worked some minutes before they could unload the boats. . . . " Once they got hold of them though, "away we went hallooing and yelling, the rest of the brigade following to cross in the boats as we got them ready." At the summit of the rise the men were "met by a volley from the rifle pits that lined the opposite bank; but the balls mostly passed over our heads, lodging in, and making splinters fly most beautifully from the pontoons we were hauling." With a yell the men of the Second continued on the descending slope toward the river.[28]

All was activity and confusion as the regiments arrived at the riverbank. In the Sixth Wisconsin some men had been detailed to row, while others were simply to find a place in a boat. There was no opportunity to be certain how many each boat would hold, and the difficulty of finding a place in the boats while under fire would have made those initial moments seem like an eternity. One member of the Sixth recounted that "we lay about three deep [in the boat] and pushed off." Dawes lamented that although the men threw themselves into the boats as instructed, "Here was our only mistake; the men were on the oars," which were lying at the bottom of the pontoons. Still the men quickly took their positions and pushed off.[29]

Generals Reynolds and Wadsworth and their staffs rode among the men of the Iron Brigade as they moved to the boats or formed into line to fire on the enemy. Lieutenant Colonel John A. Kress recounted that as bullets rained down around them, the "most unconcerned of the whole party appeared to be the two generals, who energetically smoked their cigars and maintained a calm exterior, [while] everyone around them pale or red, knit their brows or closed their lips with unusual firmness."[30]

The first pontoons in the water were from the Sixth Wisconsin and Twenty-fourth Michigan. Dawes was in one of the lead boats and the colors of the regiment were with him. He listened as the excited voices around him shouted to "Shove her off," and he heard their pride in what they were doing in yells of "The first man up the bank shall be a general" and "Show the Army why the old Sixth was chosen to lead them." Bullets slammed into the boats, sending splinters flying, and Dawes was anxious as "It was no time to quail or flinch, one halt or waver was destruction." With this in mind, Dawes "stood up in the bow of the boat I commanded, swinging my sword in one hand, and cheering the oarsmen, holding my pistol in the other to shoot them if they wavered or flinched."[31]

While the lead boats started across the river, the chaos on the shore grew worse. The Second and Seventh Wisconsin, the Nineteenth Indiana, as well as the men of the first two regiments who had not yet embarked into the boats, began to intermingle. In fact, the colonel of the Twenty-fourth Michigan crossed in a boat manned by Company A of the Sixth Wisconsin. Captain Craig Wadsworth, the impetuous son and aide of General Wadsworth, also found a spot in one of the Sixth's boats.[32]

While orders to the other three regiments had directed them to keep the enemy pinned down with fire, not all the men in those units seemed content to do that. Many were finding spots in boats that were being filled near them. Captain Henry B. Converse and First Lieutenant Alured Larke of Company A, Second Wisconsin, along with fourteen men, scrambled into one of the pontoons which had been carried down by the Second and pushed off into the river.[33]

For Colonel William W. Robinson of the Seventh Wisconsin the situation was equally fluid. Arriving at the bank, he found "the Sixth and Twenty-fourth rapidly launching boats and crossing, but most of the men of those regiments still on this bank." With the Second coming into line on his right and the enemy firing at his men, Robinson quickly commanded his regiment to form line of battle with the companies opening fire as they did so. As his orders seemed to indicate he was to wait for the boats to return from carrying the first regiments across before the Seventh embarked, Colonel Robinson was somewhat surprised when a member of Wadsworth's staff galloped up and bypassing him began to order his regiment to "Cease firing" and to "Launch the boats." Going to the right of the Seventh, Colonel Robinson learned that the staff officer had stated "the general wished the men rushed over without regard to precedence of regiments or companies." With that Robinson began to order the men to enter the boats.[34]

The lead boats of the Sixth Wisconsin were now drawing near the opposite shore. Suddenly the majority of the enemy's fire did not seem to be directed at them. As the Sixth drew within ten yards or so of the shore, the Confederates would have had to lean out of their rifle pits to fire down on them. This would expose them to the fire of the Federals and it was far safer to stay down and fire across the river or to simply lie low.[35]

The passage across the river had not been without its hazards. Mickey Sullivan noted that Private Hoel Trumbull had helped push their boat off, and while he was getting into the pontoon a bullet hit him in the head and he sank beneath the water. Sullivan watched in vain for him to come back up. Another man in the Sixth had happened upon a boat almost full and stuck in the mud. Calling for assistance, he and two comrades helped push it off the bank. One of his friends lay on the bottom of the boat, but thinking better of it, the first soldier stood in the rear of the boat. The last soldier clung to the back of the boat, waist deep in water and "it seems his is the safest position of all." That thought was dispelled when "a bullet passes through my feet and crashes through his brain. He sinks beneath the water; his hat floating down with the current."[36]

Not all the danger was from the enemy's guns. As the boats crossed, the Federal cannon posted on the heights behind them redoubled their efforts to suppress the Confederate riflemen. As they set their fuses to explode over the rifle pits, some of the shells burst prematurely and struck the boats carrying the men of the Iron Brigade. Reverend Samuel Eaton, Chaplain of the Seventh Wisconsin, related in a letter home that "Five of our Regiment, one of them the Col. were struck with shells from our own guns not properly posted, but none of them are injured. A piece struck the bottom of the boat in one case, with force sufficient to have carried it through the body."[37]

Covering fire during the crossing was coming not only from the far shore but also from the boats themselves. One member of the Sixth Wisconsin recounted how, as he watched the enemy's shore rapidly approaching, he noticed

> that now and again a rebel lifts up his head, takes a hasty look around, springs out of the works, and disappears over the brow of the hill to the rear. I bring my piece to a ready. Pretty soon I see another Johnny prepare to make his escape. He is unfortunate. We are drawing near. Just as he springs out of the pit I aim just between the shoulders as he turns his back. It is the only shot I fire in the engagement. He throws down his rifle and lies down.[38]

Only minutes after launching, the first boats of the Sixth Wisconsin arrived on the enemy shore. The point of landing for the lead boats was just downriver from the rifle pits, thus giving the men in the boats time to reform slightly before meeting the enemy. As Dawes related, "Across the river, we tumbled into the mud or water, waist deep, wade ashore, crawled and scrambled up the bank. Nobody could say who was first." Although their position masked them from the enemy's fire, the men of the Sixth Wisconsin and Twenty-fourth Michigan were not free from the danger. Reverend Eaton also commented that "there were instances in which our men after they reached the other side were shot by our own men on this side aiming to hit the rebels who were almost among them." Indeed, Dawes noted in his journal that as the men scrambled up the slope "[Gabriel] Ruby [of Company I was] killed by our own men. Volley in our backs by Seventh [Wisconsin]."[39]

This did not, however, deter the men. As Colonel Bragg wrote home:

> The Twenty-fourth Michigan were ordered across at the same time & did their duty nobly, but the Sixth were in for a fight, and they led the run, and flung out their flag, first on the enemies [*sic*] shore, and then, such cheering & shouting that you never heard—Everybody was crazy—we had been

> ordered to do it—had done it in the face of the enemy & gallantly—that old soldiers even "behaved foolishly in the exhibitions of joy."

Indeed, as one participant described in another letter home, the crossing took only a few moments, and then the men were "charging up the steep bank like so many devils."[40]

On the Federal side the confusion continued, with some men trying to fire to cover those crossing while others sought to find places in the boats. The Seventh Wisconsin was on the left flank of the brigade and was still largely on the northern bank. Its crossing was disrupted when a volley came from a concealed group of the enemy downstream. The volley hit Company K the hardest, and Captain Alexander Gordon, who commanded the company, called out, "Boys I am struck." Grabbing his belt and unfastening his accouterments, Gordon sat down quickly. As men gathered around him, a private said that the wound appeared to be in his arm, but Gordon responded that he could feel it in his chest. When he was borne to the rear, it was determined that the wound was indeed more serious. The bullet had entered his arm and passed into his body. Gordon would die shortly thereafter. Lieutenant William O. Topping of Company C fell in the same volley. They would be the only officers killed in the crossing.[41]

The Second Wisconsin was filling the remaining boats when Wadsworth dismounted and stepped into the nearest pontoon. Though his horse was hesitant to follow, Wadsworth held him firmly by the reins. Wadsworth called out to a lieutenant of the Fiftieth New York Engineers for help. The lieutenant directed some of his men to shove the horse in, which they did. The boat was then pushed off with the general in the stern, his horse swimming behind, and bullets still filling the air. It was said at that time that "General Wadsworth will never see the end of this war—he is too brave a man." Indeed, the words were true, he would not.[42]

On the far bank the men of the Sixth Wisconsin began to flush the enemy from their cover. Dawes noted that when they reached the top of the slope the men gathered "in a bunch just under the top of the bank. We rose up and rushed the rifle pits." The enemy was taken by surprise and began to run or surrender. For those who tried to run, the result was sometimes fatal. One member of the Sixth related that

> A comrade calls my attention to something that has the appearance of a man a dozen rods or so in front of us lying in a slight depression. We run out there and as we come within a few paces up springs a Johnny and starts to run to the rear. The comrade orders him to surrender. He continues to run. My musket is not loaded but he is shot down in his tracks.[43]

The men of Company A of the Second Wisconsin also reached the opposite shore, but unlike the Sixth they landed in front of the rifle pits rather than below them. Still, the men jumped out and scrambled up the bank.

With the Sixth coming from their flank, the Confederates were in no mood to contest the men from the Second. Soon the men of the Second, along with men from the Sixth, were seen scrambling from rifle pit to rifle pit, urging the enemy to surrender, or running after fugitives trying to reach the main Confederate line.[44]

Standing on the far bank, Colonel Charles S. Wainwright, commanding the First Corps artillery, watched as the Iron Brigade scooped up prisoners. Noting that "Nothing but legs could save the rebs on the bank," Wainwright watched as two Federal soldiers "push up the bank alone and took the men out of the smaller pits; they would only take their muskets away from them, tell them to run to the rear, and then throwing down the captured muskets, rush on to the next pit." Wainwright observed that these two men went as far as Smithfield in this manner.[45]

Bragg and Dawes worked hard to reform their men, as did officers of the other regiments, when they reached the far bank. It was now imperative to push on to keep the enemy from recovering and realizing what a small force they confronted. Dawes moved forward with the Sixth Wisconsin toward the "brick house," or "Smithfield." In doing so the Badgers continued to push the now dispersed men of the Sixth Louisiana back toward their main line, while also forcing the Fifth Louisiana to pull back. Reaching the building, which was as far as their orders allowed them to go, Dawes entered the house and went to the roof with the colors of the regiment. There he unfurled the flag and waved it to show the Federals on the opposite shore that success was theirs. As he did so, "such a shout of triumph as went up from ten thousand anxious spectators on the north bank of the river—it was good to hear."[46]

The Twenty-fourth Michigan had also completed crossing the river to secure the left flank. There they moved to a ravine where an enemy picket post had been. In the meantime, Wadsworth had gained the bank and rode to both the Sixth and Twenty-fourth. Reaching the Sixth he found Colonel Bragg, shook his hand, and said, "Colonel Bragg, I thank you and your gallant regiment for their noble conduct today." Riding to the Twenty-fourth, he simply took off his cap, pierced by two bullets, and said, "God bless the Twenty-fourth Michigan. God bless you all." There would later be some bad feelings in the other regiments because of Wadsworth's commending only these two regiments.[47]

With the enemy in flight, the Twenty-fourth Michigan moved to place its left flank on the river with the regiment perpendicular to it. The Nineteenth Indiana was formed to its right facing the enemy. The Seventh and Second Wisconsin continued the line, with the Sixth completing it by placing its right upon the river. This created a three-sided box with the fourth side being the river itself. With skirmishers out, the brigade made ready to defend what they had gained until reinforcements could cross on the bridge that was again being worked upon.[48]

Then it was time to take stock of the cost of the effort, and what was gained. The river had been successfully forced, and the losses among the regiments of the Iron Brigade were far less than had been anticipated. In the Sixth Wisconsin only three men were killed outright, one mortally wounded, and one officer and eleven men wounded. The Twenty-fourth Michigan had two men killed and one officer and seventeen men wounded. The Nineteenth Indiana had one man killed and three wounded. The Second Wisconsin had only two men wounded, while the Seventh Wisconsin had two officers and one enlisted man killed, and one officer and three enlisted men wounded. The total losses of the brigade were thus ten killed and thirty-nine wounded. As soon as the landing was secure the regimental surgeons crossed over to tend to the wounded.[49]

For the Confederates, due to incomplete, conflicting, or nonexistent reports, the losses were not as easy to tally. The Thirteenth Georgia, who had initially held the rifle pits, reported a loss of three men killed, one mortally wounded, and eleven wounded. The majority of these men were lost when the regiment attempted to leave its position. Captain William Seymour, then serving on the staff of General Harry Hays, who commanded the Louisiana troops, reported a loss of eighty-nine men from the Sixth Louisiana. In their muster rolls the companies of the Sixth told the grim story of the flanking of their regiment. The regiment reported eight killed, fifty-five wounded, and twenty-one missing. Some of the companies also noted their losses that day. Company A reported that "before the company was aware of [the Federal] landing, they were surrounded. Only three of the company escaped by running the gauntlet of a heavy fire from a full brigade. One was killed in the attempt to escape." Company C reported seven men taken prisoner in the retreat, while Company D reported a loss of two killed and five missing. Company F reported its captain and one man slightly wounded who managed to escape capture, but one corporal and fourteen other men who did not. Company G listed its captain as wounded during the relief of the Georgians, with two other men wounded during the retreat, and oddly stated four men captured on the 30th. Company K reported that the company "narrowly escaped capture after losing three men wounded and two taken prisoner." No losses can be found for the Fifth Louisiana.[50]

In the Federal sources, the estimates of the enemy's loss varied greatly. General Meredith's report stated that 30 of the enemy were killed, many wounded, and 200 captured. A letter to a Wisconsin paper reported that 40 of the enemy had been killed and 207 captured. More in line with probable facts, the monthly report of the Second Wisconsin stated that "30 Rebels were left dead on the ground and 135 taken prisoner." Orson B. Curtis, historian of the Twenty-fourth Michigan, wrote in later years that they killed "several, capturing 103 prisoners, including a lieutenant colonel and two other officers, as well as all of the cannon." Dawes would write in the same postwar time period that records showed 90 prisoners taken. Obviously time had little to do with the fluctuation in numbers or facts.[51]

One of those taken prisoner was of greater interest than the others. Elmer Wallace of the Twenty-fourth Michigan wrote home that among those captured was a "Jerry O'Donnel, son of the O'Donnel that keeps grocery on the corner of Woodward Ave. and Columbia St. He deserted from the 1st Mich. and will be shot of course." It was O'Donnel's fate to be captured by a regiment containing men from his own home town, Detroit.[52]

Later that morning the Confederates sent forward a flag of truce offering to suspend hostilities to allow for the burial of the dead. The men of the Iron Brigade replied that there was no need, as the job was already done. A truce between the pickets of each side was soon arranged, however, as the men of both armies could see little to be gained from such bloodshed. With the bridge finally completed, fresh troops moved across the river and the Iron Brigade was relieved and moved to a new position farther downstream. Ironically, the area to be occupied was where they fought in December of 1862. There, with the coming of night, the regiments formed to repel a counterattack and the men slept on their arms in a heavy rainstorm.[53]

The next day was spent waiting for the Confederates to attack. The regiments put up breastworks, using the available material at hand, and soon had themselves in a position "so that ten times our number could hardly drive us out." Indeed, one soldier commented that they "lay still in our rifle pits all day . . . hoping that the rebs might come and see us, this being the first time we had ever found ourselves behind anything of the kind." There was to be no attack, however, and the only show of hostilities was on the evening of April 30th when enemy batteries opened on the brigade. The losses were slight, but two sergeants in the Twenty-fourth Michigan were killed when a solid shot struck them and wounded two others.[54]

During the day of May 1st, heavy cannonading was heard upstream. It was the sound of the battle of Chancellorsville and the driving back of the Federal army. This fact was unknown to the men of the Iron Brigade, though the sound of cheering in the enemy's trenches that night hinted as to its nature. Then on May 2nd, the First Division of the First Corps was withdrawn back across the river. The Iron Brigade's pickets held their positions to the last and then moved quickly to avoid being left behind. The corps moved toward the rest of the Army, crossed the river, and took up position on the far right of the Union line. There would be no great battle there for the brigade though, as the remaining fighting would fall elsewhere.[55]

Then on the evening of May 6th, as part of the rear guard of the army, the Iron Brigade again crossed to the northern side of the river, and marched southeast toward their old camps at Falmouth. They had done what was asked of them and more, and the defeat the army suffered seemed in no way to be attached to them. The campaign was over, and although the Western men of the Iron Brigade did not know it at the time, Gettysburg was less than two months away.[56]

7

John F. Reynolds and the Iron Brigade

LANCE J. HERDEGEN

The bullet that killed Major General John F. Reynolds at Gettysburg made him an American hero and forever linked his name to the Iron Brigade. The Federal officer was shot in the opening of the infantry fighting on the morning of July 1, 1863, while urging the famous "Black Hats" forward in a desperate charge to keep Confederates from seizing McPherson's Ridge northwest of the town. Word of his death was passed from soldier to soldier even as his body was carried from the field. It was a story that was told around the coffee fires of the army camps, and, finally, in the war histories and old soldier newspapers. In the end, no one, it seemed, knew the truth of it beyond the broad outlines. There was a "great difference between battles in fact and battles in print," one veteran said of his war days, and that was certainly true of the death of John Reynolds.[1]

The event became a Gettysburg parable showcased by heroic statues and wax museum tableaus; a mingling of fable and fact made important by Reynolds's key role in the great battle and the growing awareness of American military tradition. From the very first it was an event that touched the souls of Americans on both sides. It was the kind of death that they wanted for their military heroes—the brave soldier who fell while leading his men in an epic battle. Confederates expressed sorrow over the death of such a gallant officer and puzzled over who fired the shot that killed him. New Yorkers and Pennsylvanians argued over who carried the general's body from the field. Iron Brigade men from Wisconsin, Indiana, and Michigan pointed to where Reynolds fell and told how the news reached them.

Typical in the Federal officer corps was the reaction of Reynolds's friend, George B. McClellan, who called him "remarkably brave and intelligent, an honest true gentleman." Lieutenant Frank Haskell of the Sixth Wisconsin wrote home that the fallen officer "was one of the *soldier* Generals of the army, a man whose soul was in his country's work, which he did with a

John F. Reynolds. Courtesy of the Wisconsin Veterans Museum.

soldier's high honor and fidelity." He mourned the fallen hero with a recollection of Fredericksburg: "Mounted upon a superb black horse, with his head thrown back and his great black eyes flashing fire, he was every where upon the field, seeing all things and giving commands in person." Within months of the battle, the officers of Reynolds's First Corps, seeking to be associated with the moment, began procuring "funds for raising a monument over the grave of the late Maj. Genl. Jno. F. Reynolds."[2]

The importance of the Union victory placed Reynolds in the pantheon of American heroes. An admiring Iron Brigade veteran, writing long afterward, remembered the general on the morning of Gettysburg as "careworn, and we thought very sad," but with the "high purpose of his patriotic soul . . . stamped upon every lineament." The soldiers "loved him as a child a parent," another wrote, and a more modern correspondent (obviously no equestrian) described a Reynolds "so much at ease in the saddle as to be able to pick a dime from the ground while riding at full speed." The historian of the First Corps wrote in heavy black ink that the general "took in the strong and weak points of a battlefield with the keen perception of Charlemagne . . . ," and another veteran elevated him to a figure in a morality play: "Peerless John F. Reynolds" struck down by a Confederate sharpshooter who saw "the double stars on Reynolds' shoulders and sends a leaden messenger that lifts the spirit of that faultless and dauntless soldier to the God who gave it."[3]

Even the Reynolds family added a somehow satisfying and romantic, if sorrowful, postscript. While preparing the general's body for mourning, they had discovered a ring with the inscription "Dear Kate," a name he had never mentioned. Then, as his body lay in the parlor of his sister's home in Philadelphia, a somber young woman came to the front door. She was Catherine Mary "Kate" Hewitt, she said, and told how she and the general had met in California in 1860 and planned to marry after the war. She had followed him when he was transferred to West Point and had attended the Academy of the Sacred Heart in Torresdale, Pennsylvania. The couple had agreed, she told the family, that if anything happened to him during the war, she would forsake the world and enter a convent. "Kate" soon entered the Sisters of Charity Catholic Convent in Emmitsburg, Maryland. She remained in touch with the Reynolds family until 1868, then was never heard from again.[4]

The man who became "Reynolds of Gettysburg" was born in Lancaster, Pennsylvania, September 21, 1820, a hard day's ride from the wooded ridge where he would be killed forty-two years later. His father was John Reynolds Sr., who published a Democratic newspaper, *The Lancaster Journal.* A friend of the family and business associate was soon-to-be-president James Buchanan, who, as a U.S. senator, appointed Reynolds to the U.S. Military Academy at West Point. The young man graduated in 1841 and saw service in Florida, on the frontier, and in the Mexican War, in which he was twice cited for bravery. At the time of the firing on Fort Sumter in 1861, he was serving as commandant of cadet corps at West Point. With the outbreak of the war, he sought a position in the regular army before being offered (due to the efforts of George B. McClellan) the First Brigade of the Pennsylvania Reserve Division from his home state.[5]

Already prominent in the old army, Reynolds's star rose quickly in the first months of the war. When his division was held back as a reserve during McClellan's grand advance, he served for a time as military governor at Fredericksburg, Virginia, before his brigade rejoined the Army of the Potomac outside Richmond, Virginia. In the Seven Days fighting, Reynolds won favorable mention in the early dispatches, then was ignominiously captured when his wounded horse became entangled in a swamp as he returned in the dark from posting artillery. He spent six weeks in captivity, most of it at the Libby Prison in Richmond, before being paroled. He returned to his brigade and was given command of the Pennsylvania Reserve Division when the unit's commander, General George McCall, returned home because of ill health.

During the fighting at Second Bull Run in late August 1862, his division was credited by some with preventing the Confederate army from "crushing our forces" during the subsequent retreat. When Lee moved his Army of Northern Virginia into Maryland in September 1862, Pennsylvania Governor Andrew Curtin, seeking "an active energetic officer" to take command of the thousands of Pennsylvania militiamen being gathered at Harrisburg to repel the invasion, asked for Reynolds by name. It was a job that would win no glory, but the general arrived as ordered at Harrisburg, Pennsylvania, on September 13 and set up headquarters.

But the militia was not needed. The Confederate army retreated to Virginia following the bloody fighting along Antietam Creek on September 17 and two weeks later Reynolds was back with the Army of the Potomac. He was given temporary command of the First Corps, replacing General George Meade, a fellow Pennsylvanian who had led the corps since the wounding of Joseph Hooker at Antietam. It was a difficult situation for both officers, perhaps more so for Meade. Despite a grudging friendship and mutual respect, Meade found it hard to take orders from an officer five years his junior. If he had not dropped out of the service between 1836 and 1842, he would have outranked Reynolds.[6]

The commander of the Army of the Potomac, George McClellan, in November 1862 was replaced by Ambrose Burnside, who told anyone who would listen that he was unsuited for the command and proved it a month later in the Federal defeat at Fredericksburg, Virginia. It was Meade, not Reynolds, who won favorable attention during the Fredericksburg fighting when his division briefly opened a gap in the Confederate line while Reynolds did little more than move reinforcements to the front. In the Federal defeat at Chancellorsville in May 1863, Reynolds was kept from a significant role, perhaps because he and the new army commander, General Joseph Hooker, had a falling out. A chance at advancement came the next month when, while visiting Washington, Reynolds was finally offered command of the Army of the Potomac. But he refused it when President Abraham Lincoln was unable to assure him a free hand. A young New Yorker, who saw him about that time, left a description of Reynolds as "tall, dark, slender" with "a wild look, a rolling eye. Very nervous to all appearance."[7]

June 1863 was a time of great excitement. The Confederate brigades were on the move after stunning victories at Fredericksburg and Chancellorsville. The long gray columns swung to the west and then northward toward Pennsylvania as the Army of the Potomac followed, trying to keep itself between Washington and the rebels. Philadelphia, Baltimore, and other cities were in a panic. From every quarter there were alarmed cries for the army to act and, as the Federal columns neared Pennsylvania, Lincoln surprisingly removed Hooker and ordered George Gordon Meade, then in command of the Fifth Corps, to take his place. In the turmoil and camp talk following the announcement, Reynolds put on his best uniform and went to offer Meade his congratulations. But to Colonel Charles Wainwright, who commanded the artillery of the First Corps, Reynolds confided that he had been offered command of the army a month earlier and had refused it because he was "unwilling to take Burnside and Hooker's leavings." In his journal, Wainwright wrote: "For my part, I think we have got the best man [Meade] of the two, much as I think of Reynolds. He will do better at carrying out plans than at devising them, I think."[8]

In the ranks, of course, the unexpected change in command with a battle in the offing added to the confusion. In fact, however, Meade assumed command with a quiet competency that would be recognized only later. He understood from the very first that he must attack the invading Confederate army or force it to attack him; politically there could be no other acceptable actions. Meade assigned Reynolds, his rival and friend, to continue the assignment from Hooker of directing the First, Third, and Eleventh Corps at what seemed would be the point of contact near the Pennsylvania community of Gettysburg and its network of connecting roads. To Meade the military situation held promise and danger, and he issued two orders, one calling for a general advance toward Gettysburg and the other for a possible withdrawal to a predetermined defensive position on Pipe Creek. The second order became famous as the "Pipe Creek Circular" and was later used by Meade's critics as evidence of the general commanding's hesitancy in the face of the enemy.[9]

Reynolds rode toward Gettysburg with an opportunity to play a pivotal role. In the advance with him was the small First Division of the First Army Corps, two brigades under the command of General James Wadsworth, a crusty old New York State politician-turned-soldier who was much admired by the men in ranks. The most prominent of the two organizations was the "Iron Brigade of the West" (the men making much of the fact they were in the First Brigade of the First Division of the First Army Corps) which included the Second, Sixth, and Seventh Wisconsin, Nineteenth Indiana, and Twenty-fourth Michigan. The only all-Western outfit in the Army of the Potomac, these tough soldiers had earned a reputation as hard fighters and were recognizable because of their tall regular army felt hats. Other soldiers at first called them "the big hats" or "Black Hat Brigade," but it was McClellan at South Mountain in September 1862 who declared they "stood like iron," hence an "Iron Brigade."[10]

The brigade was first under the command of Rufus King of Milwaukee and later John Gibbon, a West Pointer who was promoted from Battery B of the Fourth U.S. Artillery. It was Gibbon who trained them unmercifully under the hot sun in the second summer of the war and made the Model 1858 black felt hat and nine-button blue wool frock coat the standard for his regiments. It was on those drill fields outside Fredericksburg that John Reynolds probably had his first contact with the Westerners and a few weeks later, on the eve of Second Bull Run, he watched the "Black Hats" in their first battle.

Assigned to John Pope's Army of Virginia, the Western soldiers had been frantically marched here and there in the search for the Confederate force under Thomas "Stonewall" Jackson which attacked and pillaged the Union depot at Manassas Junction. As Gibbon's brigade marched along the Warrenton Turnpike at dusk on August 28, 1862, it had been fired on by artillery and then attacked by a heavy force of infantry. Reynolds, hearing the firing behind his marching division, rode back in the fading light to find Gibbon's "Black Hat" Brigade sharply engaged.

The Westerners had found Jackson (or more correctly, Jackson found them) and the Federals now had a chance to whip him before the arrival of the rest of the Confederate army. But the division commander, General Rufus King, who was ill, and his brigade officers failed to support the embattled Gibbon; only two regiments had been sent. "Why don't you push all these troops up?" Reynolds had asked, referring to the three nearby brigades. There was no satisfactory answer. Urging King to maintain his position and promising that he would return in the morning with his division, Reynolds galloped off in the night only to get lost. He did not find his soldiers until morning and by then it was all too late. "I did not see General Reynolds . . . and knew nothing of his proposition to support us," Gibbon said later. "His offer fully demonstrated that this fine soldier appreciated the importance of our position."[11]

But as the commander of the First Corps, Reynolds was a distant figure to the men in ranks and his ties to the Iron Brigade before the morning of July 1, 1863, were indistinct. A tough disciplinarian in the old army manner, he was not the officer of the colorful uniform or profane remark about whom the soldiers talked or wrote home. The Western men left no colorful nicknames and only a few camp stories about that "dark, silent, alert man," as one Badger described him. What they did remember was his striking military appearance and steady professionalism even if, as one officer noted in his journal, the general had a way of getting caught up in the minor administrative details of running an army corps.[12] One veteran recalled that during those hard days of long marches the general would send an aide to the regiments with word whether there was time to boil coffee. "If we did not receive that order no man started a fire, and during the whole march there was never a fire lighted in vain." The soldiers of the Old First Corps, he concluded, "were very fortunate that our general had, not only common sense, but sufficient humanity in his heart to use it."[13] Another officer said Reynolds was a "superb-looking man, dark-complexioned, wearing full black whiskers" and "sat his horse like a Centaur, tall, straight and graceful, the ideal soldier." But a Michigan veteran admitted that "perhaps few knew him intimately, for he was a strangely reticent man. . . . [But] his opponents recognized his ability and his soldiers knew that he held in reserve a latent force of clear and coolheadedness that could always be relied upon. They trusted him implicitly."[14]

It had been much the same when John Gibbon, a professional soldier, took command of the citizen-volunteers of the Western brigade. His cold and overbearing old army manner had not gone down well with the independent boys and men of the frontier. It was not until they saw him weeping over the dead and wounded of their first battle that Gibbon became "Johnny, the War Horse" and "the boss soldier." Reynolds, always the professional, commanded the respect of his soldiers, but did not develop Gibbon's knack for handling volunteers. Iron Brigade veterans never forgot that Reynolds had been ready to abandon the Nineteenth Indiana at Fredericksburg. The Hoosiers were manning an advance picket line when the general withdrawal began and Reynolds, to avoid alerting the Rebels, was prepared to leave them behind. It was through the intervention of Colonel Lysander Cutler that a successful attempt was made to bring off the pickets.[15] It was only after the general's death at Gettysburg, when his reputation was growing and the soldiers realized what had been accomplished, that his name began to appear in the letters and diaries, and even then the reference was to "General Reynolds."[16]

The Iron Brigade was third in line of march on the morning of July 1, 1863, tramping along behind the New York and Pennsylvania regiments of Lysander Cutler's Second Brigade and Hall's Second Maine Artillery. Just ahead on the Emmitsburg Road was Gettysburg, and, off to the north and west, although the marching soldiers did not know it, was the Confederate army. The soldiers of the First Division had seen Reynolds when they broke camp at Marsh Creek, just north of the Pennsylvania-Maryland line, but he had ridden ahead to confer with General John Buford, who had been using his small cavalry force to slow Confederates from moving on the town from the northwest. There were also reports of more Johnnies, in force, north of Gettysburg, but they had not yet become a factor.

Buford, whose significant role in the unfolding drama would be overshadowed by subsequent events, had been fighting his horsemen dismounted and, despite their fast breech-loading carbines, the rebels rolled them back from one ridge and then another until Gettysburg was at their backs. Buford had seen the strong position and held it to the best of his resources, but now it came down to a hard decision for Reynolds—fight here or fall back. It was about 10 A.M. and Reynolds had Wadsworth's two brigades at hand, but his next closest division was an hour from the field. Advance elements of the Eleventh Corps could not arrive until noon or later, and the Third Corps was miles away at Emmitsburg, Maryland, not close enough to be of assistance. But it was a good position, as Buford had pointed out, where Reynolds could mount a defense in depth and use the town to advantage if forced to retreat.[17] High ground south of Gettysburg also appeared promising, and an engagement might force decisive action from Meade, who seemed hesitant in consolidating his scattered army. But critics whispered later that the most compelling reason of all to stand and fight was that Reynolds faced an invading army with his home and family only fifty miles away; here was his opportunity to strike a blow.

Caught up in the decision was also the simple frustration of an ambitious professional who had not been lucky in the first two years of the war. He had led his brigade with promise in the Seven Days fighting of early 1862 only to be captured. The role of his division won praise at Second Bull Run, but it was lost in the sour aftermath of wrangling over the defeat. Reynolds had missed South Mountain and Antietam on a political assignment in Pennsylvania that did not advance his career or reputation. At Fredericksburg, even though he commanded the First Corps, it had been his friend and rival, George Meade, whose division won fame. At Chancellorsville, Hooker had given him an assignment that would win no headlines. Finally, Lincoln had offered him command of the nation's first army, but it came at a time when the president and the administration were unable to give the assurances the general felt he needed. Now, here on the rolling ridges outside Gettysburg, Reynolds was being handed a chance to play a significant role.[18]

Reynolds issued a flurry of orders. Buford and his troopers should hang on as long as possible, he said, and Wadsworth's division should come up on the run. Gallopers were sent to the other divisions of the First Corps as well as the Eleventh and Third Corps. To all the command was the same—come quick! Another aide was dispatched to Meade at army headquarters: "Tell him the enemy are advancing in strong force and that I fear they will get to the heights beyond the town before I can. I will fight them inch by inch and if driven back into town, I will barricade the streets and hold them back as long as possible."[19]

Then, Reynolds looked to what could be done. Wadsworth's division would be the first Union infantry to engage, and it was all chance that two of his best fighting brigades were in the lead (one of the speculations involving Gettysburg is what would have happened had two other brigades been in the advance). The First Division of the First Corps had led the march the previous day and ordinarily would have brought up the rear in the regular marching order on this day. It was Reynolds who ordered the division to again take the lead on the road toward Gettysburg.[20] But the head of the column was still out of sight and the general rode back to the town (getting lost briefly on a back street) before finding the Emmitsburg Road. At the Codori Farm, south of Gettysburg, he directed that the fences be knocked down so Wadsworth's men could march cross lots to the sound of Buford's fighting.

As the head of the infantry column moved northwest of the town, Reynolds followed Cutler's brigade over a low ridge marked by a Lutheran seminary, to a second parallel ridge northwest of it. Just behind the rise, he placed three of Cutler's regiments north of a road known as the Chambersburg Pike and the other two south of it. The left of the brigade's line rested against Herbst's Woodlot on McPherson's Ridge. After positioning Hall's Maine Battery by the roadway, Reynolds told Wadsworth to take charge north of the pike and that he would look out for the left. Reynolds remarked to a staff officer that he would hold the Chambersburg Pike and that General Abner Doubleday, who was commanding the First Corps and had regiments just reaching the field, should hold the Fairfield Road to the south because it posed a threat to Wadsworth's left flank.

It was about that time Reynolds saw Confederate infantry—later determined to be Brigadier General James J. Archer's brigade—moving in a thick line of battle toward Herbst's Woodlot. If the line gained the crest of McPherson's Ridge and seized the woodlot, Reynolds saw, the whole Federal position was in danger. Looking back, he could see, marching en echelon, the small regiments of the Iron Brigade steadily crossing the swale at the double-quick; it was going to be very close.

The leading regiment was the Second Wisconsin, oldest of the Iron Brigade regiments in time of service. It had been the first of the three-year volunteer regiments to reach Washington and had fought at First Bull Run. The unit's commander, Lucius Fairchild, looked ahead and saw "a light battery and a body of dismounted cavalry" engaging the enemy. "My regiment . . . became hotly engaged the moment they passed the battery," he wrote. "We pushed forward slowly, loading and firing as we went, down a slight incline, which was thickly studded with trees of a large growth, toward the enemy who seemed to be posted at the foot of the incline behind a small stream. My officers and men fell, killed or wounded, with terrible rapidity—from the instant they arrived at and passed the highest point of the ridge. We had gone but a short distance after becoming engaged when I was struck by a rifle ball which struck my left arm and made amputation necessary."[21] Not mentioned in Fairchild's account was how the mounted Reynolds had come up to urge the soldiers forward. It was just as the two lines crashed together that the general toppled from his saddle, shot in the head.

The exact location would later be questioned, but Reynolds most likely fell behind the Second Wisconsin at the east edge of Herbst's Woodlot. The bullet that killed him "entered the back of the neck, just below the coat collar, and passed downward in its course," leading his aides to believe he was looking backward when struck.[22] Unspoken was the grim thought that the fatal shot could have been fired by a Federal soldier behind him. But from the very first there was speculation the bullet that killed Reynolds was fired by a Confederate sharpshooter from a tree in the woods and that it was, somehow, an unfair and cowardly act.

Several accounts of how the general was shot, some more likely than others, were advanced. Cornelius Wheeler, a sergeant with the Second Wisconsin, said the general was "struck by a stray ball immediately after the volley" his regiment received as it "charged over the top of the ridge where Archer's Brigade was lying." He was on the right, Wheeler said, and "as the line came to a temporary halt when it reached the top of the ridge," he turned "to look for those of his company who had fallen, and glancing down the slope to the rear saw General Reynolds fall from his horse. . . ." Corporal William B. Murphy of the Second Mississippi later claimed the bullet that killed the general just might have been fired by his regiment. The line of the Second Mississippi, Murphy said, was north of the Chambersburg Pike and had driven back Cutler's brigade when "Genl. Reynold [*sic*] and staff rode up in about 100 yards to our right just over the hill in some timber to our right and our Reg. 2nd Miss, gave him one volley with our rifles and I was told that Genl Reynold was killed and nearly all of his staff were killed or wounded."[23] Other claims were advanced, but the most likely explanation was that the bullet that hit Reynolds was fired by an advancing Confederate in Herbst's Woodlot.[24]

But if the general selected the place where the infantry battle of Gettysburg opened, it was the hard veterans of the Iron Brigade who made the successful fight the general envisioned. With Reynolds down, the men of the Second Wisconsin drove through the thin woods after the broken Confederate line, finally crossing Willoughby Run at the west edge before pulling up. The other Iron Brigade regiments hammered Archer's men with a series of blows. Hundreds of the Johnnies, including Archer, surrendered or fled, and Wisconsin men boasted later that the rebels had called out "Hell! Those are the big hat devils of the Army of the Potomac! They told us we were to meet only Pennsylvania militia."[25] To the north, where Cutler's brigade was broken and was on the run, it was the last of the Iron Brigade regiments—the Sixth Wisconsin, held as a reserve with the 100 men of the Brigade Guard—that came up to drive Confederates from a railroad cut and preserve the Federal line.[26]

These successful attacks would be the key to the Union victory. Major General Oliver O. Howard of the Eleventh Corps said later that the "very energy" of the assaults had "deceived the Rebel general and made him cautious." It would be more than three hours before the Confederates came again in deep lines to drive the Union defenders back into and through Gettysburg. By then it was all too late; arriving Federal brigades were already filing onto the high ground south of the town that would give them the decisive position over the next two days.

With Reynolds dead, command fell to Major General Abner Doubleday, who decided to hold the position. Doubleday established a new line through Herbst's Woodlot, from north to south. Robinson's division of the First Corps reached the field about that time and was held in reserve on Seminary Ridge. Rowley's division (formerly Doubleday's) also arrived and about 11 A.M. Howard, riding in advance of his columns, reached Gettysburg and assumed overall command of the First and Eleventh Corps.[27]

The heavy Confederate attacks of mid-afternoon came from the northwest and north. Elements of the Eleventh Corps, fed piecemeal into the fighting north of Gettysburg, were soon in disorder or retreating, fleeing soldiers streaming to the town. The Confederates broke through at the juncture of the left of the Eleventh Corps and the adjoining right of the First Corps. The exposed right flank of the First Corps soon fell back, and, by 4:30 P.M., the whole Union line had been driven toward the town. Only a few units kept their formations—the Iron Brigade regiments among them—in the retreat through the streets of the town to a new defensive position being put together on Cemetery Hill just south of Gettysburg.

Reynolds's steady leadership was missed. Artillery Colonel Charles Wainwright wrote in his journal: "Not that I think we would not have had to fall back here had he not been killed, for the enemy outnumbered us three to one; but it would have been done in better order, with half the loss to ourselves and much more to the enemy." A Second Wisconsin man called the fatal wounding of Reynolds a "sad blow to the army" and said that "while it is not possible to see how his inspiring gallantry could have overcome the numerical majority of the enemy on this first day of the great battle, there is little doubt that his skill and courage would have added materially to our strength and that his fiery impatience would have hastened the arrival of reinforcements."[28] William Dudley of the Iron Brigade's Nineteenth Indiana said it was Reynolds's "keen prescience" that prevented the Confederates from seizing Gettysburg. By "this brilliant achievement," he said, the rebels were kept a "respectful distance" until afternoon when "the stubborn resistance to the advance of the Rebel army" allowed Federal forces to occupy the key high ground south of Gettysburg.[29]

Others suggested that Reynolds assumed more authority than Meade had given him. Even a member of the general's own staff admitted later that it has "often been hinted, rather than asserted that Reynolds was the victim of his own rashness, that he heedlessly and impetuously engaged the enemy in an overwhelming force, and was not ready to open battle nor right in doing so." But the whispers were ignored in the eulogies for the slain officer. Generals killed leading their troops, even rash generals, escape the double-sided political questions of Congressional committeemen, the sharp pens of newspaper editors, and the sniping of jealous fellow officers. From the instant of his fatal wounding, Reynolds's service at Gettysburg was lionized; a modern writer would refer to his death as "the single most tragic event of the first day's battle."[30]

One Federal officer, Colonel Thomas L. Livermore, in a postwar speech, claimed that Reynolds should have retired to a secondary position closer to the approaching Army of the Potomac. Such action would have been "in compliance with his instructions, drawing back Buford after him, without the risk of disaster." There was "no merit" in the position Reynolds selected, the colonel said, as it was "vulnerable to approach on the roads from the northeast by the enemy of whose presence in that direction he had been informed, and in it he was beyond possible support by any adequate force." But Livermore admitted that Reynolds would probably have felt the abandonment of Gettysburg was unthinkable: "His disregard of Meade's orders must be laid to the ardor of a very martial soldier, and the revolt of a patriot against the delivery of an important town of his native State to the enemy."

Samuel P. Bates, who wrote of Gettysburg a decade after the battle, suggested that Reynolds, commanding nearly half of the Union force, should have taken a less direct role because the army's "preservation and safety demanded that he should exercise care of his person." But the general knew that "collision could not long be avoided," Bates wrote. "The choice of the field and the initiative of the battle was in his eyes all important, and he determined to push to the front and decide everything from personal observation, and who will say that he did not do right?"[31]

The right and wrong of Reynolds's action, in the final result, was not as important as the perception of it as one of the shining moments of Gettysburg. The veterans of the Iron Brigade, at the time or later, never doubted for an instant the worth of their efforts on July 1, 1863, even if the cost had been frightful. In the Second Wisconsin Infantry the toll was three of four; the Sixth Wisconsin and Seventh Wisconsin, one of every two; the Nineteenth Indiana almost three of four. The largest and newest regiment—the Twenty-fourth Michigan—lost 399 of 496 men, the highest of any Federal regiment in the three days of Gettysburg.[32] Indeed, the celebrated "Iron Brigade of the West" had been shot to pieces. Within a few hours, only 671 of 1,883 men taken into the battle were still in ranks.[33]

But to the survivors, and the other veterans of both sides, and, finally, even the country, Gettysburg became the grand epic of the American Civil War and "the gallant Reynolds" the symbolic fallen knight of the Union—a brave and true American soldier struck down just as his promise was being realized. In death, he became "John Reynolds of Gettysburg," a heroic figure on a big, black horse forever shouting to the soldiers of the Iron Brigade as they ran toward the crest of a wooded ridge, "Forward Men! Forward for God's sake, and drive those fellows out of those woods!"[34]

8

"A New Kind of Murder"

The Iron Brigade in the Wilderness

SHARON EGGLESTON VIPOND

They go where the shade is, perhaps into Hades,
Where the brave of all times have led.
—Herman Melville, "The Armies of the Wilderness"[1]

Ulysses S. Grant met the Iron Brigade for the first time on March 29, 1864. Halting in the midst of his first review of the Army of the Potomac, he removed his hat in the freezing rain and made a low bow to the proud Western men who stood motionless as statues before him.[2] Even before Grant left the Western theater of the war and came to Washington to accept Lincoln's appointment as commander of the Federal armies earlier in the spring, a number of profound changes had taken place in the famed Western brigade.

Officers and men who had been with the Iron Brigade since the early days of the war had left the ranks due to death or disabling injury at Gettysburg. Massive casualties sustained in the defense of Seminary Ridge and the fight at the Railroad Cut had virtually destroyed the brigade. As a whole, it had suffered 65 percent casualties and led the casualty list for the entire Federal army for losses sustained during the three days of battle.[3] Brigade leadership also suffered heavy casualties at Gettysburg; nine of fourteen field officers had been killed or disabled.[4] The losses at Gettysburg necessitated several command changes and compelled the Federal army to supplement the Iron Brigade with non-Western army units and recruits. These forever changed the unique character and composition of the brigade.

The first of these army implants arrived on July 16, 1863, when the 167th Pennsylvania was transferred to the Iron Brigade from Seventh Corps.

This was an undisciplined and wholly unfit group of Eastern draftees who had to be threatened into marching at the point of a bayonet.[5] Fortunately, the mutinous Pennsylvanians were withdrawn from the brigade after only four weeks and their place taken by a more respected and soldierly group: the First Battalion New York Sharpshooters. These Easterners would serve with the Iron Brigade for the next eighteen months and would share the rigors of Grant's first campaign against Robert E. Lee in the spring of 1864.[6] Other than the Seventy-sixth New York—which was temporarily attached to the Iron Brigade for a few weeks in early 1864—the final group to join the brigade was Colonel Ira G. Grover and his Hoosiers of the Seventh Indiana. Unlike the other implants, these were true "Western" men, distinguished combat veterans, and Iron Brigade comrades from their First Corps days under General Joseph Hooker.[7]

Army conscripts and new recruits were also used to rebuild the ranks of the Iron Brigade after Gettysburg. Conscripts and "bounty men" were universally reviled and, more often than not, proved to be unsatisfactory soldiers. As one Wisconsin officer lamented, "What a contrast between such hounds and the enthusiastic and eager volunteers of 1861. Our men thoroughly despise these cattle and certainly the honor of the old army will not be safe in such hands."[8] Draftees and volunteer recruits, on the other hand, often worked hard to become worthy of the proud unit to which they now belonged. "We have to drill almost all the time to teach these awkward recruits," said one of the Seventh Wisconsin veterans. "There is some of them that take hold and try to learn, but the most of them are as awkward as mules." In the upcoming battles, some of "the raws," as they were contemptuously known, would eventually earn grudging acceptance from the Iron Brigade veterans.[9] One group of recruits that earned rapid acceptance was composed of fourteen Chippewa Indians, "wild from the woods," who were assigned to the Seventh Wisconsin. During the bloody months to come, they would prove themselves equal to the best skirmishers in the Army of the Potomac.[10]

The "veteran question" also caused major changes in the Iron Brigade regiments in the period after Gettysburg. Except for the Twenty-fourth Michigan, whose term of service would not expire until 1865, the other Iron Brigade regiments were due to muster out of the army in the spring and summer of 1864. As one of several reenlistment incentives, the U.S. Government offered the promise of a thirty-day furlough if three-fourths of each regiment reenlisted. The Sixth and Seventh Wisconsin enrolled three-fourths of their regiments, but the Nineteenth Indiana and the greatly reduced Second Wisconsin fell short of the goal.[11]

Early spring of 1864 brought yet another profound and disturbing change for the Iron Brigade. To the great sorrow of the proud First Corps veterans, John F. Reynolds's old corps was merged with Major General Gouverneur K. Warren's Fifth Corps and, with this action, the Iron Brigade lost forever its

Lysander Cutler.
Courtesy of the Wisconsin
Veterans Museum.

proud distinction of being the First Brigade of the First Division of the First Corps of the Army of the Potomac, and became the First Brigade in Warren's Fourth Division. Dissolution of the old First Corps produced bitter resentment among the Western men, who regarded it as "a loss of their identity purchased with blood and held most sacred." Only when they were permitted to wear their old corps badges did some of the hurt begin to subside.[12]

Thus, it was a transformed Iron Brigade which stood in the rain for Ulysses S. Grant's first review of the Army of the Potomac. The Western men had made their "final stand" at Gettysburg and although their best fighting days were indeed behind them, they remained a formidable presence within the Army of the Potomac and still retained the solid core of veteran pride that had been forged in the heat of so many desperate battles.[13] The men in the ranks had changed and most of the "Boys of '61" were gone, but the structure of the brigade was solid and contained officers who were well-known Iron Brigade veterans.[14] Major General James S. Wadsworth—the brigade's divisional commander at Gettysburg—had returned from leave in March of 1864 and was now actively engaged in preparing his Fourth Division troops for the upcoming campaign. Brigadier General Lysander Cutler—an Iron Brigade veteran and former commander of the Sixth Wisconsin—took permanent command of the brigade in March of 1864. Cutler was an experienced soldier and stern disciplinarian. The "old colonel" or "old prince," as he was called by the Sixth Wisconsin boys, was "rugged as a wolf," and the men who served under Cutler had great confidence in him, both as a man and an officer.

As the month of April 1864 drew to a close, the Iron Brigade's winter camp outside Culpeper, Virginia, was filled with rumors of Grant's plans and the Western men were surrounded by a "lively hum of preparation" for spring maneuvers against Lee's army south of the Rapidan. George McClellan was long gone and they were now Grant's Iron Brigade.[15] Most of the Western men welcomed the appointment of Grant with great satisfaction, because they hoped and believed that fighting under Grant would yield better results than had been achieved during the past three years.[16] Others were fearful of Grant's inexperience with combat in the Eastern theater of the war and the fact that he had never before confronted "Bobby" Lee on a battlefield. Many felt a deep foreboding about the upcoming campaign and believed that a "new kind of murder" was about to begin.[17]

On Tuesday, May 3, Captain Earl M. Rogers, one of Wadsworth's most trusted staff officers, felt the "ominous forebodings of war." These culminated the next afternoon with an announcement that more than 100,000 men of the Army of the Potomac would begin their march that night with four days' rations.[18] Rogers had been an officer in the Sixth Wisconsin and still maintained a close connection with his Iron Brigade comrades. He always kept an eye peeled for one Badger, in particular, a scruffy youngster named Pete Markle from Coon Slough in Bad Axe County. Over the months, Markle had become a celebrated "straggler" in the Iron Brigade and, although rarely found in regimental formation, he had amply demonstrated his courage and marksmanship at places like Bull Run, Antietam, and Gettysburg. Pete was not a shirker or coward, but simply a "free spirit" who liked to explore the countryside while his Iron Brigade comrades trudged along. The teenager whom Rogers called "an unpolished, straggling diamond" would be back in line when Grant and the Iron Brigade met up with Lee's army south of the Rapidan.[19]

The Iron Brigade spent the afternoon and evening hours of Tuesday, May 3, drilling and performing picket duty. Soon after midnight, the brigade broke camp and joined the Fifth Corps's line of march toward the Rapidan, passing by Pony Mountain and through Stevensburg on their way to the Germanna Ford river crossing. The roads were dusty, the night was hot, and the twenty-mile march took a severe toll on everyone.

The sun dawned on a beautiful, spring morning as the marching columns trudged on toward the Rapidan River crossing. As Earl Rogers rode along he saw overcoats, shirts, drawers, blankets, and portfolios "sufficient to have supplied the Confederate army" discarded by the sweating men and strewn haphazardly on both sides of the road. "When I run from Johnnys," joked one of the boys in the Twenty-fourth Michigan, "I don't want any load on."[20] Rogers saw that Pete Markle had also discarded much of his gear.

As he continued to watch, Markle wandered from the marching line and disappeared into the woods. It was a good morning to explore the Virginia countryside.

After waiting for an hour on the banks of the Rapidan while their Fifth Corps comrades filed by, the brigade finally crossed over pontoons erected by Major General George G. Meade's engineers between 9:00 and 10:00 A.M. They pulled up the Germanna Plank Road, past its junction with the Orange Court House Turnpike, and then turned east to the old Wilderness Tavern. By 4:00 P.M. on the afternoon of May 4, the Western men were bivouacked near the ruined tavern buildings at the crossroads and a detachment from the Second Wisconsin sent out on picket duty. In spite of the tiring march, the men were in high spirits and "sanguine of success" as they washed off the dust and cooked supper.[21] Only the forbidding forest which stood on the western edge of their encampment was cause for concern.

The men could see how the road disappeared into an evil-looking entanglement of scrub pine, briers, and thickets, and formed an impenetrable jungle some twenty or thirty feet high in places. Fortunately, Grant's orders had made it clear that they would pass quickly through the Wilderness and engage Lee's army only when well clear of this region of gloom. That was indeed a relief, for as the men savored their coffee and gazed at the tangled forest, they saw "the shadow of death" and could hardly imagine a more dark and terrible place to fight a battle.[22]

The heavily wooded area known as the Wilderness began near Orange Court House to the west and extended almost to Fredericksburg, some forty miles to the east. Bounded on the north by the Rapidan and Rappahannock rivers, it extended twelve miles south almost to Spotsylvania. The dense thicket was made up of scrub oaks and low-limbed pines, and because of its unique history, it did not have the characteristics of an ordinary forest. In the eighteenth and early nineteenth centuries, Virginians had carried out extensive mining operations in the area and had cut down miles of Wilderness timber in order to feed their mining furnaces and mineral forges. With the timber gone, a densely matted growth of low-limbed trees, vines, and stiff bushes had intermingled with the underbrush. To make travel within the Wilderness even more difficult, the terrain itself resembled "a choppy sea" with ridges, hillocks, and mudholes concealed beneath the undergrowth. A Confederate soldier observed that "the surface of the earth is indented occasionally with low basins, through which the rainfall, washing from the higher margins, cuts long gullies and often deep and wide washouts." One battle-hardened Yankee, waving his arm toward the surrounding woods, said simply: "This is an awful place to fight."[23]

At 4:30 A.M. the next morning, the men of Cutler's brigade rolled out of their makeshift beds, finished their coffee, and were drawn up in line for roll call. When everyone was accounted for, they filed past the large house and buildings of the Lacy Plantation, a few hundred yards south of the Orange

Turnpike, and headed for a dirt road that disappeared into the woods to the southwest.[24] Accompanied by Lieutenant George Breck's Battery L, First New York Artillery, and Lieutenant James Stewart's Battery B, Fourth U.S. Artillery, the Iron Brigade—with the Twenty-fourth Michigan in the lead—entered its place in Wadsworth's column. Within Wadsworth's division, the New York regiments of Brigadier General James C. Rice headed the column, followed by Colonel Roy W. Stone and his Pennsylvanians, and then Cutler's brigade. Stewart's Battery B contained a number of "detached" volunteers from Iron Brigade regiments, and was known as the "Iron Brigade Battery." Battery B had supported the brigade at Brawner Farm, South Mountain, Antietam, and Gettysburg.[25]

Three of Major General Gouverneur K. Warren's four divisions—Brigadier General Samuel Crawford in the lead, followed by Wadsworth, then Brigadier General James Robinson—began moving southwest down the densely wooded road toward Parker's Store, an abandoned country market that formed Warren's objective for the morning's march. The last of Warren's four divisions—that of Brigadier General Charles Griffin—headed due west, down the Orange Turnpike. Griffin's route of march called for him to cover Warren's flank from the Orange Turnpike as his divisions passed, and then fall in behind Robinson and follow the rest of Fifth Corps down the Parker's Store Road.[26]

Because Warren had allowed Brigadier General James H. Wilson and some of his Fifth Corps cavalry to move ahead to the Parker's Store crossroads, the divisions of Crawford, Wadsworth, and Robinson had to advance along the road without the protection of a cavalry screen. To compensate, Warren threw out pickets and ordered everyone to march slowly and remain alert to any sign of trouble. In spite of the fact that enemy skirmishers had already been encountered—indicating that elements of the Confederate army were certainly in the area—no serious fighting was expected in the immediate future, least of all south of the turnpike. Without any hard information to the contrary, Warren, Meade, and Grant were all operating on the belief that Lee's army was beyond Mine Run, several miles to the west, and would obligingly stay there until the Army of the Potomac had passed safely through the Wilderness.[27]

As the divisions of Crawford, Wadsworth, and Robinson weaved slowly along the Parker's Store Road, Griffin's pickets looked westward from their advance outpost on the Orange Turnpike. They saw an ominous cloud of dust forming over the deserted roadway and small moving objects that slowly materialized into horsemen. Behind the riders were foot soldiers in tattered butternut and gray, hats slouched low over their eyes, striding ahead with a swinging, determined gait. These men were not Confederate scouts or skirmishers, they were the vanguard of Lieutenant General Richard S. Ewell's Second Army Corps and formed the tip of a powerful rebel infantry column. The rest of Ewell's Confederates were moving eastward down the turnpike.

Warren and the Army of the Potomac were about to receive an unpleasant surprise.[28]

When he received Griffin's astonishing message that the enemy was attacking his pickets, Warren was deeply shocked. The Confederates were supposed to be entrenched miles away, and Warren had heard nothing from his cavalry outposts to indicate the enemy was this close—within actual striking distance![29] Warren ordered Griffin to prepare for an attack and dashed off a note to Meade and Grant at headquarters. However, before Warren could dispatch his note, another messenger arrived from Griffin warning that rebel infantry were now moving down the turnpike in force and forming in line of battle. Warren ordered Griffin to hold his position and push out a small force to determine the strength of the enemy he was facing. Griffin's skirmishers crept out from behind the Federal picket line on the Orange Turnpike and came to the edge of Saunders' Field. A chilling sight greeted them: The enemy filled the woods on the far side of the clearing and Confederate shovels and axes could be seen flying through the air as a rough line of earthworks and log breastworks began to take shape.[30]

Back at headquarters, Meade had received Warren's message and directed him to halt his columns and attack the enemy with his whole corps. Grant's supporting directive likewise ordered Warren to take immediate action: "If any opportunity presents itself of pitching into a part of Lee's army," Grant ordered, "do so *without giving time for disposition* [italics added]."[31] Disposition was the least of Warren's problems as he struggled to collect and organize his divisions: Griffin was nearly in place on the Orange Turnpike; Crawford's lead units were at the Chewning Farm near Parker's Store; Wadsworth was hacking his way through the Wilderness Run valley along—and on both sides of—Parker's Store Road; and Robinson (having barely moved since morning) was still in sight of the Old Wilderness Tavern.[32] Units of Wadsworth's Fourth Division artillery—Breck's and Stewart's batteries—were parked in a clearing near the Chewning Farm.

In order to accomplish his directive from Grant and Meade, Warren had to execute a number of difficult maneuvers: (1) Rapidly bring the marching divisions of Crawford and Wadsworth to a halt and shift them from column to line of battle facing west. Given the current order of march, Warren's line would be composed of Crawford on the left, Wadsworth in the middle, and (connecting with) Griffin on the left; (2) move Robinson's division forward and position them in reserve once a line of battle had been established; (3) link all three divisions with Griffin up on the Orange Turnpike and, finally; (4) initiate a coordinated, frontal assault on Ewell's force. Given the number of men and units involved, the proximity of the enemy force, the need for careful coordination of the linking maneuver prior to staging the attack, and the unyielding terrain which lay between him and Ewell, Warren's assignment of "pitching into" Lee's army would prove nearly impossible.

With these precipitous orders to Warren's Fifth Corps, Grant and Meade

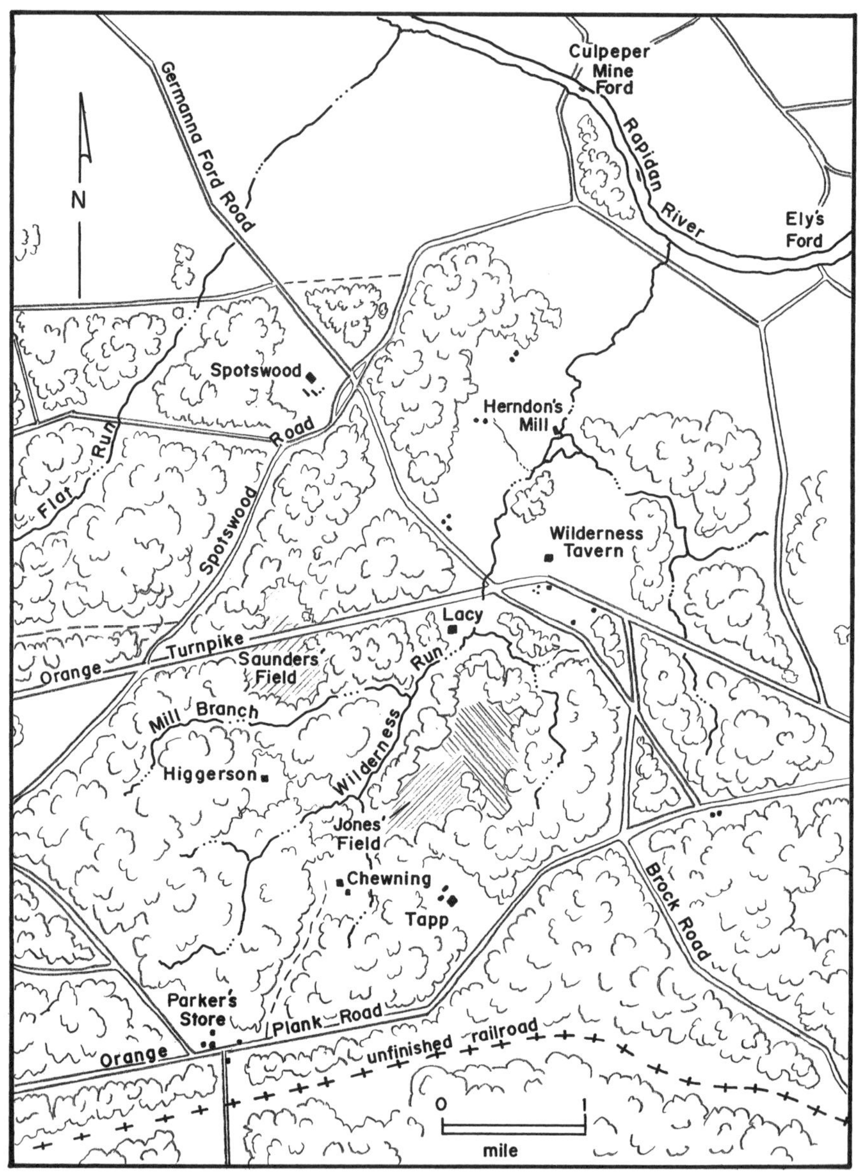

Wilderness Battlefield, Chancellorsville, Virginia.
Source: *Official Records*; *Battles and Leaders*; Rhea

abandoned their original plan of getting through the Wilderness as quickly as possible and committed their army to battle under the worst possible conditions. Since Warren's men were the nearest Federal force, they would be the first to reap the bitter fruits of this decision.

While Warren's other divisions were halting and turning northwest in preparation for the anticipated linkage, Wadsworth reformed his division on open ground at Jones' Field near the Chewning Farm.[33] Once reformed, Wadsworth's division also turned northwest and began the half-mile advance meant to accomplish Warren's planned linkage. Appointed by Wadsworth as de facto Chief of Artillery for the Fourth Division, Lieutenant James Stewart sent all of Breck's battery and the caissons of Battery B back to the Lacy House, but kept the guns and limbers of Battery B with him as he struggled through the thick woods in the wake of Wadsworth's brigades.[34] Stewart could see the terrible terrain over which Battery B and the rest of Wadsworth's division would be forced to travel, and did not want to be encumbered with another battery or caissons if a rapid withdrawal of his guns became necessary.[35]

Slugging their way through nearly impassable terrain, the men of Wadsworth's division were compelled to work forward in single columns. Because of their relative positions in the original line of march, Wadsworth's brigades would form a line of battle in which Rice was on the left, Stone in the middle, and Cutler's Iron Brigade on the right. Thus, it would be Cutler's responsibility to link his right flank with Griffin's left-most division near the Orange Turnpike. As the various regiments moved through the undergrowth, many lost their sense of direction and became mixed with other units. As Cutler's men struggled along, his units began to drift to the right, toward the Orange Turnpike.[36]

On the left of Wadsworth's division, Crawford seemed to have absorbed only that half of Warren's 7:30 A.M. message that said "Halt!" and not the other half ordering him to *expedite his connection with Wadsworth.* From 8:00 A.M. when Crawford advised Warren that he was halted in good position, until 11:15 A.M.—when he amazingly asked Warren: "Shall I abandon the position I now hold to connect with General Wadsworth?"—Crawford remained nearly immobile on the road near the Chewning Farm. Warren angrily replied: "You will move to the right as quickly as possible." Again at 11:50 A.M. Warren berated Crawford: "You must connect with General Wadsworth, and cover and protect his left as he advances."[37] Warren's sense of alarm at Crawford's tardiness was only heightened by prior staff assessments noting the vital importance of closing the half-mile gap between Wadsworth and Crawford. If this gap was not closed quickly, Wadsworth's brigades could not hold the line against an attack.[38]

To Wadsworth's right, Griffin was also frustrating Warren's efforts to link his command into a unified line and promptly attack the enemy. Griffin's reluctance, however, was based upon the firm conviction that his superiors had seriously miscalculated the size and ferocity of the Confederate force occupying the Orange Turnpike ahead of him. As a result, Griffin had been dragging his feet all morning, arguing with Warren and resisting his order to attack.[39]

Increasingly impatient with the slow progress of the linking movement, Warren ordered Wadsworth to pick up the pace of his advance and "attack the enemy at once." Wadsworth was now to push forward a heavy line of skirmishers and *not wait for the linkup with Griffin.* Warren assured him that "General Griffin will also attack. Do not wait for him, but look out for your own left flank."[40] Warren was justifiably afraid that Crawford's division—still struggling through the brush just south of Rice's position—would not arrive in time to link up with Wadsworth's left. This meant that James Rice's New Yorkers, as Wadsworth's leftmost brigade, would advance with their own left flank in the air and fully exposed to whatever threat lay hidden in the undergrowth ahead.[41] Ignoring appropriate measures for the protection and connection of these flanks would prove to be a fatal mistake.

It was now late morning and even Wadsworth was showing no inclination to hurry. Since receiving Warren's pointed order to attack "at once," Wadsworth had sent several groups of skirmishers into the underbrush to probe for Confederate pickets. Captain John A. Kellogg and Company I of the Sixth Wisconsin were designated for this morning's "reconnaissance duty."[42] As Kellogg got up to go, he shook hands with his friends and fellow officers, Phil Plummer and Rollin Converse. Plummer asked if Kellogg wanted him to send a message to his wife. "Never mind my wife," laughed Kellogg, "Look after Converse's girl!" Converse gestured toward Major Rufus Dawes and replied: "Plummer will be shot before either of us, leave your message with Dawes, he is the only man they can't kill!"[43] After zigzagging for more than half an hour through dense thickets, Kellogg's skirmishers finally encountered Ewell's pickets and engaged them in a brief but deadly fight. This action accounted for the first Iron Brigade casualties of the battle and also cost the lives of several sharpshooters in the First New York Battalion. When the surviving skirmishers made their way back to the Iron Brigade lines, Captain John Kellogg was not among them.[44]

While skirmishers tore into each other less than half a mile to their front, Cutler's men—formed into two ragged lines of battle—lay down in the woods to rest. Rufus Dawes noted, "It was a bright and pleasant morning, and the woods were filled with the twitter of birds. Colonel Bragg and all of our officers gathered under a great oak tree, and were chattering and chaffering in the highest spirits."[45] This description hardly supports the familiar picture of Federal troops floundering through the thickets in a hurried and desperate attempt to form a connected line of battle. To the contrary, many of Warren's men were relaxing from their strenuous morning maneuvers while Ewell's Confederates strengthened log breastworks and grimly prepared for the impending fight. As noon approached, 10,000 Confederate soldiers were dug in and ready on the western edge of Saunders' Field. Even better for the

Confederate cause, they had 4,500 men of General Jubal Early's division moving into supporting positions. Early's three brigades—those of Brigadier General John B. Gordon, Colonel Harry T. Hayes, and Colonel John Pegram—stood ready to fill any gaps that materialized in the rebel line ahead.[46] The Confederates' early morning work would pay significant dividends within the hour.

It was almost noon when the skirmishers' battle subsided and Warren finally managed to arrange his corps into a wavering line extending from Saunders' Field southward. Between noon and 1:00 P.M., Crawford notified Warren that the connection with Wadsworth was finally achieved, and Griffin, his earlier protests unsuccessful, moved out from behind his breastworks, advanced to the edge of Saunders' Field, and connected with Cutler's brigade which was in the woods southeast of the clearing.[47]

Saunders' Field was a clearing about 400 yards long and 800 yards wide that extended on both sides of the Orange Turnpike. A gully ran the length of the clearing, roughly north to south, and created a natural hazard for troops trying to cross it while under fire. The field sloped uphill from the gully to the western edge of the clearing and the terrain was composed of low ridges and marshy depressions. The woods south of Saunders' Field would become the location of some of the Iron Brigade's most brutal fighting of the war and ironically, for the Western men, the clearing was a *cornfield*.[48]

Although Cutler noted in his official report that the Iron Brigade line was formed and moved forward at 12:00 noon, the westward advance was chaotic and the line of battle stumbled along from noon until after 1:00 P.M., with large gaps between the Federal regiments and brigades spread across Saunders' Field.[49] On Cutler's right flank, the Seventh Indiana traversed the woods at the south edge of Saunders' Field with the Sixth Wisconsin close behind. As the line moved forward, the Seventh Indiana maintained a close connection on the right with elements of Bartlett's Third Brigade. As the Indiana and Wisconsin men plowed through the brush, the Badgers had trouble keeping up but managed to keep their eyes on the Indiana colors floating just ahead of them.[50] There was sharp firing in the front and artillery could be heard booming off to the right, over on the Orange Turnpike. Suddenly, the Wisconsin men heard the shout of Colonel Ira Grover as he ordered his Seventh Indiana to advance at the "double quick." Major Rufus Dawes of the Sixth also pushed his men forward as quickly as possible, while Colonel Bragg ran ahead to keep the colors of the Seventh Indiana in sight. On the left, the other Iron Brigade regiments picked up the pace. Still maintaining their connection with Bartlett's brigade on the right, the Western men surged across the south edge of the field as Ewell's men opened fire from the trees just ahead.[51]

Bartlett's first line leaned into the storm of bullets as though facing a strong wind. A Maine soldier in the first line remembered that a "red volcano yawned before us and vomited forth fire, and lead, and death." Together,

Cutler's and Bartlett's men threw themselves into the Confederate guns. Firing at almost point-blank range, in terrible similarity to the fight at Brawner Farm, both lines blasted away at each other as they advanced.[52] Bartlett's forward line faltered momentarily but managed to hold on until his second line pulled up, stiffened with reinforcements from Sweitzer's brigade. Reaching the edge of the field, both Cutler on the left and the reinforced line of Bartlett on the right then struck the front of Brigadier General John M. Jones's brigade. The connection between the inner flanks of these two brigades was maintained during the advance to the jump-off point and, in hitting the same target, they attacked almost in unison.[53] Federal volleys tore into Jones's outflanked Virginia regiments and both Jones and his aide, Captain Robert D. Early—nephew of General Jubal Early—tumbled, dead, from their horses. Overpowered, the leaderless Confederates fell to the rear, firing as they went.

During the furious struggle, Iron Brigade regiments captured two battle flags and 289 prisoners.[54] Private John N. Opel of the Seventh Indiana captured the colors of Jones's Fiftieth Virginia regiment and Major Albert M. Edwards of the Twenty-fourth Michigan captured the battle flag of the Forty-eighth Virginia.[55] Sergeant Abram J. Buckles of the Nineteenth Indiana rallied the Hoosiers with their regimental colors and led them in a charge on the Confederate lines.[56]

After shearing off the right of Jones's brigade, Cutler and his men pushed the Confederates for half a mile and—still connected with Bartlett on the right—they penetrated into Ewell's second line of defense composed of the brigades of Cullen A. Battle, George Doles, and Junius Daniel. As the fighting intensified, Doles's line suddenly stiffened and blocked the path of Cutler's further advance. At the same time, while fiercely engaged with Doles's four Georgia regiments, Cutler lost connection on the right with Bartlett's brigade. The connection was lost when Bartlett, reinforced by Sweitzer's first-line units, overwhelmed Battle's Alabama brigade and exuberantly swept on for several hundred yards through the woods, apparently forgetting, in the excitement of the moment, the necessity of maintaining his connection with Cutler.[57]

On the Iron Brigade's right flank, the Sixth Wisconsin felt the loss of Bartlett on the right and drifted out of alignment with the rest of the brigade. Instead of facing the enemy in a parallel line, as they should have been, the Sixth was now positioned at a forty-five degree angle to the advancing rebels. As the Wisconsin men moved forward through the dense underbrush, the roar of musketry increased and the brambles around them erupted into small fires. They staggered along half suffocated, stumbling now and then over bodies clad in gray, butternut, and blue. The Badgers were unaware of their deadly peril until they emerged from a cloud of smoke, and felt musketry burst suddenly from the area formerly occupied by Bartlett's troops.[58]

Major Phil Plummer shouted, "Look to the right!" Those were his last words. Stretching as far as the eye could see through the woods were Virginia and North Carolina troops from Brigadier General George H. Steuart's brigade, advancing rapidly and pouring a murderous volley into the disoriented Badgers. Rufus Dawes ordered the right wing of the regiment to make a change of front on the color company in order to bring his men into position to face their attackers. He yelled at Plummer to do the same with the left wing, but Plummer was dead and his men could do little more than dive into the bushes. As the rebels came on, yelling and firing, Dawes and a small group of men formed around the regimental colors and gave the enemy a "hot reception" that stopped their advance and discouraged further pursuit.[59] Dawes, Bragg, and other Sixth Wisconsin survivors now found themselves alone and lost in the woods. They lay flat on the ground, not knowing which way to go in order to rejoin their Iron Brigade comrades. Bragg crept through the bushes and, while trying to locate Grover and the Seventh Indiana, almost blundered into the middle of Lee's army. He could not find the Hoosiers, but did bring back one of the Company I boys who said he was certain Captain Kellogg had been killed in the morning skirmish. Gathering the survivors of their regiment together, Bragg and Dawes felt their way cautiously back toward the Fifth Corps lines. Captain Rollin Converse, the last of the three friends who had joked about getting shot, lay mortally wounded in the grass. He was left behind when the Badgers pulled out.[60]

Meanwhile, conditions on the left flank of Cutler's brigade were rapidly deteriorating from bad to critical. As the Nineteenth Indiana, Second Wisconsin, and Seventh Wisconsin battled the now combined weight of Doles's and Battle's brigades to the front, the left flank, anchored by the Twenty-fourth Michigan, began to give way. The Wolverines should have been supported by Colonel Andrew W. Denison's Maryland regiments from the rear and connected to Stone's Pennsylvanians on their left, but neither of these units had appeared, and the situation was now desperate.

Where were the promised reserves? Earlier in the day, Denison's Third Brigade had been detached from Robinson's division and placed in position near the Lacy House to support Wadsworth's division as it advanced. In spite of these direct orders and the fact that *they could hear and see* the terrific battle taking place in front of them, the Marylanders stood immobile.[61]

Where was Roy Stone and his Pennsylvania brigade? Stone's regiments had been connected to Cutler's left flank and Rice's right flank when the advance had first begun. However, some of Stone's men—skirmishers from the 150th Pennsylvania—veered off and joined in the Iron Brigade's forward movement, and the remainder of the brigade got into trouble almost immediately after leaving the jump-off point.[62] Cutler and Rice had rapidly moved off to the northwest (with skirmishers from the 150th), leaving Stone's flanks exposed. If that was not bad enough, the Pennsylvanians' line of march carried them across a clearing about a quarter mile below Saunders' Field in which stood Benjamin and Permelia Higgerson's farmhouse.[63] On the far side of the Higgerson clearing they plunged through dense foliage and down into the muddy morass of Mill Branch, one of the tributaries of Wilderness Run. Stone's men had been unable to keep up with the brigades of Cutler and Rice and had floundered into serious trouble. They began receiving Confederate fire when they were mired in the mud and least ready to defend themselves, or to protect Cutler's left flank, as originally planned.[64] A disgruntled soldier from the 121st Pennsylvania provided an account of this "champion mud hole of mud holes" that would be amusing, were it not for the lethal effect of the incident on both Stone's and Cutler's brigades:

> . . . our men . . . could not do much execution while floundering about in the mud and water up to their middle. . . . It was evident before long that this locality was altogether too unhealthy; and when the order to retire was given, the scrambling to get out of that mud hole was amusing as well as ridiculous. . . . During this stampede it very naturally followed that the men became somewhat confused and more or less scattered, many not being sure which way to turn.[65]

To make matters even worse, Stone and several other officers could be seen "swilling whiskey as they would water."[66] Roy Stone was drunk. When some of his frightened men scrambled out of the mud hole and took to their heels, he rode through the brambles shouting that the 143rd Pennsylvania was to blame for the rout. Soldiers of that proud unit seethed with rage as they listened to his drunken tirade. After the war one of them wrote:

> I would have like[d] to have seen a rebel shell come and took the drunken head clean from his shoulders after he got through with his abuse. Could I photograph this hell hole that we were put in, I would then ask, what in the name of justice and cause and effect, had we to do with the outflanking and envelopment of the famous old Iron Brigade. . . . Tell to the world if you can why then two fighting brigades were thus advanced to this position in this hell hole, without connection on either flank, and officers drunk.[67]

Entrapped in the mud, confused and essentially leaderless, Stone's Pennsylvanians could offer no real support to the Twenty-fourth Michigan as it fought to maintain the left flank of the embattled Iron Brigade. As Cutler succinctly put it, "Stone's brigade gave way soon after meeting the enemy, thus letting the enemy through our line."[68]

The rapidly deteriorating conditions to the front and on both right and left flanks now brought the Iron Brigade to a critical point in the Wilderness battle: First, the Western men found themselves locked in a deadly struggle to their front with the Confederate brigades of Battle and Doles. Elements of the Nineteenth Indiana, Second Wisconsin, and Seventh Wisconsin were engaged in what was virtually hand-to-hand combat with several North Carolina, Alabama, and Georgia regiments. Second, the Iron Brigade was beginning to feel severe pressure on its left as Confederates exploited the gap left by Stone's absence and pushed reinforcements into the fight against the Twenty-fourth Michigan in an attempt to turn the left flank of the brigade.[69] Finally, the unexpected loss of connection with Bartlett and the apparent disappearance of both the Seventh Indiana and Sixth Wisconsin placed the brigade's right flank in the air and dangerously exposed it to a Confederate counterattack. Where were the Hoosiers and Badgers who had anchored the Iron Brigade's right flank?

Both the Seventh Indiana and Sixth Wisconsin had encountered severe fire, and in their attempts to get reorganized and mount an offensive, they had become hopelessly jumbled and disconnected from each other and from the rest of the brigade. The Seventh Indiana had surged forward through the dense thicket, successfully engaging a strong enemy force near the Orange Turnpike, but had been flanked by Confederate reinforcements and forced to retire from the field.[70] As mentioned, the Sixth Wisconsin had tried to keep pace with the Seventh Indiana but, finding itself lost in the woods and at least a quarter of a mile away from the Hoosiers, was caught in a sudden and severe attack and forced to creep back through the bushes in an attempt to locate their Iron Brigade comrades.[71]

Complicating matters still further, the terrain and other factors had caused the remaining Iron Brigade regiments to drift into an oblique alignment with respect to the Confederate lines which they were facing. In other words, they gradually and unknowingly turned their unprotected backs and sides to an aggressive and dangerous enemy, who was even now gathering his reinforcements for a ferocious counterattack.

Considering all of these factors, and viewing matters from the Confederate perspective, General Richard S. Ewell could hardly have wished for better conditions under which to launch an aggressive counterattack on the Black Hats who formed the center of Warren's Federal line. The Western men had been brought to a standstill in front by the tenacious combination of Doles's and Battle's brigades. Both flanks were more or less open. The Marylanders who had been assigned to support the Iron Brigade were standing immobile nearly a mile back. The battle in the woods south of Saunders' Field had come down to essentially one point: In order to survive, the Iron Brigade would have to fend for itself.[72]

Brigadier General John B. Gordon and his men were the means by which Ewell would deliver a potentially fatal blow to Wadsworth's division and to those regiments of the Iron Brigade still holding the line in the woods south of Saunders' Field. Gordon's Georgia brigade had been moving into reserve positions back on the Orange Turnpike when Ewell called for their assistance, and they immediately recognized the seriousness of the situation.[73]

Gordon wheeled his brigade by the right flank and formed at right angles to the road as quickly as possible, given the dense woods and the incoming fire from advancing infantry and Federal artillery on the turnpike. As soon as his men were ready, Gordon stood in his stirrups and bellowed out the command: "Forward!" Screaming the rebel yell, Gordon's men sprinted approximately 300 yards into the melee and pierced the Federal line with a three-pronged attack. While the center of his force surged forward (i.e., the Thirty-first and Thirty-eighth Georgia regiments), Gordon split the remainder of his command (i.e., the Thirteenth, Sixtieth, and Sixty-first Georgia regiments) into two sections and wheeled them—like two "doors" on separate hinges—toward the exposed flanks of both Cutler's and Rice's brigades. Then, driving into the fray alongside of Battle's brigade, Gordon crashed the "door" closest to the turnpike directly into the open flank of the Iron Brigade with catastrophic effect.[74]

The ultimate result of the alignment situation and the Ewell-Gordon counterattack is described in Cutler's official report: "The First Brigade (Cutler's) continued to drive the enemy until it was ascertained that the troops on both flanks had left and that the enemy was closing in his rear, when he was obliged to *fight his way back* [italics added], losing very heavily in killed and wounded."[75] The Western men took severe casualties in holding the center of their line and in executing the pullback maneuver ordered by Cutler. The ground of Saunders' Field was littered with dead men clad in butternut and blue, but in the woods near the southern edge of the field, where the center and left regiments of the Iron Brigade had met Gordon's fierce counterattack, most of the dead were clad in Federal blue. There were scores of tall black hats scattered among the bodies which lay in the smoldering grass.

On the edge of the field, left behind by their comrades and lying bleeding in the grass, were two Black Hats named Jim Whitty and Mark Smith. Both had been severely wounded and each would lose a leg within the next twenty-four hours. Watching rebel soldiers emptying the pockets and knapsacks of the Iron Brigade dead, they saw a tall Confederate officer ride slowly in their direction, his horse carefully picking its way around the bodies in the grass. Whitty and Smith noticed the gold stars of a general officer so they saluted him and asked his name. He replied, "My name is Gordon, boys." They sat up and said, "We are badly wounded, General; will you get us a drink?" John B. Gordon dismounted and gave each of the men a drink from his own canteen. Before riding away he turned in his saddle and said, "I am sorry for you, boys, but such is the fortune of war."[76]

As the Federal line moved rapidly backward with Ewell's men in hot pursuit, the dry grass, leaves, and overgrown bushes in Saunders' Field were ignited by the furious musketry, and fire swept across the clearing. Men on both sides made an effort to reach the wounded, but in many cases it was hopeless. Bodies of both the living and dead were consumed by fire.[77] Cartridge boxes strapped to the waists of the wounded were ignited by the flames and men were literally blown to pieces.[78] An officer of the Twenty-fourth Michigan recalled that although the ground was covered with wounded men, he could do little more than leap over them and hurry away. He had no time to look out for anyone but himself.[79]

One of the wounded Hoosiers of the Seventh Indiana who lay near the Orange Turnpike saw fire creeping over the ground, fed by the thick carpet of dead grass and leaves. Wounded men who could still move began frantically crawling toward the road in an attempt to reach the open ground over which the flames could not travel. Some of the Iron Brigade wounded were overtaken by the flames after crawling only a few feet, and some were caught when they had almost reached the safety of the road. The ground over which the Seventh Indiana had fought earlier in the day was now charred by fire. The blackened figures were no longer discernible as human beings, although everyone knew there were friends and comrades who still lay out in that burned field.[80] The fires which swept across Saunders' Field vanished as quickly as they had appeared. Those who had attempted to save wounded comrades went back to the lines and continued the fight.

In giving the order to fall back, Lysander Cutler extricated the Iron Brigade from almost certain annihilation at the hands of Gordon's and Doles's brigades. As the survivors of each regiment fell back to the clearing around the Lacy House, Gilbert M. Woodward, a lawyer from La Crosse, Wisconsin, paused to take stock of the situation. As adjutant of the Second Wisconsin, Woodward hoped to determine the enemy's line of advance as rebels pursued the Western men back across Saunders' Field. While watching the Confederates approach, he suddenly heard a deep, bass voice: "Adjutant, what be I going to do with this flag?" Turning, Woodward saw the regimental color-bearer, Roslas E. Davidson—a farmer from Spring Green—standing all alone in the woods with the flagstaff of the Second Wisconsin clutched in his hands. Understanding that Davidson was not about to abandon his post without a direct order, Woodward yelled at him to fall back with the regiment, and together he and the brave color-sergeant of the Second Wisconsin sprinted for the rear as Confederate bullets pelted the grass around them.[81]

The question of *how* the Iron Brigade executed the pullback from the woods south of Saunders' Field to the Lacy House is one which often seems to overshadow other aspects of the brigade's involvement in the battle. Some modern writers conclude that the battle of the Wilderness was unique in that it was the *first time* that the famed Iron Brigade actually *broke down* in combat and *ran* from the enemy.[82] Even Morris Schaff, one of Wadsworth's staff officers as well as an eyewitness and participant in the pullback, said that "Bartlett's troops fell back, in great disorder, to the east of the old field [Saunders' Field] and the works they had made in the morning; most of Cutler's and those on the left did not stop till they reached the Lacy farm. . . . I recall very distinctly their condition, for I was right among them."[83]

As survivors of the Iron Brigade and the rest of Wadsworth's division and Griffin's division fell back, their retreat was covered by Stewart's and Breck's batteries, who lobbed shells into the advancing Confederates when their comrades were safely through the guns. Stewart had ordered both batteries to deploy their guns *fixed prolonge*—ready to retire fighting—so they were able to rapidly limber up and join in the Federal retrograde movement.[84] On their way back, Wadsworth's and Griffin's survivors crashed through Denison's Marylanders—still standing solidly in place.[85]

The picture of terrified men, pouring through the woods and back across Saunders' Field, is further reinforced by some Confederate accounts of the incident. For example, a member of Steuart's Confederate brigade wrote that he and his comrades saw a "wave of wild-eyed fugitives" approach and had to dive into a gully for shelter from the stampede. Members of Steuart's brigade watched "while this vast herd of fleeing Federals came rushing through and over us without firing a gun or speaking a word."[86]

While it is possible that some members of the brigade fled precipitously to the rear after (or perhaps even before) Gordon's lethal assault on the Federal line, it is not accurate to characterize this incident as one in which the courage and determination of the Western men—as a whole—somehow failed and they ignominiously "ran" from the enemy in the face of orders to stand and fight. Quite to the contrary, Cutler clearly states that the situation was such that he was forced to "fight his way back." Even aside from Cutler, who might rightly be accused of trying to cast a better light on a bad situation, other credible eyewitnesses such as Morris Schaff and Warren's aide, Major Washington Roebling, said that the Western men—while routed and forced to retire—did not betray their proud heritage and flee like a pack of "wild-eyed fugitives." Riding into the fields immediately to the west of the Lacy House, Roebling saw that Parker's Store Road was "crowded with stragglers and large crowds of soldiers [were] pouring out of the woods in great confusion and almost panic-stricken. Some said they were flanked, others said they had suddenly come upon the enemy lying concealed in two lines of battle in the thick underbrush, and that our men had broken at the first volley. *Cutler's brigade came back in good order bringing a number of prisoners* [italics added]."[87]

However traumatized Iron Brigade survivors were by their nearly fatal confrontation with Gordon's men, they were obviously not fleeing against orders or deserting their post in the face of the enemy. In spite of their battered and bloody condition, Cutler and his regimental commanders still maintained control of the Iron Brigade.[88] The Western men brought their prisoners back with them for disposal at the Lacy House and immediately began the process of regrouping, building log breastworks, and taking up positions in the rifle pits located nearby.[89]

When the Sixth Wisconsin survivors finally emerged from the woods near the Lacy House, they realized, to their horror, that their beloved regimental flag had somehow been lost in the confused retreat. Battle-hardened veterans wept bitter tears over the loss of their tattered but proud emblem. As the exhausted men pulled themselves together and prepared to go back in search of their flag, they saw Cuyler Babcock stagger all alone out of the woods. "Sergeant Major, where is our flag?" A quiet smile passed over his smoke-begrimed face as Babcock unbuttoned his coat and there—wrapped around his body—was the "dear old flag" of the Calico Sixth.[90]

Around 2:00 P.M. Grant and Meade rode up to the Lacy House and found that Wadsworth had reformed the Iron Brigade and the rest of his Fourth Division troops on the high ground in front of the house. Wadsworth's artillery—including Battery B—had collected their caissons and were now parked nearby. Wadsworth's division was facing south, in the direction of the Orange Plank Road, which ran past Parker's Store and connected with the Brock Road some miles to the east.[91]

After talking with the two commanding generals, Wadsworth managed to convince Grant and Meade to give him a chance to redeem the honor he felt had been called into question by the behavior of his men over the past several hours.[92] Grant and Meade granted Wadsworth's request and ordered him to lead an assault on Lieutenant General A. P. Hill's corps, located somewhere to the south, between the Lacy House and the Orange Plank Road. Wadsworth was given Brigadier General Henry Baxter's brigade from Robinson's Second Division for additional support, and his column would be guided by Major Roebling of Warren's staff.[93]

Sometime between 4:00 and 5:00 P.M., Wadsworth received the formal command ordering him to move his division to the south and, along with Baxter's brigade, attack the left of Hill's corps. By 6:00 P.M. Wadsworth's men, now formed in two lines of battle, had left their positions around the Lacy House and started making their way through the dense thickets toward the extreme right of the Confederate battle line, about a half-mile northeast of the Widow Tapp's farm. The first line of Wadsworth's attack formation was made up of Stone's and Baxter's brigades. Cutler and the Iron Brigade formed the second line and Rice's battered brigade made up the reserve which followed behind Cutler.[94] The advance of Wadsworth's column was hampered by more than just thick undergrowth. As the historian of the 149th Pennsylvania noted, "The shaky men, still unnerved from the morning experience, broke through the growth of bush and vines with the greatest of care. The fear of again being surprised permeated the entire force." Wadsworth had issued strict orders for absolute quiet in the ranks, and the only sound to be heard as the men advanced was the continual snapping and popping of twigs and limbs, not unlike the sound of cattle grazing through the undergrowth.[95]

As Wadsworth and his staff followed the troops through the dense foliage and toward the Confederate position, they were mortified to suddenly hear Colonel Roy Stone—apparently still drunk—shooting his revolver into the air and yelling at the top of his lungs. Wadsworth hurried Earl Rogers forward with a direct order that Stone stop firing immediately and quiet down. Not only did Stone *continue* yelling and firing, he refused to obey a second command to report at once to Wadsworth. Instead, he ordered his men to sound "cheers" for the Commonwealth of Pennsylvania.[96]

Around 6:15 P.M., Wadsworth's men encountered skirmishers of Brigadier General Edward L. Thomas's Georgia brigade.[97] Thomas was already heavily engaged with elements of Winfield Hancock's Second Corps, so the only Confederate troops available to fend off Wadsworth's assault were the 125 men of the Fifth Alabama battalion. These Alabamians had been guarding Federal prisoners and now saw their chance to get back into the fight. Spreading out in a thin line of attack, the small force fired up their rebel yell and hit Stone's and Baxter's line head on.[98] Baxter's skirmishers returned the fire but Stone's men, already rattled by what had been—in anyone's estimation—a *very* bad day, panicked and ran. As Frank Cowdrey, Wadsworth's division adjutant noted, "[Stone's] brigade broke in a disgraceful manner on seeing the fire of Baxter's skirmishers in front of them."[99] Stone's horse reared in fright and pitched him to the ground. Drunk (and apparently injured) he was carried from the field and never returned to the Army of the Potomac.[100] As the Pennsylvanians bolted from battle formation and scattered, Cutler ordered the Iron Brigade—in rank immediately behind them—to lower their bayonets and stop the panic-stricken men.[101] As one modern analyst of the battle could not help but remark, "The Iron Brigade . . . held fast, and was able to direct the fleeing troops back to the front at the point of a bayonet. . . . The [Iron] brigade had been routed for the first time earlier in the day, and it was not about to bear such humiliation again, no matter what the price."[102]

The surprise "attack" of the tiny Fifth Alabama succeeded in throwing Wadsworth's column into disarray. The Fifth Alabama's attack—combined with the gathering darkness, the delays encountered in reforming the attack formation, and difficulties in getting Stone's men back into line—had effectively cost Wadsworth any chance for the type of success, or redemption, he might have hoped would be gained from the late afternoon assault.

Facing almost due south, Wadsworth's column halted and formed in the thickets north of the Orange Plank Road. As darkness closed in, Rice moved his men up from their reserve position and deployed them on the right of Baxter's brigade. Cutler and the Iron Brigade moved into the front line, taking position on Baxter's left, and Stone's brigade moved behind them into reserve. Each brigade was in two lines.[103] The extreme right of Wadsworth's line (held by Rice) was approximately one-half mile from the Widow Tapp's field. The far left of the line (held by Cutler) was west of the Brock Road. Baxter's line at the front was parallel to the Orange Plank Road and approximately one-half to five-eighths of a mile from the roadway.[104]

The men of the Iron Brigade spent the next few hours resting on their arms and in close proximity to the enemy lines. So close were they, in fact, that skirmish lines of the opposing forces lay barely one hundred feet apart. Frequent alarms were sounded throughout the night as small fire-fights erupted without warning, and several soldiers from the Twenty-fourth Michigan were killed and wounded while serving as pickets.[105] The Western men lay upon the ground surrounded by dead and dying rebel soldiers. As Rufus Dawes of the Sixth Wisconsin remembered,

> The sufferings of these poor men, and their moans and cries were harrowing. We gave them water from our canteens and all aid that was within our power. One dying Confederate soldier cried out again and again: "My God, why hast thou forsaken me!"[106]

Earl Rogers had been looking for Pete Markle ever since the Iron Brigade and Wadsworth's staff halted for the night. As usual, Pete had fought well throughout the day but when nightfall came, the renowned straggler of the Iron Brigade had disappeared. Although initially not concerned, Rogers became worried when he realized that Markle would find the straggling conditions hard and the living poor in the Wilderness, and he began searching in earnest through the scattered groups of weary and wounded men.[107]

Back at the Lacy House the men and horses of Battery B were also settling in for a long night. They had played a minor role in the day's action because of the impassable woodland terrain, and had sustained no appreciable injuries. After covering the fallback, it had been their lot to wait and watch from the Lacy House clearing. They heard the crash of musketry until well after dark, but it would be the "awful procession of mangled men" that they would remember. This ghastly stream of human misery staggered back through the battery's position all night long.[108]

Corporal Frank Hare of the Sixth Wisconsin lay next to Rollin Converse in a field hospital behind enemy lines. Wounded in the leg at the same time as Converse, Hare stuck close to his dying captain as Confederate surgeons examined both men and announced that they were going to amputate the mangled limbs of each. Calling weakly to Corporal Hare, Converse whispered: "Frank, I'll die soon. Don't let them cut off my leg. Nothing can save me." Hare took out his pistol and warned the blood-stained surgeons that he would shoot anyone who tried to amputate the captain's leg: "Take off mine, but let him alone." Weak from blood loss, Frank Hare kept watch with his gun "at the ready" until Converse's breathing slowed and then finally stopped.[109]

After the first day of battle in the Wilderness, the men of the Iron Brigade had fought their way from the woods south of Saunders' Field through swamps and thickets, to this equally inhospitable section of the forest. In the next twenty-four hours, the Iron Brigade would come to know this small parcel of land—from Widow Tapp's field, along the Orange Plank Road, to the Brock Road—in terrible detail. Years after the war, one of Wadsworth's staff officers would write: "There are but one or two square miles upon this continent that have been more saturated with blood than was the square mile which lay in front of the Brock Road and had the Orange Plank Road as a central avenue, in the two days of the battle of the Wilderness. . . . Nearly every square yard had its fill of blood, and on nearly every square yard was Northern and Southern blood intermingled."[110] The Western men would remember this ground—and the Wilderness, as a whole—as some of the most expensive territory they had ever fought for.

Around 1:00 A.M., Wadsworth received a message from Warren notifying him that another advance would be made on A. P. Hill's corps starting at 4:30 A.M. Wadsworth was to establish his battle line on a line extending northeast and southwest, march directly southeast, and join Hancock's Second Corps in an attack upon Hill's right flank.[111]

Wadsworth and his staff had a sleepless night. Earlier in the evening, Wadsworth had discovered that his men were nearly out of ammunition and so dispatched Captain Robert Monteith, one of his aides, on a mission to locate and distribute ammunition before the division had to move out at 4:30 A.M. Monteith, using the North Star to guide him through the smoke and darkness, reached the Lacy House and headed back with a train of pack mules carrying more than twenty thousand rounds. After almost stumbling into a camp of Confederates, Monteith finally arrived at 3:00 A.M., with barely enough time to distribute the ammunition to the Iron Brigade and the rest of Wadsworth's division before the order came to move out.[112]

At 4:30 A.M., the Western men were roused from sleep and managed to gulp down a bit of cold food before silently forming up with the rest of Wadsworth's division. It was anticipated that Stewart's Battery B and Breck's battery would go along with Wadsworth's men, as they had done the previous day. But just as both batteries were pulling into line behind the infantry, they were ordered back to the Lacy House clearing. From this position, it was determined the batteries could better protect the ravine of Wilderness Run and enfilade the edge of the brush on the opposite rise of ground if the enemy should suddenly appear.[113]

Shortly before 5:00 A.M. a signal gun was sounded by Hancock's corps and the two Federal assault columns—Wadsworth on the right (minus his artillery) and Hancock on the left—began their convergence on A. P. Hill's ill-prepared defenses on Orange Plank Road.[114] If Wadsworth's four brigades retained their positions from the previous evening, then Baxter would still have been in the center with Rice to Baxter's right, Cutler's brigade to Baxter's left, and Stone's Pennsylvanians—without a commanding officer since Stone's departure—following in reserve. However, this can only be assumed since there are conflicting reports of alignment within Wadsworth's division during the advance, and this point still remains unclear.[115] As Wadsworth's men fought and hacked their way through the undergrowth, the sun rose hot and bright over the Wilderness, penetrating the deep shade and shining on the moving men. Hancock's Second Corps was also struggling through the thick underbrush on their way to the rendezvous with Wadsworth.[116]

The Federal assault columns quickly converged on Hill's corps, and heavy firing erupted on his right flank and spread across the entire Confederate line. As Cutler's men surged forward, one Pennsylvania soldier saw that "the Iron Brigade [was] in our front making plenty of music with their Enfields, driving the enemy before them and taking a line of log breastworks."[117] After some initial resistance, the Confederate line crumpled and then disintegrated into a full-fledged stampede. Theodore Lyman, one of Meade's aides, sent an encouraging message to headquarters that Hancock was "driving the enemy handsomely" and that "Birney has joined with Wadsworth."[118]

The Iron Brigade, together with Baxter's brigade, began driving the fleeing Confederates through the woods toward the Orange Plank Road. On the right, Rice's brigade was severely raked by artillery fire and fell behind for several minutes while his skirmishers tried to clear away the Confederate guns that were harassing his men.[119] Yelling with excitement and driving a pack of stampeding rebels, Cutler's and Baxter's brigades careened onto the Orange Plank Road from the north and crashed into the side of Major General David B. Birney's division of Hancock's Second Corps.

Birney's troops were almost forced off the road and men of both Federal corps became jammed and crowded in the enormous confusion.[120] Although Cutler described the massive collision as simply making "a juncture" with Second Corps, there were reports that Lieutenant General James Longstreet's Confederate First Corps was headed in that direction and neither Wadsworth nor Hancock could afford this sort of deadly entanglement in the face of an impending attack. Fortunately, Birney's and Wadsworth's hard-working brigade commanders were able to get everyone sorted out and back into their places within a relatively short time.[121]

Pulling onto the Orange Plank Road and facing west, Wadsworth's division was then formed into four lines, with the left of each line resting on the plank road. By order of General Wadsworth, the ranks were crowded closely together so as to avoid the artillery fire that had caused such damage to Rice's brigade earlier in the morning.[122] As Cutler finished his alignment and prepared to join the general advance up the Orange Plank Road, Longstreet and his Confederate First Corps burst suddenly onto the scene, taking the Western men completely by surprise. Longstreet's First Corps slammed into the Federal lines and rocked Wadsworth's and Hancock's assault columns back on their heels.[123] One of the Badgers in the Sixth Wisconsin remembered that

> Our brigade was forming its lines, the 6th Wisconsin was in the second line, a short distance in the rear of the first line. We were in oak openings, trees, but no underbrush. Just in front of our first line, the brush was thick, hiding the view to the front. Just as the command was given for the first line to advance, to our surprise, the rebel line burst forth from the brush and poured a volley into our ranks, killing and wounding many in the first line and a few in the second. The onset was not expected and no one was prepared to receive it. The second line was ordered to lie down and allow the

first line to pass over us and to the rear of us where they could recover from the shock.[124]

The stunned Badgers lay down, but before they could climb back on their feet, Longstreet's men pounced upon them and broke up the entire brigade. Fighting furiously, the Western men were forced backward, step by step, along the plank road.[125] They took temporary shelter in a ravine on the northeastern side of the plank road. At 8:15 A.M. Warren received news of Wadsworth's deadly struggle: "Wadsworth has been slowly pushed back, but is contesting every inch of ground."[126]

Pinned down, Iron Brigade survivors continued to pour round after round into the advancing Confederates until elements of the Fifteenth, Forty-fourth, and Forty-eighth Alabama worked their way around the right flank of the Western men and delivered a deadly enfilade into their ranks.[127] Caught and flanked by the Confederates as surely as they had been the day before in the woods south of Saunders' Field, the Iron Brigade was forced backward and their ranks shattered. In the deadly melee, fragments of Iron Brigade regiments got mixed in with other units and continued fighting. Some Wolverines from the Twenty-fourth Michigan retreated back to the Brock Road with Birney's troops and joined them in repulsing a Confederate charge on Hancock's position later in the morning.[128] A company of the Sixth Wisconsin was swept into a group of assorted units near the Brock Road and fought, later that afternoon, under the command of Colonel J. William Hoffman of the Fifty-sixth Pennsylvania.[129] Thirty men and several officers from Company I of the Seventh Wisconsin fell back toward the left of Wadsworth's original line of battle and found themselves fighting with Burnside's Ninth Corps behind some wooden breastworks.[130]

When Wadsworth's division shattered under the impact of Longstreet's powerful assault, his brigades were split into two retreating groups. The first group—Baxter's and Rice's brigades—was forced back through the woods but later reformed on the Orange Plank Road. The second group—Cutler's and Stone's brigades—was rallied by Cutler and returned with him to the vicinity of the Old Wilderness Tavern. It was the *first* group which Wadsworth and Rice were trying to rally when Wadsworth was mortally wounded.[131]

Wadsworth, seeing that his division was largely broken and scattered by Longstreet's assault, had ridden forward through the lines, passing through the ranks of the Fifty-sixth Pennsylvania and 149th Pennsylvania regiments. When in front of the 149th Pennsylvania, Wadsworth ordered his troops forward. Leaping his horse over the logs of some Confederate breastworks and leading the charge himself, he crashed directly into Abner Perrin's Alabama brigade of Richard H. Anderson's division in A. P. Hill's Corps. Perrin's Alabamians rose from behind their breastworks and fired a deadly volley at Wadsworth and his men. Wadsworth would not (or could not) rein in his frightened horse, and the animal dashed forward to within twenty feet of the

Confederate lines. As Wadsworth then turned in his saddle to escape, a Confederate bullet struck him in the back of the head. His blood and brain matter spattered onto the coat of Earl Rogers, who rode at his side.[132] As the general tumbled from his saddle, Rogers reportedly abandoned his own wounded mount and vaulted into Wadsworth's saddle, narrowly escaping back to the Federal lines through a hail of bullets. When asked why he did not stop Wadsworth from riding to his death, Rogers replied: "My God . . . nobody could stop him!"[133]

The men of the Iron Brigade were profoundly saddened by the old patriot's death. He had led them to their finest and bloodiest hour at Gettysburg and they never ceased to admire "Daddy Wadsworth" for his courage and sacrifice.[134] A New York aristocrat of great wealth, Wadsworth had offered his services to the government and served without pay. One of the Wolverines of the Twenty-fourth Michigan said that Wadsworth's death and his loss to the Union was equaled only by that of the Iron Brigade's beloved John F. Reynolds.[135]

Cutler and his Iron Brigade survivors—those that formed the *second* of Wadsworth's two groups of retreating brigades—were heading back through the woods toward the Old Wilderness Tavern when Cutler first received the news that General Wadsworth was dead.[136] The Iron Brigade had been driven back in the direction from which they had marched the previous afternoon and had become completely separated from the rest of the division.

In spite of the severity of the Confederate counterattack on the Orange Plank Road, the Western men regrouped and pulled back in good order, and were not pursued back through the trees and thickets by Hill's or Longstreet's men.[137] Again, as with the retreat from the woods south of Saunders' Field, some modern analysts have tended to characterize the pullback from the Orange Plank Road as "Cutler's famed Iron Brigade" ignominiously "fleeing through the woods" as though they were a "swarm of stragglers."[138] In Morris Schaff's eyewitness report he states that he did indeed encounter "swarms of stragglers" from Wadsworth's division wending their way back toward the Wilderness Tavern crossroads. However, Schaff particularly noticed one group of so-called stragglers who were *different*; they were not demoralized or fleeing like many others. "I struck off more to the left," he said, "and in a little while ran into swarms of stragglers, and pretty soon met *a group falling back under some discipline* [italics added]. Upon inquiring, I found that they belonged to Cutler's brigade of Wadsworth's division, and they told me that the division had been driven with heavy losses."[139]

Back at the Lacy House, Stewart's men of Battery B waited and watched anxiously. By mid-morning the sounds of musketry and the dense clouds of smoke rolling up above the scrubby woods began to approach their position on the Lacy House knoll. They knew, of course, that this meant the enemy was driving Federal infantry back from the Orange Plank Road. Before long, the first rush of stragglers began to emerge from the woods in their front, and the men of Battery B could distinctly hear the rebel yell echoing through the brush. Unbroken by the hoarser roar of artillery anywhere on the line, the sound of musketry was one solid, savage, "crash," "crash," "crash," without the slightest lull, extending along a line over two miles in length. Suddenly, the cannoneers saw Federal infantry emerge from the woods; it was the Iron Brigade:

> The deafening crashes and yelling continued and suddenly our infantry, the old Iron Brigade, came pell-mell out of the woods, a little to the left of our front in some confusion. . . . They had not been broken by the enemy, but their formation had been destroyed by the density of the thickets where they fought. . . . the narrow clearing was full of Cutler's disordered infantry, so we stood at a ready, pieces sighted and lanyards in hand for several minutes, expecting to see the enemy's line emerge from the brush. . . . The Johnnies . . . instead of charging, as we expected them to do, lay down in the edge of the brush and began sharpshooting at us and [at] our rallying infantry. To this we instantly replied with canister [and] they did not seriously follow our broken infantry beyond the edge of the brush.[140]

Finally arriving at Meade's and Grant's headquarters near the Wilderness crossroads, Meade ordered Cutler to report to Hancock, and so notified Warren of the change in command.[141] Upon receiving final confirmation that Wadsworth had indeed fallen in battle, Cutler assumed command of Wadsworth's division. This, in spite of the fact that most of Wadsworth's division were dead, wounded, or scattered throughout the area enclosed on the south by the Orange Plank Road and on the east by the Brock Road. All that Cutler could muster under his command were a total of 1,269 men: 529 survivors of Rice's and Stone's brigades and 740 men of the Iron Brigade.[142]

Cutler immediately set about reorganizing his Iron Brigade survivors and the remainder of Wadsworth's shattered division in the clearing around the Wilderness Tavern. Although the men soon replenished their ammunition and "stood ready for any duty which may be assigned them," no orders were forthcoming and they soon set about digging earthworks and constructing log breastworks.[143] As the afternoon wore on and darkness fell, the exhausted men cooked coffee, took out their blankets and lay down on the ground to sleep.[144]

The men of Stewart's Battery B continued their vigil on the knoll at Lacy's clearing throughout the afternoon and evening hours. In the late afternoon they saw that the woods on the southern edge of the clearing were on fire and became increasingly apprehensive about their Iron Brigade comrades who might be lying wounded and helpless in the brush. At dusk, the cannoneers saw flashing volleys of musketry light the sky like heat lightning on a summer night. Finally, Battery B limbered up and fell back to the Germanna Road for its own bivouac. They had held their position on the Lacy knoll for most of the battle and had sustained only light casualties, four men slightly hit by spent balls and none of them listed as wounded.[145]

As his men slept, Cutler became increasingly concerned about talk back at Meade's headquarters which seemed to imply that he and his brigade, after becoming separated from the rest of Wadsworth's division, had avoided getting back into the fight. Earlier in the afternoon Cutler had, of course, replenished his ammunition and readied his troops for immediate action, but the battle was waged by other Federal corps farther to the south, and Wadsworth's division—and the Iron Brigade—were not called upon for further duty that day.

After a good night's rest, Cutler's men and their comrades in Battery B got up at sunrise on Saturday morning, May 7, cleaned their weapons, washed the black powder from their faces, and cooked breakfast. When they had finished their meal, they were ordered to pack up, move to the right, and occupy the rifle pits and log breastworks that members of the brigade had constructed just two days before. As the Western men moved into line, they learned that General Cutler had been promoted to command of Warren's Fourth Division. Colonel William Robinson of the Seventh Wisconsin had (again) taken over for Cutler as commander of the Iron Brigade.[146]

As the morning of May 7 wore on, the new divisional commander's agitation was such that he wrote out and submitted a formal report to Warren. As Cutler put it, the purpose of the report was "to prevent any misapprehension as to why I came out of the woods yesterday morning." Cutler wrote:

> When they broke the men started back on the route we went in. I and all my staff commenced rallying them, but they were within half a mile of here [i.e., the Wilderness Tavern crossroads] before I got anything like order restored. I despatched [*sic*] two staff officers to find General Wadsworth and take his orders; they both ran into the rebel skirmishers. I at the same time saw the division flag with horsemen and men rallying around it, and moved to it, supposing it was division head-quarters. I moved to it and found only two of [Wadsworth's] aides with his orderlies. I immediately went to your head-quarters for instruction. I could have moved the men I had rallied on the Plank Road, and should have done so but for the above-stated facts. I was very much mortified at finding myself separated from the column, and feared that there might be some misapprehension about it.[147]

As the Western men sat in their rifle pits during the afternoon and evening hours of May 7, they could hear loud cheering from unseen Confederate forces to the south and southwest which seemed to run up and down the rebel lines for nearly half an hour. Not knowing what prompted the cheering, they nevertheless responded with loud yells of their own.[148] At 8:00 on Saturday evening, May 7, Stewart's Battery B and the Iron Brigade regiments—their survivors, at least—fell into line and moved out with Warren's Fifth Corps, heading south along the Brock Road toward Todd's Tavern some thirteen miles down the road near the Spotsylvania County courthouse. The night was very dark.[149]

The battle of the Wilderness was the first trial of strength between Robert E. Lee and Ulysses S. Grant, and preceded almost forty days of unremitting warfare. Even Grant, new to the Eastern theater of war, noted that "More desperate fighting has not been witnessed on this continent than that of the Fifth and Sixth of May."[150] The casualty figures in Cutler's division told a grim story, not only of the killed and wounded, but of the many who literally disappeared in the fire of battle. One of the Black Hats wrote home: "Many of my comrades are laying cold and ghastly corpses unburied & unmarked."[151]

Many Iron Brigade wounded were forced to endure a harrowing wagon ride to the hospital in Fredericksburg, Virginia.[152] Jim Whitty and Mark Smith, after initial tending by Confederate surgeons and amputation of a leg each, were sent bouncing along in an ambulance wagon driven by a careless orderly. One of the boys grabbed the driver and threw him in the back, the other took over the reins, and the "one-legged brigade" continued toward Fredericksburg at a slower and more careful pace. From Fredericksburg, some of the Western men were transferred to other hospitals. From his bed in a Philadelphia hospital, Hugh Perkins of the Seventh Wisconsin wrote to assure friends of his speedy recovery and described the hard fight on the fifth of May: "It was a hot place, I can tell you, but we all done our best and drove the rebels about three miles through the thickest woods you ever saw." He noted with grudging admiration, "The recruits fought like tigers."[153]

John Kellogg, who had disappeared in the skirmishers' fight on the first morning of the battle, was initially presumed dead, but like so many others, he was captured and sent south to Confederate prison.[154] However, unlike many who died in the terrible prison camps, Kellogg escaped. He returned to command the Iron Brigade at the close of the war.

Fifteen years after his disappearance in the Wilderness, the suffering family of Major Phil Plummer wrote to former Iron Brigade commander John Gibbon for help in determining where and how their son and brother had died. Gibbon, in turn, wrote a poignant letter to the editors of the *Milwaukee Sunday Telegraph* asking readers to provide information about Plummer's fate: "He is supposed to have been killed May 4, 1864 in the [W]ilderness, and his friends have heard nothing of him since, not even positively that he was killed." Gibbon's inquiry was answered one week later by none other than General (then Colonel) Bragg, Plummer's regimental commander. Although Bragg said he did not actually see Plummer fall, his testimony ended any real hope the family cherished that their lost son had somehow survived the battle. Like so many others, the body of Major Phil Plummer had simply disappeared in the inferno of the Wilderness.[155]

Earl Rogers finally located his "straggling diamond" in a Federal field hospital. Walking down the rows of wounded men, Rogers called repeatedly for "Pete Markle of Coon Slough" until finally he heard a weak voice from one of the cots answer back: "Aye, aye, sir." The surgeons had amputated

Pete's gangrene-infected leg and when Rogers shook the boy's fevered hands, he saw death "stamped in his pallid features." Years later, Rogers still remembered the "boy hero" and wrote fondly of the teenager who had gained renown as the best "straggler" in the Iron Brigade.[156]

The officers of Cutler's brigade also suffered significant casualties in the Wilderness.[157] Colonel Henry Morrow of the Twenty-fourth Michigan sustained a severe wound which temporarily disabled him from command, and it would be November before he rejoined his regiment. Lt. Colonel John Mansfield of the Second Wisconsin was wounded and temporarily taken prisoner. After his return in August of 1864, he was mustered out of the army. Colonel Ira Grover of the Seventh Indiana was wounded and missing in action. Colonel Samuel Williams of the Nineteenth Indiana was also killed. Major John Lindley of the Nineteenth reported that "While bravely leading his regiment against the enemies of his country [Williams] was struck in the breast by a cannon ball and instantly killed."[158]

But perhaps the Iron Brigade's most painful loss in the aftermath of the Wilderness campaign was that of the Second Wisconsin. The regiment, now greatly reduced in size and its officers killed (or missing) in the Wilderness, was formally detached on May 11 from the Iron Brigade and transformed into the provost guard for Cutler's Fourth Division under the command of Captain George H. Otis. At the war's onset, the Second Wisconsin had been the first of the Federal "three year regiments" to reach Washington, and thereafter had anchored the Iron Brigade with its unsurpassed record of courage, combat skill, and sacrifice. Without the men of the "Ragged Ass Second," the Iron Brigade would never again be the same.[159]

This strange and savage battle in the Virginia Wilderness marked the beginning of the end of the Civil War. When Grant led the Army of the Potomac south toward Spotsylvania on the night of May 7, the Iron Brigade knew they were inextricably part of a new kind of war—there would be no turning back from now on. The Western men had lost much at Gettysburg and still more in the Wilderness, but had sustained their proud record in spite of the transformation and travail they had undergone. New men, not all of them "Western," would carry the brigade forward to the end. And for those men of the Iron Brigade, the final and most terrible campaign in this "carnival of blood" had only just begun.[160]

The Iron Brigade Battery

An Irregular Regular Battery

SILAS FELTON

Unlike the infantry regiments of the Iron Brigade, Battery B of the Fourth U.S. Artillery, so closely associated with that brigade during the Civil War, had a long history as a regular army battery.[1] Battery B had been established as one of thirty-six companies, divided equally into four regiments, in the artillery reorganization of 1821. Only four of these companies were designated as "field" or "light" artillery to be equipped with horses.[2] Battery B was one of these, but received horses only periodically when need justified the expense. In this period there was little need for artillery, so in the Seminole War Battery B parked its guns and fought as dragoons. After a period of training and action as infantry, the soldiers served with distinction in their normal role at Monterrey and Buena Vista during the war with Mexico. At Buena Vista the battery for the first time supported Midwestern infantry regiments, a factor that set the precedent for an easy natural alliance when Brigadier General John Gibbon called for volunteers to fill battery vacancies in 1861 and 1862. With the end of the hostilities with Mexico, Battery B moved to Fort Brown, Texas, where the two leaders who most influenced the character of the organization entered the picture: Captain John Gibbon as battery commander, and James Stewart as a recruit. Gibbon is well known through his memoirs, so there is no need to dwell on him here. James Stewart, on the other hand, is a virtual unknown who needs more definition.

By design or omission James Stewart left little direct information. His writings consisted of letters to the editor of the *National Tribune* concerning Augustus C. Buell's series of articles called *The Cannoneer*, later appended to the book version, and two presentations to the Ohio Commandery of the Military Order of the Loyal Legion of the United States. The first was an

James Stewart, Battery B, Fourth United States Artillery. Frontispiece engraving from *The Cannoneer: Recollections of Service in the Army of the Potomac*, Augustus C. Buell (Washington: *The National Tribune*, 1890).

article on Battery B's role at Gettysburg and the second on the Utah Expedition. Neither tells much about him, but both reinforce his brevity and modesty in presenting his point. Heitman's *Historical Register and Dictionary of the United States Army* contains the normal brief summary given to all regular army officers. Gibbon and Buell describe some of his military achievements, and both hold him in high regard, as do the many others that mention him in reports and correspondence. But again, this covers only the military portion of his life.

The major source on Stewart is a slim *In Memoriam* volume issued by the Ohio Commandery after his death in 1905. From that volume and his pension records it appears that James Stewart was born in Edinburgh, Scotland, on May 18, 1826. He was trained as a printer in Leith, Scotland, and emigrated to the United States in 1844. There is no information on his occupation from then until he enlisted as a private in the army on October 29, 1851, or what circumstances led him to that decision. His pension records describe him with brown hair, blue eyes, and 5 feet 6½ inches tall. Existing photographs and sketches show him as short and stocky, a fireplug of a man. Stewart prospered in his new occupation, rising rapidly through corporal, sergeant, and first sergeant, and then commissioned, as chronicled later here, in an era when promotions in the peacetime army were extremely slow. His promotion to first sergeant certainly speaks well of his organizational ability and his superiors' respect for his abilities.

On the eve of the battle of Gettysburg he carefully attended to the completion of the bimonthly muster roll, and long after most batteries had discarded their artillery sabers, Stewart hauled Battery B's along in the battery wagons, inventorying them monthly. From the various comments about him, he seems to have been fond of battle, either one-on-one, or in the maelstrom of war. He also seems to have been fond of alcoholic spirits, but never to the detriment of his duties. A strict disciplinarian, he set the same high standard for himself and his men, and for this was respected throughout all levels of the military organization. One of the anecdotes of Stewart's discipline involved Private John H. Cook of the Sixth Wisconsin, called the "tough one."[3] Cook made a habit of run-ins with the authorities in the Sixth, and volunteered for Battery B in order to get away from their oppressive rule. However, things didn't improve in Battery B. One evening Cook and some of his friends shared a sutler's whiskey, became rather loud, and were warned to calm down before there was trouble. Cook's version had him already in his tent when someone dragged him outside. He said the next thing he was aware of was Lieutenant Stewart lying on the ground in front of him. Cook spent time tied over the spare wheel on a limber for that indiscretion, despite several attempted or actual escapes. The "tough one" says that he shivered every time Stewart came near.[4] But overall, Stewart used punishment sparingly, and commanded through respect rather than fear.

After the Civil War, Stewart served with the Eighteenth Infantry until his retirement on March 20, 1879. He lived in the Cincinnati area at Fort Thomas, Kentucky, and was active in the Ohio Military Order of the Loyal Legion of the United States (MOLLUS) and the Iron Brigade Association until his death on April 19, 1905. His comrades in the Ohio MOLLUS termed him "ever gentle, genial, lovable," and concluded their *In Memoriam* with "None knew him but to love him, Nor named him but to praise." He was buried in Arlington Cemetery on Easter Sunday, April 23. His tombstone there, much larger and more elaborate than the normal government stone, was provided by the Iron Brigade Association. Although retired as a captain, he had been breveted a major for action at the Weldon Railroad, and was promoted to major in retirement by an act of Congress. Now back to our story of Battery B.[5]

After the Mexican War, there was little need for artillery in Texas and, once again, Battery B served as cavalry ordered to deal with the local Indians. In 1857, while under the command of Captain John Gibbon, it marched via Fort Leavenworth to join Brevet Brigadier General Albert Sidney Johnston's forces at Camp Floyd, Utah Territory (later Fort Crittenden) for the Mormon War. With an uneasy truce in place, Battery B once again parked its artillery and became cavalry in order to guard the Pony Express route.[6] It was from the Pony Express riders that the men of Battery B received news of the fall of Fort Sumter and the start of war. When General George B. McClellan stripped the frontier of regular army units to beef up his newly formed army in the East, Battery B received its marching orders.[7] The men assisted in burning the military stores that they could not transport and then marched east on July 27, 1861. Before they left Utah, a Pony Express rider found them with news of the battle at Manassas (First Bull Run). Thoughts of "Will we make it back in time for the war?" turned to "Will there be a government left to fight for when we get there?"[8]

In that era, there was a great chasm between the top and bottom strata of the regular army. Many of the officers were West Point graduates, well educated, and often from "fine" families. They looked askance at non–West Pointers. On the other hand, the recruits were often individuals who did not fit well elsewhere in society, unlike what would later be called the "best and the brightest." As a result, the army was rigidly rule-structured, with a harsh discipline to uphold and reinforce that structure. The chief enforcer, as well as intermediary between officers and enlisted men, was the first sergeant, promoted to that post on ability rather than longevity.[9] By this time, James Stewart was first sergeant of Battery B, thus the disciplinarian for the unit. His discipline was not perfect, however, because six of his enlisted men deserted between Camp Floyd and Maryland, either to return to the South to fight for their native states or because they decided that they had not joined the army to fight a war.[10]

Battery B reached Fort Leavenworth on October 6 and departed by rail two days later for the reserve artillery camp at Camp Duncan in the District of Columbia. They arrived on October 19 and later went to Camp DuPont. The battery was, by this time, down to one officer and fifty-five enlisted men available for duty.[11] Gibbon was soon appointed chief of artillery for General Irvin McDowell's division, with responsibility for training and equipping Battery B as well as three volunteer batteries. Gibbon continued to hold the captain's billet in the battery, effectively blocking promotion of anyone else to that position throughout the war. In the meantime, the battery was commanded by a series of first lieutenants, none of whom lasted more than six months. As a start to stability, James Stewart, "the best first sergeant" Gibbon ever saw, was promoted to second lieutenant, and First Lieutenant Joseph B. Campbell was attached to the battery.[12]

The battery had been issued six light twelve-pounders (Napoleons) with a complete equipment issue, and 112 horses for full field mobility. By the November-December 1861 muster, the battery was reduced to three lieutenants and forty-seven enlisted men available for duty. At Gibbon's request, the artillery issued an appeal for volunteer replacements from the infantry ranks. Included was the gentle hint that Battery B was the battery that served with their fathers and brothers in Mexico. The response more than filled Gibbon's expectations, for apparently the volunteers had learned quickly that slogging through the mud was not much fun and riding was better, even if it was on a limber. In all, Battery B accepted ninety-one volunteers from the Second, Sixth, and Seventh Wisconsin, the Nineteenth Indiana, and the Twenty-third and Thirty-fifth New York Regiments. That number would increase over the next two years as the number of regulars steadily declined until the battery consisted of two regular officers, three noncommissioned officers, and five privates.[13]

The first seven months following the battery's arrival in the East consisted of more training and duty at Falmouth and Fredericksburg, Virginia. Significant changes in the battery's leadership included promotion of John Gibbon to brigadier general of volunteers and his assignment as commander of King's brigade; the end to the rotation of lieutenants in the battery; and the assignment to command of First Lieutenant Joseph Campbell. This period was a new learning experience for Gibbon and the old regulars. They found that their newly attached volunteers were intelligent and picked up the details of their duties and responsibilities quickly and easily. However, the regulars also learned that the volunteers had a much more informal and relaxed view of discipline. The result of the learning experience seems to have produced a well-disciplined unit that trusted its leaders, especially Lieutenant Stewart, without the blind obedience of the regular army, but retained the free-thinking flexibility to quickly adapt to any situation.[14]

In August, the battery's action started in the Virginia campaign. After skirmishing at Sulphur Springs, the battery's first real test came at Brawner Farm on August 28 and at Second Manassas on the 30th. Although they were heavily engaged in supporting Gibbon's infantry, the battery fought at a distance, and losses were light (three wounded with one of those severe, one missing, and twelve horses killed)—not yet a test of the leadership and mettle of Battery B. All that would change within a month in the Maryland campaign, first in support of Gibbon at South Mountain, and then three days later at Antietam.

At South Mountain, a section under Lieutenant Stewart moved forward with the advancing infantry, effectively countering a Confederate battery, dispersing enemy infantry, and driving sharpshooters from a house with a direct hit. The remainder of the battery later joined Stewart's section and remained in action until the fight ended after dark. Stewart lists no loss from that fight.[15] That would not hold true at Antietam.

At Antietam, the battery would again support Gibbon and his brigade. There Gibbon himself positioned the guns, with the number three gun on the Hagerstown Pike and the other five spaced across the Miller farmyard, facing southeast into Miller's cornfield. The position was far from ideal for artillery, for the fields sloped gently upward in their front, then dropped off more steeply, so that the advancing enemy did not come into full view until they were within 100 yards. The view was further blocked by the mature corn in the field in front, cover that hid enemy riflemen as they fired at the battery's men and horses. In addition to personally assisting in siting the guns Gibbon remained near the battery, perhaps recognizing this as a critical position or possibly because he was still an artilleryman at heart. For whatever reason, his presence in the eye of the storm certainly provided the artillery and infantry around him with the confidence necessary to hold the position. Gibbon would become much more involved than that.

When he saw that the gun on the pike, firing left into the cornfield, as a result of recoil and vibration was firing over its target, Gibbon rode to the gun. Unable to make himself heard over the din, he dismounted and ran the elevating screw up so that the canister swept the ground in front. As the battered Iron Brigade drifted to the rear, Battery B became the rallying point for a fresh stand, this time at almost gun muzzle range of ten to fifteen yards. Gibbon then provided what was perhaps his most valuable leadership. Lieutenant Campbell had started to withdraw the battery's left section, fearing that they would be captured. This was misunderstood as a general movement to limber to the rear. Gibbon recognized that moving the battery would imperil the position, probably could not be successfully accomplished under fire, and might cause a collapse and rout. He stopped the movement and urged both artillery and infantry to increase their fire. The continued double canister, the increased fire from the remnants of the Iron Brigade, and the arrival of reinforcements from Brigadier General Abner Doubleday stemmed the tide, then drove the attackers back. In the lull that followed, both the Iron Brigade and their battery, badly battered, were withdrawn to reorganize.

The battery would continue to be engaged through the battle, but not again at close range. Stewart listed his losses in that short, fierce fight as ten killed, twenty-nine wounded, twenty-six horses killed, and seven wounded. The killed included three regulars, one of whom was Sergeant Joseph Herzog, wounded through the leg, who committed suicide to end his suffering; four from Wisconsin and Indiana; and three from New York. Lieutenant Campbell was so severely wounded that he transferred to staff duty and did not return to field service. This moved Lieutenant Stewart into battery command, a position he retained, with the sponsorship and support of Gibbon, until late in the war despite his junior rank.[16]

By this time, only a core group of eight noncommissioned officers and eight privates remained from the regular army. The rest of the battery were attached volunteer infantrymen. But that core provided the discipline and pride that glued the unit together.

The respite after Antietam was short. In November, the battery moved to Brooks Station, and from there to the Fredericksburg campaign. There Battery B crossed the Rappahannock River below the town, again with the Iron Brigade. Although the battery did not play a significant part in the fight, it engaged in a fierce artillery duel with a Confederate battery, blowing up one caisson and disabling a gun. The battery then formed an advanced artillery picket within 200 yards of the enemy pickets, protecting the withdrawing troops. It finally withdrew from under the noses of the Confederate pickets as one of the last units across the river the night of December 15.[17] Losses were light: two men killed, six wounded, eight horses killed, four wounded and subsequently abandoned, and one wounded slightly. The battery then added an additional lieutenant, James Davison, attached from the Third U.S. Artillery to replace Lieutenant Campbell. Stewart remained in command, as Davison was the junior officer.

With the end of the Fredericksburg campaign, Battery B went into winter quarters. Knowing that he would lose his New York attached volunteers in April, due to expiration of their two-year enlistment, Stewart chose to release them early and called for replacements from the Iron Brigade. Once again the Iron Brigade regiments responded generously, even though by this time Battery B was gaining a reputation as "Bloody B." The battery was now composed of 90 percent volunteers from the Second, Sixth, and Seventh Wisconsin, the Nineteenth Indiana, and the Twenty-fourth Michigan, a new regiment that joined the brigade on the eve of Fredericksburg. It was truly the "Iron Brigade Battery." Stewart spent the winter training the new members, replacing horses, and repairing equipment for the fighting to come when the weather and roads improved.[18]

Battery B, along with most of the First Corps artillery played little part at Chancellorsville. They skirmished on the extreme left and right, but were not heavily engaged. Their losses were again light, two wounded, one of whom died of his wounds. Then after sparring and waiting, the battery moved northward to Gettysburg by steps through camps at White Oak Church, Centreville, Catlett's Station, Thornton Station, Edwards Ferry, Middletown, and Emmitsburg.

In battle, great events often mean offering an organization as sacrifice for the good of the army. Battery B was on their way to their second great event of the war, and another severe test of its leadership.

July 1, 1863, found Battery B camped north of Emmitsburg, Maryland, about two miles over the Pennsylvania border, where Marsh Creek crosses the Emmitsburg Road, approximately 6½ miles from Gettysburg. That morning, they followed Brigadier General James S. Wadsworth's First Division, First Corps, marching with General Abner Doubleday's Third Division, First Corps. The sounds of the building battle reached the men of Battery B as they marched northward. When they reached Gettysburg, they were turned west, into a position just south of the Lutheran Theological Seminary. In about an hour, at General Wadsworth's request, Colonel Charles S. Wainwright, chief of First Corps Artillery, repositioned Battery B to the railroad cut in Oak Ridge (the northern extension of Seminary Ridge), at the hinge between the First and Second Divisions of First Corps. Lieutenant Stewart split the battery and put three guns on each side of the cut with about a 75-to-100-yard gap between them. Stewart commanded the three guns on the right, Lieutenant Davison the three on the left, positioned between the railroad cut and the Chambersburg Road. Both were on the front of the slope and had open fields of fire to the west, even though there was a young orchard in front of Davison. Because of the rolling terrain, they also had a clear view of approaching Confederate troops as far away as Belmont School Road, over a mile, as they crested the intervening ridges. This gave opportunity for harassment with case shot as the Confederate reinforcements moved forward.

Stewart's half battery came into action first against the right flank of Major General Robert E. Rodes's forces attacking from Oak Hill. This drew return fire from the Confederate batteries, particularly the one on Oak Hill, although the woods to the north provided some cover. The left half battery, with Union troops directly in front, remained spectators for the most part, until the Union forces fell back to the Seminary Ridge line, clearing the field of fire. By the luck of positioning, the Sixth Wisconsin Infantry, although heavily used and reduced to a handful in the earlier action at the railroad cut, occupied the crest of the ridge behind Stewart's half battery. The 143rd Pennsylvania regiment of Colonel Roy Stone's Pennsylvania brigade supported Davison's half battery. A mixture of First (Iron Brigade) and Third (Stone's) Division troops, supported a section of Lieutenant Benjamin W. Wilber's Battery L, First New York, and Captain Greenleaf T. Stevens's Fifth Maine Battery. The remaining serviceable guns of Captain James Cooper's Battery B, First Pennsylvania, prolonged the line south to the Seminary. For the first time that day, the First Corps line had a position with strong defensive artillery support, eighteen guns in a line about 300 to 400 yards long.

The interlude ended between 3 and 4 o'clock. Brigadier General Alfred M. Scales's brigade of Major General William Dorsey Pender's division passed over the lines of Major General Henry Heth's division, crested the cover of McPherson's Ridge, and charged forward. They were fresh troops, the Thirty-eighth, Thirteenth, Thirty-fourth, Twenty-second, and Sixteenth North Carolina Regiments arrayed from their left to right. To Scales's right, beyond the seminary, were Colonel Abner Perrin's South Carolinians. Although all of Scales's brigade started their approach south of Chambersburg Road, the angle of the road and their forces to the south pushed the Thirty-eighth North Carolina into the area between the north edge of the road and the railroad cut, directly in front of Lieutenant Davison's half battery.

Scales's Brigade, although fresh, now faced concentrated artillery and rifle fire. Stewart picked at their left flank with canister as Rodes's threat had temporarily abated. With the independence of action that occurred in a well-trained and confident unit, Lieutenant Davison swung his half battery ninety degrees left, firing double canister down the length of the swale between McPherson's Ridge and Seminary Ridge, directly into the flank of the Thirteenth North Carolina and, at a greater distance, the remainder of the right and center of Scales's brigade. While canister from the front is extremely effective, by firing the length of Scales's line, Davison multiplied the chance that each ball would find one or more targets, and therefore, multiplied the destructive effect of each discharge. This move, however, exposed Davison's right flank to the fire of the Thirty-eighth North Carolina, which took a heavy toll among the cannoneers, including Davison. First Sergeant John Mitchell then took command of the left half battery.

Scales's attack was stopped with fearful destruction. The brigade lost almost all its officers, and one-third of its force was killed, wounded, or missing. However, new Confederate lines quickly moved forward, overlapping the Union left, and overrunning the Union right (Eleventh Corps) making the position untenable. Colonel Wainwright's instructions to Lieutenant Stewart were to hold the position at all cost. The troops around him got the order to withdraw and consolidate on Cemetery Ridge, just south of the town. Somehow, in the confusion, Stewart did not receive the order. Only when he saw that the supporting forces on either side were gone, and when his half battery was in danger of capture, did he, accompanied by the Sixth Wisconsin, limber to the rear across the boulders of the unfinished railroad cut and into town, leaving the dead and wounded behind. At this point, Stewart had lost contact with the left half battery. He thought that they were still in the position he had assigned, so he rode back to attempt to remove them. He found them already gone, but was injured by a shell fragment and nearly captured, before escaping across field and fence back into town. The Sixth Wisconsin's claim that day, in addition to all the glory of the charge on the railroad cut, was that they, with Battery B, were the last to leave the field. The toll for the latter moments of glory was four enlisted killed and two officers and twenty-six enlisted wounded.

Major General Winfield S. Hancock personally selected the battery's next position, astride the Baltimore Pike on Cemetery Ridge. The battery had only four effective guns remaining, and barely enough men to handle them. In this condition, Battery B participated in the battle the next two days, in a more traditional role of counterbattery, and the repulse of Major General Jubal Early's evening attack on July 2, but without a repeat of the close combat or destructive results of July 1. The toll was only two additional wounded for July 2 and 3.[19]

The remainder of 1863 was spent marching and waiting in Maryland and Virginia. Although involved in both the Bristoe Station and Mine Run campaigns, the battery was not heavily involved. The big events for the battery were the promotion of Stewart to first lieutenant on September 15, and First Sergeant John Mitchell's appointment as second lieutenant on August 15 to replace Lieutenant Davison. Battery B was now under the command of its two former first sergeants.

Battery B spent the winter at Culpeper, Virginia. For the first time since it entered the war, the battery received regular army recruits in January of 1864. Fifty-one of them came direct from the recruiting depot. Once again it was training time. The veteran noncommissioned officer core plus an experienced set of attached volunteers reduced the task to a manageable size, but the desertion rate of the new recruits indicates that they were not of the quality of the volunteers. At the same time, the battery started releasing the veteran volunteers back to their regiments. By the start of the summer campaign in May of 1864, the battery was down to about sixty of these soldiers, mostly from the Seventh Wisconsin and the Twenty-fourth Michigan, many of these men near the end of their three-year enlistments. By the close of August, all the Iron Brigade cannoneers would be gone, either mustered out or returned to their regiments. Among the latter, several were to die as infantrymen in the Wilderness and subsequent campaigns.[20]

However, before the last Iron Brigadiers departed the battery, Battery B demonstrated once more that it had something special in discipline and ability. Together, the battery, the Iron Brigade, and the remaining units of the First Corps were transferred to the newly consolidated Fifth Corps. Battery B entered the Wilderness campaign supporting General James Wadsworth's Fourth Division of the reorganized Fifth Corps, which now also included the Iron Brigade. Because of the brush and terrain, the battery played a limited part in the Wilderness. The most significant action came in covering Wadsworth's left flank when the rebels attacked through the gap between the divisions of Wadsworth and Brigadier General Samuel W. Crawford.

Three days later, the battery was in the vanguard of the Fifth Corps as it approached Spottsylvania Courthouse. After a failed attack by Brigadier General John C. Robinson's Second Division, Battery B and Capt. Augustus P. Martin's batteries were positioned to soften up the opposing positions. Initially the duel was between artillery and infantry, but after about an hour, an enemy battery opened from behind the cover of a knoll and prepared works. For the first time since Fredericksburg, Battery B had the opportunity to practice the artillerist's art of indirect fire. In this case, they timed their fuses and skimmed the projectiles off the top of the knoll so that the shells would explode over the opposing battery. Unfortunately for Battery B, the enemy battery was also practicing the exact same thing very effectively. Although Battery B silenced the enemy battery in a short time, it lost four killed and three wounded, all by artillery fire.[21]

All of the Fifth Corps batteries were at this time consolidated with those of First Corps and reduced to four guns. Then came a time of marching, maneuvering with some limited action, until Bethesda Church. There, on the afternoon of June 2, Battery B took position on the Mechanicsville Pike and engaged in a short-range canister fight with an enemy battery, silencing it in a short time. This third test of the battery's mettle came in a setting that required supreme confidence in ability and leadership, a great amount of audacity, and perhaps a fair amount of insanity.

On that afternoon, Battery B was temporarily assigned to Brigadier General Charles Griffin's First Division of the Fifth Corps. Griffin's position spread in a quarter circle south of Bethesda Church, astride the Mechanicsville Road. Brigadier General Romeyn B. Ayres's First Brigade was being harassed from in front by Confederate artillery fire, a battery well placed in the edge of a woods in advance of the enemy lines. General Griffin that day was "interfering with the artillery operations and making numerous suggestions for putting artillery in exposed positions," so much so that Colonel Wainwright seems to have been avoiding Griffin in order to protect the artillery. Griffin had apparently had enough of the enemy artillery's harassment. He asked Lieutenant Stewart (and for a regular army officer, that probably translated as an order) if he could take position in front of the Union lines and silence the battery. Stewart ordered the battery forward down the Mechanicsville Pike at a gallop, and went into battery with one section on either side of the pike, at a range of about 1,200 yards. The great danger in this move was that Battery B was approaching a battery already in action, and as Battery B moved, it was vulnerable to the latter's fire, as well as to the sharpshooting that such a move was sure to attract. A single round of artillery fire into the lead team would have piled the battery in a heap of dead horses, cannoneers, and demolished guns. A few well-placed rifle shots into the battery horses could have done the same. Luck held, however, and the Federals went into battery, immediately firing a combination of case and canister, and in a few minutes, the return fire ceased. When the smoke cleared, it was apparent that the enemy battery was badly damaged and abandoned. One infantryman termed it "The grandest thing he saw in the war." Stewart, in a rather laconic, understated report, says simply: "During the Afternoon, I was ordered to place one section on Mechanicsville Pike, the other on the right of it. The battery scarcely being in position before the enemy opened upon us with canister. We replied, and in a short time firing ceased on the part of the enemy. After dark the battery was withdrawn and placed in position to the right and in front of Bethesda Church." Stewart's losses that day were amazingly light: just one man wounded.

The following day, the three batteries attached to the First Division advanced alternately, again to clear the enemy artillery from their front. Although firing at longer range, the results were more costly to Battery B, one killed and four wounded.[22]

The remainder of the campaign of 1864 involved more artillery duels at long range, first at Cold Harbor, then in the fortifications around Petersburg. By the end of the July-August muster period, all of the battery's Iron Brigade volunteers were gone, either back to their regiments, or mustered out at expiration of their terms of service. Concurrently, the battery received eighty-seven additional recruits in August.[23]

After once again training almost an entirely new battery, Lieutenant Stewart was transferred to Battery A, Fourth U. S. Artillery, which had an open captain's billet, and on December 26, 1864, he was promoted to the captaincy he so richly deserved. Command of Battery B went to Lieutenant Mitchell, and Second Lieutenant Joseph P. Vose was attached to the battery as an additional officer. The battery ably assisted the Fifth Corps in the pursuit of Lee's Army toward Appomattox Court House, fighting at Boydton Road, Gravelly Run (where Mitchell was seriously wounded just ten days before the end, a wound that led to his death three years later), White Oak Road, and Five Forks. The battery was present and waiting at Appomattox. Stewart returned to command Battery B by special order on April 5 to honor his service with the battery.

Even though Battery B was a "Regular Battery," it is apparent that for the critical middle period of the war, the majority of its members were really attached volunteers, many of them Iron Brigade men. In addition, from the time Battery B joined McDowell's division through its service with the First Corps and until its final months with the Fifth Corps, the battery and the Iron Brigade were never far apart and usually fought together. They maintained a loose informal association that, in the heat of battle, temporarily filled shortages in the artillery ranks with infantrymen who stepped forward only for the needed moments then faded back into their regiments. The infantrymen took as much pride in the fact that they never lost a gun as the artillerymen, and rightfully so, as they provided the battery's support. The bond is probably best expressed on James Stewart's tombstone. Although Stewart was a regular army officer through and through, his tombstone was purchased and placed by the Iron Brigade Association. At its top the stone has the traditional Iron Brigade Cross, but in the center circle it is inscribed with "BAT. B, FOURTH ART. IRON BRIGADE."

Table 1. Iron Brigade Men Carried On Muster Rolls Of Battery B, Fourth U. S. Artillery

Name	Unit	Dates of Service in Battery B	Comments
Ackerman, Daniel	Seventh Wisconsin	Sep 1862 to Jun 1864	Wounded at Gettysburg, Returned in March 1864
Anderson, John R.	Nineteenth Indiana	May 1862 to Sep 1862	Killed at Antietam
Anderson, Joseph A	Nineteenth Indiana	Nov 1861 to Aug 1863	
Armstrong, Edgar B.	Sixth Wisconsin	Nov 1861 to Jun 1864	
Armstrong, James S.	Sixth Wisconsin	Nov 1861 to Dec 1862	
Bach, Theodore	Twenty-fourth Michigan	Jan 1863 to Jun 1864	Wounded at Gettysburg
Balch, William L.	Nineteenth Indiana	Mar 1862 to Oct 1863	Note A
Barber, Frederick	Seventh Wisconsin	Jan 1863 to Oct 1863	Note G
Barhydt, George W.	Seventh Wisconsin	Jan 1863 to Feb 1864	Note G
Barney, James L.	Sixth Wisconsin	Sep 1862 to Dec 1863	
Bartholomew, William	Second Wisconsin	Nov 1861 to Apr 1864	
Batman, Peter	Twenty-fourth Michigan	Jan 1863 to Jun 1864	
Beecham, Henry	Seventh Wisconsin	Sep 1862 to Jun 1864	Wounded at Bethesda Church

Name	Unit	Dates of Service in Battery B	Comments
Bell, Francis	Sixth Wisconsin	Sep 1862 to Dec 1863	
Bishop, Andrew	Seventh Wisconsin	Nov 1861 to Dec 1863	Note G
Black, James	Seventh Wisconsin	Jan 1863 to Jun 1863	
Blackley, Lyman W.	Twenty-fourth Michigan	Jan 1863 to Jun 1864	
Blain, Daniel	Nineteenth Indiana	Sep 1862 to Feb 1864	Wounded at Gettysburg, DNR
Blair, Francis P.	Seventh Wisconsin	May 1862 to Jun 1864	Note G
Branham, Benjamin F.	Seventh Wisconsin	Nov 1861 to Dec 1863	Note G
Briggs, Jonathan	Twenty-fourth Michigan	Jan 1863 to Feb 1864	
Brown, Henry	Twenty-fourth Michigan	Jan 1863 to Jun 1864	
Brunt, Andrew J.	Seventh Wisconsin	Nov 1861 to Oct 1863	Note H
Burdick, Amos G.	Second Wisconsin	May 1862 to Apr 1863	Wounded at Antietam, DNR
Burghart, Henry	Second Wisconsin	Nov 1861 to Apr 1864	
Cardy, J. Henry	Sixth Wisconsin	Nov 1861 to Jun 1863	
Casper, Peter	Nineteenth Indiana	Nov 1861 to Oct 1863	Note A, Wounded at Gettysburg
Childs, Harvey H.	Sixth Wisconsin	May 1862 to Feb 1863	
Childs, Henry L.	Sixth Wisconsin	Nov 1861 to Dec 1863	
Clark, Thomas M.	Second Wisconsin	May 1862 to Apr 1864	Wounded at Antietam
Coady, William J.	Nineteenth Indiana	Nov 1861 to Aug 1863	
Colby, Henry M.	Sixth Wisconsin	Nov 1861 to Apr 1863	Wounded at Antietam, DNR
Collins, Alphonso D. L.	Seventh Wisconsin	May 1862 to Jun 1864	Note G
Compton, John W.	Second Wisconsin	Nov 1861 to Oct 1863	Note B
Cook, John H	Sixth Wisconsin	Sep 1862 to Dec 1863	Wounded at Antietam
Coolly, Seymour W.	Sixth Wisconsin	Nov 1861 to Jun 1864	Wounded at Gettysburg
Crannels, George M.	Nineteenth Indiana	May 1862 to Feb 1863	Discharged for Disability
Dettloff, Ferdinand	Second Wisconsin	May 1863 to Jul 1864	
Dickerson, William	Nineteenth Indiana	Mar 1862 to Aug 1863	Wounded at Antietam, DNR
Dolphin, John	Seventh Wisconsin	Sep 1862 to Jun 1864	Note G
Dowling, Lawrence	Seventh Wisconsin	Nov 1861 to Jun 1864	Note G
Driggs, Job S.	Sixth Wisconsin	Sep 1862 to Dec 1863	
Dumond, David B.	Nineteenth Indiana	Sep 1862 to Oct 1863	Wounded at Gettysburg, Note A
Dunlap, Eben B.	Seventh Wisconsin	Nov 1861 to Oct 1863	Note G
Earl, William J.	Seventh Wisconsin	Nov 1861 to Aug 1863	Deserted on July 7, 1863
Eberts, Anthony	Twenty-fourth Michigan	Jan 1863 to Jun 1864	Wounded at Gettysburg
Ellis, Horace	Seventh Wisconsin	Jan 1863 to Oct 1863	Note G
Evans, Hugh	Seventh Wisconsin	Jan 1863 to Oct 1863	Note G
Fagan, Bartley	Second Wisconsin	Sep 1862 to Dec 1862	Killed in Action at Fredricksburg on December 17, 1862
Fillmore, John H.	Sixth Wisconsin	Nov 1861 to Dec 1863	Wounded at Antietam

Name	Unit	Dates of Service in Battery B	Comments
Finley, John	Sixth Wisconsin	Sep 1862 to Dec 1863	
Fort, Isaac	Sixth Wisconsin	Nov 1861 to Dec 1863	
Fort, Sylvester	Sixth Wisconsin	May 1862 to Oct 1863	Wounded at Antietam, DNR
Foster, Henry B.	Second Wisconsin	Nov 1861 to Apr 1864	
Franke, William	Twenty-fourth Michigan	Jan 1863 to May 1864	Killed in Action at Bethesda Church on May 30, 1864
Frazer, Philip	Seventh Wisconsin	Nov 1861 to Oct 1863	Note I
Freeman, Maitland J.	Seventh Wisconsin	Nov 1861 to Jun 1864	Note G
Fuller, Dennis M.	Sixth Wisconsin	Sep 1862 to Dec 1863	
Fulton, Charles S.	Seventh Wisconsin	Sep 1862 to Jun 1864	Wounded at Bethesda Church, Note G
Fulton, John H.	Seventh Wisconsin	Jul 1862 to Jun 1864	Wounded at Antietam, Note G
Gardner, William C.	Sixth Wisconsin	Nov 1861 to Feb 1864	Wounded at Gettysburg
Gleason, William J.	Second Wisconsin	May 1863 to Apr 1864	
Gohir, Edward	Twenty-fourth Michigan	Jan 1863 to Jun 1864	
Gould, Joseph P.	Nineteenth Indiana	Nov 1861 to Dec 1862	
Griffin, George	Second Wisconsin	Nov 1861 to Oct 1862	Discharged Due to Disability
Grim, Joseph D.	Nineteenth Indiana	Nov 1861 to Feb 1863	Wounded at Antietam, DNR
Grover, Theodore	Twenty-fourth Michigan	Jan 1863 to Jun 1864	Wounded at Gettyburg
Gunsolle, James	Twenty-fourth Michigan	Jan 1863 to Jun 1864	
Hansen, Charles	Second Wisconsin	May 1862 to Feb 1864	
Happe, John	Twenty-fourth Michigan	Jan 1863 to Oct 1863	Wounded at Gettysburg (lost foot)
Harris, Charles	Seventh Wisconsin	Sep 1862 to Jun 1864	Note G
Hinman, William G.	Seventh Wisconsin	Jan 1863 to Jun 1864	Note G
Hodgdon, John G.	Sixth Wisconsin	Nov 1861 to Oct 1863	Taken Sick in September 12, 1862, Note E
Hodgeman, Rufus	Seventh Wisconsin	Jan 1863 to Oct 1863	Note G
Holland, John	Second Wisconsin	Sep 1862 to Feb 1864	
Hunt, Albert C.	Seventh Wisconsin	Nov 1861 to Jun 1864	Note G
Irving, William	Twenty-fourth Michigan	Jan 1863 to Jun 1864	Killed in Action at Laurel Hill on May 8, 1864
Jenks, Charles C.	Second Wisconsin	May 1863 to Feb 1864	
Jessey, Henry C.	Seventh Wisconsin	Jan 1863 to Oct 1863	Note G
Jinkens, James M.	Nineteenth Indiana	May 1862 to Dec 1862	Deserted on January 23, 1863
Johnson, John	Second Wisconsin	Nov 1861 to Feb 1863	Wounded at Fredricksburg, Note C
Johnson, John	Seventh Wisconsin	Jan 1863 to Jun 1864	Note G
Johnson, Preston	Second Wisconsin	Nov 1861 to Apr 1863	

Name	Unit	Dates of Service in Battery B	Comments
Johnson, William L.	Sixth Wisconsin	Nov 1861 to Dec 1863	
Jones, John L.	Seventh Wisconsin	Nov 1861 to Feb 1862	
Jones, John W.	Nineteenth Indiana	Mar 1862 to Dec 1862	Deserted in January, 1863
Kellogg, Frank	Twenty-fourth Michigan	Jan 1863 to Jun 1864	
Kennedy, John W.	Nineteenth Indiana	Sep 1862 to Dec 1863	
Kingfield, Daniel	Nineteenth Indiana	Nov 1861 to Oct 1863	Note A
Klinefelter, Henry G.	Seventh Wisconsin	Mar 1862 to Oct 1864	Note G
Knight, John W.	Nineteenth Indiana	Mar 1862 to Oct 1863	Note A
Kocher, Conrad	Twenty-fourth Michigan	Jan 1863 to Feb 1864	
Lee, John J.	Seventh Wisconsin	Mar 1862 to Oct 1863	Wounded at Antietam, DNR
Lewis, James H.	Second Wisconsin	May 1863 to Apr 1864	
Livens, Charles	Seventh Wisconsin	Sep 1862 to Oct 1863	Note G
Mackey, Edwin I.	Seventh Wisconsin	Nov 1861 to Aug 1863	Wounded at Gettysburg, Note J
Malson, Nathaniel	Second Wisconsin	Nov 1861 to Apr 1863	Disch disability
Marshall, Lucius E.	Seventh Wisconsin	May 1863 to Jun 1864	Note G
McCaudria, Martin	Sixth Wisconsin	May 1862 to Oct 1862	Killed in Action at Antietam
McDaniel, Reason	Nineteenth Indiana	Mar 1862 to Jun 1864	
McDermott, John	Twenty-fourth Michigan	Jan 1863 to Jun 1864	
McDermott, John P.	Second Wisconsin	Nov 1861 to Sep 1863	Deserted on August 5, 1863
McDougall, Henry G.	Sixth Wisconsin	Nov 1861 to Feb 1864	
McLaughlin, John H.	Sixth Wisconsin	Jul 1862 to Jun 1864	Wounded at Antietam
Miles, John W.	Second Wisconsin	May 1862 to Feb 1864	
Miller, Burton	Sixth Wisconsin	May 1862 to Dec 1863	Wounded at Antietam
Milton, John H.	Seventh Wisconsin	May 1862 to Jun 1862	
Moore, James W.	Seventh Wisconsin	Sep 1862 to Jun 1864	Note G
Moore, John B	Twenty-fourth Michigan	Jan 1863 to Aug 1863	Wounded at Gettysburg and Disabled, DNR
Morris, Robert	Twenty-fourth Michigan	Jan 1863 to Jun 1864	
Moynahan, Henry	Twenty-fourth Michigan	Jan 1863 to Feb 1864	Wounded at Gettysburg
Murphy, Jeremiah	Sixth Wisconsin	May 1862 to Dec 1863	Wounded at Gettysburg
Nobles, Frank B.	Seventh Wisconsin	May 1862 to Oct 1863	Wounded at Antietam, Note G
O'Neal, John	Nineteenth Indiana	Sep 1862 to Oct 1863	Note A
Oakley, George	Twenty-fourth Michigan	Jan 1863 to Jun 1864	
Orth, John	Twenty-fourth Michigan	Jan 1863 to Jun 1864	
Packard, Elbridge E.	Second Wisconsin	Nov 1861 to Jun 1864	Wounded at North Anna, Note D
Palmer, Uriah	Sixth Wisconsin	Sep 1862 to Aug 1863	Died of Wounds Received at Gettysburg on July 21, 1863
Pattee, John A.	Twenty-fourth Michigan	Jan 1863 to Jun 1864	

Name	Unit	Dates of Service in Battery B	Comments
Patten, Charles	Twenty-fourth Michigan	Jan 1863 to Jun 1863	Died of Wounds Received at Gettysburg
Phillips, Martin	Nineteenth Indiana	Nov 1861 to Oct 1863	Note A
Phillips, William	Nineteenth Indiana	Mar 1862 to Jun 1862	Discharged for Disability
Powers, George L.	Second Wisconsin	May 1863 to Feb 1864	
Price, Thomas	Seventh Wisconsin	Sep 1862 to Jun 1864	Wounded at Spotsylvania, Note G
Priest, Alonzo	Sixth Wisconsin	Nov 1861 to Dec 1863	
Pursley, Lafayette	Nineteenth Indiana	Sep 1862 to Oct 1863	Note A
Quadt, Charles	Twenty-fourth Michigan	Jan 1863 to Jun 1864	Drowned on August 9, 1863
Reedy, Robert	Twenty-fourth Michigan	Jan 1863 to Jun 1864	
Richardson, Wesley	Seventh Wisconsin	Sep 1862 to Oct 1863	Note G
Ripley, Horace	Seventh Wisconsin	Sep 1862 to Jun 1864	Note G
Robinson, A. Wilder	Twenty-fourth Michigan	Jan 1863 to Feb 1864	Deserted in July, 1863 and Returned in January, 1864
Rogers, James H.	Seventh Wisconsin	Jan 1863 to Apr 1863	
Rowe, Perry	Nineteenth Indiana	Sep 1862 to Oct 1863	Wounded at Gettysburg (lost leg)
Russel, James	Second Wisconsin	Sep 1862 to Feb 1864	
Sanborn, John B.	Sixth Wisconsin	Nov 1861 to Jun 1864	
Scott, Cockrell	Seventh Wisconsin	Jan 1863 to Oct 1863	Note G
Seagraves, Michael	Nineteenth Indiana	Jan 1863 to Oct 1863	Note A
Shephest, Hermann	Twenty-fourth Michigan	Jan 1863 to Jun 1864	
Sheppard, Adolphus	Twenty-fourth Michigan	Jan 1863 to Feb 1864	Killed in action at Gettysburg
Shimeall, David	Second Wisconsin	Sep 1862 to Feb 1864	Wounded at Gettysburg
Small, John	Seventh Wisconsin	Sep 1862 to Jun 1864	Note G
Smith, David C.	Seventh Wisconsin	Jan 1863 to Jun 1864	Note G
Smith, Fleming	Nineteenth Indiana	Nov 1861 to Feb 1862	
Smith, George A.	Seventh Wisconsin	Jan 1863 to Oct 1863	Wounded at Gettysburg, Note G
Smith, Joseph	Twenty-fourth Michigan	Jan 1863 to Apr 1863	
Smith, Peter	Sixth Wisconsin	Sep 1862 to Dec 1863	
Smith, Willard A.	Twenty-fourth Michigan	Jan 1863 to Feb 1864	
Sowerwine, Isaac	Nineteenth Indiana	Nov 1861 to Aug 1863	Wounded at Antietam, DNR
Sprague, Charles	Sixth Wisconsin	Sep 1862 to Aug 1863	Killed in Action at Gettysburg
Stedman, Arthur	Nineteenth Indiana	Nov 1861 to Feb 1864	Wounded at Gettysburg
Stillman, Benjamin H.	Seventh Wisconsin	Nov 1861 to Oct 1863	Note G
Stone, John	Second Wisconsin	Sep 1862 to Sep 1863	Deserted on August 5, 1863
Thornton, William E	Twenty-fourth Michigan	Jan 1863 to Jun 1864	
Thorp, James	Seventh Wisconsin	Nov 1861 to Dec 1861	
Thorpe, Edgar A.	Second Wisconsin	Nov 1861 to Apr 1864	
Thurstan, Ahaz R.	Seventh Wisconsin	Jan 1863 to Oct 1863	Note G

Name	Unit	Dates of Service in Battery B	Comments
Vandecar, Isaac L.	Twenty-fourth Michigan	Jan 1863 to Apr 1864	Killed in Action at Laurel Hill on May 8, 1864
Velie, Abram	Twenty-fourth Michigan	Jan 1863 to Jun 1864	
Walker, George E.	Twenty-fourth Michigan	Jan 1863 to Feb 1864	Wounded at Gettysburg
Wallace, Patrick	Seventh Wisconsin	Sep 1862 to Apr 1863	Wounded at Fredricksburg, Note K
Weed, Minot S.	Twenty-fourth Michigan	Jan 1863 to Jun 1864	
Wemple, Mynderd	Sixth Wisconsin	Nov 1861 to Feb 1863	Deserted on November 5, 1862
Wilkinson, Andrew J.	Seventh Wisconsin	Jan 1863 to Oct 1863	Note G
Williams, Winfield S.	Seventh Wisconsin	May 1863 to Jun 1864	Note G
Wills, William H.	Twenty-fourth Michigan	Jan 1863 to Oct 1863	Dropped Due to Disability
Wine, James	Nineteenth Indiana	Sep 1862 to Feb 1864	
Wingate, Philip A.	Nineteenth Indiana	Sep 1862 to Dec 1862	Deserted in January, 1863
Young, Claus	Nineteenth Indiana	Sep 1862 to Oct 1863	Wounded at Antietam, Note A
Young, Smith	Sixth Wisconsin	Sep 1862 to Oct 1863	Wounded at Antietam, Note F
Zimmerman, William W.	Nineteenth Indiana	Nov 1861 to Aug 1863	Drowned on August 15, 1863

Table 1—Notes

1. DNR: "Did Not Return" to Battery B after event mentioned, even though person remained on the muster roll.

2. The muster roll dates from-to are for the period that the names appeared on Battery B's rolls. That does not mean that the person was present, because members were normally carried if sick, wounded, or missing, until their status was verified, sometimes a year after the event.

3. Killed and wounded are from the muster rolls and returns. Therefore, only those seriously wounded and noted on these documents are included.

4. There is some variation in spelling of names between muster roll editions, and between muster rolls, state rosters, and unit histories. The spelling used here is usually from the muster rolls.

A. The section of muster roll containing these personnel is missing from the September to October, 1863 roll.

B. The muster roll shows Compton sick on September 17, 1862. He was probably wounded at Antietam that day. He was carried as sick through August, 1863, and then shown as disabled in September and October, and then dropped from the rolls.

C. Arm amputated.

D. Died on May 25, 1864 from wounds received at North Anna River.

E. Carried as sick until he died of disease.

F. Wounded at Antietam, carried as such on all muster rolls through Oct, 1863, then shown disabled. Wisconsin rosters show killed at Antietam.

G. Muster roll section missing for November through Dec, 1863. Probably all of these individuals served with Battery B through December, 1863.

H. Wounded at Sulfur Springs, Virginia on August 24, 1862. Left arm amputated. Released as disabled in October, 1863.

I. Wounded on April 30, 1863 at Pollock's Mill Crossing. Right leg amputated on June 28, 1863. Died on October 1, 1863 of wound and complications.

J. Deserted on July 17, 1863.

K. Discharged for disability on March 8, 1863.

Table 2. Non–Iron Brigade Members of Battery B—Killed or Wounded

Name	Unit	Comments
Berkitz, Herman	New Recruit, U.S. Army	Wounded at Spotsylvania, DNR
Bowers, George C.	New Recruit, U.S. Army	Wounded at Bethesda Church on June 3, 1864
Brown, Henry	Twenty-third New York Infantry	Killed In Action at Antietam
Brown, John	Battery B, U.S. Army Regulars	Killed In Action at Antietam
Campbell, Lt. Joseph B.	Battery B, U.S. Army Regulars	Wounded at Antietam, DNR
Clark, James C	Thirty-fifth New York Infantry	Wounded at Antietam, DNR
Cunningham, James	New Recruit, U.S. Army	Wounded at Gravelly Run
Davison, Lt. James	Battery B, U.S. Army Regulars	Wounded at Gettysburg, DNR
Evans, Addison	Twenty-third New York Infantry	Wounded at Antietam, DNR
Freitong, Adolph	New Recruit, U.S. Army	Killed In Action at Gravelly Run
Givens, Warren	New Recruit, U.S. Army	Wounded at Bethesda Church on June 3, 1864, DNR
Goodman, Lt. Thomas	Battery B, U.S. Army Regulars	Killed In Action at Spotsylvania
Hathaway, Charles	Twenty-third New York Infantry	Wounded at Antietam, DNR
Herzog, Joseph	Battery B, U.S. Army Regulars	Killed In Action at Antietam
Hogan, Patrick	Battery B, U.S. Army Regulars	Killed In Action at Fredricksburg
Lyons, Henry P.	Battery B, U.S. Army Regulars	Killed In Action at Antietam
McAlona, Robert	Thirty-fifth New York Infantry	Wounded at Antietam
McCabe, Patrick	Battery B, U.S. Army Regulars	Wounded at Second Bull Run, DNR
Mitchell, Lt. John	Battery B, U.S. Army Regulars	Wounded at Gravelly Run
Moore, William I.	Thirty-fifth New York Infantry	Wounded at Antietam
Morgan, Joseph J. E.	Thirty-fifth New York Infantry	Probably Killed In Action at Antietam
Sheahan, John	Battery B, U.S. Army Regulars	Killed In Action at Gettysburg, While Serving as General John Gibbon's Aide
Springer, Charles	Thirty-fifth New York Infantry	Probably Killed In Action at Antietam
Stewart, Lt. James	Battery B, U.S. Army Regulars	Wounded at Gettysburg
Tea, Richard	Battery B, U.S. Army Regulars	Wounded at Petersburg

In Peace and War

Union Veterans and Cultural Symbols— The Flags of the Iron Brigade

RICHARD H. ZEITLIN

The battle flags of the Iron Brigade became important cultural symbols in the eyes of Wisconsinites because of their ability to evoke an emotional response from those who viewed them. Particularly during the lifetime of the Civil War generation, the flags of the Iron Brigade, along with the banners of other famous state units, played an integral role in a variety of significant events.

The political managers who controlled the Iron Brigade flags emphasized differing themes after the war. Depending upon their own needs, political leaders made use of the battle flags graphically to illustrate particular social developments. The Iron Brigade's battle flags were actively deployed for twenty-three years following 1865, during electoral campaigns, veterans' rallies, for charitable fund-raising, and for pension legislation purposes. The Iron Brigade's flags symbolized—as few other emblems could—patriotism, courage, sacrifice, and pride.

In the years immediately following the Civil War, state leaders used the flags of the Iron Brigade to encourage charitable donations for sick and wounded soldiers. Wisconsin Radical Republicans used the flags to dramatize the Reconstruction issue, to blame the South and the Democratic party for starting the war, as well as to attract veterans into their own political camp. The flags became "Bloody Shirt" relics highlighting wartime divisions. In the mid-1870s, however, the flags became features at the mass gatherings and rallies held during the nation's Centennial celebrations where they represented patriotism, national union, and civic virtue. After 1880, the battle flags helped attract state veterans into the ranks of regimental associations and into military fraternities such as the Grand Army of the Republic (GAR) by symbolizing comradeship and sociability. Once organized, the veterans successfully lobbied Congress for the adoption of pension legislation on behalf of Union soldiers which, ultimately, cost the federal treasury hundreds of millions of dollars.

The long and enthusiastic use which the flags experienced after the war finally took its toll on the delicate objects. The flags deteriorated despite attempts to repair them. To preserve the value that the banners obviously possessed, state officials retired the symbols of sacrifice in 1888. Thereafter, the flags of the Iron Brigade were treated as holy relics by legislators who authorized public museums to house the collection. Museums then justified their own educational missions, as well as the need for funding, for the care, preservation, and display of the revered objects.

The context of the immediate post-1865 period set the stage for the peacetime career of the Iron Brigade's battle flags. The end of the Civil War reintroduced more than 70,000 veterans into the social, economic, and political life of Wisconsin. In terms of establishing a meaningful perspective on this number of people, the total number of votes cast by Wisconsinites in 1864, a presidential year, amounted to 149,342. In other words, if they chose to exercise their franchise, veterans represented a very sizable portion of Wisconsin's electorate.[1]

The ex-soldiers faced important adjustment problems when they returned home. The number of wounded men has never even been officially counted. As with wounds, sicknesses contracted in the South continued to kill or incapacitate. Limbless, blind, injured, diseased, and otherwise handicapped soldiers returned to a society where social service agencies hardly existed. The widows and orphans of soldiers were especially hard-pressed. Jobs, trades, and farms had been taken over by others during the war, leaving the task of reentering the economy to the veterans' own resources.

Considering the size of the veteran population, the war experiences they had shared, and the readjustment challenges they faced, it is not surprising that politicians eagerly sought to become "the soldier's friend." Bounty equalizations, pensions for those obviously disabled by wounds and disease, benefits for widows and dependents, creation of a state-supported soldiers' orphans' home, and preferential consideration for government jobs became issues in which veterans took a keen interest. When Lucius Fairchild, the ex-colonel of the Second Wisconsin Infantry who had lost his left arm at Gettysburg, took office as governor in January 1866, the level of political activities associated with veterans' affairs increased. Fairchild and his associates helped to organize Civil War veterans, encouraging them to vote as a bloc, and, especially, to tie their futures to the Republican party.

Fairchild used the Civil War battle flags to further his career. They became advertising devices in emotional anti-Southern, anti-Democratic political activities—Bloody Shirt campaigns—through which Fairchild and his supporters attained and kept themselves in office. A dynamic and impassioned speaker, the thirty-four-year-old Fairchild became a regionally important politician, the first of Wisconsin's seven soldier-governors, a national force within veterans' circles, and the state's first chief executive to be elected to three consecutive terms. While railroad, lumber, and commercial interests undoubtedly dominated state politics in the years following the war, some citizens and a number of politicians preoccupied themselves with Civil War themes.[2]

Rather than confront potentially divisive questions such as those engendered by immigration, industrialization, monopolization, the concentration of wealth, urbanization, and labor unrest, Fairchild and his supporters (and even some of his rivals) remained complacently identified with issues stemming from the Civil War. Sharp partisanship, of course, remained a feature of postwar state politics, and the desire on the part of leading members of both major political parties throughout the North to please the approximately 2,500,000 Union veterans (and potential voters) had important consequences at all levels of government. To be sure, the effective organizing of the veterans did not occur overnight. Nearly twenty years passed before the ex-soldiers were welded into a truly recognizable unified national pressure group. Organizing took place in fits and starts, and initial successes during the period 1865–1869 were followed by a decade of failures. Throughout this era, the Civil War battle flags played an important role.

Early in 1866, Fairchild helped organize the Wisconsin chapter of the Soldiers' and Sailors' National Union League, an association formed by Eastern veterans.[3] Nearly all Union League members from Wisconsin, as elsewhere, were active Republicans. The Union League lobbied for veterans' preference in jobs and aid for disabled soldiers. But the organization quickly affiliated itself with Radical Republicans in Congress and joined their efforts to thwart President Andrew Johnson's Reconstruction program for the defeated Confederate states.[4] Wisconsin's Union League members became, with few exceptions, a leadership cadre of Radical Republican veteran activists who helped to form and promote another military society with a broadly based Western membership: the Grand Army of the Republic, or GAR.

Between February and May of 1866, Fairchild initiated contact with Illinois soldier-politicians who had founded the GAR and who were associated with John A. Logan, ex-commander of the Fifteenth Corps, a leading congressional Radical, and soon to be National GAR Commander.[5] James K. Proudfit became Wisconsin's commander as the Badger State organized the first GAR department outside Illinois. The GAR adopted the trappings of a fraternal benevolent society with a secret initiation ritual.[6] In 1866 Fairchild helped recruit Eastern veterans—who had been attracted to Soldiers' and Sailors' Union Leagues and similar organizations—to the GAR during a massive veterans' rally held in Pittsburgh to support congressional Republican Radicals.[7]

In July 1866, Fairchild organized an elaborate ceremony in Madison to commemorate the end of the war and to show off the strength and popularity of the soldier element. Iron Brigade battle flags and veterans were prominently featured. On July 4, contingents of veterans from each Wisconsin regiment were assembled at the state capitol, and they selected a color guard to carry the unit's banners. The flags would be formally presented to the state by the men who bore them during the war. Fairchild invited military figures and guests from across the nation.[8]

Officials of local units of government, as well as Wisconsin congressmen and senators, attended the Madison gathering. Some 20,000 people flocked to Wisconsin's capital city on the appointed day, clogging local roads while tripling the population of the city. Rain showers let up and the Fourth of July dawned clear, cool, and beautiful. Madisonians draped flags from their homes while church bells pealed and cannon salutes sounded. It was "a day that will ever be remembered in the history of Madison," noted a *Wisconsin State Journal* reporter. The parade moved down State Street before returning to the Capitol Park. Bands blared while citizens and guests fell in behind the detachment of veterans carrying the regimental colors, led by the flags of the "glorious Iron Brigade." There "was one feature in the procession which riveted the attention of all," noted a reporter. "It was the . . . battle flags . . . some torn until only a few shreds were left. . . . "[9]

Fairchild accepted the flags in the name of the state and delivered a ringing speech in which he promised the veterans that their flags would be installed at the capitol "as monuments of glory" for as "long as this government shall stand. . . . " After the ceremony, the flags were taken to the capitol and "placed in different offices and in the rooms of the State Historical Society" in such a manner that they could be "seen but not handled."[10]

In August, Fairchild joined Senator Timothy O. Howe; one-legged Milwaukee soldier-politician, Congressman Halbert E. Paine; Jerry Rusk; and ex-governor Edward Salomon for a series of pro-Radical meetings denouncing Democrats and President Johnson.[11] In Madison shortly thereafter, Wisconsin Radical Republicans hung captured Confederate flags upside down "in token of subjugation" while the governor harangued a crowd in the Assembly chambers.[12] Prior to the fall election, Governor Fairchild allowed a group of Wisconsin battle flags to appear at a veterans' political gathering in Burlington. Fairchild requested that Jacob S. Crane, organizer of the rally and a former officer of the Forty-third Wisconsin, "send a careful man" to Madison to pick up the flags: "They are too sacred to be entrusted to a common carrier."[13]

To preserve the Union victory, won at such enormous cost, Wisconsin's Radical politicians continually urged veterans and other citizens to vote Republican.[14] Healthy Republican majorities vindicated the Bloody Shirt campaign technique in 1866, although Democrats still retained a number of seats in the Wisconsin Senate. In fact, throughout the period 1860–1890 the Republican party could not take its victories for granted, either on the state or national levels. Democrats remained electorally competitive, possibly because of their strong base among some ethnic groups and among Southerners.[15]

In May of 1868, Fairchild convened the meeting of the Wisconsin Soldiers' and Sailors' Association in Milwaukee. He secured from the soldiers their endorsement for the Republican party in the coming election and had himself selected to lead the state delegation to the National Soldiers' and Sailors' Convention scheduled to gather in Chicago at the same time that the Republican National Convention would be nominating a presidential candidate.[16] Fairchild, Proudfit, Rusk, and Judge W. H. Sessions, an ex-captain of the Twenty-first Wisconsin, carried a group of Wisconsin battle flags, including those of the Iron Brigade's Second Regiment, to Chicago.[17]

At the national soldiers' gathering, Fairchild was chosen as the presiding officer. Wisconsin's governor, in association with GAR Commander John Logan, convinced the assembled veterans to declare their "active support" of the Republican party as "the only political organization which . . . is true to the principles of loyalty, liberty, and equality before the law."[18] With the Republican party thus endorsed as the official veterans' party, conventioneers selected Ulysses S. Grant as the ex-soldiers' candidate for president.[19]

The veterans then held a parade, with Fairchild and the Wisconsin delegation following the tattered Civil War flags as they marched to the Crosby Opera House where the Republican convention was in full swing. Thousands of Chicago residents cheered the parading ex-soldiers and their flags. Fairchild informed the conventioneers of the veterans' preference. GAR Commander and Congressman Logan nominated Grant, whom the delegates unanimously chose as the Republican candidate for president.[20]

Fairchild then formed Wisconsin Soldiers' Grant and Colfax Clubs. The governor toured Wisconsin rallying ex-soldiers and other citizens in support of Grant and his running-mate Schuyler Colfax. The Radicals missed no opportunity to equate the Democrats with civil war and treason. "Every rebel, every Copper head, every draft sneak, every dirty traitor," noted Governor Fairchild, would be voting for Democrats, as would members of the Ku Klux Klan.[21] The dividing line between the parties, explained the soldiers' friend at a veterans' gathering in Madison, "was drawn just about where it was during the war—between the loyal blue and the traitor gray."[22] Grant carried Wisconsin overwhelmingly. Fairchild then sought an unprecedented third term as governor, turning for support to the veterans.

Governor Fairchild brought Iron Brigade flags to local GAR gatherings to stimulate attendance.[23] Among veterans, Fairchild's theme remained focused on Civil War animosities. The Democrats, in Fairchild's view, had "encouraged rebellion," supported the South, and, therefore, had "blood on their heads."[24] The governor won re-election by a healthy majority.[25]

Fairchild began his final term as governor by requesting that Wisconsin legislators authorize an expenditure to construct glass cases for the Civil War battle flags. He asked that the quartermaster general provide the cases "in order to preserve the valued relics."[26] Legislators acted positively on the matter in March 1870, passing an "Act relating to the preservation of the colors and flags of our late regiments."[27]

The Milwaukee firm of Fisher and Reynolds constructed the cases, and the banners went on display in the State Historical Society's rooms in the capitol later that year.[28] A unique feature of the arrangement involved the fact that the historical society did not gain title to the Civil War banners. Rather, the flags remained under the control of the quartermaster general's office—an executive department. Fairchild and his allies had scant interest in leaving the battle flags permanently in a museum. The arrangement with the State Historical Society was not intended to interfere with the business of politics.

Throughout Fairchild's tenure as governor, Bloody Shirt campaign oratory proved to be an effective vote-getter, although it was never the only technique in that capable soldier's political repertoire. By the 1870s, however, Civil War issues appeared to be somewhat less immediate than they had been during the hectic 1865–1869 period. The voting populace had begun to show apathy toward Civil War enmities as the new decade dawned. Fairchild sought a foreign appointment after the Republicans selected ex-Major General Cadwallader C. Washburn of La Crosse as the party's gubernatorial candidate. A Washburn rally, billed as a soldiers' reunion, took place in La Crosse during early June 1871. Fairchild sent twenty-two Wisconsin Civil War battle flags, including a stand from each Iron Brigade regiment. Three hundred veterans showed up. The flags drew attention because of their "honorable scars, received where bullets flew with remarkable celerity and alarming frequency," but the rally fizzled.[29]

Nonetheless, Washburn carried the state, although his administration was later hampered by the nationwide economic depression of 1873, unenviable association with the scandals of the Grant era, and passage of an unpopular liquor-control measure. The battle flags made an appearance at the Society of the Army of the Tennessee Convention held in Madison in July 1872; but four years passed before they would again appear in public as a group.[30] During that time, Fairchild departed for a diplomatic post in Europe, while the GAR, like veterans' organizations across most parts of the nation, experienced a rapidly declining membership—dropping to a mere 253 in Wisconsin during 1875.[31] In 1873, the Democrats overwhelmingly captured the Wisconsin governorship and the Assembly.

During the administration of Governor William R. Taylor of Dane County, the Democratically controlled Wisconsin legislature passed an act amending the 1870 battle flag preservation law. The act of March 1875 required that Wisconsin's Civil War flags "shall not be removed" from their cases, "except as such removal may be required for their safety and better preservation."[32] The new law thus removed the Civil War flags from the political arena, as Democrats locked the artifacts of the Bloody Shirt into glass cases.

Democrats naturally recognized the potential of an ex-soldier voting bloc and they strove to offset the initial Republican advantage in appealing to the veteran element. When the "incarceration law" took the battle flags from the hands of Republican GAR men and Bloody Shirt politicians, the resurgent Democrats made an effort to court the veterans in order to enlarge their own party's following. Democratic veteran leaders espoused an end to war-generated bitterness between North and South. They emphasized the social aspect of military fraternal gatherings by sentimentally recollecting the comradeship shared by all Union soldiers regardless of their political affiliation.

Democratic control of the Wisconsin Assembly and statehouse lasted two years until Harrison Ludington, the Republican mayor of Milwaukee, helped defeat Governor Taylor and the Democrats by the narrowest of margins.[33] Shortly after Ludington took office in 1876, legislators amended the act which prohibited state Civil War flags from leaving their cases. The 1876 legislation authorized two uses for the battle flags: They could now attend festivities associated with the nation's Centennial, and more importantly, "upon application of the officers commanding," they could be "used at reunions of . . . regiments, batteries, or detachments . . . or [by] any military or regimental organization."[34]

The 1876 law freed the battle flags from cases and democratized their use. For the next decade, the flags traveled about the state to reunions and celebrations. Leaders of the moribund GAR focused on the social programs, fraternal parades, and "camp fires" which became popular gatherings. The battle flags helped attract veterans and other citizens to these events (and, incidentally, helped the GAR survive long enough to achieve a reorganization and a luxurious regeneration during the 1880s). Battle flags appeared at Centennial celebrations in Madison, La Crosse, Sheboygan, Oconomowoc, Sturgeon Bay, Menasha, Oconto, and Kewaskum. In addition to the historic banners, Centennial celebrators borrowed Civil War tents, muskets, and the surplus cannons parked around the capitol.[35]

Iron Brigade flags attended veterans' reunions at Menomonie in 1877 and at Durand in 1878. In 1879 they were present at the reunion of the Association of Soldiers and Veterans of Dunn, Pepin, Pierce, and Buffalo counties held in Menomonie. In May 1879, the flags of the Second, Eighth, and Thirty-first Infantry were taken to a Memorial Day gathering in Prairie Du Chien.[36] The fact that at least one of the Iron Brigade flags was "not in condition to be used" did not faze reunion organizers.[37]

Indeed, the tempo of Civil War veterans and other military gatherings in Wisconsin, as elsewhere, increased dramatically as the decade of the 1870s drew to a close. In Hartford, Connecticut, for example, when state battle flags were transferred to newly constructed cases in the capitol from their depository at the local armory in September 1879, approximately 100,000 citizens showed up to watch and cheer as the flags moved by. A *New York Times* story called it "the greatest popular demonstration ever witnessed in the State."[38] A reunion sponsored by the Chicago Union Veterans Club likewise drew crowds of over 100,000 when it gathered in Aurora, Illinois, in the late summer of 1879.[39]

In Wisconsin, as in other states, numerous militia units also sprang up. "At no time since the war," reported Adjutant General Edwin E. Bryant in September 1879, "has so much interest been manifested in military organizations as at present." The stage was now set for the transformation of veterans' groups from scattered soldier clubs and the nearly defunct GAR—whose membership in Wisconsin during 1879 had dwindled to 135—into a national lobby able to influence elections and, therefore, legislation and the composition of governmental agencies.[40] The closely matched strength of the major political parties, and especially the popular social aspect of the military gatherings, combined to bring forth a new era in veterans' affairs. The battle flags played a role in these developments, because, as one Wisconsin reunion organizer put it, the veterans "have a desire to march under the old flags once more."[41]

Other factors contributed to the revived interest in soldiers' organizations. One of these was increased leisure time, as the boys of 1861–1865 approached their middle years and had established themselves economically. The national penchant for joining groups revealed itself in 260 new secret organizations, including numerous veterans' societies, which formed during 1880–1896. Older fraternal orders such as the Odd Fellows also experienced rapid growth. Nostalgic memories of the war experience, which included heady recollections of comradeship, heroism, and sacrifice—as one veteran put it in 1880, "the most precious memories of our lives"—no doubt encouraged soldiers' organization membership, along with the growing popularity of Memorial Day as a holiday. Perhaps most important, however, was a revival of interest in national Civil War pensions for Union veterans, together with an appreciation of the need for a strong lobbying organization to obtain them. The Arrears Act of January 25, 1879, for example, established the precedent for substantially broadening existing pension legislation, making available sizable chunks of arrears (ranging from $953.62 to $1,121.51) for 138,195 ex-soldiers not previously qualified to receive payments.[42] In other words, a series of favorable circumstances operated to encourage and rejuvenate veterans' organizations at this particular juncture. And, as in every age, whenever and wherever crowds of voters gathered or organized, politicians were sure to be found.

Wisconsin veterans convincingly demonstrated their collective strength in June 1880. Following a year of intense planning, veteran activists formed the Wisconsin Soldiers and Sailors Reunion Association. The GAR—after repudiating overt political involvement, graded membership, and its Radial Republican views—undertook a compilation of names and addresses of veterans residing in Wisconsin.

Governor William E. Smith supported the veterans by speaking on behalf of the reunion. The governor also authorized State Quartermaster General Edwin Bryant to "thoroughly repair" the state battle flags which would be prominently displayed during the gathering.[43] In fact, the veterans were urged to attend the five-day affair because the flags would be in attendance:

"Let the storm tattered flags riven by shot and shell on a hundred fields of battle, once more be unfolded to the breeze. . . ."[44]

The Great Reunion took place June 7–12, 1880. Although the weather was disagreeably warm, muggy, and frequently rainy, the gathering attracted huge crowds. Veterans, families, spectators, and hucksters doubled Milwaukee's population of 150,000. Citizens who "came to see the old veterans," packed every hotel in the city as well as those in nearby Racine, Waukesha, and Oconomowoc. Food supplies ran short. As one reporter noted, "it was a difficult matter to get square meals or anything better than rye bread and beer."[45] The tent camp for veterans at North Point sheltered between 20,000 and 30,000 veterans in rain-soaked, muddy conditions that probably recalled old campaigns. Each ex-soldier provided his own blanket, tin cup, plate, and eating utensils, as well as fifty cents per day. The veterans brought whatever parts of their old uniforms they still possessed—or could fit into—and were required to supply army-type slouch hats or fatigue caps. Milwaukee residents decorated their homes with flowers and banners.[46]

On June 9, a giant parade of the greatest reunion of soldiers held anywhere since the war took place.[47] Former President Grant and General Philip H. Sheridan were the guests of honor. They led the procession of members of Wisconsin regiments, numbering about 25,000 men, while more than 100,000 viewers cheered. "It was a great seething surging mass of humanity," recorded the *Milwaukee Sentinel*: "The men who had forgotten for fifteen years that they were heroes . . . have now been reminded of it again."[48] As usual, the battle flags seemed to capture the emotional essence of the Civil War experience. The *Sentinel*'s reporter observed: "Hats went off as the column swung by, and cheers went up that seemed to make the ground tremble. When the flags torn by shot and shell were borne by, a quiver went through the vast assemblage and a moment after, the wildest excitement prevailed."[49]

On June 12, the veterans broke camp and the battle flags were returned to their glass cases in the "state historical rooms" at the capitol.[50] The flags had thus served again to inspire veterans and other citizens. They had been repaired for the second time since returning from the war. Nor did they rest long in their cases. In September, selected banners were displayed at a reunion in Port Washington. In October, flags and cannon went to Chilton "for use of the Garfield and Arthur Club and the town generally." In June, 1881, "cannon, tents, and colors" traveled to Sturgeon Bay for a local reunion.[51]

The most important effects of the Great Reunion of 1880, other than demonstrating the numerical strength and popular support that organized veterans could generate, was in the creation of regimental associations. The formal organization of these associations was planned in advance by reunion leaders.[52] The regimental associations formed a local grapevine through which the ex-soldiers might be rallied or informed on issues which, like pensions, would be of particular interest to them. They could be marshaled for social gatherings, or for future organizing into the ranks of the Grand Army of the

Republic. With good reason, one reunion organizer noted that the "boys have grown more thoughtful. Hence it is that . . . reunions are becoming more general, and we look forward to them with deeper interest as the years wear away."[53]

The case of the Iron Brigade illustrates the phenomenon. During the Great Reunion, Iron Brigade veterans formed the Iron Brigade Association, a "semi-civic society." Organizers included Iron Brigade members and such Fairchild allies as John A. Kellogg, Joseph H. Marston of Appleton, and Jerome A. Watrous, a newspaperman and professional writer from Fond du Lac who moved to Milwaukee in 1879 where he became associate editor and later editor-in-chief of the *Milwaukee Telegraph*. Over the next several decades, Watrous acted as the secretary of the Iron Brigade Association as well as the "pen" of the state GAR, eventually becoming its commander. Representatives from the Iron Brigade's Nineteenth Indiana and Twenty-fourth Michigan regiments were also present.[54]

The ex-soldiers chose as president of their association General John Gibbon, a regular army officer who had commanded the Iron Brigade at Brawner Farm, South Mountain, and Antietam. Because Gibbon was stationed on the Pacific Coast and could therefore not be expected to attend reunions on a regular basis, the choice of first vice president became crucial. (It was he who selected the date and site of the group's reunions.) Congressman Edward S. Bragg, former colonel of the Sixth Wisconsin, was elected to fill the important post, and each of the five regiments in the brigade provided a vice president with less power than the senior vice president.[55]

Bragg chose to hold the first reunion of the Iron Brigade Association in Milwaukee during September 1882. The brigade's battle flags were "nailed to the wall" of the Stanley and Camp Jewelry Store on Wisconsin Avenue and Broadway, headquarters of the reunion association, to "give a martial appearance." As one veteran said to a *Sentinel* reporter: "Twenty years ago I saw that old flag on South Mountain and it was a sorry day for some of our boys."[56] The general meeting took place at City Hall, and some 250 of the Iron Brigade's approximately 700 survivors attended. Governor Rusk, Congressman Bragg, and General Gibbon addressed the assembled veterans. So did Lucius Fairchild, who had returned home after spending a decade in European diplomatic posts. Fairchild became the association's second vice president. The speakers urged Iron Brigade members to support future reunions and to join the GAR.[57]

The veterans received commemorative Iron Brigade cigars, while Hattie A. Aubery, the teen-aged daughter of Cullen "Doc" Aubery, a newspaper boy attached to the Iron Brigade during the war, recited a poem and presented a handmade white silk guidon to the men. Father and daughter were elected honorary members of the Iron Brigade Association.[58]

Bragg chose La Crosse for the next reunion. The *Fond du Lac Democrat* stressed the social, nonpolitical aspect of the event, promising good fellowship and "entertainment for all."[59] He advertised the presence of the Civil War flags to encourage attendance. "The flags of the . . . old brigade will be present," General Bragg noted. "It will do us all good to see those torn and tattered battle flags." The governor of Michigan, however, refused to allow the flags of the Twenty-Fourth Michigan to appear at La Crosse because "the flags are so old and rotten that but a few handlings would entirely destroy them."[60]

The reunion was well attended despite the absence of the Michigan flags. Reunion activities included other pleasantries. The veterans spent the morning of September 14 listening to poems, recitals by local glee clubs, and singing "The Battle Cry of Freedom—which made the walls tremble." As evidence of the new democratic spirit among the veterans, Bragg invited James Patrick "Mickey" Sullivan, a private during the war, to present his humorous stories of life in the ranks of the Iron Brigade. Sullivan became the first enlisted man to formally participate in the reunion association's programs. His appearance set a notable precedent. Subsequent Iron Brigade reunions always featured nonofficer presentations.[61]

A parade of Iron Brigade veterans attracted "great throngs of citizens" along its route. The Wisconsin regimental battle flags accompanied the veterans in line while bands and local militia companies marched in support. The *Milwaukee Sentinel* called it an "imposing spectacle."[62] Dancing and singing provided the evening's entertainment. Under Chinese lanterns and electric lights, Bragg did solo performances of "Tenting On the Old Camp Ground" and the "Red, White, and Blue." "Good feelings ruled supreme at this reunion," concluded the editor of the *La Crosse Republican and Leader*.[63]

Cracks in the facade of social fellowship of the Iron Brigade Association, and in the nonpolitical orientation of military fraternal organizations, began to appear in 1884. In January, Lucius Fairchild, who was considering a run for the U.S. Senate, and several other Iron Brigade members invited the association to hold its reunion in Madison. However, after a lengthy delay, Bragg declined their offer and instead chose Lancaster as the site of the meeting.[64] Politics may well have influenced the Democratic senior vice president's decision, since the 1884 presidential election promised to be yet another exceptionally close contest between the major political parties. Grover Cleveland, Democrat of New York, was an attractive candidate and, shortly thereafter, he became president by a bare majority.

In any case, Lancaster prepared to host the Iron Brigade reunion on August 28, the anniversary of the battle of Brawner Farm. Nearly 200 veterans attended the gathering. Rain prevented a parade, but the veterans attentively listened to speeches. As usual, the battle flags were attached to the windows of the hall.[65] After the official meeting, Iron Brigade veterans attended a "camp fire"—an evening picnic replete with songs and stories. Afterward, Lucius Fairchild invited the association to hold its next reunion in Madison.[66]

During early 1885, Fairchild made the rounds of local veterans' reunions, such as those hosted by Company D of the Seventh Wisconsin in Stoughton and another in Berlin shortly thereafter, urging members to attend the gathering in Madison during September. Fairchild's presence at these local affairs was always appreciated. As he explained to a family member: "I am now a 'buster' on campfire speeches—as I have been since my return from Europe . . . and the boys go off their heads in cheering."[67]

Fairchild carefully organized the Madison reunion of the Iron Brigade Association. The governors of Michigan and Indiana agreed to be there, as did Congressman Robert M. La Follette. Railroad discounts helped encourage attendance. Some 350 Iron Brigade veterans showed up for the elaborate two-day reunion. The Assembly Chamber in the state capitol provided seating for the official meeting, while Camp Randall was the site of a "Bean Banquet."[68] Iron Brigade member and State Adjutant General Chandler P. Chapman of Madison designed a special badge consisting of a "five armed iron Maltese Cross suspended by a blue ribbon" to give each Iron Brigade veteran attending the reunion.[69]

About 1,000 veterans and spectators crammed the packed Assembly Chamber as General Bragg introduced Jerry Rusk, "the soldier-governor," who gave a welcoming speech. Rusk—who was to be Wisconsin's second three-term governor—declared that he "loved all Union soldiers." The "bebadged crowd" next called on General Fairchild to give an extemporaneous speech, responding with "three cheers" at its conclusion. Fairchild noted that other duties interfered with his position as the second vice president of the Iron Brigade Association and requested that Gil Woodward replace him. Two Iron Brigade flags stood behind the speakers, while "around the chamber extending out over the auditorium, are thirteen regimental flags, whose tattered appearance and half obliterated inscriptions tell of many a hard fought battle. . . . "[70]

Fairchild's decision to remove himself from the second vice presidency was not commented upon in the press. But it meant that the ex-governor was now at liberty to seek higher office within the Iron Brigade Association, in opposition to the Democrat, Edward Bragg. As Republican State Senator Levi E. Pond of Westfield, a GAR activist and Iron Brigade veteran, confidentially noted to Fairchild the following July: "Do you think that General Bragg ought to be continued in his present office in the Iron Brigade Association? I do not, for I am disgruntled with some of his speeches and acts in Congress. He seems to have a greater loyalty to party than to the old soldiery."[71]

Fairchild did seek high office in the GAR. He became state commander in 1886 and national commander in 1887, by which time GAR membership totaled nearly 400,000.[72] Fairchild strongly supported pension legislation, and along with other GAR members, such as William T. Sherman, revived the Bloody Shirt issue in opposition to Democratic President Cleveland. Fairchild, the GAR, and Bloody Shirt activists helped influence the course of

Iron Brigade Reunion at Oshkosh, Wisconsin, August 31, 1886.
Courtesy of the Wisconsin Veterans Museum.

national veterans' politics during the latter 1880s, particularly during the presidential election of 1888.[73]

In some respects, Democratic politicians provided their Republican critics with the excuse they sought to reintroduce politics, however subtly, into local and national veterans' affairs. At the 1886 Iron Brigade Reunion Association meeting held in Oshkosh during late August, for example, Democrats monopolized the proceedings. Bragg selected the meeting date to partly conflict with the state GAR encampment in Lake Geneva. The fiery ex-Iron Brigade commander, who was running for Congress in the Second District, opened the well-attended meetings by eulogizing General George B. McClellan, the Democratic candidate in 1864.[74]

Iron Brigade survivors marched behind their Civil War banners on September 1. "The tattered war colors were cheered at different points along the march," reported the *Oshkosh Northwestern*.[75] Photographers Cook Ely and O. H. Mazer recorded the event. An evening ball demonstrated "that the old boys had not forgotten how to dance."[76] But Fairchild and Bragg did not greet each other, for both were preparing for the contest they must have known lay ahead.

President Cleveland opened the next round in a struggle which marked the reentry of organized veterans into politics. In early 1887, Cleveland signed a pension bill for Mexican War veterans while vetoing the Dependent Pension Bill for Civil War soldiers.[77] Mexican War pension applicants, furthermore, did not have to prove that they had not borne arms against the United States during 1861–1865, thus paving the way for ex-Confederates to receive payments. GAR activists responded quickly. Democrats like Bragg, Callis, and Gibbon supported the president's actions. Republicans, on the other hand, used the veto to show that Cleveland and the Democrats were "Rebels at heart."[78] "Now who are those Mexican soldiers?" rhetorically asked one GAR man in 1887: "I think that you will agree . . . that $^4/_5$ of the pensioners of the Mexican War were men that you and I fought against [in the Civil War]; and the first man who received a pension under the act was a rebel Brigadier General. And I tell you, when we see those men who fought against us taking money out of the treasury of the United States that we made it possible to put in there, it is time we made an earnest demand for what we believe to be our rights."[79]

Commander Fairchild requested that all of the nearly 400,000 GAR members and nearly 1,000,000 other Union veterans still alive write to their Congressmen and express their opinions concerning Cleveland's veto of the Dependent Pension Bill. As a nominally nonpartisan organization, the GAR took no official position on the matter—probably in recognition of its approximately 25 percent Democratic membership.[80]

Presidential vetoes of other Civil War pension bills further contributed to Cleveland's reputation of being unfriendly to Union veterans, as did his decision not to attend the 1887 national encampment of the Grand Army of the Republic, his much-publicized fishing trip on Memorial Day, and his appointment of ex-Confederate officers to governmental positions. Many veterans no doubt recalled that Cleveland had hired a substitute to serve in his stead during the war.

But the final act which unified many veterans against Grover Cleveland involved Civil War battle flags—Confederate ones. In June, the president directed the secretary of war to return all captured Confederate banners in Federal possession to the respective Southern states. When the order became public, GAR National Commander Lucius Fairchild was on a speaking tour of posts in the East. Appearing before the Alexander Hamilton Post of Harlem, New York, on June 15, on the occasion of the completion of a Memorial Hall to house that state's Civil War flags, the one-armed Fairchild delivered an angry and unforgettable speech denouncing President Cleveland's action: "May God palsy the hand that wrote the order! May God palsy the brain that conceived it! And may God palsy the tongue that dictated it! I appeal to the sentiment of the nation to prevent this sacrilege."[81]

"I have never seen a body of men more excited than were the old soldiers there," Fairchild told his wife. "Many . . . stood with their eyes full of tears. . . ."[82] Fairchild's "three palsies" speech received tremendous national attention, drawing both criticism and praise. The Wisconsin GAR supported Fairchild, as did other state GAR organizations, although the national GAR commandery made no official response. President Grover Cleveland immediately rescinded the order, but the damage had already been done.[83] As James "Stumps" Tanner, a two-time New York GAR commander and member of the GAR's pensions committee, pointed out, the president's mistake could be turned into political capital by anti-Cleveland forces. He wrote to Fairchild in August:[84]

> As the years placed themselves between us and the period of the war all were conscious that the *sentiment* [italics in original] of those days was at least dormant if not dead and gone. But one day the President was impelled to interfere with the battle flags . . . and lo and behold there was an upheaval and he saw that in the opinion of the country he had laid impious hands on the Holy of Holies in our Patriotic Temple and he took the back track. Now, what is the lesson? Certainly this: The man of proven patriotic endeavor and achievement still *has* an advantageous standing before the people at large. We are political fools if we do not take advantage of this patriotic revival.

The stage was thus set for the Bloody Shirt revival which culminated in the presidential election of 1888. Cleveland and the Democrats were placed on the defensive, and the "soldier vote" was viewed as a potentially decisive factor in the campaign.

The Iron Brigade Association's reunion of September 1887 was a preview of what lay ahead. The reunion took place at the Milwaukee armory building, with the battle flags in attendance. The veterans posed for "soldier photographer" H. H. Bennett of Kilbourn City, sang Army songs, and swapped stories. All seemed normal until Fairchild ally Henry B. Harshaw of Madison introduced a motion to elect association officers by ballot and proposed that John Gibbon not be reelected president. "It was as if a bomb had suddenly been thrown into the room," noted a reporter. The gathering devolved into "the stormiest meeting the brigade association has ever had. . . ." Amid scenes of "great disorder and confusion," Iron Brigade veterans discussed the Harshaw motion.

GAR Adjutant Phil Cheek and Governor Rusk's Quartermaster General, Earl Rogers, led a drive to replace Gibbon with Lucius Fairchild. Democrats Gilbert Woodward and Henry Sanford opposed the dump-Gibbon move. The anti-Gibbon forces, of course, were really attempting to unseat Bragg—the senior vice president—since Gibbon was basically a figurehead. Bragg saw the move for what it was, "an excuse to throw General Bragg overboard."[85]

There was a "hornet's nest in the neighborhood of the little general," reported the *Fond du Lac Commonwealth* as the free-for-all discussion continued.[86] Finally, the veterans cast their votes and Gibbon was reelected, along with Bragg. The latter, however, chose to step down as senior vice president, since he did not want to "sow seeds of discord over points of view."

W. W. Robinson of Chippewa Falls, wartime colonel of the Seventh Wisconsin and a Fairchild ally, thereupon became first vice president. As Bragg explained to a *Milwaukee Sentinel* reporter, "It is all due to the G.A.R. men, on account of the stand I took on the dependent pension bill matter."[87]

President Cleveland's reelection campaign was effectively opposed by Republican veteran organizers. In Wisconsin, both Governor Rusk and ex-Governor Fairchild vigorously campaigned for the election of Benjamin F. Harrison of Indiana, who had been a brigadier general in the war. In the emotional campaign, Cleveland's hiring of a substitute to take his place during the Civil War was endlessly rehashed and condemned, as were his appointments of Confederate officers to federal positions, his supposedly pro-Southern "Cotton Lord" tariff policy, and his veto of the Dependent Pension Bill. Republican veterans barraged Cleveland with Bloody Shirt invective, connecting seemingly unrelated issues—such as the tariff—to Civil War animosities.[88]

A plurality of Wisconsinites and enough other American citizens, particularly those in key states, responded by voting for Harrison. The "soldier vote," and the votes of those men who looked favorably upon the ex-soldiers, was viewed at the time (and since) as providing the Republicans with their narrow margin of victory in the four-candidate race.[89] Not unexpectedly, President Harrison signed a liberal pension bill for Union veterans shortly after taking office. In 1888, the Grand Army of the Republic stood at the pinnacle of its success.

When the GAR held its national encampment in Milwaukee in 1889, politicians watched in awe as nearly 10,000 Wisconsin veterans and numerous detachments from other states paraded sixteen abreast while a quarter of a million citizens cheered them.[90] The most notable absences, however, were the state battle flags. Governor Rusk had retired them before he left office in 1889 to become secretary of agriculture in Harrison's cabinet. When the veterans requested special permission to take a group of Civil War banners—including those of the Iron Brigade—to Gettysburg in 1888, on the twenty-fifth anniversary of the battle, he refused, noting the irreplaceable nature of the artifacts. Rusk observed: "I look upon them as being too precious to risk their destruction."[91] Rusk placed the battle flags in the custody of the State Historical Society "as trustee of the State."[92] Thereafter, society director Reuben G. Thwaites did not permit Wisconsin's Civil War battle flags to appear at public events.

The flags now took up residence in the historical society's rooms in the newly completed south wing of the capitol building.[93] The age of protection and careful preservation had arrived, twenty-three years after the Civil War ended. Repairs had been carried out over the years, but the flags were in delicate condition by the 1880s. The parades, reunions, and exhibits that the flags participated in had obviously contributed to their sorry condition. Indeed, as far as can be determined by present-day examination and from photographic evidence, it seems likely that veterans and others anxious to have a memento had "souvenirized" parts of certain banners by cutting pieces of fabric from their delicate folds.

There was, in fact, no longer any need to keep the state battle flags actively deployed. Indeed, their value would be enhanced by preserving them so they could be used for educational and other purposes. Even though the battle flags had been retired, in other words, they continued to serve as political and cultural symbols of unique significance.

Reuben Gold Thwaites, for example, supported an effort to create a Civil War soldiers' memorial hall to house the state's Civil War artifacts, including the battle flags. In 1895, after an initial failure, state legislators authorized the construction of a "fireproof structure to protect and accommodate the collections of the State Historical Society of Wisconsin including the state historical museum and the records and relics of the late Civil War."[94] Section four of the act stated: ". . . all property of the State now held in trust by the State Historical Society of Wisconsin and occupying any part of the State Capitol, shall be transferred to said new building. . . . The Governor is hereby authorized . . . to place in said building . . . such battle flags and trophies of the Civil War as are in possession of the State."[95]

The State Historical Society building opened on the University of Wisconsin campus in 1900. The historical society, however, soon clashed with the GAR over control of the battle flag collection. State GAR Commander David G. James of Richland Center, veteran of Shiloh, survivor of Andersonville prison, and soon to be state senator, became critical of the historical society's battle flag display after visiting the new facility. Wandering about "in vain for some time" in search of the flags, James required the assistance of a custodian to locate the display. Then he discovered the flags in a hard-to-reach, overheated room "that served as a light shaft" on the "top story of the building." James informed his old comrades of the "distasteful" situation. The GAR then urged legislators to order the flags back to the capitol. Dutifully, the legislature passed an "act to provide for a memorial hall at the Capitol" to display war "mementos" and "relics" while "providing for a return of the battle flags to the Capitol building" in April 1901.[96]

The proposed memorial hall would not only display Civil War artifacts, but also serve as state GAR headquarters. The battle flags would be placed in the rotunda of the capitol in glass cases. "All laws in contravention of this act," directed state lawmakers, "are repealed."[97] Thus, the battle flags had helped endow two museums.

But the flags experienced another change of environment. On the evening of February 27, 1904, calamity struck the state capitol. A malfunctioning gas jet in the second-story cloakroom kindled a fire. Faulty water mains, injuries to Madison's fire chief, and other confusions prevented early quenching of the blaze. Thereafter, the fire could not be extinguished. Governor La Follette and 200 university students carried books and papers out of the flaming building. Next day, little remained of the "splendid building but the great dome and the ruined walls," reported the *Wisconsin State Journal*.[98]

While fire raged, Jacob Barr, a traveling salesman from Chicago, and Elmore Elver, a Madison hotel proprietor, had rushed into the flame-engulfed capitol. They broke open the flag cases in the rotunda and carried "the sacred relics" to the safety of nearby snowbanks.[99] The flags traveled back to the historical society for safekeeping.

Wisconsin's battle flags remained at the historical society for a decade while designers, architects, masons, and laborers built a new and larger state capitol.[100] By 1914, much of the work had been completed. In June, the aging Boys in Blue of the Grand Army of the Republic held their annual encampment in the Assembly Chamber, and Governor Francis E. McGovern ordered the battle flags back to the capitol for the occasion.[101]

The elderly veterans appreciated Governor McGovern's gesture of kindness "best of all." The old soldiers stood guard beside the gauze-covered flags, which were posted along the east wall of the Assembly Chamber. "No patriotic address during our encampment could equal in eloquence the silent presence of those old war-time banners of ours—worn and faded, torn and bullet-riddled, yet beautiful," wrote Jerome Watrous.[102] After the meeting, the battle flags were deposited in the governor's vault while work continued on the north wing of the capitol, where the new GAR Memorial Hall would be located.[103]

Workers completed decorating the GAR Memorial Hall in March 1917. Large glass-fronted cases were built to house the battle flag collection, and in December the flags were brought up from the governor's vault.[104] On Flag Day—June 14, 1918—the GAR Memorial Hall was dedicated.[105]

Iron Brigade veteran Jerome Watrous presented a dedication speech entitled, "Looking Over Our Old Battle Flags." He reviewed the major developments which had occurred in the United States since 1865. Involvement in the Spanish-American War and now in the Great War in Europe, he explained, had underscored the importance of national unity achieved by the veterans of his own generation. New generations had grown up since the Civil War, while tens of thousands of newly arrived immigrants had become citizens. What, asked Watrous, would remind these men and women of the supreme test of the Union and its staggering costs? As the old men of the GAR passed away, how would the boys of 1861–1865 be remembered? It was the battle flags that would remain immortal: "Those . . . old, faded, torn emblems of our great, strong nation." The flags had come to represent the Civil War veterans' very experience. As Watrous concluded: "We had been woven into the colors."[106]

Epilogue

The flags of the Iron Brigade remained undisturbed in their glass cases on the fourth floor of the Wisconsin State Capitol for nearly fifty years. The GAR Memorial Hall Museum passed into control of the Wisconsin Department of Veterans Affairs in 1945. In 1964, the flags were cataloged by curators from the State Historical Society during a general upgrading of the museum displays.

Thirteen years later, a Smithsonian Institution consultant visited the GAR Museum to examine the state battle flag collection, which was sadly in need of conservation by then. Funding proposals to support conservation treatment were rejected by Washington-based endowment agencies, but private donations from a variety of individuals and groups helped launch the Wisconsin Civil War Battle Flag Conservation Project in 1981. State legislators voted first to provide matching funds, and, once the project generated widespread and positive media attention, ongoing appropriations. Donors were encouraged to support specific flags with which they had a personal interest or association. Twelve Iron Brigade flags were among the first to be conserved and photographers documented the work.

As of March 1997, four Wisconsin Iron Brigade flags remain untreated. An 1861 national flag belonging to the Sixth Wisconsin Infantry, reduced to shreds by its hard service, is one. A brigade banner from the veterans' reunion era of the late nineteenth century is another. A small First Corps flag remains. And, most importantly, the Tiffany contract presentation flag given to the Iron Brigade in recognition of their valorous service at Gettysburg is not yet conserved. Funds to treat the presentation flag have been raised, although a conservator familiar with the special needs of the unique object has yet to be identified.

The battle flags of the Twenty-fourth Michigan have also received attention. The 1990 "Save the Flags" program generated support from reenactment groups and the state's general fund. Of the six flags associated with the Michigan contingent of the Iron Brigade, two have been conserved, including the unit's first national color and a state color which participated in the battles from the Wilderness to the Weldon Railroad. The flags are stored in a climate-controlled environment.

Two flags of the Nineteenth Indiana are stored in a flat climate-controlled space at the Indiana War Memorial in Indianapolis. Although not conserved, the stand of colors from the Nineteenth Indiana has been provided with an environment that promotes the long-term well-being of the artifacts. As with the banners from Wisconsin and Michigan, Indiana's Iron Brigade flags are in the control of an agency of the state government.

Notes

Introduction

1. Charles A. Stevens, *Berdan's U.S. Sharpshooters in the Army of the Potomac, 1861–1865* (St. Paul, Minnesota: Price-McGill Company, 1892), 277–78. It should be noted that Charles Stevens is not an entirely impartial observer. His brother was George H. Stevens, the Lieutenant Colonel of the Second Wisconsin.

2. Commanding the brigade at the Brawner Farm battle, John Gibbon wrote: "This fight was the 'baptism of fire' of my brigade and we paid for it a heavy penalty. Out of the 1,800 men I took into action, about one third were killed or wounded in the space of one hour and a half." John Gibbon, *Personal Recollections of the Civil War* (New York: G. P. Putnam's Sons, 1928), 55.

3. Stephen W. Sears, *Landscape Turned Red: The Battle of Antietam* (New York: Ticknor and Fields, 1983), xi.

4. See James McPherson's discussion of the value of "putting the story together" in his article "What's the Matter with History?" in James M. McPherson, *Drawn with the Sword: Reflections on the American Civil War* (New York: Oxford University Press, 1996), 231–53.

1. John Brawner's Damage Claim

1. There are three detailed accounts of the battle at Brawner Farm: Alan D. Gaff, *Brave Men's Tears: The Iron Brigade at Brawner Farm* (Dayton: Morningside House, Inc., 1988); John J. Hennessy, *Return to Bull Run* (New York: Simon & Schuster, 1993), 153–93; Alan T. Nolan, *The Iron Brigade*, third edition (Bloomington: Indiana University Press, 1994), 80–98.

2. The physical descriptions of the farm area are based on close personal examination of the ground, maps, and participants' descriptions. *Maps*: (1) "Map of the Battle-Grounds of August 28–29–30, In the Vicinity of Groveton, Prince William County, Va., Made by Authority of the Hon. G. W. McCrary, Sec. of War, Surveyed in June 1878 by Bvt. Maj. Gen. G. K. Warren, Major of Engineers, 1878, U.S.A." National Archives, Washington, D.C.; (2) U.S. War Department, *The War of the Rebellion: A Compilation of the Official Records of the Union and Confederate Armies*, ser. I, Volume 12, Part 2 Supplement, facing page 1052; (3) Esposito, Col. Vincent J., ed., *Atlas to Accompany Steele's American Campaigns* (West Point: United States Military Academy), map 60; (4) U.S. Army Corps of Engineers, United States Department of the Interior Geological Survey, *Gainesville Quadrangle* (Washington, 1953); (5) Rufus R. Dawes, *Service with the Sixth Wisconsin Volunteers* (Marietta: E. R. Alderman and Sons, 1890), 66; and (6) Gibbon, *Personal Recollections*, 53. *Participants' descriptions*: Theron Haight, *Gainesville, Groveton and Bull Run*, War Papers, Wisconsin Commandery, Military Order of the Loyal Legion, Volume 2 (Milwaukee: 1896), 345–56. Personal examination of the ground, now a part of Manassas National Battlefield Park, establishes that it is unchanged since 1862 with the exception of an additional barn, miscellaneous trees and bushes, and the wood which is larger now, north and south, with an extension in the northeast corner. The farmhouse and barn are postwar but located where the 1862 buildings were. The remnants of an orchard are visible.

3. *Petition of John C. Brawner, Prince William County, Southern Claims Commission*, Commission No. 1335, Office No. 13, Report No. 1, U.S. National Archives (Washington, D.C.), hereinafter identified as "Brawner Claim File."

4. Robert Underwood Johnson and Clarence Clough Buel, eds., *Battles and Leaders of the Civil War*, Volume 2 (New York: Century, 1884–87), 510.

5. *Official Records*, Volume 2, 1.

6. These early months of the war are well described in James M. McPherson, *Battle Cry of Freedom* (New York: Oxford University Press, 1988).

7. *Official Records*, Volume 12, Part 3, 580, 584.

8. See note 1, above.

9. The difficult question of numbers is discussed in Nolan, *The Iron Brigade*, 78, 84, 88, 89. See also Gaff, *Brave Men's Tears*, 156–60.

10. Johnson and Buel, *Battles and Leaders*, 510.

11. Gibbon, *Personal Recollections*, 54.

12. *Official Records*, Volume 12, Part 2, 657; Isaac R. Trimble, "Trimble's Report of Operations of His Brigade from 14th to 29th of August, 1862," *Southern Historical Society Papers*, 8 (1880), 306–309; Abner Doubleday Journal, Harpers Ferry Center Library, Harpers Ferry, West Virginia.

13. Johnson and Buel, *Battles and Leaders*, 510.

14. Nolan, *The Iron Brigade*, 95–96; Gaff, *Brave Men's Tears*, 156–60.

15. Henderson, G. F. R., *Stonewall Jackson and the American Civil War* (New York: Grosset, 1936), 451.

16. Chapter 116, Forty-First Congress, Session III, "An Act Making Appropriations For The Support Of The Army For The Year Ending June Thirty, Eighteen Hundred And Seventy-Two, And For Other Purposes," Sections 2–6, 524–25.

17. See note 3 above. The facts concerning the claim appear in the Brawner Claim File.

18. *Official Records*, Volume 2, 911–12.

19. Nolan, *The Iron Brigade* (New York: The Macmillan Company, 1961).

20. Dawes, *Service with the Sixth Wisconsin*, 60; *Official Records*, Volume 12, Part 2, 845.

21. K. P. Williams, *Lincoln Finds a General*, Volume 1 (New York: The Macmillan Company, 1950), 318–20.

22. *Official Records*, Volume 12, Part 2, 645.

23. Joseph Mills Hanson to Fred W. Cross, 21 December 1846, Manuscript File, Manassas National Battlefield Park, Manassas, Virginia.

24. Gibbon, *Personal Recollections*, 53–54.

25. *Official Records*, Volume 12, Part 3, 661.

2. "They Must Be Made of Iron"

Kent Gramm wishes to thank the Aldeen Fund for its generosity in providing travel for the research on this essay.

1. Alan D. Gaff, *Brave Men's Tears: The Iron Brigade at Brawner Farm* (Dayton: Morningside House, Inc., 1988).

2. George H. Otis, *The Second Wisconsin Infantry*, Alan D. Gaff, ed. (Dayton: Press of Morningside Bookshop, 1984), 255.

3. William J. K. Beaudot and Lance J. Herdegen, *An Irishman in the Iron Brigade: The Civil War Memoirs of James P. Sullivan, Sergt., Company K, 6th Wisconsin Volunteers* (New York: Fordham University Press, 1993), 57.

4. Philip Cheek and Mair Pointon, *History of the Sauk County Riflemen, Known*

As Company "A," Sixth Wisconsin Veteran Volunteer Infantry, 1861–1865 (Gaithersburg: Butternut Press, 1909), 44.

5. Alan T. Nolan, *The Iron Brigade: A Military History* (Ann Arbor: Historical Society of Michigan, 1961), 114–15. It should be noted that officers generally mustered into their new ranks several months after their commissions were issued.

6. Cheek and Pointon, *Sauk County Riflemen*, 46.

7. Beaudot and Herdegen, *Irishman*, 59.

8. John Gibbon, *Personal Recollections of the Civil War* (Dayton: Morningside House Inc., 1988), 71–75.

9. Rufus R. Dawes, *Service with the Sixth Wisconsin Volunteers* (Marietta: E. R. Alderman and Sons, 1890), 79.

10. Otis, *Second Wisconsin Infantry*, 39.

11. Ibid., 29.

12. Dawes, *Service with the Sixth Wisconsin*, 79–80.

13. Cheek and Pointon, *Sauk County Riflemen*, 47.

14. Coughing was the nineteenth-century equivalent of the wolf whistle.

15. Clarence Clough Buel and Robert Underwood Johnson, *Battles and Leaders of the Civil War*, Volume 2, (New York: Thomas Yoseloff, 1956), 557.

16. Ibid., 566.

17. Nolan, *The Iron Brigade*,122.

18. John Michael Priest, *Before Antietam: The Battle for South Mountain* (Shippensburg, Pa: White Mane Publishing Co., 1992), 265.

19. *Official Records*, Volume 19, 252.

20. Dawes, *Service with the Sixth Wisconsin*, 81.

21. Otis, *Second Wisconsin Infantry*, 61.

22. Lance J. Herdegen, *The Men Stood Like Iron* (Bloomington: Indiana University Press, 1997), Chapter 17 and note 4 above. On Colwell being "determined to die," see *Milwaukee Sentinel*, October 31, 1862.

23. *Official Records*, Volume 19, 253.

24. Ibid., 250.

25. Cheek and Pointon, *Sauk County Riflemen*, 48.

26. Beaudot and Herdegen, *Irishman*, 60–61.

27. Ibid., 61.

28. Cheek and Pointon, *Sauk County Riflemen*, 48.

29. Priest, *Before Antietam*, 268.

30. Dawes, *Service with the Sixth Wisconsin*, 82.

31. Herdegen, *Men Stood Like Iron*.

32. Ibid., Chapter 17; note 12 above; and Nolan, *The Iron Brigade*, 336. The wording, based on McClellan's recollection, is impossible to verify. But it was after the Antietam campaign that the name became common, and other accounts in addition to this one place the origin of the name at South Mountain. The Cincinnati correspondent wrote, "This brigade has done some of the hardest and best fighting in the service. It has been justly termed the Iron Brigade of the West." See Herdegen, *Men Stood Like Iron*, and note 12 above. Although not as famous, there were two other brigades with this name: John Porter Hatch's Iron Brigade and Joseph O. Shelby's "Iron Brigade of the West." See Mark M. Boatner III, *The Civil War Dictionary*, revised edition (New York: David McKay Company, Inc., 1988), 428; and *Historical Times Illustrated Encyclopedia of the Civil War*, Patricia L. Faust, ed. (New York: Harper and Row, 1986), 673.

33. Hugh C. Perkins, "'Dear Friend,' Letters of a Civil War Soldier," ed. Marilyn Gardner, *The Christian Science Monitor* (April 6, 1983, and April 7, 1983).

34. *Official Records*, Volume 19, 1053.

35. Herdegen, *Men Stood Like Iron*, 147.

36. Beaudot and Herdegen, *Irishman,* 62–63.

37. Buel and Johnson, *Battles and Leaders*, 576; Dawes, *Service with the Sixth Wisconsin,* 82–83.

38. Nolan, *The Iron Brigade,* 127; Cheek and Pointon, *Sauk County Riflemen,* 49; Herdegen, *Men Stood Like Iron.*

39. Lance Herdegen, in conversation 30 April 1996; *Official Records,* Volume 19, 257, 1053; Dawes, *Service with the Sixth Wisconsin,* 83–84.

40. Herdegen, *Men Stood Like Iron.*

41. Dawes, *Service with the Sixth Wisconsin,* 84.

42. Cheek and Pointon, *Sauk County Riflemen,* 50.

43. *Official Records,* Volume 19, 215.

44. Dawes, *Service with the Sixth Wisconsin,* 84.

45. Buel and Johnson, *Battles and Leaders*, 575.

46. Bruce Catton, *Glory Road* (New York: Doubleday, 1952), 251.

47. Gibbon, *Personal Recollections,* 79–80.

48. Buel and Johnson, *Battles and Leaders,* 576.

49. Ibid., 580.

50. Dawes, *Service with the Sixth Wisconsin,* 85–86.

51. George Washington Partridge, Jr., *Letters from the Iron Brigade*, ed. Hugh L. Whitehouse (Indianapolis: Guild Press of Indiana, 1995), 58.

3. "I Dread the Thought of the Place"

Scott Hartwig wishes to thank Marc Storch for sharing information from his files on the Second Wisconsin Infantry at Antietam.

1. Dawes, *Service with the Sixth Wisconsin*, 87.

2. Harries, "In the Ranks at Antietam," in *Second Wisconsin Infantry*, 260. The strength of the brigade was reported by Lieutenant Frank Haskell, aide-de-camp to Gibbon, who stated in a letter home that the brigade lost 47.5 percent of its strength at Antietam. This gives a strength of 800 men. The figure of 800 is a relatively accurate number given that, in the midst of a campaign, precise numbers of those present always fluctuated. This figure comes from Frank Haskell, who was adjutant of the brigade at that time and would, presumably, have a good idea as to exact figures. See *Haskell of Gettysburg*, Frank L. Byrne, ed. (Madison: State Historical Society of Wisconsin, 1970), 48.

3. These casualty numbers are approximate. During the period from Brawner Farm to South Mountain, a number of men returned to the ranks from illness and other causes, the numbers of which the author does not have statistics for. The number of deserters from the ranks of the Nineteenth Indiana was not available to the author and this may account for some discrepancies. However, even with those additions, the count of deserters in Iron Brigade regiments was still very low in comparison to other Federal infantry units after the battle of Antietam.

4. Sydney Meade Journal, State Historical Society of Wisconsin; Edward Bragg to "My Dear Wife," 13 September 1862, Edward S. Bragg Papers, State Historical Sociey of Wisconsin; Henry B. Young to "Delia," 13 September 1862, Henry Young Papers, State Historical Society of Wisconsin; Byrne, *Haskell of Gettysburg*, 48.

5. William W. Dudley to Ezra A. Carman, 16 July 1895, Record Group 94, *Antietam Studies*, U.S. National Archives; Rufus R. Dawes to Ezra A. Carman, 4 January 1893, *Antietam Studies*. Dudley erred in placing the Second Wisconsin in the first line, or left of the brigade at its bivouac. All available evidence indicates that the Sixth Wisconsin was in the first line and led the brigade advance on the 17th.

6. Gibbon, *Personal Recollections*, 80.

7. Dawes, *Service with the Sixth Wisconsin*, 87; Edward Bragg to Ezra A. Carman, 26 December 1894, *Antietam Studies*; Rufus R. Dawes Journal, undated, State Historical Society of Wisconsin. There is some question regarding who led the column, the Sixth or Second Wisconsin. Lt. Colonel Dudley remembered that the Second Wisconsin did. But Major Dawes, Gibbon, and William Harries recalled that the Sixth Wisconsin did, and I have accepted the opinion of the majority.

8. Dawes Journal; Harries, "In the Ranks at Antietam," 261; Dawes, *Service with the Sixth Wisconsin*, 87. Although Dawes recorded that the shell burst in the "very center" of the regiment, Colonel Bragg, in a letter to his wife on 21 September 1862, wrote that it struck in the rear division. See Bragg to "My Dear Wife." For the fact that the shell burst in Company A, see James Perry Diary, State Historical Society of Wisconsin.

9. John Gibbon, "Antietam Eighteen Years After," *Milwaukee Sunday Telegraph* (5 December 1880).

10. Gibbon, "Antietam Eighteen Years After." William Harries wrote that Bragg said, "Steady on the right, Sixth." See Harries, "In the Ranks at Antietam," 261; Dawes Journal.

11. Gibbon, "Antietam Eighteen Years After"; Gibbon, *Personal Recollections*, 82.

12. George Fairfield, a member of Hooe's company, wrote: "At [Second] Bull Run he had to go to the front to lead his company forward into line and you would have thought he was trying to sneak up on a wild turkey." George Fairfield to "Sister," 2 October 1862, Fairfield Papers, State Historical Society of Wisconsin; *Official Records*, Volume 19, Part 1, 254; Gibbon, *Recollections*, 82; Dawes, *Service with the Sixth Wisconsin*, 13.

13. Dawes Journal; Gibbon, *Personal Recollections*, 82; Ezra A. Carman and Emmor B. Cope, Revised 1905, Antietam Battlefield Map, U.S. Library of Congress.

14. Dawes Journal; Bragg to Carman, 26 December 1894, *Antietam Studies*. But according to Lyman Holford, of Company C, at least some men from this company remained on the skirmish line until they were fired into by friendly troops. See Lyman Holford Diary, Manuscript Division, U.S. Library of Congress.

15. Bragg to Carman, 26 December 1894, *Antietam Studies*; Dawes, *Service with the Sixth Wisconsin*, 88; Dawes, "On the Right at Antietam," in *Service with the Sixth Wisconsin*, 333. In his paper "On the Right at Antietam," Dawes writes that Brown gave the order in a "loud, nervous voice." He altered this in *Service with the Sixth Wisconsin* to, with a "loud imperative voice," no doubt because "nervous" might have been interpreted to imply that Brown was less than brave. Curiously, in his journal Dawes merely stated that Brown was killed in Miller's peach orchard, and offered no other details.

16. Bragg to Carman, 26 December 1894, *Antietam Studies*; Dawes, *Service with the Sixth Wisconsin*, 88; Dawes, "On the Right at Antietam," 334; Dawes Journal.

17. Dawes, "On the Right at Antietam," 333; Dawes to Carman, 7 July 1896, *Antietam Studies*. In another letter to Carman on 14 January 1899, Dawes wrote that the cornstalks were ten to twelve feet high. This seems rather excessive and I have accepted his earlier estimate of height.

18. *Official Records*, Volume 19, Part 1, 255; Ezra A. Carman, *History of the Antietam Campaign*, Carman Papers, Manuscript Division, U.S. Library of Congress, 77.

19. *Official Records*, Volume 19, Part 1, 255; Bragg to Carman, 26 December 1894, *Antietam Studies*; Dawes, *Service with the Sixth Wisconsin*, 13, 99.

20. Bragg to "Wife," 21 September 1862, Bragg Papers; Bragg to Carman, 26 December 1894, *Antietam Studies*; *Official Records*, Volume 19, Part 1, 255.

21. Dawes, *Service with the Sixth Wisconsin*, 89; Dawes Journal. In his published accounts of the battle, Dawes refrained from identifying the artillery fire that killed Bode and wounded Ticknor as "friendly fire."

22. Nineteenth-century cornfields were not dense or planted in straight rows. Stalks grew in large clumps, and thus, one could easily dash around the stalks and through the cornfield. Dawes Journal; Dawes, *Service with the Sixth Wisconsin*, 89. Bragg wrote his wife that "the men discovered the ball hole in my side pocket and saw the red lining & were sure I was shot through the body." Bragg to "Wife," 21 September 1862, Bragg Papers.

23. Dawes, *Service with the Sixth Wisconsin*, 89. For Captain Hooe's proficiency in drill see Dawes, *Service with the Sixth Wisconsin*, 13.

24. Lyman Holford Diary; Volume 19, Part 1, 229, 248; James Stewart, "Short Stories," *Milwaukee Sunday Telegraph* (26 January 1895); Stewart to Carman, 18 September 1896, *Antietam Studies*. See also John Gibbon, "Genl 'Johnny' Gibbon," *Milwaukee Sunday Telegraph* (5 December 1880). Stewart may have confused straw with hay when noting that the limbers were placed behind "straw stacks."

25. *Official Records*, Volume 19, Part 1, 248, 251, 257; Dudley to Carman, 16 July 1895, *Antietam Studies*.

26. Otis, *Second Wisconsin Infantry*, 57, 63; "Report of Acting Adjutant James D. Wood, Second Wisconsin Infantry," in *Supplement to the Official Records of the Union and Confederate Armies*, Janet B. Hewett, Noah A. Trudeau, and Bryce A. Suderow, eds. (Wilmington: Broadfoot Publishing Co., 1994), 540–41; Dawes to Carman, 7 July 1896, *Antietam Studies*; Dawes Journal; Dawes, *Service with the Sixth Wisconsin*, 90. Only in his journal did Dawes write that he sent Huntington to Captain Plummer. In his published account, he stated he sent Huntington to Kellogg.

27. Dawes Journal; Dawes, *Service with the Sixth Wisconsin*, 90. Dawes never mentioned that Huntington did not give Kellogg the complete order in any of his published accounts of the battle.

28. Dawes Journal.

29. Dawes, *Service with the Sixth Wisconsin*, 90.

30. Dawes Journal; Dawes, *Service with the Sixth Wisconsin*, 90; Carman, *History of the Antietam Campaign*, 79; Hewett, Trudeau, and Suderow, *Supplement to the Official Records*, 541.

31. Dawes Journal; Dawes, *Service with the Sixth Wisconsin*, 90; Carman, *History of the Antietam Campaign*, 81–82. See also: Dawes to Carman, 2 November 1898, *Antietam Studies*; and Hewett, Trudeau, and Suderow, *Supplement to the Official Records*, 541.

32. Carman, Chapter 15, *History of the Antietam Campaign*, 77–78; Dudley to Carman, 16 July 1895, *Antietam Studies*; George S. Hoyt to Carman, 22 January 1895, *Antietam Studies*; *Official Records*, Volume 19, Part 1, 251, 257.

33. Carman, *History of the Antietam Campaign*, 82; *Official Records*, Volume 19, Part 1, 229. Stewart's report omitted a number of details that he later related in correspondence to Carman. See Stewart to Carman, 18 September 1896, *Antietam Studies*; and Stewart, "Short Stories."

34. Hoyt to Carman, 2 January 1895, *Antietam Studies*; *Official Records*, Volume 19, Part 1, 258; Hugh Perkins to "Friend," 26 September 1862 (letter loaned to author by Hugh Perkins Jr.); Carman, *History of the Antietam Campaign*, 83. Carman does not state that the Seventh Wisconsin engaged Starke's brigade, and writes that only the skirmishers of the Nineteenth Indiana threatened Starke's rear. Carman did a masterful job of balancing innumerable conflicting accounts he received from veterans, but I believe here he erred. The accounts from the Seventh Wisconsin indicate that they had indeed engaged Starke, and letters from veterans in Starke's brigade confirm that a Union force on their left and rear forced their retreat. The actions of the Nineteenth Indiana during this time are not known with

any precision. Possibly, as Carman states, its skirmishers engaged Starke's men, but the main body of the regiment did not change front to the east until after Starke's retreat, when Hood's division counterattacked.

35. Hugh Perkins to "Friend," 26 September 1862.

36. Dawes Journal; Dawes, *Service with the Sixth Wisconsin*, 91; Frank Holsinger, "How It Feels To Be Under Fire," in *The Blue and the Gray*, Henry Steele Commager, ed., Volume 1 (Indianapolis: Bobbs Merrill Co., Inc., 1973), 316; Hugh Perkins to "Friend," 21 September 1862, letter loaned to the author by Hugh Perkins Jr.

37. Dawes, *Service with the Sixth Wisconsin*, 91, 214–15; Dawes Journal; Bragg to Carman, 26 December 1894, *Antietam Studies*.

38. Dawes Journal; Dawes, *Service with the Sixth Wisconsin*, 91; Dawes to Carman, 10 November 1898, *Antietam Studies*.

39. Dawes, *Service with the Sixth Wisconsin*, 91; Dawes Journal; Gibbon, *Personal Recollections*, 84. Although Dawes wrote that he collected 200 men in his published accounts of the battle, in his journal he gave the number as 60, which seems more likely. See also Dawes to Carman, 14 February 1898, *Antietam Studies.*

40. *Official Records*, Volume 19, Part 1, 229; Carman, *Antietam Studies*, 109; Stewart, "Short Stories."

41. *Official Records*, Volume 19, Part 1, 229; Gibbon, *Personal Recollections*, 84; Stewart, "Short Stories." Although Stewart wrote that Campbell was wounded almost immediately, in his official report he stated that in "less than twenty minutes" after going into action, Campbell was wounded. Gibbon's account supports the fact that Campbell was not wounded immediately.

42. Gibbon, *Personal Recollections*, 82–83.

43. Gibbon, *Personal Recollections*, 83; Gibbon, "Gen'l 'Johnny' Gibbon."

44. *Official Records*, Volume 19, Part 1, 251, 258; Hoyt to Carman, 22 January 1895, *Antietam Studies*; Dudley to Carman, 16 July 1895, *Antietam Studies*; Carman, *History of the Antietam Campaign*, 112.

45. *Official Records*, Volume 19, Part 1, 251; Dudley to Carman, 16 July 1895, *Antietam Studies*. Dudley called the charge "foolhardy," but this was after thirty years of reflection. No doubt it was, but it also reflected the élan and aggressive spirit of the brigade. Bob Patterson, "Reminiscences of Antietam," in Henry C. Marsh Papers, Indiana State Library; Henry Marsh to "Father," September 1862, Henry C. Marsh Papers [date of the letter is obscure].

46. Carman, *History of the Antietam Campaign*, 113; *Official Records*, Volume 19, Part 1, 251–52.

47. Gibbon, "Genl 'Johnny' Gibbon"; Dawes Journal; Dawes, *Service with the Sixth Wisconsin*, 92; Dawes to Carman, 14 January 1899, *Antietam Studies*. Dawes wrote in his journal that Ely had only fifteen men. He adjusted this in his postwar account to eighteen. I accepted the lower figure because Dawes recorded this closer to the event.

48. Otis, *Second Wisconsin Infantry*, 62–63; Hewett, Trudeau, and Suderow, *Supplement to the Official Records*, 541; Sydney Meade Diary, State Historical Society of Wisconsin. Meade evidently intended to enter the numbers of losses, for beneath his statement that losses were very heavy he wrote "there being killed & wounded," but recorded no numbers.

49. The precise time that these two regiments were recalled is difficult to establish. In his after-action report, Dudley said they moved back to the North Woods at 2 P.M. In a 16 July 1895 letter to Carman he wrote that they were relieved by Sumner's corps and then moved back. However, Dawes recorded in his journal that the rest of the brigade reached the North Woods shortly after Captain Ely and the Second Wisconsin arrived there. See also: *Official Records*, Volume 19, Part 1, 258; and Hoyt to Carman, 22 January 1895, *Antietam Studies*. Hoyt wrote that they were relieved by fresh troops, but was not sure whether they were of the Second or Twelfth Corps.

They were probably Goodrich's brigade of the Twelfth Corps, since Sumner did not come up until later in the morning. See *Official Records*, Volume 19, Part 1, 189.

50. Dawes Journal; Dawes, *Service with the Sixth Wisconsin*, 92.

51. Dawes Journal.

52. Bragg to Carman, 26 December 1894, *Antietam Studies*; Hoyt to Carman, 22 January 1895, *Antietam Studies*. Another incident that illustrated the pugnacity of the brigade involved troops from the Second Corps brigade of Brigadier General Willis Gorman. Gorman's brigade had relieved Gibbon's brigade at South Mountain on the night of September 14th. However, Gorman had refused to send a regiment forward to relieve the Sixth Wisconsin, which was in the woods on the side of the mountain, stating that "all men are cowards in the dark." When Gorman's men fled the slaughter of their division (i.e., Sedgwick's) in the West Woods, during the fighting on the 17th, they attempted to pass through the skirmish line posted by Gibbon with the remnants of his brigade. Dawes recalled that "some men of the Second Wisconsin had pronounced Gorman's brigade stragglers, and were proposing to stop them and not allow them to go through our line to the rear," citing their failure to relieve the Sixth Wisconsin at South Mountain as the reason. See Dawes to Carman, 2 February 1899, *Antietam Studies*.

53. *Official Records,* Volume 19, Part 1, 66, 252.

54. Dawes, *Service with the Sixth Wisconsin*, 108.

55. Ibid., 94–95; Bragg to "Wife," 21 September 1862, Bragg Papers.

56. Otis, *Second Wisconsin Infantry*, 63; Henry Young to "Wife," 18 September 1862, Young Papers, State Historical Society of Wisconsin; Bragg to Carman, 26 December 1894, *Antietam Studies*; James Perry Diary; "From the Wisconsin Third," *Wisconsin State Journal* (2 December 1862).

57. *The Medical and Surgical History of the Civil War*, Volume 12 (Wilmington, NC: Broadfoot Publishing Company, 1990), 882; Hugh Perkins to "Friend," 26 September 1862.

58. Dawes, *Service with the Sixth Wisconsin*, 99; Bob Patterson, "Reminiscences of Antietam."

59. Otis, *Second Wisconsin Infantry*, 306, 320; Henry Young to "Wife," 18 September 1862 and 4 October 1862; Henry Marsh to "Father," 20 September 1862; Byrne, *Haskell of Gettysburg*, 48; Perkins to "Friend," 26 September 1862. For desertions of the Sixth and Seventh Wisconsin, the author is indebted to Marc Storch, who provided a list from his records.

60. Dawes, *Service with the Sixth Wisconsin*, 153.

4. John Gibbon and the Black Hat Brigade

1. Gibbon, *Personal Recollections*; John Gibbon, *The Artillerist's Manual, Compiled from Various Sources, and Adapted to the Service of the United States* (New York: D. Van Nostrand, 1859). A second revised and enlarged edition was published in 1863.

2. William H. Harries, "Gainesville, Virginia, Aug. 28, 1862," in *Glimpses of the Nation's Struggle, Military Order of the Loyal Legion of the United States*, Volume 6 (St. Paul: H. L. Collins Co., 1909), 198. The theme of seeing others being promoted ahead of him was repeated throughout his letters to his wife. See Gibbon Papers, The Historical Society of Pennsylvania, Philadelphia, Pennsylvania. See also Steven J. Wright and Blake A. Magner, "John Gibbon: The Man and the Monument," *The Gettysburg Magazine* 13 (July 1995), 120.

3. Gibbon, *Personal Recollections.*

4. Nolan, *The Iron Brigade*, 41.

5. Gibbon Papers, Box 1, Folder 2.

6. Nolan, *The Iron Brigade*, 51–52; Gibbon, *Personal Recollections*, 35–37.

7. Gibbon, *Personal Recollections*, 35–36.

8. Ibid., 37–38.

9. Dawes, *Service with the Sixth Wisconsin*, 44.

10. Otis, *Second Wisconsin Infantry*, 45.

11. William H. Harries, "In the Ranks at Antietam," *Glimpses of the Nation's Struggle, Military Order of the Loyal Legion of the United States*, Volume 4 (St. Paul: H. L. Collins, 1898), 556–57.

12. Gibbon Papers, Box 1, Folder 3.

13. Gibbon, *Personal Recollections*, 39–40.

14. Ibid., 30–31.

15. Gibbon's Report, *Official Records*, Volume 12, Part 2, 105–106; Gibbon Papers, Box 1, Folder 3; Otis, *Second Wisconsin Infantry*, 52–53.

16. Nolan, *The Iron Brigade*, 65–67; *Official Records*, Volume 12, Part 2, 123–24.

17. Gibbon Papers, Box 1, Folder 4.

18. Otis, *Second Wisconsin Infantry*, 55.

19. *Official Records*, Volume 12, Part 2, 378. For detailed accounts of the battles of Brawner Farm and Second Bull Run see: Gaff, *Brave Men's Tears*; Nolan, *The Iron Brigade*, 80–98; appropriate reports in *Official Records*, Volume 12; as well as Nolan's and Gaff's contribution to this work.

20. Gibbon, *Personal Recollections*, 54.

21. Gibbon Papers, Box 1, Folder 4.

22. Dawes, *Service with the Sixth Wisconsin*, 71; Nolan, *The Iron Brigade*, 106.

23. Dawes, *Service with the Sixth Wisconsin*, 72.

24. Gibbon Papers, Box 1, Folder 4; *Official Records*, Volume 12, Part 2, 379–80.

25. *Official Records*, Volume 12, Part 2, 38.

26. Harries, "In the Ranks at Antietam," 556.

27. Gibbon Papers, Box 1, Folder 4.

28. The regiment, the Twenty-fourth Michigan, joined the brigade on October 8, 1862, following a great deal of effort by Gibbon to keep the brigade one of exclusively Western troops. See Nolan, *The Iron Brigade*, 117–18, 159.

29. Dawes, *Service with the Sixth Wisconsin*, 81.

30. *Official Records*, Volume 19, Part 1, 247–48. For detail about the opening stages of the Maryland campaign and the battle of South Mountain, see Nolan, *The Iron Brigade*, 113–30; and Kent Gramm's contribution to this work. Gibbon also wrote extensively on the subject in his *Personal Recollections* and in his letters to his wife.

31. Gibbon Papers, Box 1, Folder 4; *Official Records*, Volume 19, Part 1, 52.

32. Gibbon, *Personal Recollections*, 79–80; Nolan, *The Iron Brigade*, 130. In the Gibbon Papers at The Historical Society of Pennsylvania, Philadelphia, Pennsylvania, there are numerous references by Gibbon in correspondence with his wife and others. After the war Madeleine Dahlgren, widow of Admiral John A. Dahlgren and mother of slain Union cavalryman Colonel Ulric Dahlgren, made her home at The Mountain House and built the large stone chapel located across the road as a final resting place for her first husband. The imposing nature of the structure has led many unsuspecting battlefield visitors to incorrectly surmise that it was there at the time of Gibbon's meeting with General Sumner. Today The Mountain House is preserved as part of a large restaurant.

33. *Official Records*, Volume 19, Part 1, 248.

34. Ibid., 229. For more detail of the actions of Gibbon and his brigade at the

battle of Antietam, see appropriate reports in *Official Records,* Volume 19; Nolan, *The Iron Brigade* 131–48; Gibbon, *Personal Recollections*; and D. Scott Hartwig's contribution to this book.

35. Harries, "In the Ranks at Antietam," 556.

36. Gibbon Papers, Box 1, Folder 4.

37. Ibid., Box 1, Folder 5.

38. Dawes, *Service with the Sixth Wisconsin,* 106. Actually, Dawes was mistaken in that Gibbon had not yet been promoted to major general, but rather given the "promotion" of divisional command. Gibbon was not promoted to Major General of Volunteers until June 7, 1864.

39. Gibbon, *Personal Recollections*, 107–108. For details about this issue, see Nolan, *The Iron Brigade*, 168–75.

40. Frank A. Haskell, *The Battle of Gettysburg* (Madison: Wisconsin History Commission, 1910), 26–27.

41. Ibid., 14.

42. The greatest criticism of Haskell came from the Philadelphia Brigade Survivors' Association who spent nearly thirty years defending their position and actions during the battle of Gettysburg.

43. Haskell, *Battle of Gettysburg,* 16–17.

44. Ibid., 20.

45. Gibbon Papers, Box 2 contains correspondence regarding the site of Gibbon's final resting place, as well as newspaper articles prematurely announcing that he had chosen to be buried in Wisconsin. This box also contains numerous letters, articles, reunion ribbons, and other material which supports the belief that Gibbon remained very close to veterans of the Iron Brigade.

46. The Military Order of the Loyal Legion of the United States Commandery-in-Chief Scrapbook #6, Entry 300, Civil War Library and Museum, Philadelphia, Pennsylvania.

47. Charles A. Woodruff, "In Memory of Major General John Gibbon, Commander-in-Chief," *Personal Recollections of the War of the Rebellion: Addresses Delivered Before the Commandery of the State of New York, Military Order of the Loyal Legion of the United States,* Volume 2 (New York: G. P. Putnam's Sons, 1897), 292.

5. "The Dread Reality of War"

1. "Heroism," *Littell's Living Age*, Volume 116 (February 8, 1873), 347.

2. Gerald E. Linderman, *Embattled Courage* (New York: The Free Press, 1987), 2.

3. U.S. National Archives, Record Group 393, *Records of U.S. Army Continental Commands, Gibbon's Brigade, General Orders*.

4. *Wisconsin Daily Patriot* (June 27, 1862), 2.

5. Henry Marsh Manuscript, Indiana Division, Indiana State Library, Indianapolis, Indiana.

6. *Wisconsin Daily Patriot* (August 18, 1862), 2.

7. *Wisconsin State Journal* (December 7, 1863), 1.

8. N. P. Milner, trans., *Vegetius: Epitome of Military Science* (Liverpool: Liverpool University Press, 1993), 87.

9. S. A. Stouffer et al., *The American Soldier: Combat and Its Aftermath* (Princeton: Princeton University, 1949), 77, 98.

10. *Milwaukee Sunday Telegraph* (February 25, 1899), 5. The Second Wisconsin had fought at Bull Run on July 21, 1861, but its experience there had been as a virtually untrained militia regiment and bore little resemblance to the combat situation encountered in 1862. See Alan D. Gaff, *If This Is War: A History of the Cam-*

paign of Bull's Run by the Wisconsin Regiment Thereafter Known as the Ragged Ass Second (Dayton: Morningside House, Inc.), 1991.

11. *National Tribune* (December 21, 1902), 3

12. United States 46th Congress, 1st Session, Senate Executive Document 37. *Proceedings and Report of the Board of Army Officers Convened by Special Order No. 78*, Headquarters of the Army, Adjutant General's Office, Washington, April 12, 1878, "In the Case of Fitz John Porter, Together with Proceedings in the Original Trial and Papers Relating Thereto" (Washington: Government Printing Office, 1879), 586.

13. *Milwaukee Sunday Telegraph* (September 7, 1884), 3.

14. E. B. Quiner, *Correspondence of Wisconsin Volunteers, 1861–1865*, Wisconsin State Historical Society, Madison, Wisconsin, Volume 8, 133.

15. Gilbert M. Woodward letter in Robert Hughes Manuscript, State Historical Society of Wisconsin, Madison, Wisconsin.

16. *Milwaukee Sunday Telegraph* (September 23, 1883), 2.

17. Ibid. (May 6, 1888), 3.

18. Ibid. (November 4, 1883), 3.

19. *Wisconsin State Register* (September 13, 1862), 2.

20. *National Tribune* (December 11, 1902), 5.

21. *Wisconsin State Journal* (October 6, 1862), 2.

22. Rufus R. Dawes, "Skirmishes of the Rappahannock and Battle of Gainesville," T. C. H. Smith Manuscript, Ohio Historical Society, Columbus, Ohio.

23. *Janesville Daily Gazette* (December 22, 1862), 2.

24. *Grant County Herald* (September 30, 1862), 1.

25. John St. Clair Manuscript, State Historical Society of Wisconsin, Madison, Wisconsin.

26. *Randolph County Journal* (September 12, 1862), 4.

27. Solomon Meredith Manuscript, Indiana Historical Society, Indianapolis, Indiana.

28. *Elkhart Review* (October 25, 1862), 2.

29. Otis, *Second Wisconsin Infantry*, 55.

30. Gaff, *Brave Men's Tears*, 164–65.

31. *Official Records*, Volume 12, Part 1, 382.

32. W. H. Church Manuscript, State Historical Society of Wisconsin, Madison, Wisconsin.

33. *Milwaukee Sunday Telegraph* (November 30, 1884), 3.

34. Nathaniel Rollins Diary, State Historical Society of Wisconsin, Madison, Wisconsin.

35. *Milwaukee Sunday Telegraph* (September 23, 1883), 2.

36. George Fairfield Diary, State Historical Society of Wisconsin, Madison, Wisconsin.

37. William P. Maxson, *Campfires of the Twenty-third New York* (New York: Davies and Kent, 1863), 77.

38. *Milwaukee Sunday Telegraph* (May 16, 1884), 3.

39. Ibid. (November 4, 1883), 3.

40. Otis, *Second Wisconsin Infantry*, 57.

41. *Wisconsin State Register* (September 13, 1862), 2; Dawes, *Service with the Sixth Wisconsin*, 68.

42. Gaff, *Brave Men's Tears*, 156–58.

43. Dawes, *Service with the Sixth Wisconsin*, 70.

44. Catherine Merrill, *The Soldier of Indiana in the War for the Union*, Volume 1 (Indianapolis: Merrill and Co., 1866), 593.

45. Cheek and Pointon, *Sauk County Riflemen*, 45.

46. Nolan, *The Iron Brigade*, 105–107.

47. *Milwaukee Sentinel* (October 8, 1862), 2.
48. Nolan, *The Iron Brigade*, 110.
49. Quiner, *Correspondence*, Volume 2, 261.
50. Dawes, *Service with the Sixth Wisconsin*, 75; U.S., *Congressional Record*, Volume 14, Part 4, Appendix, 140.
51. Dawes, *Service with the Sixth Wisconsin*, 68.
52. *Wisconsin State Journal* (September 18, 1862), 2.
53. *Prairie du Chien Courier* (September 11, 1862), 2.
54. Quiner, *Correspondence*, Volume 4, 12.
55. William N. Jackson Diary, Indiana Historical Society, Indianapolis, Indiana.
56. *Wisconsin State Journal* (October 25, 1862), 2.
57. John Gibbon Manuscript, The Historical Society of Pennsylvania, Philadelphia, Pennsylvania.
58. *Daily State Sentinel* (September 12, 1862), 2.
59. *Grant County Witness* (September 25, 1862), 1.
60. *Elkhart Review* (September 13, 1862), 3.
61. *Milwaukee Sentinel* (September 24, 1862), 1.
62. *Grant County Herald* (September 11, 1862), 2.
63. *Milwaukee Sentinel* (September 13, 1862), 1.
64. *Wisconsin State Register* (September 6, 1862), 3.
65. Eugene H. Berwanger, ed., "'absent So long from those I love': The Civil War Letters of Joshua Jones," *Indiana Magazine of History*, Volume 88 (September 1992), 234.
66. Marsh Manuscript; *Wisconsin State Journal* (September 17, 1862), 2.
67. Nolan, *The Iron Brigade*, 114–15.
68. *Wisconsin State Journal* (October 25, 1862), 2.
69. Frank A. Haskell Manuscript, State Historical Society of Wisconsin, Madison, Wisconsin.
70. "Personal War Sketches of the Members of Tom Cox Post 132, Department of Wisconsin, Grand Army of the Potomac," Grant County Historical Society, Lancaster, Wisconsin.
71. *Milwaukee Sunday Telegraph* (August 24, 1895), 2.
72. Ibid. (August 22, 1886), 3.
73. Ibid.
74. *Personal War Sketches.*
75. *Milwaukee Sentinel* (October 8, 1862), 2; Nolan, *The Iron Brigade*, 129.
76. Dawes, *Service with the Sixth Wisconsin*, 84.
77. Ibid.
78. Nolan, *The Iron Brigade*, 137–39.
79. Gibbon, *Personal Recollections*, 90.
80. Otis, *Second Wisconsin Infantry*, 260.
81. Quiner, *Correspondence*, Volume 2, 308.
82. Dawes, *Service with the Sixth Wisconsin*, 93.
83. *Prairie du Chien Courier* (October 23, 1862), 3.
84. *Wisconsin State Journal* (October 4, 1862), 2.
85. Nolan, *The Iron Brigade*, 142.
86. Alan D. Gaff and Maureen Gaff, *Our Boys: A Civil War Photograph Album* (Evansville: Windmill, 1996), 22–23.
87. *Janesville Daily Gazette* (December 22, 1862), 2.
88. Quiner, *Correspondence*, Volume 4, 22.
89. Edward S. Bragg Manuscript, State Historical Society of Wisconsin, Madison; *Milwaukee Sentinel* (October 8, 1862), 2.
90. Gaff and Gaff, *Our Boys*, 20–21.

91. Reuben Huntley Manuscript, State Historical Society of Wisconsin, Madison, Wisconsin.

92. Quiner, *Correspondence*, Volume 2, 286.

93. Margaret Ryan Kelley, "A Soldier of the Iron Brigade," *Wisconsin Magazine of History*, Volume 22 (1938–1939), 308.

94. *Wisconsin State Register* (September 13, 1862), 2; *Roster of Wisconsin Volunteers* (Madison: Democrat Printing, 1886), Volume 1, 366.

95. Quiner, *Correspondence*, Volume 2, 307.

96. Sullivan Green Manuscript, State Historical Society of Wisconsin, Madison, Wisconsin.

97. *Milwaukee Sunday Telegraph* (April 29, 1888), 3.

98. *Personal War Sketches.*

99. Julius Murray Manuscript, State Historical Society of Wisconsin, Madison, Wisconsin.

100. *Wisconsin State Journal* (December 16, 1862), 2.

101. Quiner, *Correspondence*, Volume 2, 308.

102. Cornelius Wheeler Manuscript, State Historical Society of Wisconsin, Madison,Wisconsin.

103. Elisha B. Odle Manuscript, Fredericksburg and Spotsylvania National Military Park, Fredericksburg, Virginia.

104. *Milwaukee Sunday Telegraph* (September 28, 1879), 2.

105. Gibbon, *Recollections*, 38, 40.

106. Gaff, *Brave Men's Tears*, 156–57.

107. Nolan, *The Iron Brigade*, 131.

108. *Indianapolis Daily Journal* (October 5, 1862), 2.

109. Cheek and Pointon, *Sauk County Riflemen*, 52.

110. *Milwaukee Sunday Telegraph* (September 26, 1896), 3.

111. *Milwaukee Sunday Telegraph* (July 27, 1895), 8.

112. *Grant County Herald* (September 30, 1862), 1; *Milwaukee Sunday Telegraph* (July 25, 1886), 3.

113. Cheek and Pointon, *Sauk County Riflemen*, 46–47.

114. *Milwaukee Sunday Telegraph* (May 10, 1885), 3.

115. *Milwaukee Sunday Telegraph* (July 27, 1895), 8.

116. Alan D. Gaff, *On Many a Bloody Field: Four Years in the Iron Brigade* (Bloomington: Indiana University Press, 1996), 154.

117. *Richmond Palladium* (April 14, 1864), 2.

118. George Fairfield Diary.

119. *Official Records*, Volume 19, Part 1, 255.

120. Quiner, *Correspondence*, Volume 2, 296.

121. Berwanger, "absent So long," 234.

122. Edwin Brown Manuscript, privately owned.

123. Quiner, *Correspondence*, Volume 3, 269.

124. *Milwaukee Sunday Telegraph* (May 20, 1883), 2.

125. *Official Records*, Volume 19, Part 1, 252.

126. Gaff, *Bloody Field*, 196.

127. Ibid., 183.

128. *Wisconsin State Journal* (September 26, 1862), 2.

129. *Milwaukee Sentinel* (September 24, 1862), 1; *Milwaukee Sunday Telegraph* (August 24, 1895), 2.

130. *Milwaukee Sunday Telegraph* (September 26, 1896), 1.

131. Otis, *Second Wisconsin Infantry*, 257.

132. Quiner, *Correspondence*, Volume 8, 392.

133. Frank A. Haskell Manuscript.

134. Although Colonel Robinson did not leave the service until 1864, his resignation followed the breaking open of his Brawner Farm wound.

135. Frank A. Haskell Manuscript; *The Weekly Teller* (June 11, 1885), 1.

6. "Like So Many Devils"

Marc and Beth Storch wish to extend their thanks to Keith Bohannon for his assistance with sources for the Georgia troops who faced the Iron Brigade; to Noel Harrison for his help in viewing and preserving the site of Fitzhugh's Crossing; and to the Vernon County Historical Society of Wisconsin for their kind assistance with this research.

1. Cheek and Pointon, *Sauk County Riflemen*, 65.

2. Elmer Wallace Letters, 9 May 1863, and 11 May 1863, John Fuller Collection; Cornelius Wheeler Papers, 8 May 1861, State Historical Society of Wisconsin.

3. Rufus Dawes Journal. It is interesting to note that in his book, *Service with the Sixth Wisconsin* (135), Dawes states that it was the Sixth and Seventh Wisconsin that quelled the mutiny. Dawes modifies his actual journal and letter entries often in the book, however; sometimes to protect an individual, sometimes to correct an error made at the time. In this case, however, members of the Second also noted their participation in this event.

4. Wallace Letters, 11 May 1863. Some members of the brigade comment that no fires were allowed for fear of alerting the enemy, but they are contradicted by Wallace and others.

5. Elon Brown Journal, 28 April 1863, State Historical Society of Wisconsin.

6. *Official Records*, Volume 25, Part 1, 273.

7. Dawes Papers; Letter from Edward Bragg (n.d. but circa 1890). Bragg is in error in his memory of it being the Barnard House they were to occupy. That building had been destroyed in the December 1862 fight at Fredericksburg. Instead, it was the residence known as Smithfield that was to be their destination.

8. Ibid.; Elon Brown Journal, 28 April 1863.

9. Ibid.; Dawes Letters, 1 May 1863.

10. Quiner, *Correspondence*, Volume 8, 136.

11. *Official Records*, Volume 25, Part 1, 262.

12. Wallace Letters, 11 May 1863.

13. The Iron Brigade Crossed the river at Fredericksburg. See John A. Kress, n.d., Fairchild Papers, Wisconsin State Historical Society, 3; Beaudot and Herdegen, *Irishman*, 76.

14. *Official Records*, Volume 25, Part 1, 262.

15. Ibid.; Henry C. Matrau, *Letters Home: Henry Matrau of the Iron Brigade*, ed. Marcia Reid-Green (Lincoln: University of Nebraska Press, 1993), 53.

16. Cheek and Pointon, *Sauk County Riflemen*, 62; Quiner, *Correspondence*, Volume 8, 375.

17. Dawes Letters, 1 May 1863.

18. *National Tribune*, "Chancellorsville, Jno. T. Davidson" (June 19, 1890); Dawes Letters, 1 May 1863.

19. Cheek and Pointon, *Sauk County Riflemen*, 63; Curtis, *Twenty-fourth Michigan*, 125; Quiner, *Correspondence*, Volume 8, 375.

20. Wallace Letters, 11 May 1863; Matrau, *Letters Home*, 54.

21. The Iron Brigade Crossed the river at Fredericksburg, 3.

22. Ibid., 2; *Official Records*, Volume 25, Part 1, 267; Quiner, *Correspondence*, Volume 8, 375. There is some difference of opinion as to how many boats were actually in the water. Kress states that when the twentieth boat was placed in the

water, the enemy opened fire and drove off the engineers. Henry Matrau saw only one boat in the water. If it is assumed that each boat could hold a company, then the figure of twenty boats would not have required the Second Wisconsin to carry more boats to the river. Perhaps some had been damaged, or Meredith might have wanted to ensure that enough men could cross in the first wave.

23. Henry C. Walker to J. W. Johnston, 9 May 1863, copy in Civil War Miscellany, Personal Papers, Georgia State Archives, Atlanta, Georgia.

24. William Seymour, *The Civil War Memoirs of Captain William Seymour*, E. Terry Jones, ed. (Baton Rouge: Louisiana State University Press, 1991), 48; Quiner, *Correspondence*, Volume 8, 407; Wallace Letters, 11 May 1863; E. Terry Jones, *Lee's Tigers* (Baton Rouge: Louisiana State University Press, 1987), 150.

25. Dawes Letters, 1 May 1863; Bragg Letters, 8 May 1863; Cheek and Pointon, *Sauk County Riflemen*, 62; *Milwaukee Sunday Telegraph* (August 7, 1887).

26. Dawes Letters, undated letter from Bragg to Dawes.

27. Beaudot and Herdegen, *Irishman*, 77.

28. *Wisconsin State Journal* (May 14, 1863); Quiner, *Correspondence*, Volume 8, 136; *Oshkosh Northwestern* (June 11, 1863).

29. Cheek and Pointon, *Sauk County Riflemen*, 64; Dawes, *Service with the Sixth Wisconsin*, 137.

30. The Iron Brigade Crossed the river at Fredericksburg. See Fairchild Papers, Wisconsin State Historical Society, 3.

31. *National Tribune* (February 6, 1890); Dawes Letters, 1 May 1863.

32. Cheek and Pointon, *Sauk County Riflemen*, 64; Henry Greenleaf Pearson, *James S. Wadsworth of Geneseo: Brevet Major General of United States Volunteers* (New York: 1913), 182.

33. Quiner, *Correspondence*, Volume 8, 137.

34. *Official Records*, Volume 25, Part 1, 273.

35. Quiner, *Correspondence*, Volume 8, Part 1, 137, 407.

36. Beaudot and Herdegen, *Irishman*, 77; *Milwaukee Sunday Telegraph* (July 1, 1888).

37. Samuel Eaton Letters, 8 May 1863, State Historical Society of Wisconsin.

38. *Milwaukee Sunday Telegraph* (July 1, 1888).

39. Dawes Letters, 1 May 1863; Eaton Letters, 8 May 1863; Dawes Journal, 29 April, 1863.

40. Bragg Letters, 8 May 1863; Wheeler Papers, 8 May 1863.

41. Quiner, *Correspondence*, Volume 8, 408.

42. General Wadsworth was shot to death while leading a desperate charge during the battle of the Wilderness on May 6, 1864. See Pearson, *Wadsworth*, 182.

43. *National Tribune* (February 6, 1890); *Milwaukee Sunday Telegraph* (July 1, 1888).

44. Quiner, *Correspondence*, Volume 8, 137.

45. Charles S. Wainwright, *A Diary of Battle, The Personal Journals of Colonel Charles S. Wainwright, 1861–1865*, ed. Allan Nevins (Gettysburg: Stan Clark Military Books, 1962), 186.

46. Dawes Letters, 1 May 1863.

47. Dawes Letters, undated letter from Bragg to Dawes; Cheek and Pointon, *Sauk Country Riflemen*, 66; Curtis, *Twenty-fourth Michigan*, 126.

48. *Official Records*, Volume 25, Part 1, 267.

49. Quiner, *Correspondence*, Volume 8, 375; *Official Records*, Volume 25, Part 1, 173; *Milwaukee Sunday Telegraph* (March 25, 1888); Lucius Fairchild Papers, 30 April 1863, State Historical Society of Wisconsin. Note that the losses for the Second, Sixth, and Seventh Wisconsin are taken from reports at the time of the event. There are no exact statements of losses for the Twenty-fourth Michigan and

the Nineteenth Indiana that do not include the days which followed the crossing. It is known that on April 30, two men were killed and two wounded in the Twenty-fourth and, thus, they are subtracted from the official report of losses. Elmer Wallace of the Twenty-fourth Michigan also confirms eighteen men wounded in the crossing. The Nineteenth Indiana does not state it suffered any losses in the days after the crossing, so it is assumed all of its losses occurred at that time.

50. Seymour, *Civil War Memoirs*, 49; Hewett, Trudeau, and Suderow, *Supplement to the Official Records*, Part 2, Volume 24, 47–108.

51. *Official Records*, Volume 25, Part 1, 267; *Oshkosh Northwestern* (June 11, 1863); "April 1863 Monthly Return," Series 1200, State Historical Society of Wisconsin; Curtis, *Twenty-fourth Michigan*, 126; *National Tribune* (February 6, 1890).

52. Wallace Letters, 11 May 1863. The *Michigan Soldier and Sailors Roster* lists no Jerry O'Donnel, but does show a James O'Donnel in the First Michigan (three-month) regiment, who mustered out August 7, 1861, in Detroit. It seems unlikely that the men of the Twenty-fourth Michigan would be mistaken as to the identity of the man captured.

53. Nathaniel Rollins Journal, 29 April 1863, State Historical Society of Wisconsin; Quiner, *Correspondence*, Volume 8, 136; Cornelius Wheeler Papers, 8 May 1863, State Historical Society of Wisconsin.

54. Fairchild Letters, 1 May 1863; Wheeler Papers, 8 May 1863; Curtis, *Twenty-fourth Michigan*, 127.

55. Wheeler Letters, 8 May 1863.

56. Ibid.

7. John F. Reynolds and the Iron Brigade

1. Edward J. Nichols, *Toward Gettysburg: A Biography of General John F. Reynolds* (College Station: Pennsylvania State University Press, 1958); Steve Sanders, "Enduring Tales of Gettysburg: The Death of Reynolds," *Gettysburg Magazine*, Issue 14 (January 1996), 27–36; Michael A. Riley, *"For God's Sake, Forward!": Gen. John F. Reynolds, USA* (Gettysburg, Pennsylvania: Farnsworth House Military Impressions, 1995); John Gibbon, *Recollections of the Civil War*, 401; Rufus R. Dawes, *Service with the Sixth Wisconsin Volunteers* (Marietta, Ohio, 1890), 166. "Across our track as we hurried on, passed some officers carrying in a blanket the body of our corps commander, General John F. Reynolds," Dawes wrote.

2. Frank A. Haskell, *The Battle of Gettysburg*, Madison, Wisconsin History Commission, 1910, 14; *McClellan's Own Story*, William C. Prime, ed., (New York: Charles L. Webster, 1887), 140; Circular, January 3, 1864, Culpeper Court House, Virginia, Correspondence of the Iron Brigade, State Historical Society of Wisconsin.

3. R[obert] K. Beecham, *Gettysburg, The Pivotal Battle of the Civil War* (Chicago: A. C. McClurg and Co., 1911), 72; "Carleton" [Charles Carleton Coffin], "Saving the Nation: The Story of the War Retold for Our Boys and Girls," *National Tribune*, March 26, 1885; W. C. Storrick, *The Battle of Gettysburg: The Country, the Contestants, the Results*, fifteenth ed. (Harrisburg, Pa.: Horace McFarland Co., 1955), 17; J. H. Stine, *History of the Army of the Potomac* (Philadelphia: Rogers Printing Co., 1982), 455; Jerome A. Watrous, *Richard Epps and Other Stories*, Milwaukee, Wis., 1906, 100.

4. Nichols, *Toward Gettysburg*, 211–12; Riley, *Forward*, 53–54; Kent Gramm, *Gettysburg: A Meditation on War and Values* (Bloomington: Indiana University Press, 1994).

5. Ibid., 75–76.

6. Ibid., 119.

7. Nichols, *Toward Gettysburg*, 220–23; Edward P. Adams, letter to his father, from Washington, July 3, 1863, Edward R. Adams Papers, Carroll College Institute for Civil War Studies, Waukesha, Wisconsin.

8. Wainwright, *A Diary of Battle*, 227.

9. Storrick, *Battle*, 17; Stine, *Potomac*, 455, quoting Maj. J. G. Rosengarten. For a discussion of the strategic situation, see Edwin B. Coddington, *The Gettysburg Campaign: A Study in Command* (New York, 1968), 209–41.

10. Nolan, *The Iron Brigade*.

11. Gibbon, *Recollections*, 57; Gaff, *Brave Men's Tears*, 141; *Official Records*, Volume 12, Part 2, 393; *Official Records*, Volume 12, Part 1, 198.

12. Wainwright, *A Diary of Battle*, 218.

13. Beecham, *Gettysburg*, 120.

14. Frederick L. Hitchcock, *War from the Inside* (Philadelphia, 1904), 101; Curtis, *History of the Twenty-fourth Michigan*, 422.

15. Nolan, *The Iron Brigade*, 185–87; Cutler's Report, *Official Records*, Volume 31, 456. Credit for the successful effort to withdraw the pickets is given to Lieutenant Clayton Rogers of the Sixth Wisconsin, an aide to General Abner Doubleday. See Lance J. Herdegen, "The Lieutenant Who Arrested a General," *Gettysburg Magazine* (January 1991), 25–32

16. An example was found in the journal of Rufus Dawes of the Sixth Wisconsin where, in writing of his regiment's pontoon boat crossing at FitzHugh's Crossing during Chancellorsville, he called it "Reynolds' Crossing." The only contemporary mention of Reynolds by Dawes was in a letter: "General Abner Doubleday now commands our division, and General John F. Reynolds commands our corps." Dawes, *Service*, 101; Rufus Dawes Journal, Newberry Library, Chicago, Rufus R. Dawes papers, State Historical Society of Wisconsin; Beecham, *Gettysburg*, 120.

17. Charles H. Veil, *The Memoirs of Charles Henry Veil*, Herman J. Viola, ed. (New York: Orion Books, 1993), 28–30.

18. Nichols, *Toward Gettysburg*, 183.

19. George Meade, *The Life and Letters of George Gordon Meade, Volume II*, ed. George Gordon Meade (New York: Charles Scribner's Sons, 1913), 35–36; Coddington, *Gettysburg*, 267.

20. *Official Records*, Volume 27, 244.

21. Lucius Fairchild, unfinished manuscript, Lucius Fairchild Papers, State Historical Society of Wisconsin.

22. Veil, *Memoirs*, 29.

23. Otis, *Second Wisconsin*, 285. The Murphy account is in a June 20, 1892, letter to Rufus Dawes of the Sixth Wisconsin. Rufus R. Dawes Papers, State Historical Society of Wisconsin. Sanders, "Death of Reynolds," 27–36.

24. Sanders, "Death of Reynolds," 27–36.

25. Otis, *Second Wisconsin Infantry*, 285; Watrous, *Epps*, 101. The most used quotation is "There are those d—d black hatted fellows again; taint no militia, it's the Army of the Potomac!" from Cheek and Pointon, *Sauk County Riflemen*, 78.

26. Herdegen and Beaudot, *In the Bloody Railroad Cut*, 168–213.

27. Stine, *Potomac*, 457.

28. Wainwright, *A Diary of Battle*, 239; William H. Harries, manuscript, "The Iron Brigade in the First Day's Battle at Gettysburg," Jerome A. Watrous Papers, State Historical Society of Wisconsin. The manuscript was prepared for an October 8, 1895, address to a Loyal Legion meeting in St. Paul, Minnesota. It was reprinted in Otis, *Second Wisconsin Infantry*, 275.

29. Wainwright, *A Diary of Battle*, 239; William W. Dudley, *The Iron Brigade at Gettysburg, 1878, Official Report of the Part Borne by the 1st Brigade, 1st Division, 1st Army Corps* (Cincinnati, Ohio, 1879), 10.

30. Robert S. Shue, *Morning at Willoughby Run, July 1, 1863* (Gettysburg, Pennsylvania: Thomas Publications, 1995).

31. Joseph G. Rosengarten, "Reynolds, hero of the First Day, by one of his staff," *New York Times Magazine*, June 29, 1913; Thomas L. Livermore, *Gettysburg Papers*, Volume 1, Morningside House, Dayton, Ohio, 1995, 118; Samuel P. Bates, *The Battle of Gettysburg* (Philadelphia: T. H. David and Co., 1875), 475–76. Livermore served as an officer with the Fifth New Hampshire and as colonel of the Eighteenth New Hampshire and wrote *Numbers and Losses in the Civil War in America, 1861–65*, published in 1900.

32. John W. Busey and David G. Martin, *Regimental Strengths and Losses at Gettysburg* (Hightown, New Jersey, 1986), 265–66. The authors cite lower numbers, but rank the Twenty-fourth Michigan as the Union regiment with the greatest total loss at Gettysburg (363); the Union regiment with the greatest number killed (67), and the regiment with the greatest number wounded (210).

33. Dawes, *Service with the Sixth Wisconsin*, 184; Nolan, *The Iron Brigade*, 256, 365–66*n*68; Dudley, *The Iron Brigade at Gettysburg*, 117.

34. Coddington, *Gettysburg*, 269; Sanders, "Death of Reynolds," 27; Charles Veil to D. McConaughy, 7 April 1864, Gettysburg College Civil War Institute, copy in Gettysburg National Military Park Library.

8. "A New Kind of Murder"

Sharon Vipond wishes to extend thanks to Don Pfanz and Lance Herdegen for their support and advice on this chapter. She also wishes to acknowledge support received from staff at the Fredericksburg and Spotsylvania National Military Park and staff of the Bently Historical Library at the University of Michigan.

1. Herman Melville, "The Armies of the Wilderness," *Selected Poems of Herman Melville*, ed. Robert Penn Warren (New York: Random House, 1967), 134.

2. The incident with Grant is described in Rufus R. Dawes, *Service with the Sixth Wisconsin Volunteers* (Marietta: E. R. Alderman and Sons, 1890), 241–42.

3. Alan T. Nolan, *The Iron Brigade: A Military History*, third edition (Bloomington: Indiana University Press, 1994), 256, 365–66*n*; William F. Fox, *Regimental Losses in the American Civil War* (Albany: Albany Publishing Company, 1889), 117.

4. Nolan, *The Iron Brigade*, 256–57, 266–67, 285–89.

5. See Dawes, *Service with the Sixth Wisconsin*, 194; Nolan, *The Iron Brigade*, 263–64; Orson B. Curtis, *History of the Twenty-fourth Michigan of the Iron Brigade, Known as the Detroit and Wayne County Regiment* (Gaithersburg: Olde Soldier Books, Inc., 1988), 200.

6. Nolan, *The Iron Brigade*, 264, 367*n*4. For background and history of the First Battalion New York Sharpshooters, see: Frederick H. Dyer, *A Compendium of the War of the Rebellion*, Volume 3 (New York: Thomas Yoseloff, 1959), 1405; and *The War of the Rebellion: A Compilation of the Official Records of the Union and Confederate Armies*, Volume 27 (Washington, 1891), Part 3, 451, 675, 692, 795; *Official Records*, Volume 29, Part 1, 217, 667, 678, 688, 692; and *Official Records*, Volume 29, Part 2, 119, 599.

7. Curtis, *Twenty-fourth Michigan*, 216; *Official Records*, Volume 33, 785; Nolan, *The Iron Brigade*, 114, 171, 197, 233, 277, 357*n*1; Dawes, *Service with the Sixth Wisconsin*, 247–48; Dyer, *Compendium*, Volume 3, 1120; *Official Records*, Volume 27, Part 1, 281–84, 284–85.

8. Dawes, *Service with the Sixth Wisconsin*, 202; Curtis, *Twenty-fourth Michigan*, 201. See also Frank Wilkeson, *Recollections of a Private Soldier in the Army of the Potomac* (New York, 1887), 25–26.

9. Nolan, *The Iron Brigade*, 264–65; Dawes, *Service with the Sixth Wisconsin*, 241. Hugh Perkins "'Dear Friend,'" (see *Christian Science Monitor*, April 7, 1983); Matrau, *Letters Home*, 75.

10. Dawes, *Service with the Sixth Wisconsin*, 248–49, 265.

11. Nolan, *The Iron Brigade*, 267–70; Dawes, *Service with the Sixth Wisconsin*, 232–36; Curtis, *Twenty-fourth Michigan*, 205.

12. Curtis, *Twenty-fourth Michigan*, 222; Cheek and Pointon, *Sauk County Riflemen*, 89.

13. Doubleday coined the phrase "final stand," when writing about the Iron Brigade's defense of Seminary Ridge at Gettysburg. See Report of Abner Doubleday, *Official Records,* Volume 27, Part 1, 250.

14. Dawes, *Service with the Sixth Wisconsin*, 243; Perkins, "'Dear Friend,'" (see *Christian Science Monitor*, April 7, 1983); Matrau, *Letters Home*, 74–75, 76; Wilkeson, *Recollections*, 26. Table 3 shows the command structure of the First Brigade when it left Culpeper, Virginia on May 3, 1864.

Table 3. Command Structure of First Brigade on May 3, 1864

Name	Unit
Brigadier Gen. Lysander Cutler	4th Division, 1st Brigade
Lt. Colonel John Mansfield	Second Wisconsin
Colonel Edward S. Bragg	Sixth Wisconsin
Colonel Ira G. Grover	Seventh Indiana
Colonel William W. Robinson	Seventh Wisconsin
Colonel Samuel J. Williams	Nineteenth Indiana
Colonel Henry A. Morrow	Twenty-fourth Michigan
Captain Volney J. Shipman	First New York Battalion Sharpshooters
Lieutenant James Stewart	Battery B, Fourth U.S. Artillery

15. Dawes, *Service with the Sixth Wisconsin*, 25, 216, 239, 240, 242, 274; Herdegen and Beaudot, *In the Bloody Railroad Cut*, 58, 118–24, 131, 330–31; Nolan, *The Iron Brigade*, 266. For further background information on Wadsworth, see Boatner, *Civil War Dictionary*, 882–83 and Ezra J. Warner, *Generals in Blue: Lives of Union Commanders* (Baton Rouge: Louisiana State University Press, 1964), 532. For further background information on Cutler, see Boatner, *Civil War Dictionary*, 110, and Warner, *Generals in Blue*, 216–17.

16. See Perkins, "'Dear Friend,'" (see *Christian Science Monitor*, April 7, 1983); Andrew A. Humphreys, *The Virginia Campaign of '64 and '65* (New York, 1883), 7–9; Curtis, *Twenty-fourth Michigan*, 221–22. See also Dawes, *Service with the Sixth Wisconsin*, 239–40; Rogers, "General Wadsworth," 2; Charles Royster, *The Destructive War: William Tecumseh Sherman, Stonewall Jackson, and the Americans* (New York: Alfred A. Knopf, 1991), 333, 336, 338.

17. Buell quotes William A. Holland of the Pennsylvania Reserves as saying that the men in his unit were veterans of many battles, "but the Wilderness fighting was 'a new kind of murder.'" Buell goes on to say, "The same was true of Wadsworth's troops, the Iron Brigade, and others, as their survivors have often told me since the war." Augustus C. Buell, *The Cannoneer: Recollections Of Service In The Army Of The Potomac* (Washington: The National Tribune, 1890), 161. See Donald L. Smith, *The Twenty-fourth Michigan of the Iron Brigade* (Harrisburg: Stackpole Company, 1962), 184–85.

18. Rogers, "General Wadsworth," 2. On April 30, 1864, the Army of the Potomac had 99,438 men "present for duty equipped." Together with the 19,331

men of Burnside's Ninth Corps, Grant's total number of troops was 118,769. See *Official Records*, Volume 33, 1036 and Gordon C. Rhea, *The Battle of The Wilderness, May 5–6, 1864* (Baton Rouge: Louisiana State University Press, 1994), 34–35.

19. For background of Earl Rogers see Herdegen and Beaudot, *In the Bloody Railroad Cut*, 141,145, 179, 246–48. The story of Pete Markle is contained in Bona [Earl M.] Rogers, "Markle, Straggler," *Milwaukee Sunday Telegraph* (October 2, 1887), 8. See also Herdegen and Beaudot, *In the Bloody Railroad Cut*, 46–47, 166, 245–46. "Bad Axe" County was renamed as Vernon County in 1863.

20. Rogers, "General Wadsworth," 2; George W. Burchell to [Burchell Family], 13 May 1864, Sullivan Dexter Green Papers, Bentley Historical Library, University of Michigan.

21. Alexander B. Pattison, *Civil War Diary*, May 4, 1864, Fredericksburg and Spotsylvania National Military Park; Cheek and Pointon, *Sauk County Riflemen*, 89; Curtis, *Twenty-fourth Michigan*, 230; Pearson, *Wadsworth*, 258. Comments on "high spirits" are from Captain John Witherspoon Manuscript, as quoted by Smith, *Twenty-fourth Michigan*, 184.

22. William Swinton, *Campaigns of the Army of the Potomac* (New York, 1866), 417; Robert Monteith, "The Battle of the Wilderness and Death of General Wadsworth," in *War Papers Read Before The Commandery of the State of Wisconsin, Military Order of the Loyal Legion of the United States*, 1 (Milwaukee, 1891), 411; Wilkeson, *Recollections*, 39–42.

23. Swinton, *Campaigns*, 428–29; Morris Schaff, *The Battle of the Wilderness* (Boston, 1910), 55–63; S. D. Thruston, "Report of the Conduct of General George H. Steuart's Brigade from the 5th to the 12th of May, 1864, Inclusive," *Southern Historical Society Papers*, 14 (1886), 147; Wilkeson, *Recollections*, 41–42.

24. Curtis, *Twenty-fourth Michigan*, 230; Pattison, *Diary*, May 5, 1864. Curtis says that the brigade was awakened at 4:30 A.M. However, Alexander Pattison, captain of Company A, Seventh Indiana, noted that they did not break camp until 8:00 A.M., so the brigade probably did not began actual movement until then. The correct name of the plantation house is "Ellwood" but is typically called the "Lacy House" in contemporary accounts and later descriptions of the battle. See "Historic Structures Report for Ellwood (Lacy) House," as noted in Noel G. Harrison, *Gazetteer of Historic Sites Related to the Fredericksburg and Spotsylvania National Military Park* (Fredericksburg and Spotsylvania National Military Park, 1986), 264.

25. Curtis, *Twenty-fourth Michigan*, 230; Buell, *The Cannoneer*, 159. See also Nolan, *The Iron Brigade*, 40–41, 160, 273; and Silas Felton, "The Iron Brigade Battery at Gettysburg," *The Gettysburg Magazine* (July 1994), 56–70.

26. Report of Lysander Cutler, August 13, 1864, in *Official Records*, Volume 36, Part 1, 610; Meade's general orders of May 2 specified that Warren's Fifth Corps, "after crossing [the Rapidan] will move to the vicinity of the Old Wilderness Tavern, on the Orange Court-House pike. The corps will move the following day past the head of Catharpin Run, crossing the Orange Court-House plank road at Parker's Store." See "Orders for May 2, 1864," *Official Records*, Volume 36, Part 2, 332.

27. Warren to Humphreys, *Official Records*, Volume 36, Part 2, 413; Rhea, *Battle of The Wilderness*, 95–98.

28. See Rhea, *Battle of The Wilderness*, 99; Jenkins to Locke, *Official Records*, Volume 36, Part 2, 415; Schaff, *Battle of the Wilderness*, 126.

29. See Rhea, *Battle of the Wilderness*, 110–15; and Gregory A. Mertz, "No Turning Back: The Battle of The Wilderness, Part I—The Fighting on May 5, 1864," *Blue and Gray Magazine*, Volume 12 (April 1995), 11, 14–15.

30. Warren to Humphreys, *Official Records*, Volume 36, Part 2, 413; Locke to Griffin, *Official Records*, Volume 36, Part 2, 417; Report of William B. White, *Official Records*, Part 1, 575.

31. Meade to Grant, *Official Records*, Part 2, 403; Grant to Meade, *Official Records*, Volume 36, Part 2, 403; Schaff, *Battle of the Wilderness*, 128.

32. Report of John C. Robinson. *Official Records*, Volume 36, Part 1, 593.

33. Wadsworth to Griffin (?), *Official Records*, Volume 36, Part 2, 420.

34. See Wainwright, *A Diary of Battle*, 348–49.

35. Buell, *The Cannoneer*, 159–60.

36. Report of William S. Tilton, *Official Records*, Volume 36, Part 1, 559.

37. Crawford to Locke, *Official Records*, Volume 36, Part 2, 417–18; Warren to Crawford, *Official Records*, Part 2, 418–19.

38. Roebling to Warren, *Official Records*, Volume 36, Part 2, 418. Washington A. Roebling was one of Warren's staff officers.

39. Schaff, *Battle of the Wilderness*, 134–35.

40. Locke to Wadsworth, *Official Records*, Volume 36, Part 2, 420.

41. Schaff, *Battle of the Wilderness*, 134.

42. John A. Kellogg was a prosecuting attorney in Mauston, Wisconsin when the war broke out. When Rufus Dawes was elected Captain of Company K ("The Lemonweir Minute Men"), Kellogg was named his first lieutenant. See Dawes, *Service with the Sixth Wisconsin*, 6; Herdegen and Beaudot, *In the Bloody Railroad Cut*, 67, 75–76, 123, 205, 258; Nolan, *The Iron Brigade*, 286, 380*n*61.

43. Dawes, *Service with the Sixth Wisconsin*, 259. Rollin P. Converse was one of the best-loved officers in the Sixth Wisconsin. Born in New York state and working as a clerk in Prescott, Wisconsin when the war broke out, Converse rose rapidly through the ranks from sergeant to captain of Company B ("The Prescott Guards"), and was cited for "conspicuous bravery" at Gettysburg. Philip W. Plummer and his brother, Thomas, were Englishmen who came to America with their father in the years before the war. Both served as lieutenants in Company C ("The Prairie du Chien Volunteers") before the popular Phil Plummer was promoted to Captain of Company G ("The Beloit Star Rifles"). See Herdegen and Beaudot, *In the Bloody Railroad Cut*, 59–60, 64, 123, 207, 217.

44. John A. Kellogg, *Capture and Escape: A Narrative of Army and Prison Life* (Madison: Democrat State Printer, 1908), 10–11.

45. Dawes, *Service with the Sixth Wisconsin*, 259.

46. John B. Gordon, *Reminiscences of the Civil War* (New York: Charles Scribner's Sons, 1904), 237–39. See also Report of Richard S. Ewell, *Official Records*, Volume 36, Part 1, 1070–1071.

47. Crawford to Locke, *Official Records*, Volume 36, Part 2, 420; Edward Steere, *The Wilderness Campaign* (Harrisburg: Stackpole Company, 1960), 154.

48. The clearing took its name from the Saunders family who lived nearby, and was also called "Palmer's Field" and "Sanders' Field." See Harrison, *Gazetteer of Historic Sites*, 260–61; and Schaff, *Battle of the Wilderness*, 149–50. One of the Iron Brigade's deadliest battles of the war was fought in David R. Miller's cornfield near Sharpsburg, Maryland on September 17, 1862. The battle in the "Bloody Cornfield," as it came to be known, claimed the lives of many Iron Brigade men during the Battle of Antietam. Captain John Kellogg and Company I were also deployed as skirmishers on the morning of September 17. See Dawes, *Service with the Sixth Wisconsin*, 88–95; Nolan, *The Iron Brigade*, 137–42.

49. Crawford to Locke, *Official Records*, Volume 36, Part 2, 420; Cutler, *Official Records*, Volume 36, Part 1, 610.

50. It is extremely difficult to pinpoint the precise position and alignment of Cutler's brigade at the moment of the westward advance. Later descriptions of the battle by Iron Brigade veterans paint a confusing and contradictory picture, perhaps mirroring the battlefield conditions they remembered. Sorting through the various official and unofficial accounts, the following is a reasonably accurate description of

the brigade's alignment and positioning relative to the positions of individual regiments within the Iron Brigade, the brigades which formed Cutler's left and right flanks, and the troops designated to support the Federal advance.

- *Position of individual regiments within the Iron Brigade*. The brigade was formed into two lines of battle. From left to right, in the first line of battle, were the Twenty-fourth Michigan, Nineteenth Indiana, Second Wisconsin, and Seventh Indiana. In the second line, the Seventh Wisconsin supported the Second Wisconsin and the Sixth Wisconsin was placed directly behind the Seventh Indiana. Several accounts mistakenly interchange the positions of the Seventh Indiana and Seventh Wisconsin regiments, but Rufus Dawes of the Sixth Wisconsin clearly states that "Colonel Ira B. Grover's Seventh Indiana regiment was directly in front of us, in the first line of battle, and it was our duty to follow them at a distance of one hundred paces." See Dawes, *Service with the Sixth Wisconsin*, 259. Merit Welsh of the Seventh Indiana, in writing the official report for the regiment (Colonel Grover was missing in action in the May 5 engagement), also notes that the "Seventh Indiana [formed] extreme right of brigade and of the division, and [connected] to General Griffin's division, of Fifth Corps." See Report of Merit C. Welsh, *Official Records*, Volume 36, Part 1, 616–17.
- *Brigades forming Cutler's left and right flanks*. Some accounts of the battle place the Iron Brigade on the left of Wadsworth's division, but Cutler clearly states that when the divisions of Cutler, Stone, and Rice moved forward, Cutler was on the right, Stone in the center, and Rice on the left, next to Crawford. Donald Smith, in his excellent history of the Twenty-fourth Michigan, picks up Orson Curtis' incorrect alignment for Cutler's brigade. Curtis also confuses the positions of the Seventh Indiana and Seventh Wisconsin. See Smith, *Twenty-fourth Michigan*, 183; Curtis, *Twenty-fourth Michigan*, 230–231; Cutler, *Official Records*, Volume 36, Part 1, 610; Schaff, *Battle of the Wilderness*, 140, 151.
- *Supporting troops for the Federal advance*. As Bartlett advanced, he was to be supported by troops from Colonel Jacob B. Sweitzer's Second Brigade of Griffin's First Division. Support for Cutler's advance was to be provided by troops from Brigadier General John C. Robinson's Second Division. While Sweitzer's brigade was already in place, and near enough to Bartlett to provide immediate support if needed, the brigade designated by Robinson to support Cutler (i.e., Denison's Third Brigade) was still back at the Lacy House. Tilton, *Official Records*, Volume 36, Part 1, 559; Robinson, *Official Records*, Part 1, 592–93.

51. Dawes, *Service with the Sixth Wisconsin*, 259–60; Cheek and Pointon, *Sauk County Riflemen*, 90; E. S. Bragg, "Letter from Gen. Bragg," *Milwaukee Sunday Telegraph* (July 20, 1879), 2. Bragg stated that the Sixth advanced without any "objective point, except the sound of irregular musketry in front, indicating where the hunt would be found."

52. See Rhea, *Battle of the Wilderness*, 153.

53. Steere, *Wilderness Campaign*, 153.

54. Cutler, *Official Records*, Volume 36, Part 1, 610.

55. Welsh, *Official Records*, Volume 36, Part 1, 616; Curtis, *Twenty-fourth Michigan*, 231.

56. "He Kept His Colors Flying," in *Deeds Of Valor: How America's Civil War Heroes Won The Congressional Medal Of Honor*. eds. W. F. Beyer and O. F. Keydel (Detroit: Perrien-Keydel Company, 1903), 316–17. In his official report, Cutler stated that the Iron Brigade captured three battle flags, but this number is not supported by the Army of the Potomac's official report of battle flags captured in the Wilderness campaign. Only John N. Opel of the Seventh Indiana was given credit—and a Con-

gressional Medal of Honor—for his feat of bravery. Neither Edwards nor Buckles is mentioned in the official record of battle honors or roll of Medal of Honor recipients. See "Report of Colors Captured From the Enemy by the Fifth Army Corps from May 4 to November 1, 1864," *Official Records*, Volume 36, Part 1, 545, and "Medals of Honor Awarded for Duty Services," *Official Records*, Volume 36, Part 1, 1020–1021.

57. Steere, *Wilderness Campaign*, 163–64; Rhea, *Battle of the Wilderness*, 154–55.

58. Bragg, "Letter from Gen. Bragg," 2.

59. Dawes, *Service with the Sixth Wisconsin*, 260–61.

60. Ibid., 260–61; Cheek and Pointon, *Sauk County Riflemen*, 90; *Milwaukee Sunday Telegraph*, "Captain Rollin Converse and Corporal Hare" (July 27, 1879), 3.

61. For example, Graham states: "[We] formed in line of battle, and advanced through a dense pine wood, supporting General Wadsworth (Fourth Division). Moved about 2 miles in a southerly [*sic*] direction, when heavy skirmishing followed, and *a terrific battle took place in our immediate front* [italics added] between the enemy and General Wadsworth's command. At 1.40 P.M. General Cutler's brigade, which was in our immediate front, was overpowered, and fell back in confusion." Unfortunately, Denison was seriously wounded during the battle and left no report to explain his version of these events. Colonel Richard Bowerman, who commanded the Fourth Maryland, one of Denison's regiments, assumed command of the brigade on May 8. See Report of Samuel A. Graham, *Official Records*, Volume 36, Part 1, 60; Robinson, *Official Records*, Volume 36, Part 1, 593; Locke to Robinson, *Official Records*, Volume 36, Part 2, 417; Steere, *Wilderness Campaign*, 149; Graham, *Official Records*, Volume 36, Part 1, 601; Report of Richard N. Bowerman, *Official Records*, Volume 36, Part 1, 600–604; William W. Swan, "Battle of the Wilderness," *Papers of the Military Historical Society of Massachusetts*, Volume 4 (Boston: Military Historical Society of Massachusetts, 1891), 151–52.

62. See Thomas Chamberlin, *History of the One Hundred and Fiftieth Regiment of Pennsylvania Volunteers* (Philadelphia: F. McManus, Jr. and Company, 1905), 207; Richard E. Matthews, *149th Pennsylvania Volunteer Infantry Unit in the Civil War* (Jefferson: McFarland and Company, Inc., 1994), 134–35.

63. The family name of "Higgerson" is also known in some accounts of the battle as "Hagerson." See Harrison, *Gazetteer of Historic Sites*, 255–56.

64. Pearson, *Wadsworth*, 264; Matthews, *149th Pennsylvania*, 135.

65. *Survivor's Association, 121st Regiment Pennsylvania Volunteers* (Philadelphia, 1906), 76–77.

66. Rhea, *Battle of the Wilderness*, 162.

67. Ibid., 163.

68. Cutler, *Official Records*, Volume 36, Part 1, 611. One might also ask: Where was Crawford's division on the left? Crawford had not been effective in getting his Third Division troops redeployed from their position at Chewning's Farm, and when he finally did get moving, he sent only the one brigade of Colonel William McCandless to make the linkage and then, only after so much delay that it was of little or no use to Wadsworth and the beleaguered Rice. See Buell, *The Cannoneer*, 160–61; Pearson, *Wadsworth*, 260–61; Smith, *Twenty-fourth Michigan*, 184; Curtis, *Twenty-fourth Michigan*, 231–32.

69. Curtis relates a curious story about an incident that supposedly happened at this point in the battle. He says that the Iron Brigade was attacked by and then engaged in "a sharp fight" with its Confederate counterpart, the "Stonewall Brigade." However, during the battle on May 5, the Stonewall Brigade fought on and near the Spotswood Road, north of the Orange Turnpike. According to all accounts, the Stonewall Brigade apparently never fought *south* of the Turnpike on that day and probably never came in contact with the Iron Brigade or the Twenty-fourth

Michigan. See Curtis, *Twenty-fourth Michigan*, 231–33; Rhea, *Battle of the Wilderness*, 125,179–82; James I. Robertson Jr., *The Stonewall Brigade* (Baton Rouge: Louisiana State University Press, 1963), 218–19; John O. Casler, *Four Years in the Stonewall Brigade* (Oklahoma City: State Capital Printing Company, 1893), 312–13; Thruston, "George H. Steuart's Brigade," 149.

70. Welsh, *Official Records*, Volume 36, Part 1, 617; Pearson, *Wadsworth*, 155.

71. Dawes, *Service with the Sixth Wisconsin*, 260–61; Cheek and Pointon, *Sauk County Riflemen*, 89–91; Pearson, *Wadsworth*, 155.

72. Rhea, *Battle of the Wilderness*, 160.

73. Report of John B. Gordon, *Official Records*, Volume 36, Part 1, 1076–1077.

74. Ibid., 1076–1077; George W. Nichols, *A Soldier's Story of His Regiment and Incidentally of the Lawton, Gordon, Evans Brigade* (Jesup, Georgia: 1898), 141–42; F. L. Hudgins, "With the 38th Georgia Regiment," *Confederate Veteran* 26 (1918), 163; Alton J. Murray, *South Georgia Rebels* (St. Mary's, 1976), 148–49. The notion of *a simultaneously executed three-pronged attack* may be an exaggeration on Gordon's part. Thus, it may be more plausible to conclude that if Gordon actually struck in three directions, he must have executed a *sequence* of maneuvers. Steere's analysis of Gordon's maneuver is probably the most accurate: *Wilderness Campaign*, 168–71. See also Rhea's discussion of the debate surrounding the exact point of Gordon's attack in *Battle of the Wilderness*, 161, and J. B. Gordon's own explanation (and diagram) of the maneuver in *Reminiscences of the Civil War*, 239–41.

75. Cutler, *Official Records*, Volume 36, Part 1, 610–11.

76. Jerome A. Watrous, "Some Short Stories," *Milwaukee Sunday Telegraph* (September 1, 1894), 1. Almost everyone, in both armies, took the belongings of the dead. See Wilkeson, *Recollections*, 55.

77. Robert Garth Scott, *Into the Wilderness with the Army of the Potomac* (Bloomington: Indiana University Press, 1985), 68.

78. See Mary Genevie Green Brainard, *Campaigns of the One Hundred and Forty-Sixth Regiment, New York State Volunteers; Also Known As Halleck's Infantry, and Fifth Oneida and Garrard's Tigers* (New York: G. P. Putnam's Sons, 1915), 195.

79. Burchell to [Burchell Family], 13 May 1864.

80. The story of the Seventh Indiana wounded is recounted by Schaff in *Battle of the Wilderness*, 165–66. See also Curtis, *Twenty-fourth Michigan*, 236.

81. Schaff, *Battle of the Wilderness*, 138; "Roster of the Second Wisconsin Infantry," in George H. Otis, *The Second Wisconsin Infantry* (Dayton: Press of Morningside Bookshop, 1984), 72, 305, 342.

82. For example, see Scott, *Into the Wilderness*, 62; Rhea, *Battle of the Wilderness*, 161; Steere, *Wilderness Campaign*, 171.

83. Schaff, *Battle of the Wilderness*, 157.

84. Buell, *The Cannoneer*, 159–60; Report of Charles S. Wainwright, *Official Records*, Volume 36, Part 1, 640.

85. Graham, *Official Records*, Volume 36, Part 1, 601.

86. See Rhea, *Battle of the Wilderness*, 169, for a description of this situation and the "wave of wild-eyed fugitives" from Bartlett's and Cutler's Federal brigades.

87. Washington A. Roebling's Report in The Gouverneur K. Warren Collection, New York State Archives, Albany, New York, as quoted by Schaff in *Battle of the Wilderness*, 157–58.

88. Fifth Corps's casualty reports indicate that Wadsworth's division was more badly damaged than Griffin's. See "Return of Casualties in the Union Forces, Battle of the Wilderness, 5–7 May 1864," *Official Records*, Volume 36, Part 1, 123, 125; Steere, *Wilderness Campaign*, 177; Scott, *Into the Wilderness*, 69.

89. Pearson, *Wadsworth*, 264; Schaff, *Battle of the Wilderness*, 159; Cutler,

Official Records, Volume 36, Part 1, 611; Dawes, *Service with the Sixth Wisconsin*, 261; Cheek and Pointon, *Sauk County Riflemen*, 91; Curtis, *Twenty-fourth Michigan*, 233.

90. Jerome A. Watrous, "Some Short Stories," *Milwaukee Sunday Telegraph* (October 6, 1894), 8.

91. Buell, *The Cannoneer*, 151.

92. Pearson, *Wadsworth*, 266, 268.

93. Robinson, *Official Records*, Volume 36, Part 1, 593; Report of Richard Coulter, *Official Records*, Volume 36, Part 1, 595–96; Pearson, *Wadsworth*, 268; Schaff, *Battle of the Wilderness*, 198.

94. Report of Frank H. Cowdrey, *Official Records*, Volume 36, Part 1, 615; Schaff, *Battle of the Wilderness*, 198; Coulter, *Official Records*, Volume 36, Part 1, 596.

95. See Matthews, *149th Pennsylvania*, 143.

96. Earl Rogers provided Wadsworth's biographer with a description of this incident. See Pearson, *Wadsworth*, 269–70; Matthews, *149th Pennsylvania*, 143–44.

97. Cope to Warren, *Official Records*, Volume 36, Part 2, 421. Cope's message said, in part, that Wadsworth had engaged Hill's corps and was "driving the enemy."

98. William H. Parker, A. P. Hill's Chief of Staff, described the attack by the tiny Fifth Alabama in a 1908 letter published in William L. Royall, *Some Reminiscences* (New York: Neale Publishing Company, 1909), 30.

99. Cowdrey, *Official Records*, Volume 36, Part 1, 615.

100. Ibid., 615. See also Report of Edward S. Bragg, *Official Records*, Volume 36, Part 1, 637; Cutler, *Official Records*, Volume 36, Part 1, 611.

101. Cowdrey, *Official Records*, Part 1, 615. Later, under Bragg's steady command, the demoralized Pennsylvanians would pull themselves together and again become a "soldierly body of troops." See Rogers, "General Wadsworth," 2.

102. Scott, *Into the Wilderness*, 91.

103. Cowdrey, *Official Records*, Volume 36, Part 1, 615; Cutler, *Official Records*, Volume 36, Part 1, 611; Coulter, *Official Records*, Volume 36, Part 1, 596.

104. Schaff, *Battle of the Wilderness*, 198.

105. Cheek and Pointon, *Sauk County Riflemen*, 91; Curtis, *Twenty-fourth Michigan*, 234.

106. Dawes, *Service with the Sixth Wisconsin*, 261.

107. Rogers, "Markle, Straggler," 8.

108. Buell, *The Cannoneer*, 161.

109. *Milwaukee Sunday Telegraph*, "Captain Rollin Converse and Corporal Hare," 3.

110. Swan, "Battle of the Wilderness," 144.

111. Warren to Wadsworth, *Official Records*, Volume 36, Part 2, 458.

112. Monteith, "The Battle of the Wilderness," 412–13; Rogers, "General Wadsworth," 2; Monteith, "The Wilderness, One of the Fiercest and Bloodiest Battles of the War of the Rebellion," *Milwaukee Sunday Telegraph* (January 17, 1886), 3.

113. The Lacy House stood on a relatively high piece of ground. The knoll upon which Stewart and Breck placed their batteries faced south and looked down into a little valley that contained Wilderness Run, a stream that meandered across the battlefield. See Buell, *The Cannoneer*, 164; Wainwright, *A Diary of Battle*, 351.

114. Cutler, *Official Records*, Volume 36, Part 1, 611; Pearson, *Wadsworth*, 272.

115. Cowdrey was uncertain of the alignment and could say only that "I think each brigade was in two lines." Curtis, however, implies more than one line and states that "General Rice's Brigade [formed] the first line and the Iron Brigade the second and third." Richard Coulter of the Eleventh Pennsylvania (who assumed command of Baxter's brigade after he was wounded later in the day on May 6)

reported that Cutler was on Baxter's left and Rice was on Baxter's right, with the Twelfth Massachusetts deployed forward as skirmishers. See Cowdrey, *Official Records*, Volume 36, Part 1, 615; Curtis, *Twenty-fourth Michigan*, 235; Coulter, *Official Records*, Volume 36, Part 1, 596.

116. Matthews, *149th Pennsylvania*, 145; Francis A. Walker, *History of the Second Army Corps in the Army of the Potomac* (New York: Charles Scribner's Sons, 1886), 422.

117. Quoted by Matthews from an article in the *National Tribune* by George Goshorn of the 149th Pennsylvania. See Matthews, *149th Pennsylvania*, 145. The Iron Brigade used 1861 Springfield and Austrian Lorenz muskets, not Enfields. See Herdegen and Beaudot, *In the Bloody Railroad Cut*, 363–66.

118. Lyman to Meade, *Official Records*, Volume 36, Part 2, 439.

119. Report of J. William Hofmann, *Official Records*, Part 1, 623–24. Hofmann commanded the Fifty-sixth Pennsylvania in Rice's brigade. See also Cowdrey, *Official Records*, Volume 36, Part 1, 615.

120. Dawes, *Service with the Sixth Wisconsin*, 262

121. Cutler, *Official Records*, Volume 36, Part 1, 611.

122. Ibid., 611; Dawes, *Service with the Sixth Wisconsin*, 261–62; Steere, *Wilderness Campaign*, 354; Alexander S. Webb, "Through the Wilderness," *Battles and Leaders*, 158. Other accounts state that the division was arranged into six, rather than four, lines of battle. See Chamberlin, *One Hundred and Fiftieth Pennsylvania*, 214–15; see also note 120 above.

123. Monteith, "Battle of the Wilderness," 414.

124. Cheek and Pointon, *Sauk County Riflemen*, 92.

125. Welsh reported that the "rebels charging in front and on right flanks caused us to slowly retire, losing the ground gained this day." See Welsh, *Official Records*, Volume 36, Part 1, 617.

126. Cope to Warren, *Official Records*, Volume 36, Part 2, 459. Cope was an aide on Warren's staff. On May 6, he was temporarily assigned to Wadsworth's staff.

127. Cheek and Pointon, *Sauk County Riflemen*, 92; Cutler, *Official Records*, Volume 36, Part 1, 611; William F. Perry, "Reminiscences of the Campaign of 1864 in Virginia," *Southern Historical Society Papers*, 7 (February 1879), 52–54.

128. Curtis, *Twenty-fourth Michigan*, 235.

129. Hofmann, *Official Records*, Volume 36, Part 1, 624.

130. B. M. Barnes, "The Wilderness: Another Account of What Took Place at the Plank Road," *The National Tribune* (August 6, 1889), 1.

131. Cutler, *Official Records*, Volume 36, Part 1, 611; Cowdrey, *Official Records*, Volume 36, Part 1, 615; Schaff, *Battle of the Wilderness*, 253.

132. There are various stories of how Wadsworth was mortally wounded. Rather than attempting to reconcile these various accounts, I have followed the version given by Pearson in his biography of the general, which was informed by the eyewitness account of Earl Rogers, Wadsworth's closest aide. See Webb, "Through the Wilderness," 160; Pearson, *Wadsworth*, 283–84; Schaff, *Battle of the Wilderness*, 271; Hofmann, *Official Records*, Volume 36, Part 2, 624; Monteith, "Battle of the Wilderness," 414; Rogers, "General Wadsworth," 2; Chamberlin, *One Hundred and Fiftieth Pennsylvania*, 212.

133. Dawes, *Service with the Sixth Wisconsin*, 262. After Wadsworth's death, rumors circulated that Rogers had actually vaulted from his horse to retrieve a watch from the dead general, but Rogers always denied this. See Herdegen and Beaudot, *In the Bloody Railroad Cut*, 246–48; Rogers, "General Wadsworth," 2.

134. James P. Sullivan, "Old Company K" in Beaudot and Herdegen, *Irishman*, xiii, 86; Dawes, *Service with the Sixth Wisconsin*, 129.

135. Cheek and Pointon, *Sauk County Riflemen*, 92–93; Pearson, *Wadsworth*, 176–77; Z. Boylston Adams, "In the Wilderness," *Military Order of the Loyal Legion of the United States, Civil War Papers, Commandery of The State of Massachusetts*, Volume 2 (Boston: Military Order of the Loyal Legion of the United States, 1900), 391. The comparison to Reynolds was made by Curtis in *Twenty-fourth Michigan*, 235.

136. Wadsworth was mortally wounded on the morning of May 6 but did not die until May 8. At the time, however, Cutler and many others were understandably confused as to whether or not Wadsworth was actually dead. In fact, the first rumors of the general's death began circulating after Wadsworth's horse was shot out from under him (apparently, the first of several horses to be killed under him that day), but Wadsworth was not mortally wounded until about two hours later. See Schaff, *Battle of the Wilderness*, 236; Rogers, "General Wadsworth," 2.

137. Dawes, *Service with the Sixth Wisconsin*, 262; Schaff, *Battle of the Wilderness*, 237.

138. For example: Scott, *Into the Wilderness*, 137; Rhea, *Battle of the Wilderness*, 308; Steere, *Wilderness Campaign*, 355.

139. Schaff, *Battle of the Wilderness*, 235.

140. Buell, *The Cannoneer*, 164–65.

141. Cutler to Locke, *Official Records*, Volume 36, Part 2, 458 (the first of four messages from Cutler to Locke on May 6); Cutler to Locke, *Official Records*, Volume 36, Part 2, 459 (second of four messages).

142. Cutler to Locke, *Official Records*, Volume 36, Part 2, 459. This third of four messages from Cutler to Locke notes that "the balance of the division is scattered and gone, except what I have with me."

143. Cutler to Locke, *Official Records*, Volume 36, Part 2, 459 (fourth and final message from Cutler to Locke); Schaff, *Battle of the Wilderness*, 236.

144. Curtis, *Twenty-fourth Michigan*, 235; Cowdrey, *Official Records*, Volume 36, Part 1, 615; Cheek and Pointon, *Sauk County Riflemen*, 93.

145. Buell, *The Cannoneer*, 166–67.

146. Cheek and Pointon, *Sauk County Riflemen*, 93; Curtis, *Twenty-fourth Michigan*, 235; Matrau, *Letters Home*, 77–78. During Wadsworth's previous absence from the division—July, 1863 to April, 1863—Cutler had shared divisional command with James C. Rice and Henry S. Briggs. When Cutler was serving as division commander during this time period, Robinson took over command of the Iron Brigade. See Nolan, *The Iron Brigade*, 266, 370*n*9.

147. Cutler, *Official Records*, Volume 36, Part 1, 611.

148. A member of the Thirty-eighth Georgia Regiment in Gordon's brigade remembered the Confederate cheering happened on Friday night, May 5, rather than Saturday night, May 6. See Hudgins, "With the 38th Georgia Regiment," 163.

149. Curtis, *Twenty-fourth Michigan*, 235, 238; Cheek and Pointon, *Sauk County Riflemen*, 93; Dawes, *Service with the Sixth Wisconsin*, 262; Cutler, *Official Records*, Volume 36, Part 1, 611; Buell, *The Cannoneer*, 175; Wainwright, *Official Records*, Volume 36, Part 1, 641.

150. Ulysses S. Grant, *Personal Memoirs of U. S. Grant* (New York: C. L. Webster, 1894), 534.

151. Matrau, *Letters Home*, 77. Table 4 (below) summarizes casualty figures for the Iron Brigade regiments and other units of Cutler's brigade during the Wilderness battle. Figures are reported as of May 7, 1864, and taken from "Return of Casualties in the Union Forces, Battle of the Wilderness, 5–7 May 1864," *Official Records*, Volume 36, Part 1, 125.

Table 4. Return of Casualties for First Brigade, May 5–7, 1864

Unit	Killed		Wounded		Captured and Missing		Totals
	Officers	Men	Officers	Men	Officers	Men	
Seventh Indiana	1	15	3	89	4	50	162
Nineteenth Indiana	1	13	2	76	1	10	103
Twenty-fourth Michigan	2	12	3	45	1	41	104
Second Wisconsin	2	4	2	14	1	17	40
Sixth Wisconsin	3	5	1	39	1	14	63
Seventh Wisconsin	3	24	7	148	0	35	217
First NY Battalion SS	0	1	0	27	0	7	35
Battery B, Fourth U.S.	0	0	0	0	0	0	0
Total First Brigade	12	74	18	438	8	174	724

152. Some of the Iron Brigade wounded were cared for behind Confederate lines in a field hospital at Locust Grove. Locust Grove was near Robertson's Tavern on the Orange Turnpike, near the western edge of the Wilderness battlefield. See Bragg, "Letter from Gen. Bragg," 2; Harrison, *Gazetteer of Historic Sites*, 260.

153. Watrous, "Some Short Stories," 1; Perkins, "'Dear Friend,'" (see *Christian Science Monitor*, April 7, 1983).

154. Dawes, *Service with the Sixth Wisconsin*, 295–96. Kellogg was held prisoner in both Charleston, South Carolina, and Macon, Georgia. See Kellogg's entire recounting of his imprisonment in Kellogg, *Capture and Escape.*

155. John Gibbon, Letter to the Editor, *Milwaukee Sunday Telegraph* (July 13, 1879), 2; Bragg, "Letter from Gen. Bragg," 2.

156. Rogers, "Markle, Straggler," 8.

157. Table 5 (below) shows the names of all First Brigade officers killed or mortally wounded in the Wilderness battle. See "Officers Killed or Mortally Wounded," *Official Records*, Volume 36, Part 1, 133.

Table 5. First Brigade Officers Killed or Mortally Wounded in the Wilderness

Name	Unit
Captain George P. Clayton	Seventh Indiana
Lieutenant James L. Converse	Sixth Wisconsin
Captain Rollin P. Converse	Sixth Wisconsin
Lieutenant James Holmes	Seventh Wisconsin
Lieutenant William B. Hutchinson	Twenty-fourth Michigan
Captain George Hutton	Twenty-fourth Michigan
Captain Jefferson Newman	Seventh Wisconsin
Lieutenant William Noble	Second Wisconsin
Major Philip W. Plummer	Sixth Wisconsin
Captain John R. Spoerry	Second Wisconsin
Colonel Samuel J. Williams	Nineteenth Indiana

158. Nolan, *The Iron Brigade*, 274–75; Otis, 294; Curtis, *Twenty-fourth Michigan*, 231, 280–81; Pattison, *Diary*, May 6, 1864. Table 6 (below) shows command changes resulting from the Wilderness campaign. Note: Volney Shipman was replaced by Alfred Parry (*) later in May 1864. See roster of officers, May 31, 1864, in *Official Records*, Volume 36, Part 1, 203.

Table 6. Command Changes in Fourth Division and First Brigade, May 5–7, 1864

Name	Unit	Successor	Reason
Brig Gen James Wadsworth	Fourth Division	Brig Gen Lysander Cutler	Wadsworth killed in action
Brig Gen Lysander Cutler	First Brigade, Fourth Division	Col William Robinson	Cutler took Division command
Lt Col John Mansfield	Second Wisconsin	Maj George Otis	Mansfield wounded and missing in action
Col Ed Bragg	Sixth Wisconsin	Lt Col Rufus Dawes	Bragg took Third Brigade command
Col William Robinson	Seventh Wisconsin	Lt Col Mark Finnicum	Robinson took Fourth Brigade command
Col Ira Grover	Seventh Indiana	Lt Col William Banta	Grover missing in action
Col Samuel Williams	Nineteenth Indiana	Maj John Lindley	Williams killed in action
Col Henry Morrow	Twenty-fourth Michigan	Lt Col William Wight	Morrow wounded in action
Capt Volney Shipman	First NY Battalion Sharpshooters	Capt Alfred Parry	*
Lieut James Stewart	Battery B, Fourth United States Artillery	none	n/a

159. Nolan, *The Iron Brigade*, 275; Otis, *Second Wisconsin Infantry*, 99; "Comrade" [pseud.], "The Old Second," *Milwaukee Sunday Telegraph* (June 22, 1879), 2; Alan D. Gaff, "Introduction," *Second Wisconsin Infantry*, 7–12. See Gaff, *If This Is War*, 278*n*2, for origin of the nickname "Ragged Ass Second."

160. Dawes, *Service with the Sixth Wisconsin*, 291, 305; Royster, *The Destructive War*, 336; Don Lowry, *No Turning Back: The Beginning of the End of the Civil War, March-June, 1864* (New York: Hippocrene Books, 1992), 248–50; Noah Andre Trudeau, *Bloody Roads South: The Wilderness to Cold Harbor, May-June, 1864* (Boston: Little, Brown and Company, 1989), 321–22.

9. The Iron Brigade Battery

Silas Felton wishes to thank Bob Younger for his encouragement and support and also Mike Meier of the National Archives for leading him through the treasures hidden there.

1. There is a running discussion on whether artillery units should be called "batteries" or "companies." All such tactical units were officially designated "companies" by the U.S. Army until 1861, despite the unofficial designation of "batteries" both in common usage and official correspondence. With the formation of the Fifth Regiment of Artillery, the legislation was passed authorizing the regiment to designate tactical units as batteries. For that reason, the designation "battery" rather than "company" will be the term used in this chapter. See William E. Birkhimer, *Historical Sketch of the Organization, Administration, Materiel, and Tactics of the Artillery, United States Army* (Washington, D. C.: James J. Chapman, 1884; reprint, New York: Greenwood Press Publishers, 1968), 69.

2. Ibid., 54–75. Four more were later so designated, but the number fluctuated based on funding and perceived need.

3. Battery B had two John Cooks. In addition to the volunteer mentioned here, they had a fifteen-year-old regular army bugler who won the Congressional Medal of Honor for serving a gun at Antietam.

4. John H. Cook, *Cook's Time in the Army*, handwritten account of war experiences, John H. Cook Papers, Wisconsin State Historical Society, Madison.

5. Augustus Buell, "The Story of a Cannoneer," *National Tribune* (October 10, 1889, through April 3, 1890), with additional articles on May 15, May 22, and June 12, 1890; Augustus Buell, *The Cannoneer: Story of a Private Soldier* (Washington: *National Tribune*, 1890); John Gibbon, *Personal Recollections of the Civil War* (New York: G. P. Putnam's Sons, 1928, reprinted Dayton: Morningside Bookshop, 1977); James Stewart, *Battery B, Fourth United States Artillery at Gettysburg*, Sketches of War History, 1861–1865, Papers Prepared for the Ohio Commandery of the Loyal Legion of the United States, Volume 4 (Cincinnati: The Robert Clarke Company, 1896, reprinted; Wilmington, NC: Broadfoot Publishing Company, 1991), 180–93; James Stewart, *A Prologue—The Utah Campaign*, Sketches of War History, 1861–1865, Papers Prepared for the Commandery of the State of Ohio, Military Order of the Loyal Legion of the United States, Volume 5 (Cincinnati: The Robert Clarke Company, 1903, reprinted Wilmington, NC: Broadfoot Publishing Company, 1992), 1–17; James Stewart, Letters to the Editor, *National Tribune* (November 21, 1889, and December 26, 1889); James Stewart, Pension Record, Records of the Pension Office, Record Group 15, U.S. National Archives; Francis B. Heitman, *Historical Register and Dictionary of the United States Army, From Its Organization, September 29, 1789, to March 2, 1903*, Volume 1 (Washington: Government Printing Office, 1903, reprinted Gaithersburg, Md.: Olde Soldier Books, Inc., 1988), 924; *In Memoriam: Companion James Stewart, Major U. S. Army (retired)*, Military Order of the Loyal Legion of the United States, Commandery of the State of Ohio, Circular No. 16, Series of 1905, Whole No. 647, (n.p., n.d.).

6. The telegraph was pushing rapidly westward, but had reached only as far as Fort Kearney, Nebraska. The Pony Express still filled the gap between the end of the telegraph lines and California. See Gibbon, *Personal Recollections*, 3–6.

7. Ibid., 3–10; Buell, *The Cannoneer*, 11–16. For a discussion of the validity of material presented in Buell's book, see Silas Felton, "Pursuing the Elusive Cannoneer," *The Gettysburg Magazine* 9 (July 1993), 33–39. Donald R. Moorman, *Camp Floyd and the Mormons: The Utah War* (Salt Lake City: University of Utah Press, 1992), 23–110.

8. Gibbon, *Personal Recollections*, 6–10.

9. August V. Kautz, *Customs of Service for Non-Commissioned Officers and Soldiers* (Philadelphia: J. B. Lippincott & Co., 1864; reprinted, n.p., n.d.), 131–49.

10. Returns for the Fourth U.S. Artillery, July, September, October 1861, U.S. National Archives Microfilm 727, reel 29. The Returns are a monthly account sheet of the status of Regular Army personnel only, and the unit's equipment. The Returns also have a block for Record of Events, a synopsis of where the battery had been that month and often comments on what had happened. This group of returns shows Battery B leaving Camp Floyd with two officers and sixty-nine enlisted men. They lost six men to desertion, two to sickness, and two had their enlistment expire before they reached Maryland.

11. Returns, October 1861. Gibbon had departed for volunteer duty, and four enlisted men were present, but not available for duty.

12. *Muster Roll, Company B, Fourth U.S. Artillery, August 31, 1861–October 31, 1861*, Records of the Adjutant General's Office, Record Group 94, National Archives. Muster Rolls were produced bi-monthly on the last day of the month. They

recorded all assigned and attached personnel, any losses or gains and the reason, and comments pertinent to record-keeping for the unit. They also had a small block for Record of Events, although in the case of Battery B, it was not regularly filled out. Gibbon, *Personal Recollections*, 13.

13. Returns, August, September, October, November, and December 1863; Muster Rolls, October 31–December 31, 1863.

14. Gibbon, *Personal Recollections*, 11–15. Gibbon goes to some length to illustrate his point of how pleasant it was to receive intelligent volunteers.

15. John Gibbon, Report of the Battle of South Mountain, *Official Records*, Volume 19, Part 1, 247–49; Buell, *The Cannoneer*, 32–33; Gibbon, *Personal Recollections*, 76–79; Dawes, *Service with the Sixth Wisconsin*, 80–86.

16. Muster Rolls, September-October, 1862; Returns, September 1862; Stewart, *Official Records*, Volume 19, Part 1, 229–31; John Gibbon, Report of the Battle of Antietam, *Official Records*, Volume 19, Part 1, 248–49; Buell, *The Cannoneer*, 33–43; Gibbon, *Personal Recollections*, 81–91; Dawes, *Service with the Sixth Wisconsin*, 87–93.

17. Muster Rolls, November-December 1862; Returns, December, 1862; James Stewart, Report of the Battle of Fredricksburg, *Official Records*, Volume 21, Part 1, 468–69; Curtis, *History of the Twenty-fourth Michigan*, 91–95.

18. Muster Rolls, January-February, March, April 1863.

19. Muster Rolls, July-August, 1863; Returns, July 1863; Buell, *The Cannoneer*, 61–100; Dawes, *Service with the Sixth Wisconsin*, 174–80; Wainwright, *A Diary of Battle*, 229–55; James Stewart, "Battery B. Fourth United States Artillery at Gettysburg"; Alfred M. Scales, Report of Gettysburg Campaign, *Official Records*, Volume 27, Part II, 669–70; William L. J. Lowrance, Report of the Gettysburg Campaign, *Official Records*, Volume 27, Part II, 671–73.

20. Returns, January 1864; Muster Rolls, January, February, March, April, May, June 1864.

21. Returns, May 1864; Muster Rolls, May-June 1864; Buell, *The Cannoneer*, 174–83; Wainwright, *A Diary of Battle*, 357–59.

22. Muster Rolls, May-June 1864; Buell, *The Cannonneer*, 207–19; Wainwright, *A Diary of Battle*, 395–405; James Stewart, Report, Summer Campaign, 1864, in Hewett, Trudeau, and Suderow, *Supplement to the Official Records*, 604.

23. Returns, August, 1864; Muster Rolls, July-August 1864.

10. In Peace and War

Richard Zeitlin wishes to acknowledge the help of the following individuals: H. Michael Madaus, Edward M. Coffman, William F. Thompson, and John M. Cooper.

1. State of Wisconsin, *Annual Reports of the Adjutant General and the Quartermaster General of the State of Wisconsin, 1865* (Madison, 1865), 20–21. Wisconsin was credited with providing 91,379 soldiers during 1861–1865. Of that number 12,301 died from all causes; 5,782 men reenlisted and were, therefore, counted twice. Thus, 73,296 Wisconsinites survived the war (a mortality rate of approximately 14 percent). See also Fox, *Regimental Losses*, 526; State of Wisconsin, Charles H. Estabrook, ed., *Wisconsin Losses in the Civil War; A List of Names of Wisconsin Soldiers Killed in Action, Mortally wounded, or Dying from other Causes in the Civil War* (Madison: Commission on Civil War Records, 1915), passim; State of Wisconsin, Adjutant General's Office, *Roster of Wisconsin Volunteers in the War of the Rebellion*, 2 Volumes, (Madison, 1886), passim; Charles R. Tuttle, *Illustrated History of Wisconsin* (Madison, 1875), 609, 618; State of Wisconsin, "Wisconsin Vote in Presidential Elections, 1848–1980," *Wisconsin Blue Book*, 1981, 702.

2. Robert C. Nesbit, *Wisconsin: A History* (Madison, 1973), 303, 314–20, 362–73, 381.

3. Mary R. Dearing, *Veterans in Politics: The Story of the G.A.R.* (Baton Rouge, 1952), 69.

4. Ibid.

5. Dearing, *Veterans in Politics*, 94; *Wisconsin State Journal*, February 26, May 26, 1866; George F. Dawson, *Life and Service of Gen. John A. Logan* (New York, 1888), 123–25; Mary H. Stephenson, *Dr. B.F. Stephenson, Founder of the Grand Army of the Republic* (Springfield, Illinois, 1894), passim; Major Oliver M. Wilson, *The Grand Army of the Republic Under Its First Constitution: Its Birth and Organization* (Kansas City, 1905), passim.

6. Robert B. Beath, *History of the Grand Army of the Republic With Introduction by Lucius Fairchild* (New York, 1888), 537–39; Grand Army Publishing Company, *Soldiers and Citizens Album*, 2 Volumes (Chicago, 1891), 2, 768.

7. Wisconsin GAR, *Proceedings of the First Annual Encampment by Department of Wisconsin* (Madison, 1867). See also J. Worth Carnahan, *Manual of the Civil War and Key to the Grand Army of the Republic and Kindred Societies* (Chicago, 1897), 18–25; and Beath, *Grand Army of the Republic*, 41–43.

8. Beath, *Grand Army of the Republic*, 26–31; Fairchild to Soldiers and Sailors Convention, 23 September 1866, in Fairchild Papers, Wisconsin State Archive; Governor Hacheld to Fairchild, 12 September 1866, in Fairchild Papers; Dearing, *Veterans in Politics*, 98.

9. *Wisconsin State Journal*, July 5, 1866.

10. "Address Delivered July 4, 1866, Upon the Formal Delivery of the Battle Flags to the State," in Fairchild Papers.

11. *Report of Wisconsin Adjutant General*, 1867, 442.

12. *Wisconsin State Journal*, August 9, 1866.

13. *Wisconsin State Journal*, August 13, 1866.

14. Fairchild to J. S. Crane, 10 October 1866, in Fairchild Papers.

15. Sam Ross, *The Empty Sleeve: A Biography of Lucius Fairchild* (Madison: State Historical Society of Wisconsin for the Wisconsin Civil War Centennial Commission, 1964), 93; Dearing, *Veterans in Politics*, 105, 111; Fairchild to T. O. Howe, 24 July 1866, in Fairchild Papers.

16. Nesbit, *Wisconsin*, 363–64; Ross, *Empty Sleeve*, 96. See also Edward Gambill, *Conservative Ordeal: Northern Democrats and Reconstruction, 1865–1869* (Ames, Iowa, 1981), passim; and George Lankevitch, "The G.A.R. in New York State, 1865–1898" (Doctoral dissertation, Columbia University, 1967), 53–55.

17. *Milwaukee Sentinel*, May 13, 1868.

18. *Wisconsin State Journal*, May 20, 1868.

19. "Platform of Principles Adopted by the Soldiers' and Sailors' National Convention at Chicago, May 19, 1868," in Fairchild Papers; Frank A. Flower, *History of the Republican Party* (Springfield, Illinois, 1884), 293–94; *Milwaukee Sentinel*, May 20, 1868.

20. *Milwaukee Sentinel*, May 20, 1868; Ross, *Empty Sleeve*, 97–98.

21. Ibid.

22. *Wisconsin State Journal*, May 25, July 22, 1868; Flower, *Republican Party*, 302–303; *Soldiers and Citizens Album*, 2:769; Beath, *Grand Army of the Republic*, 539–40; "Importance of the Election, 1868," in Fairchild Papers.

23. *Wisconsin State Journal*, August 5, 1868; Ross, *Empty Sleeve*, 101–102.

24. Ross, *Empty Sleeve*, 122; Dearing, *Veterans in Politics*, 191–93; *Soldier's Record*, July 24, 1869; Henry Casson, *"Uncle Jerry": The Life of Jeremiah M. Rusk* (Madison, 1895), 156–57; *Wisconsin State Journal*, February 6, 1869.

25. *Campaign Scrapbook, 1870*, in Fairchild Papers.

26. State of Wisconsin, *Annual Messages of Wisconsin Governors* (Madison, 1870), 9.

27. State of Wisconsin, *Laws of Wisconsin: Acts of A General Nature Passed By The Legislature in 1870 Together With Resolutions and Memorials* (Madison, 1870), Chapter 82.

28. *Report of Wisconsin QMG, 1870*, 78; Tuttle, *History of Wisconsin*, 614; Daniel S. Durrie, *A History of Madison The Capital of Wisconsin* (Madison 1874), 319; Clifford Lord and Carl Ubbelohde, *Clio's Servant: The State Historical Society of Wisconsin, 1846–1954* (Madison, 1967), 55–56.

29. *La Crosse Republican and Leader*, June 17, 1871; *Milwaukee Sentinel*, June 9, 10, 1871.

30. Ibid.; Society of the Army of the Tennessee, *Report of the Proceedings of the Society of the Army of the Tennessee at the Annual Meeting Held at Madison, Wisconsin, July 3 and 4, 1872* (Cincinnati, 1877), 64–65; Durrie, Madison, 349–50; "Speech before Society of the Army of the Tennessee, July 4, 1872," in Fairchild Papers.

31. Wisconsin GAR published figures for GAR membership in Wisconsin from 1875 (the first year records were kept) to 1888. See Wisconsin GAR, *Proceedings of 1889*, 62–64.

32. *Annual Messages of Wisconsin Governors, 1874*, 9; *Laws of Wisconsin, 1875*, Chapter 142.

33. *Wisconsin Blue Book, 1981*, 703. Fewer than 1,000 votes separated Taylor and Ludington in 1875.

34. *Laws of Wisconsin, 1876*, Chapter 208.

35. *Wisconsin State Journal*, July 5, 1876. See also P. C. Priest to Harrison Ludington, 1 May 1876; Nathan Cole to Harrison Ludington, 19 May 1876; Floyd C. Babcock to Harrison Ludington, 21 June 1876; R. M. Wright to Harrison Ludington, 7 June 1876; E. B. Crofoot to Harrison Ludington, 22 June 1876; and N. Thatcher to Harrison Ludington, 5 June 1876, in Department of the Executive, Administration, Military Correspondence 1844–1910, Wisconsin State Archives (hereinafter cited as Governor's Military Correspondence).

36. George Tonnar to Harrison Ludington, 4 May 1877; Militus Knight to Governor William E. Smith, 3 May 1878; N. Brush and E. L. Doolittle to Governor William E. Smith, 29 August 1879; George Tonnar to Governor William E. Smith, 16 September 1879; William H. Evans to Governor William E. Smith, 28 May 1879; and George H. Otis to William Smith, 21 May 1879, all in Governor's Military Correspondence.

37. Militus Knight to G. W. Burchard, September 15, 1879, Governor's Military Correspondence.

38. *New York Times*, September 20, 1879.

39. Chicago Union Veterans Club to Governor William E. Smith, 16 August 1879, in Department of Executive, Administration, Civil War Memorials, Wisconsin State Archives; *Chicago Tribune*, August 22, 23, 1879.

40. Wisconsin GAR, *Proceedings*, 1889, 2–64.

41. William H. Evans to William E. Smith, 28 May 1879, Governor's Military Correspondence.

42. B. H. Meyer, "Fraternal Beneficiary Societies in the United States," in the *American Journal of Sociology*, Volume 6 (March 1901), 655; Hosea W. Rood, "The Grand Army of the Republic and The Wisconsin Department, Origin of the G.A.R.," *Wisconsin Magazine of History*, Volume 6 (March 1923), 293; Dearing, *Veterans in Politics*, 191–93, 243–46; Frank H. Heck, "The Grand Army of the Republic in Minnesota, 1866–1880," *Minnesota History*, Volume 16 (December 1935), 432; and Frank H. Heck, *The Civil War Veteran in Minnesota Life and Politics* (Oxford, Ohio,

1941), 11, 23; Lankevitch, "G.A.R. in New York State," 15–17, 104; William H. Glasson, *Federal Military Pensions in the United States* (New York, 1918), 148–49, 166; William H. Glasson, *History of Military Pension Legislation in the United States* (New York, 1900), 88–109; George F. Cram and R. A. Tenney, *Pensions, Who Are Entitled to Them and How They May be Obtained* (Chicago, 1890); R. A. Tenney, *Pension Laws* (Chicago, 1886), 60–63; "Laws and Statutes Now in Force," Section 4692, Revised Statutes 1862, and Section 4693, Revised Statutes 1865, 13–14; Speech of Col. E. F. Brown of Ohio, *Journal of the National G.A.R. Encampment, 1880* (Columbus, 1881), 661–62; Edward R. Noyes, "The Ohio G.A.R. and Politics from 1866–1900," *Ohio State Archeological and Historical Quarterly*, Volume 55 (April–June 1946), 79; *Milwaukee Sentinel*, June 7, 1880.

43. Wisconsin Soldiers Reunion Executive Committee to Governor William E. Smith, 19 April 1880, Governor's Military Correspondence; *Report of Wisconsin QMG, 1880*, 3; C. K. Pier, compiler, *Wisconsin Soldiers and Sailors Reunion Roster* (Fond du Lac: Wisconsin Soldiers Reunion Association, 1880), 273.

44. Pier, *Reunion Roster*, 273; *Racine Journal*, June 2, 1880; *Milwaukee Sentinel*, June 7, 1880.

45. *Milwaukee Sentinel*, June 12, 1880.

46. *Milwaukee Sentinel*, June 12, 1880; *Racine Journal*, June 2, 1880; Frank A. Flower, *History of Milwaukee*, Volume 2 (Chicago: Western Historical Company, 1881), 784.

47. Jerome A. Watrous Papers, Wisconsin Veterans Museum, Clippings.

48. *Milwaukee Sentinel*, June 12, 1880; Dearing, *Veterans in Politics*, 263.

49. *Milwaukee Sentinel*, June 11, 1880.

50. *Report of Wisconsin QMG*, 1880, 3.

51. Blake to Governor William E. Smith, 9 September 1880; D. G. Marsh to Secretary of State, 15 October 1880; both in Governor's Military Correspondence.

52. *Racine Journal*, June 2, 1880; *Milwaukee Sentinel*, June 11, 1880.

53. Pier, *Reunion Roster*, 247.

54. *Milwaukee Sentinel*, June 9, 11, 12, 1880; *National Tribune*, June 15, 1922; Watrous, *Richard Epps*; Jerome A. Watrous, ed., *Memories of Milwaukee County*, 2 Volumes (Milwaukee, 1909).

55. *Milwaukee Sentinel*, July 23, 1882.

56. *Milwaukee Sentinel*, September 15, 1882.

57. *Milwaukee Sentinel*, September 18, 21, 1882; John Stahel to J. M. Rusk, 1 June 1882; both in Governor's Military Correspondence.

58. *Milwaukee Sentinel*, September 21, 1882; Cullen B. ["Doc"] Aubery, *Echoes From the Marches of the Famous Iron Brigade* (Milwaukee, n.d.), 61, 67; Ross, *Empty Sleeve*, 186. See also Cullen B. Aubery, *Twenty-Five Years on the Streets of Milwaukee After Dark; Together with Sketches and Experiences as a Newsboy in the Army of the Potomac* (Milwaukee, 1897); and Cullen B. Aubery, *Recollections of the Newsboy in the Army of the Potomac, 1861–1865*, (n.p.,n.d.).

59. *Milwaukee Sentinel*, August 7, 15, 1883.

60. *Milwaukee Sentinel*, August 15, 1883; E. S. Bragg and J. A. Watrous, "Reunion of the Iron Brigade—La Crosse, August 7, 1883" (n.p., n.d.); W. Shakespeare to J. A. Watrous, 30 August 1883, in Secretary of State, Administrative Department, Elections and Records, Iron Brigade Reunions, 1883–1884, Wisconsin State Archives.

61. *La Crosse Morning Chronicle*, September 15, 1883; *La Crosse Republican and Leader*, September 15, 1883.

62. *Milwaukee Sentinel*, September 14, 1883.

63. *La Crosse Republican and Leader*, September 15, 1883.

64. *Milwaukee Sentinel*, January 14, 1884; *Grant County Herald*, August 1, September 4, 1884.

65. *Milwaukee Sentinel,* August 29, 1884.

66. *Grant County Herald,* September 4, 1884.

67. Fairchild to "Dear Charlie," in Fairchild Papers.

68. *Milwaukee Sentinel,* August 2, September 12, 1885; *Wisconsin State Journal,* September 15, 16, 1885.

69. *Milwaukee Sentinel,* September 16, 17, 1885.

70. *Wisconsin State Journal,* September 15, 16, 1885; *Milwaukee Sentinel,* September 16, 1885.

71. Pond to Fairchild, 15 July 1886, in Fairchild Papers; *Soldiers and Citizens Album,* 2:398.

72. Lucius Fairchild to the Department of Wisconsin GAR Members, 30 March 1886, in Fairchild Papers; Beath, *Grand Army of the Republic,* 325, 332, 540; J. M. Rusk to S. S. Burdette, 15 March 1886, in Jeremiah M. Rusk Papers, 1861–1898, Wisconsin State Archives.

73. Dearing, *Veterans in Politics,* 321–32, 325, 329, 339; Donald L. McMurry, "The Soldier Vote in Iowa in the Election of 1888," *Iowa Journal of History and Politics,* 18 (July 1920), 343; Donald L. McMurry, "The Political Significance of the Pension Question, 1885–1897," *Mississippi Valley Historical Review,* 9 (1921–1922), 19; Noyes, "The Ohio G.A.R. and Politics," 79; John A. Logan, *The Great Conspiracy* (New York, 1886), 658–69; Grand Army of the Republic, *Journal of the National G.A.R. Encampment,* 1887, 40–45. For recent assessments of the pension issue see: Richard F. Bensel, *Sectionalism and American Political Development, 1880–1980* (Madison, 1984); Theda Skoctol, *Protecting Soldiers and Mothers: The Political Origins of Social Policy in the United States* (Cambridge, Mass.: London, 1992), 102–152.

74. *Oshkosh Northwestern,* August 31, September 1, 1886; *Milwaukee Sentinel,* August 29, 31, 1886.

75. *Oshkosh Northwestern,* September 1, 1886.

76. *Oshkosh Northwestern,* August 31, September 2, 1886.

77. Grover Cleveland to House of Representatives, February 3, 11, 1887, in James D. Richardson, ed., *Messages and Papers of the Presidents* Volume 8 (Washington, 1898), 543, 549–57.

78. *Evening Wisconsin* (Madison), February 17, 1887; *Milwaukee Sentinel,* September 15, 1887; John Gibbon to E. S. Bragg, 28 July 1887, in Edward S. Bragg Papers, Wisconsin State Archives; L. E. Peterson to Lucius Fairchild, 18 June 1887, in Fairchild Papers.

79. *Journal of the National G.A.R. Encampment, 1887,* 219–20.

80. National Headquarters GAR, Circular No. 4, 1887, in Fairchild Papers; *Milwaukee Sentinel,* February 17, 1887; Wisconsin GAR, *Proceedings,* 1888, 24–25; Robert M. La Follette to Lucius Fairchild, 20 February 1887, in Fairchild Papers; Lucius Fairchild to *Madison Democrat,* February 16, 1887, in Fairchild Papers, Scrapbooks, reel 2; John C. Black to S. S. Burdett, 5 August 1885, *Journal of the National G.A.R. Encampment,* 1886, 269–70; Black to Lucius Fairchild, 22 September 1887, in Fairchild Papers.

81. *New York Sun,* June 15, 16, 1887; Lankevitch, "G.A.R. in New York State," 214.

82. Fairchild to "Dear Frank," 19 June and 21 June 1887, in Fairchild Papers.

83. Peterson to Fairchild, 18 June 1887, in Fairchild Papers; E. W. Whitaker to Fairchild, 18 June 1887 in Fairchild Papers; "An Old Veteran of 7 Years Service and No Pension" to General Fairchild, June 1887, in Fairchild Papers; Michael Griffin to J. M. Rusk, 16 June 1887, in *Military Correspondence*; Dearing, *Veterans in Politics,* 342–44; Ross, *Empty Sleeve,* 208–209; Grover Cleveland to Secretary of War, 16 June 1887, in Richardson, *Messages and Papers,* Volume 8, 579.

84. James Tanner to Lucius Fairchild, 15 August 1887, in Fairchild Papers.

85. James Tanner to Lucius Fairchild, 15 August 1887, in Fairchild Papers.

86. *Fond du Lac Commonwealth*, September 16, 1887.

87. *Milwaukee Sentinel*, September 15, 1887.

88. *Chicago Tribune*, October 3, 4, 1887; Dearing, *Veterans in Politics*, 362–65; Grover Cleveland, "Third Annual Message, December 6, 1887," in Richardson, *Messages and Papers*, Volume 8, 580–85; James L. Hutson, "A Political Response to Industrialism: The Republican Embrace of Protectionist Labor Doctrines," *Journal of American History*, 70 (June, 1983), 35–37; Logan, *Great Conspiracy*, 658–69; Rusk to G. H. Brintonell, 2 August 1888, in Rusk Papers; "Speech at Waupaca, 1888," and John C. Black to Fairchild, 22 September 1887, in Fairchild Papers; Heck, *Minnesota Veterans*, 150; "Harrison and Cleveland in 1864," in Rusk Papers.

89. McMurry, "Soldier Vote in Iowa," 33; *Wisconsin Blue Book, 1983–1984*, 686.

90. *Milwaukee Sentinel*, August 28, 1889.

91. Rusk to L. E. Pond, 21 May 1888, in the Rusk Papers.

92. Reuben Gold Thwaites to George E. Bryant, 9 January 1903, State Historical Society Administration, General Correspondence, Wisconsin State Archives.

93. Lord and Ubbelohde, *Clio's Servant*, 74.

94. *Laws of Wisconsin*, 1895, Chapter 298.

95. *Laws of Wisconsin*, 1895, Chapter 298.

96. *Laws of Wisconsin*, 1901, Chapter 125; Wisconsin G.A.R. *Proceedings*, 1901, 63; D. G. James, "The Sixteenth Wisconsin Infantry at Shiloh, Tenn., April 6 and 7, 1862," in F. H. Magdenburg, comp., *Wisconsin at Shiloh: Report of the Commission* (Milwaukee, 1909), 33–45.

97. Ibid.

98. *Wisconsin State Journal*, February 27, 1904; George E. Bryant, *The Capitol Fire* (Madison, 1904).

99. *Wisconsin State Journal*, February 27, 1904.

100. *Proceedings*, State Historical Society of Wisconsin (1914), 46; Lord and Ubbelohde, *Clio's Servant*, 206; Bryant, *The Capitol Fire*; George E. Bryant, *Classic and Beautiful Our Proposed Capitol* (Madison, 1905).

101. *Proceedings*, State Historical Society of Wisconsin (1914), 46; Lord and Ubbelohde, *Clio's Servant*, 142–43; Wisconsin GAR, *Proceedings*, 1914, 127–28; Hosea W. Rood, *A Little Flag Book* (n.p., 1919), 38.

102. Wisconsin GAR, *Proceedings*, 1914, 127–28.

103. Lord and Ubbelohde, *Clio's Servant*, 504; Rood, *Little Flag Book*, 38; Hosea W. Rood, *Memorial Day Annual, 1916* (Madison, 1916), 20; *Laws of Wisconsin*, 1909, Chapter 47.

104. Hosea W. Rood, January 10, March 17, April 20, 1917, in Rood Diary, 1917, Archives, Wisconsin Veterans Museum.

105. Rood to GAR Patriotic Instructors, 21 May 1918, in Rood Papers, Wisconsin Veterans Museum.

106. J. A. Watrous, "Looking Over Our Old Battle Flags," and J. A. Watrous, "Program for the Dedication of the Grand Army Memorial Hall in the Capital, Madison, Wisconsin, June 14, 1918," both in Archives, Wisconsin Veterans Museum.

Bibliography

Official Records and Reports

State of Wisconsin. Adjutant General's Office. *Roster of Wisconsin Volunteers in the War of the Rebellion.* 2 Volumes. Madison, 1886.

State of Wisconsin. *Annual Messages of Wisconsin Governors.* Madison, 1870.

State of Wisconsin. *Annual Reports of the Adjutant General and the Quartermaster General of the State of Wisconsin, 1865.* Madison, 1865.

State of Wisconsin. *Annual Report of the Quartermaster General of the State of Wisconsin, 1870.* Madison, 1870.

State of Wisconsin. *Annual Report of the Quartermaster General of the State of Wisconsin, 1880.* Madison, 1880.

State of Wisconsin. *Department of the Executive, Administration, Military Correspondence. 1844–1910.* Wisconsin State Archives.

State of Wisconsin. *Laws of Wisconsin: Acts of A General Nature Passed By The Legislature in 1870 Together With Resolutions and Memorials.* Madison, 1870.

State of Wisconsin. *Secretary of State, Administrative Department, Elections and Records, Iron Brigade Reunions, 1883–1884.* Wisconsin State Archives.

State of Wisconsin. *Wisconsin Blue Book.* Madison, 1981.

State of Wisconsin. Charles H. Estabrook, ed., *Wisconsin Losses in the Civil War; A List of Names of Wisconsin Soldiers Killed in Action, Mortally wounded, or Dying from other Causes in the Civil War.* Madison: Commission on Civil War Records, 1915.

U.S. Army Corps of Engineers. United States Department of Interior Geological Survey. *Gainesville Quadrangle.* Washington, D.C.: 1953.

U.S. Congress. Chapter 116. Forty-First Congress, Session III. "An Act Making Appropriations For The Support Of The Army For The Year Ending June Thirty, Eighteen Hundred and Seventy-Two, And For Other Purposes."

U.S. Congress. 46th Congress. 1st Session. Senate Executive Document 37. *Proceedings and Report of Army Officers Convened by Special Order No. 78.* Headquarters of the Army. Adjutant General's Office. Washington, D. C. April 12, 1878, "In the Case of Fitz John Porter, Together with Proceedings in the Original Trial and Papers Relating Thereto." Washington: Government Printing Office, 1879.

U.S. National Archives. *John C. Brawner Petition to Southern Claims Commission.* Commission No. 1335, Office No. 13, Report No. 1.

U.S. National Archives. Record Group 15. *Records of the Pension Office.*

U.S. National Archives. Record Group 94. *Antietam Studies.*

U.S. National Archives. Record Group 393. *Records of the U.S. Army Continental Commands, Gibbon's Brigade, General Orders.*

U.S. National Archives. *Returns for the Fourth United States Artillery for July, September, and October 1861.* National Archives Microfilm 727, Reel 29.

U.S. National Archives. *Muster Roll, Company B, Fourth United States Artillery. August 31, 1861–October 31, 1861.* Records of the Adjutant General's Office, Record Group 94.

U.S. National Archives. Bvt. Mag. Gen. G. K. Warren. "Map of the Battle Grounds of August 28–29–30, In the Vicinity of Groveton, Prince William County, Va., Made by Authority of Hon. G.W. McCrary, Sec. of War, Surveyed in June 1878."

U.S. War Department. *The War of the Rebellion: A Compilation of the Official Records of the Union and Confederate Armies.* 130 Volumes. Washington: Government Printing Office, 1880–1901.

General Reference Materials

Birkhimer, William E. *Historical Sketch of the Organization, Administration, Materiel, and Tactics of the Artillery, United States Army.* Washington: James J. Chapman, 1884. Reprinted. New York: Greenwood Press Publishers, 1968.

Boatner, Mark M., III. *The Civil War Dictionary.* Revised Edition. New York: David McKay Company, Inc., 1988.

Busey, John W., and David G. Martin. *Regimental Strengths and Losses at Gettysburg.* Hightown, New Jersey: 1986.

Carman, Ezra A., and Emmor B. Cope. Antietam Battlefield Map. Revised 1905. U.S. Library of Congress.

Carnahan, J. Worth. *Manual of the Civil War and Key to the Grand Army of the Republic and Kindred Societies.* Chicago, 1897.

Dyer, Frederick H. *A Compendium of the War of the Rebellion.* New York: Thomas Yoseloff, 1959.

Esposito, Col. Vincent J., editor. *Atlas to Accompany Steele's American Campaigns.* West Point: United States Military Academy, 1956.

Faust, Patricia L., editor. *Historical Times Illustrated Encyclopedia of the Civil War.* New York: Harper and Row, 1986.

Flower, Frank A. *History of Milwaukee.* 2 Volumes. Chicago: Western Historical Company, 1881.

Fox, William F. *Regimental Losses in the American Civil War.* Albany: Albany Publishing Company, 1889.

Harrison, Noel G. *Gazetteer of Historic Sites Related to the Fredericksburg and Spotsylvania National Military Park.* 2 Volumes. Fredericksburg: Fredericksburg and Spotsylvania National Military Park, 1986.

Heitman, Francis B. *Historical Register and Dictionary of the United States Army, From Its Organization, September 29, 1789, to March 2, 1903.* Volume 1. Washington: Government Printing Office, 1903.

Hewett, Janet B., Noah A. Trudeau, and Bryce A. Suderow, editors. *Supplement to the Official Records of the Union and Confederate Armies.* Wilmington: Broadfoot Publishing Company, 1994.

Johnson, Robert Underwood, and Clarence Clough Buel, editors. *Battles and Leaders of the Civil War.* 4 Volumes. New York: Century, 1887–88.

Kautz, August V. *Customs of Service for Non-Commissioned Officers and Soldiers.* Philadelphia: J. B. Lippincott & Co., 1864.

Livermore, Thomas L. *Gettysburg Papers.* Volume 1. Dayton: Morningside House, 1995.

The Medical and Surgical History of the Civil War. Wilmington, NC: Broadfoot Publishing Company, 1990.

Nesbit, Robert C. *Wisconsin: A History.* Madison: University of Wisconsin Press, 1973.

Pier, C. K., compiler. *Wisconsin Soldiers and Sailors Reunion Roster.* Fond du Lac: Wisconsin Soldiers Reunion Association, 1880.

Quiner, Edwin B. *Correspondence of Wisconsin Volunteers, 1861–1865.* 10 Volumes. Scrapbook Index. Madison: Wisconsin State Historical Society, n.d.

Richardson, James D., editor. *Messages and Papers of the Presidents.* Volume 8. Washington, 1898.

Society of the Army of the Tennessee. *Report of the Proceedings of the Society of* the Army of the Tennessee at the Annual meeting Held at Madison, Wisconsin, July 3 and 4, 1872.* Cincinnati, 1877.

Tuttle, Charles R. *Illustrated History of Wisconsin.* Madison, 1875.

Warner, Ezra J. *Generals in Blue: Lives of Union Commanders.* Baton Rouge: Louisiana State University Press, 1964.

Wisconsin GAR. *Proceedings of the First Annual Encampment by Department of Wisconsin.* Madison, 1867.

Wisconsin GAR. *Proceedings of the First Annual Encampment by Department of Wisconsin.* Madison, 1889.

Books, Articles, and Periodicals

Adams, Z. Boylston. "In the Wilderness." In *Military Order of the Loyal Legion of the United States, Civil War Papers, Commandery of The State of Massachusetts.* Volume 2. Boston: Military Order of the Loyal Legion of the United States, 1900.

Aubery, Cullen B. ["Doc"]. *Echoes From the Marches of the Famous Iron Brigade.* [Milwaukee, n.d.] Reprinted 1988. Gaithersburg: Ron R. Van Sickle Military Books, 1988.

Aubery, Cullen B. ["Doc"]. *Recollections of the Newsboy in the Army of the Potomac, 1861–1865.* N.p., n.d.

Aubery, Cullen B. ["Doc"]. *Twenty-Five Years on the Streets of Milwaukee After Dark; Together with Sketches and Experiences as a Newsboy in the Army of the Potomac.* Milwaukee, 1897.

Bates, Samuel P. *The Battle of Gettysburg.* Philadelphia: T. H. David and Company, 1875.

Beath, Robert B. *History of the Grand Army of the Republic With Introduction by Lucius Fairchild.* New York, 1888.

Beaudot, William J. K., and Lance J. Herdegen. *An Irishman in the Iron Brigade: The Civil War Memoirs of James P. Sullivan, Sergt., Company K, 6th Wisconsin Volunteers.* New York: Fordham University Press, 1993.

Beecham, R.[obert] K. *Gettysburg, The Pivotal Battle of the Civil War.* Chicago: A. C. McClurg and Company, 1911.

Bensel, Richard F. *Sectionalism and American Political Development, 1880–1980.* Madison, 1984.

Berwanger, Eugene H., editor, "'absent So long from those I love': The Civil War Letters of Joshua Jones." *Indiana Magazine of History.* Volume 88 (September 1992).

Beyer, W. F. and O. F. Keydel, editors. *Deeds Of Valor: How America's Civil War Heroes Won The Congressional Medal Of Honor.* Detroit: Perrien-Keydel Company, 1903.

Bragg, Edward S., and Jerome A. Watrous. "Reunion of the Iron Brigade—LaCrosse, August 7, 1883." N.p., n.d.

Brainard, Mary Genevie Green. *Campaigns of the One Hundred and Forty-Sixth Regiment, New York State Volunteers; Also Known As Halleck's Infantry, and Fifth Oneida and Garrard's Tigers.* New York: G. P. Putnam's Sons, 1915.

Bryant, George E. *The Capitol Fire.* Madison, 1904.

Bryant, George E. *Classic and Beautiful Our Proposed Capitol.* Madison, 1905.

Buell, Augustus C. "The Story of a Cannoneer." *National Tribune* (October 10, 1889, through April 3, 1890).

Buell, Augustus C. *The Cannoneer: Recollections Of Service In The Army Of The Potomac.* Washington: *The National Tribune*, 1890.

Byrne, Frank L., editor. *Haskell of Gettysburg*. Madison: State Historical Society of Wisconsin, 1970.

Casler, John O. *Four Years in the Stonewall Brigade*. Oklahoma City: State Capital Printing Company, 1893.

Casson, Henry. *"Uncle Jerry": The Life of Jeremiah M. Rusk*. Madison, 1895.

Catton, Bruce. *Glory Road*. New York: Doubleday, 1952.

Chamberlin, Thomas. *History of the One Hundred and Fiftieth Regiment of Pennsylvania Volunteers*. Philadelphia: F. McManus, Jr. and Company, 1905.

Cheek, Philip, and Mair Pointon. *History of the Sauk County Riflemen, Known As Company "A," Sixth Wisconsin Veteran Volunteer Infantry, 1861–1865*. Gaithersburg: Butternut Press, 1909.

Coddington, Edwin B. *The Gettysburg Campaign: A Study in Command*. New York: Charles Scribner's Sons, 1968.

Cram, George F., and R. A. Tenney. *Pensions, Who Are Entitled to Them and How They May be Obtained*. Chicago, 1890.

Curtis, Orson B. *History of the Twenty-Fourth Michigan of the Iron Brigade, Known as the Detroit and Wayne County Regiment*. Detroit: Winn and Hammond, 1891.

Dawes, Rufus R. *Service with the Sixth Wisconsin Volunteers*. Marietta: E. R. Alderman and Sons, 1890.

Dawes, Rufus R. "On the Right At Antietam." In *Service with the Sixth Wisconsin Volunteers*. Edited by Alan T. Nolan. Dayton: Morningside Press, 1984.

Dawson, George F. *Life and Service of Gen. John A. Logan*. New York, 1888.

Dearing, Mary R. *Veterans in Politics: The Story of the G.A.R.* Baton Rouge: Louisiana State University Press, 1952.

Dudley, William W. *The Iron Brigade at Gettysburg, 1878, Official Report of the Part Borne by the 1st Brigade, 1st Division, 1st Army Corps*. Cincinnati, 1879.

Durrie, Daniel S. *A History of Madison The Capital of Wisconsin*. Madison, 1874.

Flower, Frank A. *History of the Republican Party*. Springfield, 1884.

Gaff, Alan D. *Brave Men's Tears: The Iron Brigade at Brawner Farm*. Dayton: Morningside House, Inc., 1988.

Gaff, Alan D. *If This Is War: A History of the Campaign of Bull's Run by the Wisconsin Regiment Thereafter Known as the Ragged Ass Second*. Dayton: Morningside House, Inc., 1991.

Gaff, Alan D. *On Many a Bloody Field: Four Years in the Iron Brigade*. Bloomington: Indiana University Press, 1997.

Gaff, Alan D., and Maureen Gaff. *Our Boys: A Civil War Photograph Album*. Evansville: Windmill, 1996.

Gambill, Edward. *Conservative Ordeal: Northern Democrats and Reconstruction, 1865–1869*. Ames, Iowa, 1981.

Gibbon, John. *The Artillerist's Manual, Compiled from Various Sources, and Adapted to the Service of the United States*. New York: D. Van Nostrand, 1859.

Gibbon, John. *Personal Recollections of the Civil War*. New York: G. P. Putnam's Sons, 1928.

Gibbon, John. *Personal Recollections of the Civil War*. Rev. ed. Dayton: Morningside House Inc., 1988.

Glasson, William H. *Federal Military Pensions in the United States*. New York, 1918.

Glasson, William H. *History of Military Pension Legislation in the United States*. In *Columbia University Studies in History, Economic, and Public Law*. Volume 12. Number 3 (New York, 1900).

Gordon, John B. *Reminiscences of the Civil War*. New York: Charles Scribner's Sons, 1904.

Gramm, Kent D. *Gettysburg: A Meditation on War and Values*. Bloomington: Indiana University Press, 1994.

Grand Army Publishing Company. *Soldiers and Citizens Album.* 2 Volumes. Chicago, 1891.

Grant, Ulysses S. *Personal Memoirs of U. S. Grant.* 2 Volumes. New York: C. L. Webster, 1894.

Haight, Theron. *Gainesville, Groveton and Bull Run.* Milwaukee: War Papers, Wisconsin Commandery, Military Order of the Loyal Legion, 1896.

Harries, William H. "Gainesville, Virginia, Aug. 28, 1862." In *Glimpses of the Nation's Struggle, Military Order of the Loyal Legion of the United States.* Volume 6. St. Paul: H. L. Collins Co., 1909.

Harries, William H. "In the Ranks at Antietam." In *The Second Wisconsin Infantry.* Edited by Alan D. Gaff. Dayton: Press of the Morningside Bookshop, 1984.

Haskell, Frank A. *The Battle of Gettysburg.* Madison: Wisconsin History Commission, 1910.

Heck, Frank H. "The Grand Army of the Republic in Minnesota, 1866–1880." *Minnesota History.* Volume 16 (December 1935).

Heck, Frank H. *The Civil War Veteran in Minnesota Life and Politics.* Oxford, Ohio, 1941.

Henderson, G. F. R. *Stonewall Jackson and the American Civil War.* New York: Grosset, 1936.

Hennessy, John J. *Return to Bull Run.* New York: Simon & Schuster, 1993.

Herdegen, Lance J. *The Men Stood Like Iron.* Bloomington: Indiana University Press, 1997.

Herdegen, Lance J., and William J. K. Beaudot. *In the Bloody Railroad Cut at Gettysburg.* Dayton: Press of Morningside Bookshop, 1990.

Hitchcock, Frederick L. *War from the Inside.* Philadelphia, 1904.

Holsinger, Frank. "How It Feels To Be Under Fire." In *The Blue and the Gray.* Edited by Henry Steele Commager. Volume 1. Indianapolis: Bobbs Merrill Company, Inc., 1973. 314–17.

Humphreys, Andrew A. *The Virginia Campaign of '64 and '65.* New York, 1883.

Hutson, James L. "A Political Response to Industrialism: The Republican Embrace of Protectionist Labor Doctrines," *Journal of American History.* Volume 70 (June 1983), 35–37.

In Memoriam: Companion James Stewart, Major U.S. Army (Retired). Military Order of the Loyal Legion of the United States, Commandery of the State of Ohio. Circular No. 16. Series of 1915. Whole No. 647.

James, D. G. "The Sixteenth Wisconsin Infantry at Shiloh, Tenn., April 6 and 7, 1862." F. H. Magdenburg, compiler. *Wisconsin at Shiloh: Report of the Commission.* Milwaukee, 1909.

Jones, E. Terry. *Lee's Tigers.* Baton Rouge: Louisiana State University Press, 1987.

Kelley, Margaret Ryan. "A Soldier of the Iron Brigade." *Wisconsin Magazine of History.* Volume 22 (1938–1939), 308.

Kellogg, John A. *Capture and Escape: A Narrative of Army and Prison Life.* Madison: Democrat State Printer, 1908.

Linderman, Gerald E. *Embattled Courage.* New York: The Free Press, 1987.

Logan, John A. *The Great Conspiracy.* New York, 1886.

Lord, Clifford, and Carl Ubbelohde. *Clio's Servant: The State Historical Society of Wisconsin, 1846–1954.* Madison, 1967.

Lowry, Don. *No Turning Back: The Beginning of the End of the Civil War, March-June, 1864.* New York: Hippocrene Books, 1992.

Matrau, Henry C. *Letters Home: Henry Matrau of the Iron Brigade.* Edited by Marcia Reid-Green. Lincoln: University of Nebraska Press, 1993.

Matthews, Richard E. *149th Pennsylvania Volunteer Infantry Unit in the Civil War.* Jefferson: McFarland and Company, Inc., 1994.

Maxson, William P. *Campfires of the Twenty-third New York.* New York: Davies and Kent, 1863.

McClellan, George B. *McClellan's Own Story.* William C. Prime, editor. New York: Charles L. Webster, 1887.

McMurry, Donald L. "The Political Significance of the Pension Question, 1885–1897." *Mississippi Valley Historical Review.* Volume 9 (1921–1922).

McMurry, Donald L. "The Soldier Vote in Iowa in the Election of 1888." *Iowa Journal of History and Politics.* Volume 18 (July 1920).

McPherson, James M. *Battle Cry of Freedom.* New York: Oxford University Press, 1988.

McPherson, James M. *Drawn with the Sword: Reflections on the American Civil War.* New York: Oxford University Press, 1996.

Meade, George. *The Life and Letters of George Gordon Meade, Volume II.* Edited by George Gordon Meade. New York: Charles Scribner's Sons, 1913.

Melville, Herman. "The Armies of the Wilderness." In *Selected Poems of Herman Melville.* Edited by Robert Penn Warren. New York: Random House, 1967.

Merrill, Catherine. *The Soldier of Indiana in the War for the Union.* Indianapolis: Merrill and Company, 1866.

Mertz, Gregory A. "No Turning Back: The Battle of the Wilderness, Part I—The Fighting on May 5, 1864." *Blue and Gray Magazine.* Volume 12 (April 1995), 8–12, 14–15, 19–23, 47–53.

Mertz, Gregory A. "No Turning Back: The Battle of the Wilderness, Part II—The Fighting on May 6, 1864." *Blue and Gray Magazine.* Volume 12 (June 1995), 8–15, 18–20, 48–50.

Meyer, B. H. "Fraternal Beneficiary Societies in the United States." *American Journal of Sociology.* Volume 6 (March 1901).

Milner, N. P., translator. *Vegetius: Epitome of Military Science.* Liverpool: Liverpool University Press, 1993.

Monteith, Robert. "The Battle of the Wilderness and Death of General Wadsworth." In *War Papers Read Before The Commandery of the State of Wisconsin, Military Order of the Loyal Legion of the United States.* Volume 1. Milwaukee: Military Order of the Loyal Legion of the United States, 1891.

Moorman, Donald R. *Camp Floyd and the Mormons: The Utah War.* Salt Lake City: University of Utah Press, 1992.

Murray, Alton J. *South Georgia Rebels.* St. Mary's: Alton J. Murray, 1976.

Nichols, Edward J. *Toward Gettysburg: A Biography of General John F. Reynolds.* College Station: Pennsylvania State University Press, 1958.

Nichols, George W. *A Soldier's Story of His Regiment and Incidentally of the Lawton, Gordon, Evans Brigade.* Jesup, Georgia: 1898.

Nolan, Alan T. *The Iron Brigade: A Military History.* Third edition. Bloomington: Indiana University Press, 1994. Originally published by Macmillan, 1961.

Noyes, Edward R. "The Ohio G. A. R. and Politics from 1866–1900." Volume 55. *Ohio State Archeological and Historical Quarterly.* Volume 55 (April-June 1946).

Otis, George H. *The Second Wisconsin Infantry.* Edited by Alan D. Gaff. Dayton: Press of Morningside Bookshop, 1984.

Partridge, George Washington, Jr. *Letters from the Iron Brigade.* Edited by Hugh L. Whitehouse. Indianapolis: Guild Press of Indiana, 1995.

Pearson, Henry Greenleaf. *James S. Wadsworth of Geneseo: Brevet Major General of United States Volunteers.* New York, 1913.

Perkins, Hugh C. "'Dear Friend,' Letters of a Civil War Soldier." Edited by Marilyn Gardner. *The Christian Science Monitor* (April 6, 1983, and April 7, 1983).

Porter, Horace. *Campaigning With Grant.* New York: The Century Company, 1897.

Priest, John Michael. *Before Antietam: The Battle for South Mountain.* Shippensburg, Pa.: White Mane Publishing Co., 1992.

Rhea, Gordon C. *The Battle of The Wilderness, May 5–6, 1864*. Baton Rouge: Louisiana State University Press, 1994.

Riley, Michael A. *"For God's Sake, Forward!": Gen. John F. Reynolds, USA*. Gettysburg: Farnsworth House Military Impressions, 1995.

Robertson, James I., Jr. *The Stonewall Brigade*. Baton Rouge: Louisiana State University Press, 1963.

Rood, Hosea W. "The Grand Army of the Republic and The Wisconsin Department, Origin of the G.A.R." *Wisconsin Magazine of History*. Volume 6 (March 1923).

Rood, Hosea W. *A Little Flag Book*. N.p., 1919.

Rood, Hosea W. *Memorial Day Annual, 1916*. Madison, 1916.

Ross, Sam. *The Empty Sleeve: A Biography of Lucius Fairchild*. Madison: State Historical Society of Wisconsin for the Wisconsin Civil War Centennial Commission, 1964.

Royall, William L. *Some Reminiscences*. New York: Neale Publishing Company, 1909.

Royster, Charles. *The Destructive War: William Tecumseh Sherman, Stonewall Jackson, and the Americans*. New York: Alfred A. Knopf, 1991.

Schaff, Morris. *The Battle of the Wilderness*. Boston, 1910.

Scott, Robert Garth. *Into the Wilderness with the Army of the Potomac*. Bloomington: Indiana University Press, 1985.

Sears, Stephen W. *Landscape Turned Red: The Battle of Antietam*. New York: Ticknor and Fields, 1983.

Seymour, William. *The Civil War Memoirs of Captain William Seymour*. Edited by E. Terry Jones. Baton Rouge: Louisiana State University Press, 1991.

Shue, Robert S. *Morning at Willoughby Run, July 1, 1863*. Gettysburg: Thomas Publications, 1995.

Skoctol, Theda. *Protecting Soldiers and Mothers: The Political Origins of Social Policy in the United States*. Cambridge, MA: London, 1992.

Smith, Donald L. *The Twenty-fourth Michigan of the Iron Brigade*. Harrisburg: The Stackpole Company, 1962.

Steere, Edward. *The Wilderness Campaign*. Harrisburg: The Stackpole Company, 1960.

Stephenson, Mary H. *Dr. B. F. Stephenson, Founder of the Grand Army of the Republic*. Springfield, 1894.

Stevens, Charles A. *Berdan's U.S. Sharpshooters in the Army of the Potomac, 1861–1865*. St. Paul, Minnesota: Price-McGill Company, 1892.

Stewart, James. *Battery B, Fourth United States Artillery at Gettysburg*. Sketches of War History, 1861–1865. Papers Prepared for the Ohio Commandery of the Loyal Legion of the United States. Volume 4. Cincinnati: Robert Clarke Company, 1896.

Stewart, James. *A Prologue—The Utah Campaign*. Sketches of War History, 1861–1865. Papers Prepared for the Ohio Commandery of the Loyal Legion of the United States. Volume 5. Cincinnati: Robert Clarke Company, 1903.

Stine, J. H. *History of the Army of the Potomac*. Philadelphia: Rogers Printing Company, 1892.

Storrick, W. C. *The Battle of Gettysburg: The Country, the Contestants, the Results*. Fifteenth edition. Harrisburg: Horace McFarland Company/Mount Pleasant Press, 1955.

Stouffer, S. A., et al. *The American Soldier: Combat and Its Aftermath*. Princeton: Princeton University, 1949.

Survivor's Association, 121st Regiment Pennsylvania Volunteers. Revised edition. Philadelphia, 1906.

Swan, William W. "Battle of the Wilderness." *Papers of the Military Historical Society of Massachusetts*. Series 1, 1891. Volume 4. Boston: Military Historical Society of Massachusetts, 1881–1918.

Swinton, William. *Campaigns of the Army of the Potomac*. New York, 1866.
Tenney, R. A. *Pension Laws.* Chicago, 1886.
Trudeau, Noah Andre. *Bloody Roads South: The Wilderness to Cold Harbor, May-June, 1864*. Boston: Little, Brown and Company, 1989.
Veil, Charles H. *The Memoirs of Charles Henry Veil.* Edited by Herman J. Viola. New York: Orion Books, 1993.
Wainwright, Charles S. *A Diary of Battle, The Personal Journals of Colonel Charles S. Wainwright, 1861–1865*. Edited by Allan Nevins. Gettysburg: Stan Clark Military Books, 1962.
Walker, Francis A. *History of the Second Army Corps in the Army of the Potomac*. New York: Charles Scribner's Sons, 1886.
Watrous, Jerome A. *Richard Epps and Other Stories.* Milwaukee, 1906.
Watrous, Jerome A., editor. *Memoirs of Milwaukee County*. 2 Volumes. Milwaukee, 1909.
Wilkeson, Frank. *Recollections of a Private Soldier in the Army of the Potomac*. New York, 1887.
Williams, K. P. *Lincoln Finds a General*, 5 vols. New York: The Macmillan Company, 1950–59.
Wilson, Oliver M. *The Grand Army of the Republic Under Its First Constitution: Its Birth and Organization.* Kansas City, 1905.
Woodruff, Charles A. "In Memory of Major General John Gibbon, Commander-in-Chief." *Personal Recollections of the War of the Rebellion: Addresses Delivered Before the Commandery of the State of New York, Military Order of the Loyal Legion of the United States.* Volume 2. New York: G. P. Putnam's Sons, 1897.
Wright, Steven J. and Blake A. Magner, "John Gibbon: The Man and the Monument." *The Gettysburg Magazine.* Volume 13 (July 1995).

Newspapers and Magazines

Blue and Gray Magazine
Chicago Tribune
Confederate Veteran
Daily State Sentinel
Elkhart Review
Evening Wisconsin [Madison]
Fond du Lac Commonwealth
Gettysburg Magazine
Grant County Herald
Grant County Witness
Indiana Magazine of History
Indianapolis Daily Journal
Janesville Daily Gazette
LaCrosse Morning Chronicle
LaCrosse Republican and Leader
Littell's Living Age
Milwaukee Sentinel
Milwaukee Sunday Telegraph
National Tribune
New York Sun
New York Times
New York Times Magazine
Oshkosh Northwestern
Prairie du Chien Courier
Racine Journal
Randolph County Journal
Richmond Palladium
Soldier's Record
Southern Historical Society Papers
Weekly Teller
Wisconsin Daily Patriot
Wisconsin Magazine of History
Wisconsin State Journal
Wisconsin State Register

Unpublished Letters, Manuscripts, and Other Materials

Edward R. Adams Papers. Civil War Institute. Carroll College. Waukesha, Wisconsin.
Antietam Studies. Record Group 94. U.S. National Archives.
Edward S. Bragg Papers. State Historical Society of Wisconsin.

Edward S. Bragg Papers. Wisconsin State Archives.
Edwin Brown Manuscript. Privately owned.
Elon A. Brown Papers. State Historical Society of Wisconsin.
George W. Burchell Letters. Sullivan Dexter Green Collection. Bentley Historical Library. University of Michigan.
Ezra A. Carman Papers. Manuscript Division. U.S. Library of Congress.
W. H. Church Manuscript. State Historical Society of Wisconsin.
John H. Cook Papers. State Historical Society of Wisconsin.
Correspondence of the Iron Brigade. State Historical Society of Wisconsin.
Rufus R. Dawes Journal. Newberry Library. Chicago, Illinois.
Rufus R. Dawes Manuscript. T. C. H. Smith Collection. Ohio Historical Society.
Rufus R. Dawes Papers. State Historical Society of Wisconsin.
Abner Doubleday Journal. Harpers Ferry Center Library.
Samuel Eaton Letters. State Historical Society of Wisconsin.
Lucius Fairchild Papers. State Historical Society of Wisconsin.
George Fairfield Papers. State Historical Society of Wisconsin.
John Gibbon Manuscript and Papers. The Historical Society of Pennsylvania.
Sullivan Green Manuscript. State Historical Society of Wisconsin.
Joseph Mills Hanson Papers. Manuscript File. Manassas National Battlefield Park.
William H. Harries Manuscript. Jerome A. Watrous Papers. State Historical Society of Wisconsin.
Frank A. Haskell Manuscript. State Historical Society of Wisconsin.
Lyman Holford Diary. Manuscript Division. U.S. Library of Congress.
Robert Hughes Manuscript. State Historical Society of Wisconsin.
Reuben Huntley Manuscript. State Historical Society of Wisconsin.
William N. Jackson Diary. Indiana Historical Society.
John A. Kellogg Letters. Series 1200. Sixth Wisconsin File. State Historical Society of Wisconsin.
George Lankevitch. "The G.A.R. in New York State, 1865–1898." Doctoral dissertation. Columbia University, 1967.
Henry C. Marsh Papers. Indiana Division. Indiana State Library.
Sydney Mead Journal. State Historical Society of Wisconsin.
Solomon Meredith Manuscript. Indiana Historical Society.
Military Order of the Loyal Legion of the United States Commandery-in-Chief Scrapbook #6, Entry 300, Civil War Library and Museum, Philadelphia, Pennsylvania.
Julius Murray Manuscript. State Historical Society of Wisconsin.
Elisha B. Odle Manuscript. Fredericksburg and Spotsylvania National Military Park.
Bob Patterson Manuscript. Henry C. Marsh Papers. Indiana Division. Indiana State Library.
Alexander B. Pattison Diary. Fredericksburg and Spotsylvania National Military Park.
James Perry Diary. State Historical Society of Wisconsin.
"Personal War Sketches of the Members of Tom Cox Post 132, Department of Wisconsin, Grand Army of the Potomac." Grant County Historical Society.
Nathaniel Rollins Diary. State Historical Society of Wisconsin.
Hosea W. Rood Diary (1917). Archives. Wisconsin Veterans Museum.
Hosea W. Rood Papers. Archives. Wisconsin Veterans Museum.
Jeremiah M. Rusk Papers, 1861–1898. Wisconsin State Archives.
John St. Clair Manuscript. State Historical Society of Wisconsin.
Henry Walker Letters. Civil War Miscellany, Personal Papers. Georgia State Archives.
Elmer Wallace Letters. John Fuller Collection. Private Collection.
Jerome A. Watrous. "Looking Over Our Old Battle Flags." Archives. Wisconsin Veterans Museum.
Jerome A. Watrous. "Program for the Dedication of the Grand Army Memorial Hall

in the Capital, Madison, Wisconsin, June 14, 1918." Archives. Wisconsin Veterans Museum.
Jerome A. Watrous Papers. State Historical Society of Wisconsin.
Cornelius Wheeler Papers. State Historical Society of Wisconsin.
Henry B. Young Papers. State Historical Society of Wisconsin.

Contributors

ALAN T. NOLAN is the historian of the Iron Brigade and a native Hoosier. He is Chairman of the Board of Trustees of the Indiana Historical Society, a Fellow of the Company of Military Historians, and a founder and former President of the Indianapolis Civil War Round Table. Since its original publication in 1961, his classic history *The Iron Brigade* has been named by *Civil War Times Illustrated* as one of the "100 best books ever written on the Civil War." He has also written *Lee Considered: General Robert E. Lee and Civil War History* (Main Selection of History Book Club and Book of the Month Alternate Selection) and the contemporary novel *As Sounding Brass,* and has contributed essays to *The First Day at Gettysburg, The Fredericksburg Campaign: Decision on the Rappahannock*, and a 1996 anthology on Robert E. Lee. He is the author of articles in such publications as *Civil War Times Illustrated, Civil War, Indiana Magazine of History, Virginia Cavalcade, Virginia Magazine of History and Biography, The American Historical Review*, and *Gettysburg Magazine*. He has lectured widely on Civil War topics, including appearances at the Smithsonian Institution and various colleges and universities. He has been granted an honorary doctorate from Indiana University (1993) and the Nevins-Freeman award by the Chicago Civil War Round Table (1994). He has appeared in *The Civil War Journal* series on cable television's Arts and Entertainment Network. An attorney and graduate of Indiana University and the Harvard Law School, he lives in Indianapolis, Indiana.

SHARON EGGLESTON VIPOND was born and raised in northwestern Wisconsin. She is a graduate of the universities of Wisconsin and Minnesota with undergraduate degrees in history and English and a doctorate in communications. A member of the Milwaukee Civil War Round Table, Iron Brigade Association, and Wisconsin State Historical Society, she works as an educational technology specialist for Oracle Corporation and lives with her husband and family in Woodstock, Georgia.

SILAS FELTON is a retired U.S. Air Force maintenance officer and the author of several articles on Battery B, including "The Iron Brigade Battery at Gettysburg." He lives in Dayton, Ohio.

ALAN AND MAUREEN GAFF have been researching and writing on Civil War subjects for almost thirty years and have authored and edited six books.

Their publications include *Brave Men's Tears: The Iron Brigade at Brawner Farm*; *The Second Wisconsin Infantry*; *Adventures on the Western Frontier*; *If This Is War: A History of the Campaign of Bull's Run*; and *Our Boys: A Civil War Photograph Album*. The last two books won Awards of Merit from the State Historical Society of Wisconsin. Their most recent publication—*On Many a Bloody Field*—is a unique history of the Nineteenth Indiana Regiment of the Iron Brigade and a History Book Club Selection. They live in Fort Wayne, Indiana.

KENT GRAMM is the author of *Gettysburg: A Meditation on War and Values* and the novel *Clare*. He has taught in the University of Wisconsin system and at Wheaton College, Ottawa University, Indiana Wesleyan University, and the University of Giessen (Germany). He is current J. Omar Good Distinguished Visiting Professor at Juniata College in Huntingdon, Pennsylvania, and lives in Lake Geneva, Wisconsin.

D. SCOTT HARTWIG is a graduate of the University of Wyoming and historian at Gettysburg National Military Park. He has authored numerous articles, essays, and books, including *The Battle of Antietam and the Maryland Campaign of 1862: A Bibliography*. His most recent book is *A Killer Angels Companion*, a historical analysis of Michael Shaara's Pulitzer Prize–winning novel. He lives in Gettysburg, Pennsylvania.

LANCE J. HERDEGEN is a former executive with United Press International and director of the Institute for Civil War Studies at Carroll College in Waukesha, Wisconsin. He is the author of *The Men Stood Like Iron* (Indiana University Press, 1997) and co-author of the award-winning books *In the Bloody Railroad Cut at Gettysburg* (selection of the History Book Club) and *An Irishman in the Iron Brigade*. He was featured in *The Civil War Journal* series on cable television's Arts and Entertainment Network. He lives in Milwaukee, Wisconsin.

MARC AND BETH STORCH were both born and raised in Wisconsin and have spent the past ten years researching the Iron Brigade as well as other Wisconsin regiments in the Civil War. They have written several articles on the Iron Brigade and assisted many historians and artists in their work related to the brigade. They are currently working on a regimental history of the Second Wisconsin Volunteer Infantry. They live in Laurel, Maryland.

STEVEN J. WRIGHT is Curator of the Civil War Library and Museum and the author of two books and more than 200 reviews and articles on subjects ranging from the American Civil War and Indian Wars to Lake Superior shipwrecks. His book *The Irish Brigade* was published in 1992. He and his wife Irene, a children's librarian, live in Philadelphia, Pennsylvania.

RICHARD H. ZEITLIN was born and raised in New York City and is a graduate of Queens College. A history major, Zeitlin earned an M.S. and Ph.D. in American diplomatic and military history at the University of Wisconsin–Madison. A longtime student of the Civil War, he is presently Director of the Wisconsin Veterans Museum and is particularly interested in the history of veterans groups. He and his wife and family live in Madison.

Index